The Oxfordshire Record Society
Volume 72

A Vicar's Wife in Oxford, 1938–1943

THE OXFORDSHIRE RECORD SOCIETY

The Society was founded in 1919. Its objectives are to publish transcripts, abstracts and lists of primary sources for the history of the county of Oxfordshire and generally to extend awareness and understanding of archives relating to Oxfordshire. The Society welcomes proposals for volumes for publication. There are no restrictions on time period or topic.

The publication programme of the Society is overseen by an Editorial Committee, established in 2017.

Its members are:
                Elizabeth Gemmill, BA, PhD
                Barbara Tearle, LLB, MSt, MCLIP
                Kate Tiller, DL, MA, PhD, FSA, FRHistS (*Chair*)
                Simon Townley, BA, PGCE, DPhil, FSA

Ex officio:
                Professor Robert Evans (Chairman, ORS)
                Paul Gaskell (Secretary, ORS)

Information about the Society, its publications and how to make a proposal for a publication may be found on its website: http://www.oxfordshire-record-society.org.uk/

Details of previously published volumes are available from the Society.

A Vicar's Wife in Oxford, 1938–1943

The Diary of Madge Martin

Edited by Patricia and Robert Malcolmson

The Boydell Press
Oxfordshire Record Society
Volume 72

© Oxfordshire Record Society 2018

All rights reserved. Except as permitted under current legislation
no part of this work may be photocopied, stored in a retrieval system,
published, performed in public, adapted, broadcast,
transmitted, recorded or reproduced in any form or by any means,
without the prior permission of the copyright owner

First published 2018

An Oxfordshire Record Society publication
Published by Boydell & Brewer Ltd
PO Box 9, Woodbridge, Suffolk IP12 3DF, UK
and Boydell & Brewer Inc.
668 Mt Hope Avenue, Rochester, NY 14620–2731, USA
website: www.boydellandbrewer.com

ISBN 978-0-902509-74-0

A CIP catalogue record for this book is available
from the British Library

The publisher has no responsibility for the continued existence or accuracy of URLs for
external or third-party internet websites referred to in this book, and does not guarantee
that any content on such websites is, or will remain, accurate or appropriate

This publication is printed on acid-free paper

Printed and bound in Great Britain by
TJ International Ltd, Padstow, Cornwall

Contents

	List of Illustrations	*page* vi
	List of Maps	vii
	Foreword	viii
	Acknowledgements	ix
	Editorial Practice	xi
	Abbreviations	xiii
	Introduction	1
1	From Peace to War: September 1938–September 1939	17
2	Prelude to Bloodshed: September 1939–May 1940	52
3	In Danger: May 1940–September 1940	78
4	Battlegrounds: September 1940–May 1941	107
5	Matters New, Matters Old: May 1941–September 1941	134
6	A Mixture of Frailties: October 1941–June 1942	154
7	Better Times? June 1942–December 1942	180
8	Carrying On: January 1943–December 1943	204
	Epilogue	241
	Appendix A: Madge Martin and John Hall	245
	Appendix B: Madge Martin's Reading	249
	Bibliography	255
	Index	259

Illustrations

Plates (between pages 114 and 115)

1   Madge Martin on holiday in Kitzbühel, 1937
2   Mrs Danna Martin with sons Harry and Robert, 1940
3   Doris Dandridge with Marina, 1937
4   Nita Holland and Nancy Barrett with their families in the University Parks, 1940
5   Nick and Joy Nicholls, 1937
6   John Hall and Madge Martin at Eynsham Station, March 1936
7   Robert Martin and troops, 1942 (*courtesy of* Oxford Mail)
8   Ruth Hendewerk, 1937
9   Mrs Setterington in the garden, 1944
10–13   Drawings by Madge Martin
14   Red Cross volunteers at Worcester College, 1942
15   Cadena Café, 44–46 Cornmarket Street (*Courtesy of Oxfordshire County Council–Oxfordshire History Centre*)
16   Rubber salvage, 1942 (©Imperial War Museum (D 8933))

The front and back covers and Plates 1–5, 8–9, and 14 are reproduced by courtesy of Mrs Priscilla Ramsey, to whom grateful thanks are given for permission to use them. Plates 6 and 10–13 are courtesy of the owner of Madge Martin's diaries, to whom similar thanks are given. Permission to use other images is individually acknowledged.

Maps

Map 1 Oxford City Centre	*pages* 10–11
Map 2 Greater Oxford	12–13
Map 3 The Oxfordshire Region	14–15
Map 4 Beyond Oxfordshire	16

Foreword

Since 1919 the Oxfordshire Record Society has fulfilled its aim of making available records of the county for the benefit of all those interested in its history. Its seventy and more volumes have interspersed staple sources of public life and administration with more personal and local records ranging from medieval manorial life to the Civil War period to Victorian friendly societies, and culminating in a major synthesis of Oxfordshire history and archaeology in the *Historical Atlas of Oxfordshire*. As ORS plans celebrations for its centenary, it passes another major landmark, the move to publishing its volumes with Boydell & Brewer, an independent, employee-owned publisher with an excellent reputation for producing high-quality scholarly volumes. We look forward to working with them.

The events chronicled in the diary printed in this volume had not taken place when ORS was founded. One hundred years later they are part of the county's history.

Madge Martin, whose diary for some of the war years is published here, lived in Oxford throughout her long adult life. Her diary presents a turning point in twentieth-century history and in Madge's own life. Although Oxford itself was scarcely touched by the physical devastation of World War II, the people – and Madge – underwent the same deprivations and stresses as the rest of the country.

In their commentary the editors, Patricia and Robert Malcolmson, have ably drawn out the social changes that Madge Martin experienced in those years, whilst at the same time trying to maintain the social and cultural routines of her life. Her intensely personal account of wartime life is played out within a framework of parish life and wartime volunteering in central Oxford where her husband, Robert Martin, was vicar of St Michael at the North Gate. Two leisure themes emerge that dominated their lives in Oxford and Oxfordshire. She and her husband loved nothing more than walking in the country. They were able to continue their excursions during the war years. The diary provides glimpses of a public transport system – bus and rail – that enabled them to travel to Lewknor or Henley-on-Thames, Kingham or Burford, enjoy a substantial walk and return to Oxford in time to indulge their other passion. This was for the performing arts, where their enthusiasm went beyond frequent attendance at the theatre and cinema. They often entertained members of the Oxford Repertory Company and had an occasional entrée backstage at the theatre. While focusing on the effects of war on one person's life, the diary also opens up themes in Oxford and the county's life for future investigation.

Kate Tiller *Barbara Tearle*
Chair, ORS Editorial Committee *ORS Volume Editor*

Acknowledgements

Our first – and very important debt – is to Juliet Gardiner, who alerted us a few years ago to the existence of Madge Martin's diaries and their potential for publication. Were it not for Juliet's timely and pertinent advice, it is unlikely that we would have embarked on this project.

We are also grateful to a member of Madge Martin's family for permission to publish substantial portions of her diary, and to her niece, Priscilla Ramsey, for permission to reproduce photographs from the Martins' family album.

Our second debt of thanks is to the Oxfordshire Record Society for its favourable response to our proposal to publish an edition of several years of Madge Martin's diaries. We are especially grateful to Paul Gaskell, the Society's Hon. Secretary, for his vital support. He approved and arranged for all of her manuscript diaries for the six years 1938 through 1943 to be copied and made available to us, at the Society's expense. This, for us, was crucial. Without these copies to work on at home, we would not have been able to proceed with our work as editors.

We had the pleasure of spending three weeks in 2016–17 working in Oxford at the Oxfordshire History Centre. The assistance we received was outstanding, from all members of the OHC's staff. They were invariably attentive, helpful, and well-informed. While we did not learn the names of all those who lent us a hand, we would like to mention with appreciation Mark Lawrence, Mark Priddey, and Linda Haynes (who kindly transcribed for us some passages in Madge's diaries that could not be copied), and the conservator Rosemary Hamilton, who arranged for us to have access to one important file that was not in ideal physical condition. The excellence of the Oxfordshire History Centre is indisputable. While there we were always able to use our time productively.

The other people who helped us in various ways include Lindsay McCormack, the archivist at Lincoln College; cartographer Giles Darkes, who is responsible for the fine maps; photographer Colin Dunn of Scriptura; Malcolm Graham and members of the Editorial Committee of the Oxfordshire Record Society; Anne Baker, who in June 2017 invited us to tour her house, once occupied by Madge and Robert Martin, at 1 Wellington Place; our friend Ann Stephenson in London, a researcher on family history; Priscilla Ramsey for her recollections of the Martin family and for giving us a copy of Madge Martin's memoir, 'A Yorkshire Childhood 1899–1913'; and Helen Blum and Heather Goldik at the Nelson Public Library in British Columbia, who efficiently managed our many requests for books through the province's Interlibrary Loans system.

We have left to the last acknowledging the key contributions of Barbara Tearle, a member of the Council of the Oxfordshire Record Society and our editor in 2017–18. Barbara was a major and highly constructive participant in the production of this volume. She read some of the original diaries and contributed valuable suggestions as to how selections might be made. She offered helpful comments on our editorial approaches and annotations, and pursued additional research on our behalf, which led to some new and useful findings. Her sharp eye detected numerous errors in transcribing, which we were glad to be able to correct. Barbara was also active in arranging the production of the maps, photographs, and bibliography. All told, her work as supervisory editor was exemplary – and is deeply appreciated by us, her Canadian friends.

Nelson, British Columbia
March 2018

Editorial Practice

To publish Madge Martin's diary in its entirety would be unthinkable. For a start, much of it, like many other diaries that go on for years, is repetitious. The same matters come up again and again. She at times remarked that one day seemed to her much like any other – and she wrote something in her diary virtually every day during these years. Our principles and criteria for making selections are identified from time to time as the volume unfolds.[1] All chapters present selections, although Chapter 1 starts by reproducing, without deletions, everything that she wrote for ten consecutive weeks; Chapter 3 reproduces all her diary entries between 13 May and 17 August 1940, a time of great stress for almost everyone; and most of what she wrote in September/October 1940 appears in Chapter 4. Other chapters print numerous weeks of her diary unabridged. When a day is not represented by a diary entry, it can be assumed that the entry exists but is not reproduced.

We have chosen to start the diary in September 1938, as the prospect of war was appearing all too likely to many Britons and Madge's diary suddenly takes on an air of urgency. We conclude at the end of 1943, when military victory seemed assured, and with Madge in a hopeful frame of mind – though, as time would show, victory was still further away than many people expected.

Editors of diaries make many decisions that affect a book's character. The creation of chapters below is entirely a matter of editorial decisions. In some respects they are responses to variations in the quality of Madge's writing. Our goal as editors has been principally to reveal and reconstruct a life and times during years of crisis – that is, to portray the life of one individual in the context of her household, her local society, and her nation at war. The routines of a diarist's life – sometimes grinding routines – and her everyday concerns need to be reported, but not, we think, repeatedly. And these should be balanced against life's novelties, excitements, dangers, special events, extraordinary incidents, and the like. For the most part we allow Madge's diary to speak for itself, leaving readers to form their own opinions about its author and her commitments and attitudes. However, because so many of her entries are not fully reproduced in this volume, from time to time we

---

1 The need for selections in publishing lengthy modern diaries by previously unknown authors can usually only be avoided when a diarist has clearly self-edited, thereby minimizing repetitions and matters of recurrent routine. This, for example, is the case with Dewsbury diarist Kathleen Hey: Patricia and Robert Malcolmson, eds, *The View from the Corner Shop: The Diary of a Yorkshire Shop Assistant in Wartime, Kathleen Hey* (London: Simon & Schuster, 2016). Occasionally a non-repetitious diary is about the right length for a book; or perhaps a book-length portion of a manuscript diary can be extracted from a larger text and reproduced without any other abridgements. Every modern diary is likely to call for a somewhat different editorial approach.

present passages and commentary that are intended to provide both links between the printed selections and depictions of experiences that would otherwise not be disclosed. On one occasion in Chapter 1 (following 27 November 1938), some two and a half months into this edition of her diary, we pause to reflect on Madge's character and some persistent features of her life that readers may find helpful to keep in mind as they digest her writing for the years from the beginning of the war.

The footnotes in this book have several purposes, the main ones being to elaborate on topics mentioned in the diary and to clarify issues that are no longer self-explanatory. Some notes present passages from diary entries that are not otherwise reproduced. Other notes draw upon entries from Robert Martin's diary, which covers the same period as Madge's, except the first half of 1940, the volume for which is missing, or from his *St Michael at the North Gate, Oxford, Parish Magazine*, which he wrote and had printed each month.[2] The *Oxford Mail* (a daily) and *Oxford Times* (a weekly) often provide further details on events and incidents mentioned in the diary. We use square brackets in the text mostly to report factual information about places, people, public performances, and events – information that was taken for granted by Madge, and who had no reason to include it in a diary that she wrote largely or entirely for her own satisfaction. While her writing is largely error-free, we have silently corrected mistakes in spelling, mainly of proper names, spelt out some initials in full and altered some of her punctuation in the interest of clarity (she uses dashes, for example, to excess).

The great majority of the sources we have drawn upon, whether manuscript or printed, including local newspapers and *Kelly's Directory* of Oxford for 1939 and 1943, are held in the Oxfordshire History Centre in Temple Cowley, Oxford. The other main sources of value are online records commonly used for family research, including the census for 1901 and 1911 and the 1939 Register of Households and their inhabitants made in September of that year.[3]

2   OHC, Acc. 5374.
3   Barbara Tearle has been vastly helpful in supplying us with information from these records.

Abbreviations

ARCM	Associate of the Royal College of Music
ARP	Air Raid Precautions
ATS	Auxiliary Territorial Service
BBC	British Broadcasting Corporation
BEF	British Expeditionary Force
chap.	chapter
G & S	Gilbert and Sullivan operettas
GMT	Greenwich Mean Time
GWR	Great Western Railway
HM Forces	His Majesty's Forces
HMS	His Majesty's Ship
lb	pound weight
MO	Mass Observation
NFS	National Fire Service
OHC	Oxfordshire History Centre
OU	Oxford University
OUDS	Oxford University Drama Society
oz, ozs	ounces
POW	prisoner of war
RAF	Royal Air Force
RASC	Royal Army Service Corps
RE	Royal Engineers
RVS	Royal Voluntary Service
TB	tuberculosis
USA	United States of America
VE Day	Victory in Europe, 8 May 1945
VJ Day	Victory over Japan, 15 August 1945
WVS	Women's Voluntary Services
YMCA	Young Men's Christian Association

A Note on Currency, Weights, and Distances

Money

12 pennies = 1 shilling
20 shillings = £1
A penny was written as '1d', a shilling as '1s'. In this edition sums of money are written, for example, as '£3 12s 0d' for three pounds and twelve shillings.

Weights

16 ounces (oz) = 1 pound weight (lb)
1lb = 453.6 grams

Distances

1 mile = 1.6 km

Introduction

> Everyone has her or his own story and at the same time is part of history. Lives consist of public concerns and personal issues and the interconnections between the two.
>
> Juliet Gardiner, *Joining the Dots: A Woman in her Time*
> (London: William Collins, 2017), p. 186

By the later 1930s, Madge Martin was a veteran diary writer. She had started with a pocket schoolgirl's datebook-diary when she was in her mid-teens, and continued, with some gaps, for most of the rest of her life. Her writing was especially full during the 1930s and early 1940s. On 1 January 1929 she began her diary with the words: 'I have not kept a diary for three years – but I am having another shot.' Only one diary survives from earlier in the 1920s, for 1922, so some volumes must have been lost. There is none for 1934, yet it is almost certain that she was keeping a diary that year as well, since diaries survive for all other years in that decade. Madge wrote a diary entirely – or almost entirely – for herself, with apparently no intention of showing it to anyone else. On one occasion she referred to it as a 'very *secret* diary' (24 November 1929). Exceptionally, and only once, did she write about willingly sharing her diary with another person: on 29 November 1931 she visited her close friend, Vera Dyer, who also lived in Oxford, 'where we read our 1929 diaries together'.

When Madge Setterington (her birth name) began diary-writing in 1916, just after her 16th birthday, she had a lot to put on record, even if the tiny format of her printed diary volume gave her little space to write much. Madge had been born in Leeds on 20 December 1899, and in 1916 was living with her parents and two younger sisters, Nita and Nancy, at 14 Clarence Gardens, Dollis Park, Church End, Finchley, London.[1] Also living in the house for a good chunk of the previous year

---

1   Madge's diary for 17 September 1931 indicates that she spent 'the historic years of 1913 and 1914' in Newcastle, where, on holiday at that time, she revisited her old school,

were two young soldiers, Robert Martin, whose 21st birthday was in January 1916, and 'Nick' (i.e., Leonard Nicholls). Both had been billeted with the Setterington family on 20 March 1915 (20 March 1931).

The very first entry in Madge's diary, before the dates for 1916 are printed in the volume, is from 23 December 1915 and reads: 'Mr Martin ordered to Front. Great misery!' Amid girlish comments about difficult teachers, boring lessons, days when 'nothing happened', her jottings revealed that a serious romance was unfolding. By 10 January 1916 she had received two letters from Mr Martin – soon usually known as Rob – who also sent his ring to be taken care of. 'I am very proud indeed to take care of such a wonderful thing.' Soon it was followed by her first Valentine from him and a blue handkerchief ('Je les aime beaucoup', 14 February 1916); a thirteen-page letter (31 March); and, finally, after many delays and disappointments – on 26 April 'Mr Martin did not come so we are all in deep misery' – on 29 April 1916 his return to London on leave. '*Rejoice ye! … Rob has really and truly come. I can't believe it at all and it's too lovely for anything … Hurrah!*' Another brief military leave resulted in a punt ride for the two of them at Richmond, 'simply too delicious for words' (5 May).

A few weeks later, on 11 June 1916, Robert wrote to Madge's father, Mr Charles Setterington, a school master and later school inspector, requesting the then 16-year-old Madge's hand in marriage. As well as professing his great love for Madge and his desire to spend his life with her, Robert pointed out that he could support her on his private income of £400 a year, then a tidy sum (and more than Charles Setterington's annual salary), plus anything else that he might later earn.[2] While Madge's youth may well have been a concern, Robert must have been seen by her parents as a fine catch. In short order Madge's father approved the marriage, desiring only that Robert's mother give her endorsement. Charles's reply made Robert 'the happiest member of the British Expeditionary Force'.[3]

Rutherford College 'where I spent the unhappy term of summer 1914'. Madge grew up mostly in Yeadon, a large village just north-west of Leeds. Her father was headmaster of a boys' school there. ('A Yorkshire Childhood 1899–1913', a typescript memoir written by Madge in her seventies. Her niece, Priscilla Ramsey, kindly sent us a copy of this evocative 58-page account of Madge's early years in the North.)

2   Oxfordshire History Centre (OHC), P5/C3/1. Robert's father, a tea planter, died in 1895, shortly after his birth in Ceylon. He undoubtedly left a legacy for his infant son. A few months later the widowed Mrs Martin, 'Danna', returned to England, where she in due course settled in Bedford with her children; she did not remarry. Robert attended Bedford School, 1904–14, an independent school for boys, and was subsequently commissioned into the Bedfordshire Regiment.

3   Ibid, letter of 16 June 1916. In his letter of 11 June, Robert had also justified his proposal for marriage to teenage Madge on the grounds that Edith, Mr Setterington's wife, had been only 16 when they had married, and 'who could have a better example of a perfectly happy union'. This was factually wrong – Edith was in her mid-twenties when she married – and

On 17 July 1916, Madge put her hair up for the first time, a rite of passage to adulthood for young women in the early twentieth century – and one especially appropriate, perhaps, for an engaged woman (albeit a secret engagement at this time). On the very same day she received the alarming news that Robert had been wounded.[4] He had sustained a head wound as a result of a training accident with a bomb, and was granted medical leave, which was twice extended, the second time, on 23 November 1916, for two additional months.

This long leave, of over six months, did much more than aid Robert's recuperation: it cemented his deepening relationship with Madge. Over these months they were – especially by the standards of many engagements at this time – rarely out of each other's company.[5] Together they devoured the joys of life as any young couple might. The day he was released from hospital (20 July 1916) Robert bought Madge a 'most lovely picture' on Bond Street, and then, after having his wound re-dressed, the two of them travelled to Devon to visit his family at Bigbury-on-Sea, one of several visits there, where many happy days were spent at the beach sea bathing. These days were 'like fairy dreams', Madge gushed (27 July 1916), though the timid teenager also allowed that she was 'Dreadfully shy. Very brave I was indeed' (22 July). Back in London, with Robert billeted again with her family, the romance continued with outings to the cinema and the theatre, a visit to Hampton Court, and lots of shopping, including the purchase of a gramophone at Harrods (21 September 1916) and subsequent listening to many recordings. On one occasion that year (3 November 1916), in a sort of premonition of their future lives, they went to Oxford where they 'had tea in the Cadena Café, then looked round Lincoln College, and saw some others. Lovely place altogether.' (Robert had entered Lincoln College as an undergraduate in October 1914, though he didn't stay for long. It and the Cadena Café featured prominently in the Martins' later lives in Oxford.)

This fast-moving courtship concluded with marriage on 17 July 1917 at St Mary's Finchley.[6] It was followed by a honeymoon in Eastbourne; Lieutenant Robert Martin's return to the Army and duty in France; and his later release from military service on grounds of ill-health – he was declared 'permanently unfit' by

---

it is hard to make sense of such an inaccurate statement on Robert's part (which Charles Setterington did not correct in his reply).
4   Robert Martin's injury was a head wound incurred during a bombing training accident that killed one man and injured four others (OHC, file P5/C3/1, letter to Mrs Martin 14 July 1916 from Colonel Henry Senton, British Expeditionary Force).
5   OHC, P5/C3/1 as well as Madge Martin Diary, 1916, passim.
6   A newspaper account of the service – 'Khaki Wedding at Finchley' – states that Robert 'was severely wounded on the Somme in the great battle of last July, and has been in England ever since' (*Hendon and Finchley Times*, 20 July 1917, p. 8. We are indebted to Barbara Tearle for this reference). In fact, there is no evidence that Robert was involved in the Battle of the Somme. His injuries – not apparently 'severe' – were sustained in a training accident, though he may have been re-injured when he returned to France after his marriage.

a Medical Board in September 1918.[7] The young couple moved to their first flat at 22 Beaumont Street in Oxford a little over a year after their marriage. Robert returned to Lincoln College and read History; he received a (shortened) BA in 1919. Thereafter he studied theology and in 1923 was inducted as a priest and appointed as temporary curate, and later, in 1927, as Vicar, at St Michael at the North Gate (see Map 1). By then Madge and Robert were living in a flat at 129b High Street, Oxford, their residence until 1936.

Madge was a much-loved and, it appears, cosseted wife. She was also, by her own admission, a rather shy person who was most content with her family and girl friends. She eschewed leadership roles. A young woman of modest education – though she excelled in English literature and composition[8] – her schooling ended at the end of the summer term in 1916. Common enough for middle-class girls at the time, her formal instruction included such respectable subjects and activities for young ladies as French dictation, literature, needlework, grammar, botany, arithmetic, scripture, tennis, and gym. She had a gift for sketching, and enjoyed fashion drawing – drawings of her new outfits (clothes for her were a longstanding interest) often filled the margins and spare pages of her diaries. She attended some evening art classes after the conclusion of her formal schooling.[9] Occasionally in later years she drew posters for some church or local event, and dressed dolls, sometimes in period costume, for charitable sales (a fairly common recreation once wartime restrictions made manufactured toys very scarce). At least once she entertained a sick child by drawing paper dolls and their clothes.

As a reticent and somewhat socially insecure woman with scant scholarly credentials, at least by university standards – though she was a reader, adept with words, and an enthusiast for the performing arts – Madge sometimes found it a struggle to live in Oxford, a high-powered, sometimes intimidating city, full of people brimming with self-confidence and a sense of their intellectual superiority. Madge's background was comfortable enough, but not privileged nor noticeably intellectual. One gets a sense from her diary that in cerebral and self-assured Oxford she felt at times like a fish out of water. Her contacts with College life were minimal, aside from dramatic and musical performances. Madge seemed generally to be more relaxed when she was away from Oxford, usually on holiday, almost always with Robert, commonly for at least a month a year both before and during the war. She also loved her frequent, usually day trips, to London.

---

7   Most of the evidence not from Madge's diary concerning Robert's early years is in OHC, P5/C3/1, a file that is arranged more or less chronologically. The extent to which he may have been dogged by ill-health during the next two or three decades is unclear.

8   Even as a teenager Madge was showing herself to be a decent writer in her love letters to Robert (OHC, P5/C2/1).

9   Her teenage education is documented (including school reports) in OHC, P5/C3/1, item 62 and P5/2J/01.

Madge's rather mixed feelings about Oxford – and not just its academic superiority – were conveyed as well in a remark in her diary for 29 September 1944. 'Oxford townspeople', she wrote, 'are very tough under a fairly friendly manner, and on the whole I don't like them much. There *are* many exceptions, of course.' She felt, it seems, a certain distaste for – or at least alienation from – the city, while at the same time (as many entries in this book attest) admiring and enjoying much that Oxford had to offer. Many and varied aspects of its society and wartime culture are documented in her diary.

* * *

A key fact about Madge Martin is that she had no children. This was a central backdrop to her way of living, and how she was able to choose to spend her time. She married very young and was, by all accounts, happily married to an attentive, considerate, and affectionate man – but no child arrived. During the years of this edition of her diary (1938–1943) she is entirely silent on the matter. There are scattered indications from various years of her affection for young children, some written in relation to herself. On 7 February 1929, she 'had a wire from Dick to say Nita [her sister] has a son [Christopher]. Gosh. How I wish I had.' At that time, in her thirtieth year, she had been married for almost twelve years. She always wrote affectionately of her niece, Sally, born in 1936, but more often of boys: on 14 April 1931 'I felt absurdly happy, because I had a beaming smile from a small boy I like.' Years later, on 5 January 1944, she was thinking back to over twenty years earlier, around 1923, when 'John [Hall] was a sweet little twelve-year-old whom I should have liked to have adopted.' (Much more on John will follow.) A few weeks later, on 5 March 1944, she was again explicit about her maternal desires after meeting the three-year-old son of a friend: 'What wouldn't I give to have one like him.' This was a rare disclosure of maternal feelings that had, to her regret, been thwarted.

There is one occasion when, out of the blue, Madge spoke head-on about this fact of childlessness. She was writing in her diary on the last day of 1930, a few days after her 31st birthday. 'It has been a very happy year all round. I love Robert more every year, and I wouldn't mind growing older if only I had a baby. I wonder if I ever shall? It is my only real sorrow. Others come and go. Never mind,' – and here she tried to buck herself up – 'I'm sure we couldn't be happier.' One can imagine the sense of emptiness she probably carried with her for years but almost never wrote about – and on this crucial matter there is no further evidence in her writing that would permit anything but speculation.

If two of the key facts of Madge's life were an early marriage (she met her husband-to-be when she was only 15) and childlessness, a third was her intense emotional relationship with a boy she met in November 1923 (9 November 1941), when he was 12 and she almost 24. This close relationship – close for her, certainly – was to last for over twenty years. The boy – and later young man – was John Hall, born on 22 April 1911. She first got acquainted with him as an appealing choirboy.

John and his sister, Susie, lived with their widowed mother at 74 Argyle Street. He was – or at least became – an accomplished singer. His talents were noted in a clipping from the press she pasted into her diary (8 April 1936) – his rendition of 'He was despised' from the *Messiah* was praised as a 'beautiful alto solo [that] was worthy of the best tradition of St Michael's church'. He was also, at various times from the 1920s until the mid-1930s, a member of the local Madrigal Society, a rugby player, and, for Madge, a frequent companion.

Madge wrote about John Hall with an emotional intensity that she revealed about no one else. These 'turbulent feelings' persisted, on and off, for years, and clearly into the early 1940s. John Hall appears again and again in Madge's writing – sometimes in a positive light, at other times as a disturber of her serenity. They routinely talked with each other, occasionally for hours. Sometimes they argued, on at least one occasion about women's rights or social privilege, for example, though we are told nothing about the substance of their discussions. He often upset her. He sometimes disappointed her. He could easily make her angry. He was regularly in her thoughts, and rarely in a neutral way. Their friendship was, for her – or at least so it often seems from her diary – a vital feature of life. It would be not unreasonable to suggest that she was, to a degree, obsessed with him. Given this remarkable and charged friendship, which is a major strand of Madge's diary from around the time she was 30, Appendix A is devoted to an interpretation of its character and dynamic. (Theirs is the sort of relationship that is likely to be recorded *only* in a private diary, and not in a diary that was expected to be read by third parties, such as those written during the war for Mass Observation, even with the assurance of anonymity.[10])

From early 1936 the Martins lived at 1 Wellington Place, a short walk from St Michael's Church. This was a large house in St Giles on the St John's College estates. It was built around 1843, with later additions in the 1870s. Its three storeys included four bedrooms on the first floor and a large unfinished attic with the potential for two more bedrooms.[11] On pages following her diary entry for 12 January 1936, she described the décor and general appearance of the house's main rooms. On moving from their flat on the High Street, she and Robert had purchased (it seems) lots of new furniture and had not stinted on redecorating, though at one point she was worrying that they were spending too much (10 January 1936).[12] (This was a rare

---

10 Aside from Nella Last, who wrote at extraordinary length and was prepared to write about almost anything, the only published Mass Observation diarist who dealt with numerous intimate matters was Olivia Cockett, and some of her most personal disclosures were in her pre-MO writing. See Robert Malcolmson, ed., *Love and War in London: A Woman's Diary 1939–1942, Olivia Cockett* (Waterloo, Ontario: Wilfred Laurier University Press, 2005).

11 We are grateful to its present occupant, Anne Baker, for allowing us to inspect the interior of 1 Wellington Place, and to her neighbour, Ross McKibbon, for helping us contact her.

12 It is likely that Robert's income at this time, from various sources, some private, others ecclesiastical, was around – or even at least – £1,000 a year. Like most households with

occasion when she seemed particularly budget-conscious.) 'Please God, grant us peace and happiness in this, our dream home,' she wrote the day they moved in (16 January 1936). Except when she was travelling, 1 Wellington Place was where Madge produced all of her diary that is presented in this volume.

When she was in Oxford, Madge Martin spent almost all her time in or near the centre of the city, which was full of colleges, shops, cafés, cinemas, and theatres. This was *her* neighbourhood, with which she was intimately familiar. Only occasionally did she venture by foot more than a mile from her Oxford home. She usually travelled by bus beyond the city centre, often for country walks in Oxfordshire and occasionally into the neighbouring counties of Berkshire, Buckinghamshire, or Gloucestershire.

* * *

While most of the people in Madge's diary are identified when they first appear, here are the ones who were most prominent in her life, aside from her husband, Robert, and John Hall (and his sister, Susie), who have already been introduced.

(1) Madge's mother, Edith Setterington, a widow since 1933.

(2) Robert's mother, Danna, a widow since 1895, referred to as 'Mrs Martin' at the beginning of the diary.

(3) Madge's younger sister, Nita (born January 1903), her husband, Richard (or Dick) Holland, and their son Christopher (or Kit). Their home was in London.

(4) Madge's sister, Nancy (born June 1908), almost nine years younger than Madge, her husband, Norman Barrett, and their children Roger and Sally. They also lived in London.

(5) Robert's older brother, Harry (born 1889), and his adult daughters, Diana (born 1915), Pamela (born 1916) and June (born 1920).

(6) Madge's two most prominent unmarried friends in the 1930s and early 1940s, Vera Dyer and Muriel Smith, both in their mid-thirties when war broke out. The latter, a schoolteacher in London, was often found irritating by Madge. (Each woman was referred to as 'my friend' and given small legacies in Madge's will of 5 December 1988.)

(7) Peter Bleiben (born 1903) and his wife, Winifred (born 1901). He was Vicar of Holy Trinity, Headington Quarry and had been Robert's curate for several years in the 1930s. Outside of family, they were the only couple who were regular friends of the Martins. They also appear to have been childless.

such an income, the Martins had a telephone, a convenience that only a smallish minority of households enjoyed. They had no car; they did not need one to get around from their centrally located residence, and Robert did not have a driver's licence.

(8) Ruth Hendewerk (born 1897), a German refugee living in Oxford. By later 1943 she was residing in the Martins' house (she, too, was remembered in Madge's 1988 will).

(9) Doris Dandridge (born 1904), a married woman with a home in Oxford, who was Madge's domestic servant during the 1930s and for most of the years covered by this book.

(10) Leonard Nicholls (born 1890), known as 'Nick'. He had been billeted with Robert at the Setteringtons' home in 1915 and remained a friend, though during the Second World War he was living mostly in Nigeria, where he was employed in the civil service.

(11) Pansy (also known as Panny) Telford, Robert's younger sister, born in Worthing in 1896, shortly after their father's death. She was married to David Telford (born 1893), an accountant, had three daughters, and lived in Dublin.

Many of the other persons named in the diary made only passing appearances, as brief visitors to 1 Wellington Place, or as people Madge visited, or as acquaintances encountered in public places. A shared characteristic of quite a few of these people is that they were connected in some way with the Church of St Michael at the North Gate, where Robert Martin was Vicar.[13] The following people whose names appear at least once in the diary were (probably or certainly) among these 'worshippers': Mrs Acton, George Anderson (a visiting American priest), Mrs Bazett-Jones, the Blencowe family, Mrs Booth, Miss Bourdillon, Mrs Busby and her daughter Ruth, Mrs and Miss Butler, the Buttrum family, David Calcutt, Mrs Claringbold, Mr and Mrs Corry, Vera Dyer, Miss Egerton, the Gray family, John and Susie Hall, Miss Hardman, Elsie Harris, Mr and Mrs [Cottrell] Horser, Agnes Jennings, Mr Jennings, Peggy Longfield, Mr and Mrs Potter, Adrian Rushworth, the Russell family, Mrs Sever, Muriel Smith, and Olive Whittaker.[14] Around two-thirds of the people named in the diary, excluding family members and actors and actresses, were probably known to Madge Martin through the Church of St Michael at the North Gate.

* * *

---

13 While the parish, located in the City centre, had few residents, less than 300, many people came to St Michael's from further afield in Oxford to attend church and/or join in some of its activities. Robert reckoned that at the beginning of the war almost 700 households had some sort of association with his church. (R.R. Martin, *The Church and Parish of St Michael at the Northgate, Oxford* [Oxford, 1967], p. 180.)

14 The main sources for this paragraph concerning St Michael's at the North Gate are the following, all held in the Oxfordshire History Centre: Parish Council Minutes 1942–1944, PAR211/3/A1/3; Vestry Minutes 1871–1955, PAR211/2/A1/5; Parish Registers, PAR211/1/R5/1 and PAR211/1/R3/7; and the *Parish Magazine*, Acc. 5374. Barbara Tearle very generously examined these sources on our behalf and passed along her findings.

Every diary from the later 1930s and 1940s reflects the particular interests, limitations, and perspectives if its author. Some diaries report a lot of war news; others focus more on the immediate everyday concerns of the diarist him- or herself. Some diaries are relatively uncensored and include confidences and opinions that may have been disclosed nowhere else; others are more detached in tone, even feeling at times like exercises in reportage. Many diaries were written every day, or almost every day; others were more like letters, composed only when the writer felt that he or she had something new or significant to say – this was a manner of self-editing that usually downplayed daily, repetitive, unremarkable routine. Most assiduous diarists had a sharp eye for some features of living, even while they may have been indifferent – even virtually blind – to others.

Any diary of an expansive nature that was sustained over a period of years usually reveals, albeit often intermittently and incrementally, a multi-faceted portrait of its producer's social connections, tastes, values, satisfactions, ambitions, mood swings, and frustrations. This is very much the case with Madge Martin and her diary. She wrote almost daily for years, sometimes close to a couple of hundred words per day, occasionally more. Her writing is succinct and precise and never rambling (English was her strong subject at school). Like all diarists, she was more interested in some topics than others. Some aspects of her experiences were mentioned repeatedly; others were infrequently recorded, usually because they were not commonplace. She almost always provided basic facts concerning the many films and plays she attended; by contrast, she never named the newspapers she read on Sunday (and she did, apparently, read more than one) and she had little interest in public policy. There is much in her diary about daily and weekly routines; and as times changed from the later 1930s, these changes, especially in public affairs – and there were many compelling ones – often provoked responses and reflections and self-disclosures never before written down.

So, while some matters recurred again and again, others were new experiences. Life posed new challenges. New threats had to be dealt with. Major, perhaps unprecedented, events triggered feelings previously concealed or suppressed. These fraught years when Madge was continuing to write her diary were bound to reveal a lot about her character, her close relations, and her everyday world in Oxford.

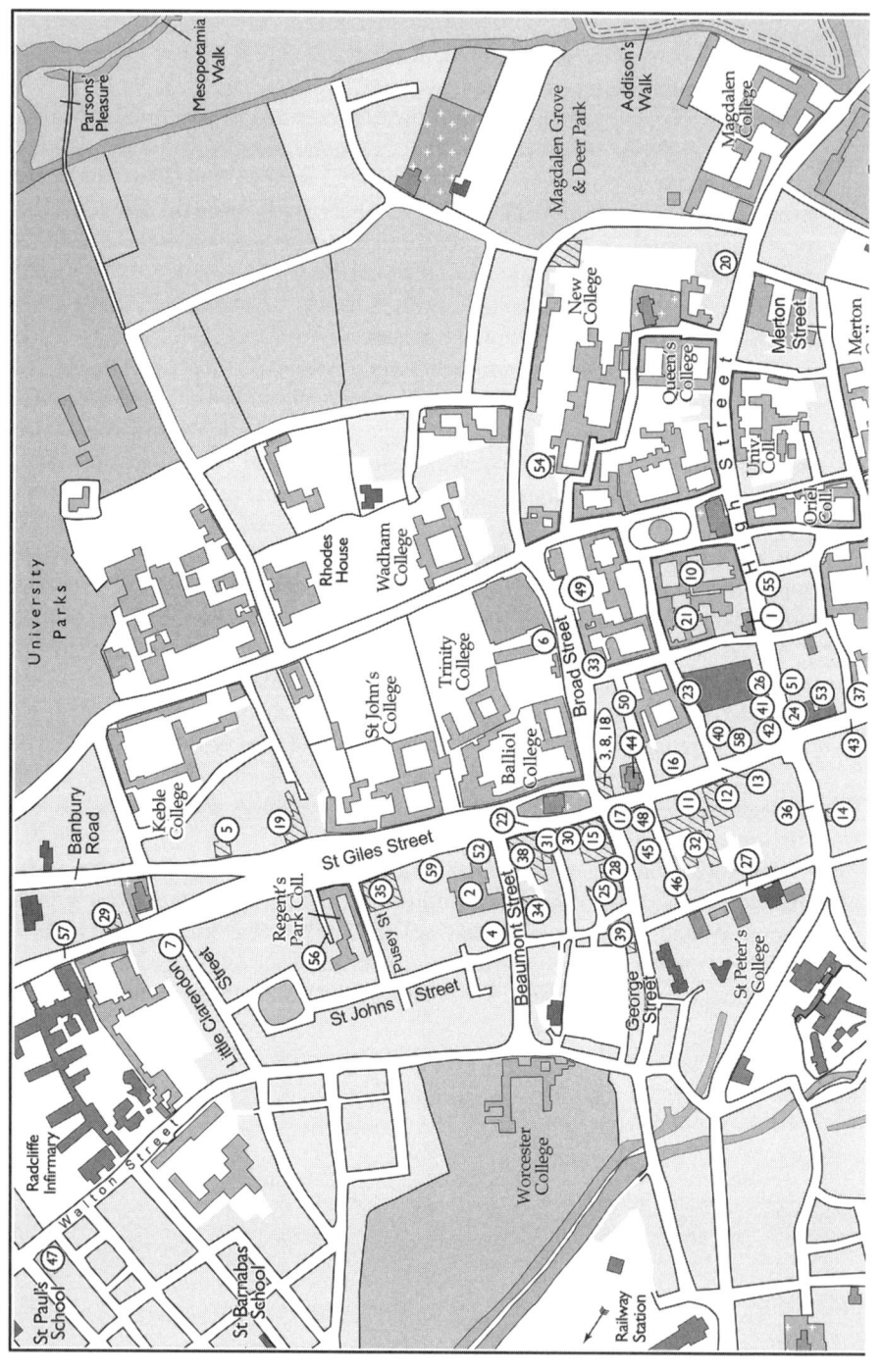

INTRODUCTION 11

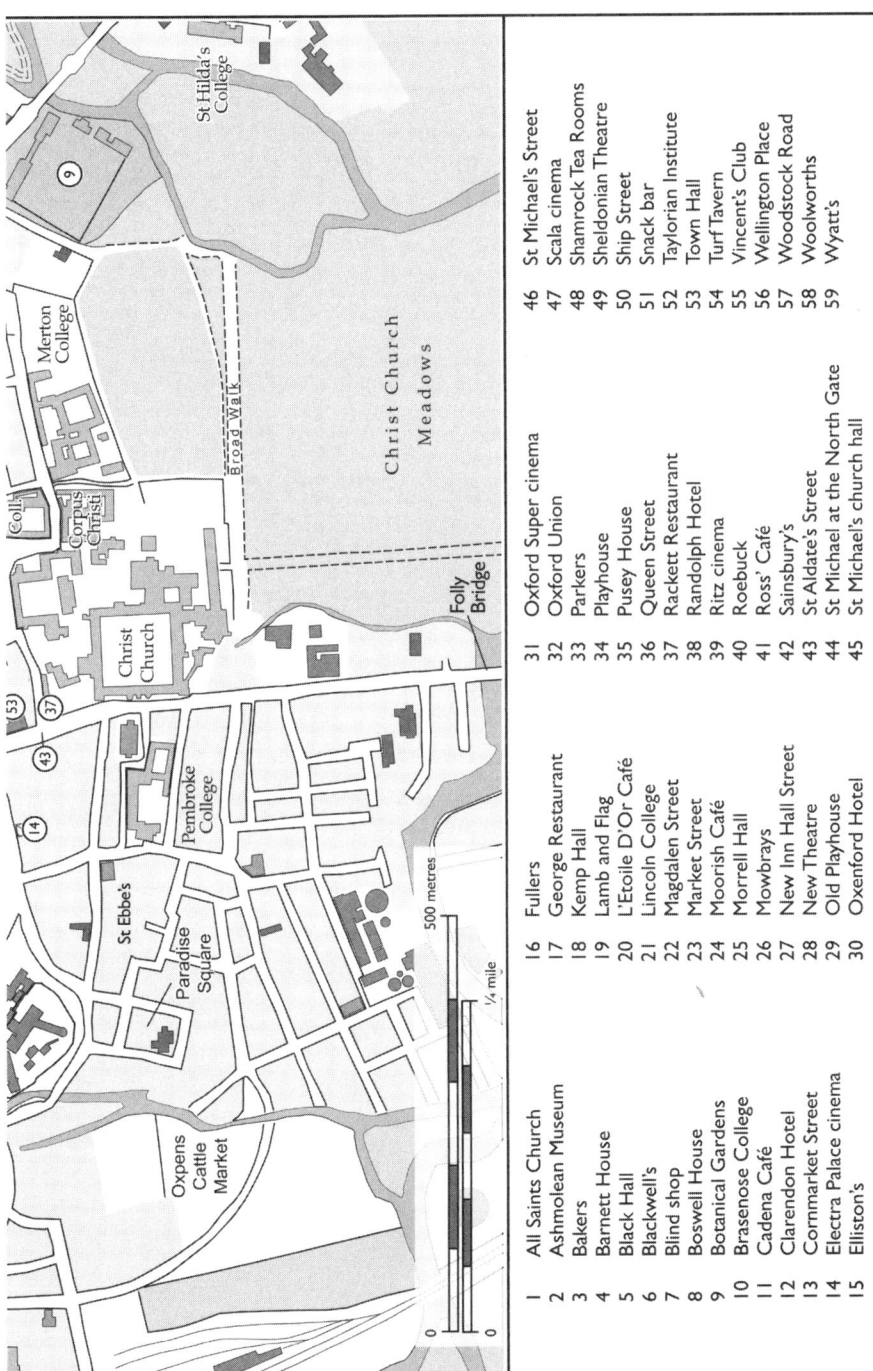

Map 1 Oxford City Centre
The principal streets and places in central Oxford frequently visited by Madge Martin.

1 All Saints Church
2 Ashmolean Museum
3 Bakers
4 Barnett House
5 Black Hall
6 Blackwell's
7 Blind shop
8 Boswell House
9 Botanical Gardens
10 Brasenose College
11 Cadena Café
12 Clarendon Hotel
13 Cornmarket Street
14 Electra Palace cinema
15 Elliston's
16 Fullers
17 George Restaurant
18 Kemp Hall
19 Lamb and Flag
20 L'Etoile D'Or Café
21 Lincoln College
22 Magdalen Street
23 Market Street
24 Moorish Café
25 Morrell Hall
26 Mowbrays
27 New Inn Hall Street
28 New Theatre
29 Old Playhouse
30 Oxenford Hotel
31 Oxford Super cinema
32 Oxford Union
33 Parkers
34 Playhouse
35 Pusey House
36 Queen Street
37 Rackett Restaurant
38 Randolph Hotel
39 Ritz cinema
40 Roebuck
41 Ross' Café
42 Sainsbury's
43 St Aldate's Street
44 St Michael at the North Gate
45 St Michael's church hall
46 St Michael's Street
47 Scala cinema
48 Shamrock Tea Rooms
49 Sheldonian Theatre
50 Ship Street
51 Snack bar
52 Taylorian Institute
53 Town Hall
54 Turf Tavern
55 Vincent's Club
56 Wellington Place
57 Woodstock Road
58 Woolworths
59 Wyatt's

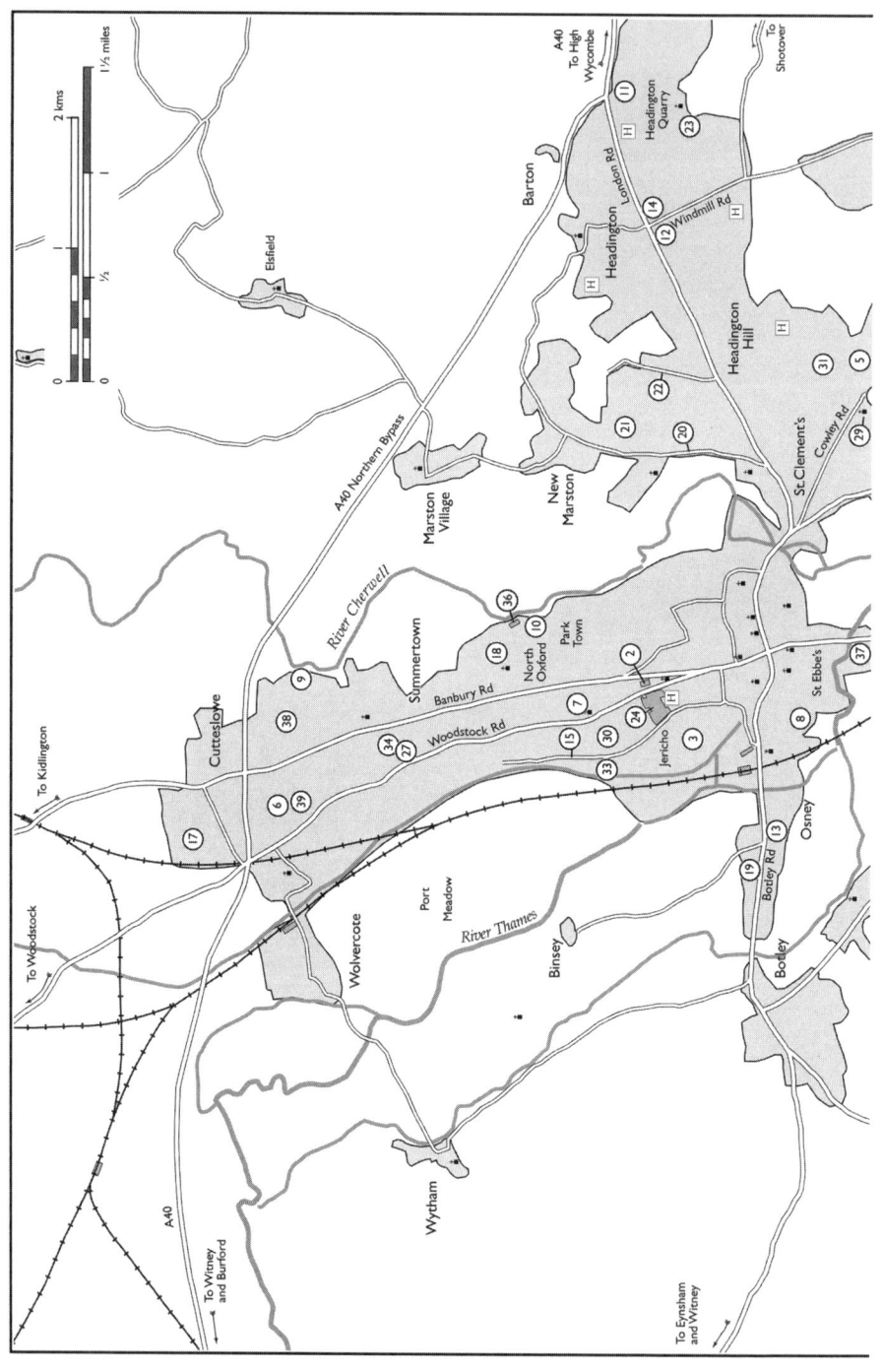

INTRODUCTION

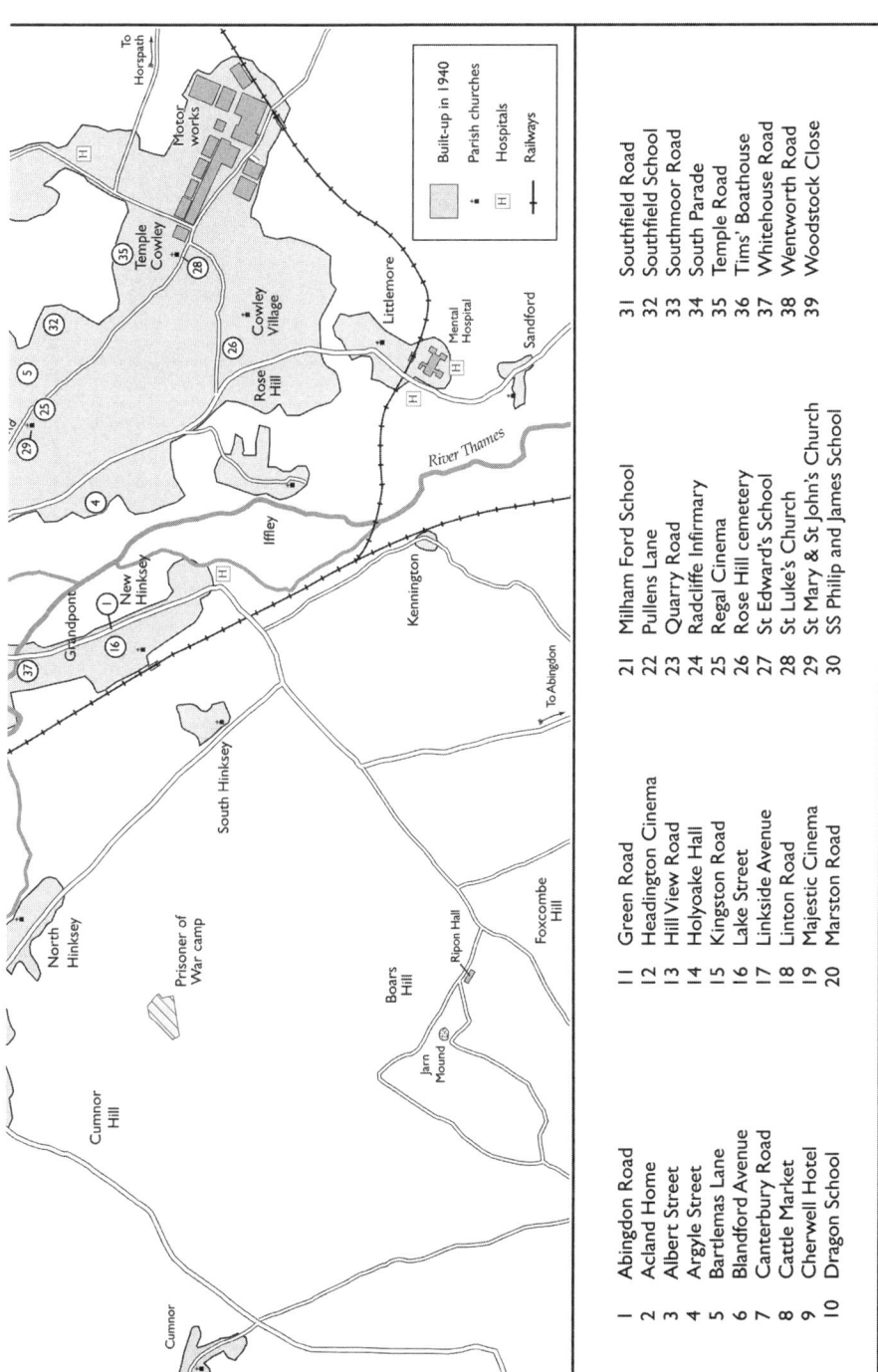

Map 2 Greater Oxford

The area outside Oxford city centre showing the principal places mentioned in the diary.

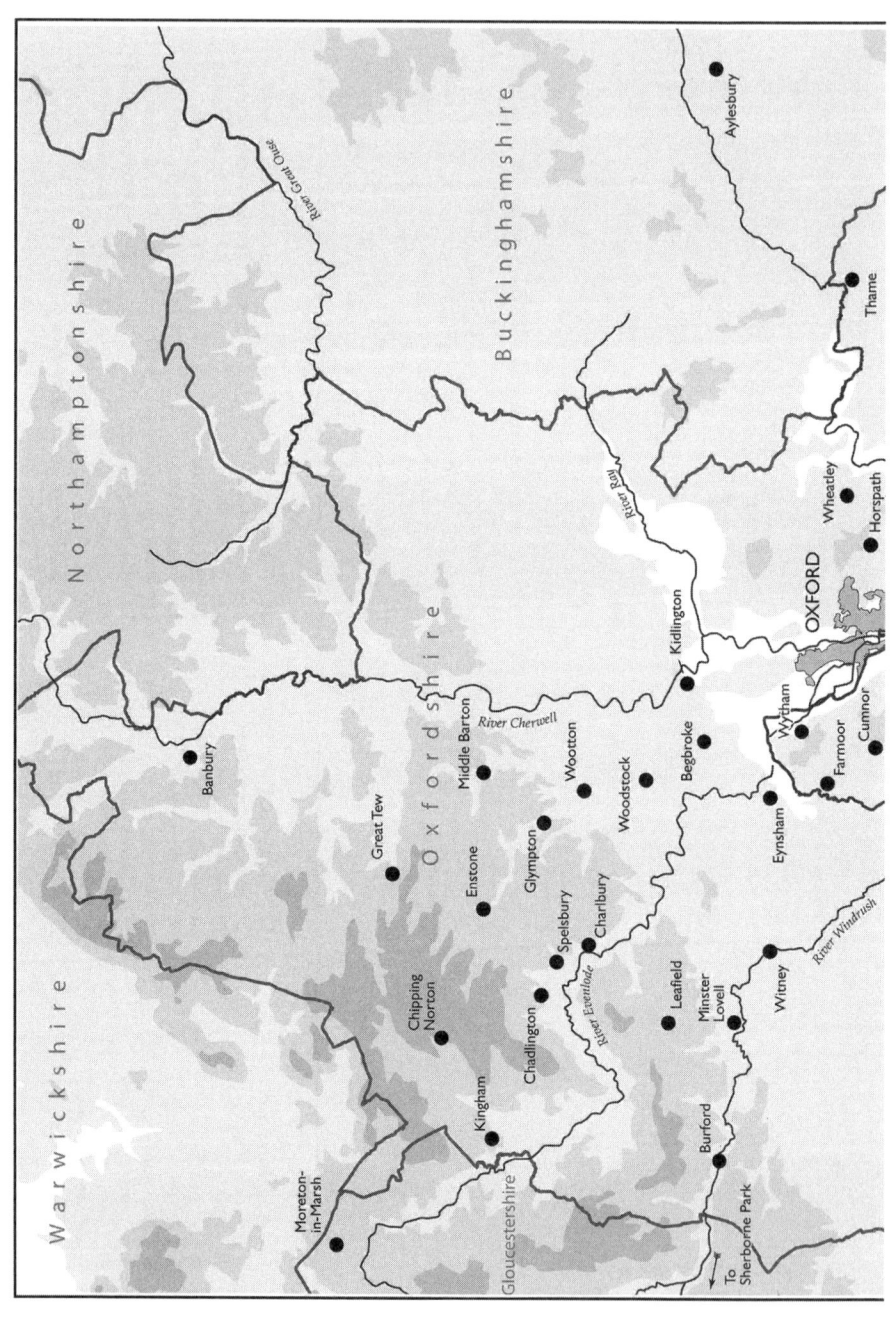

INTRODUCTION

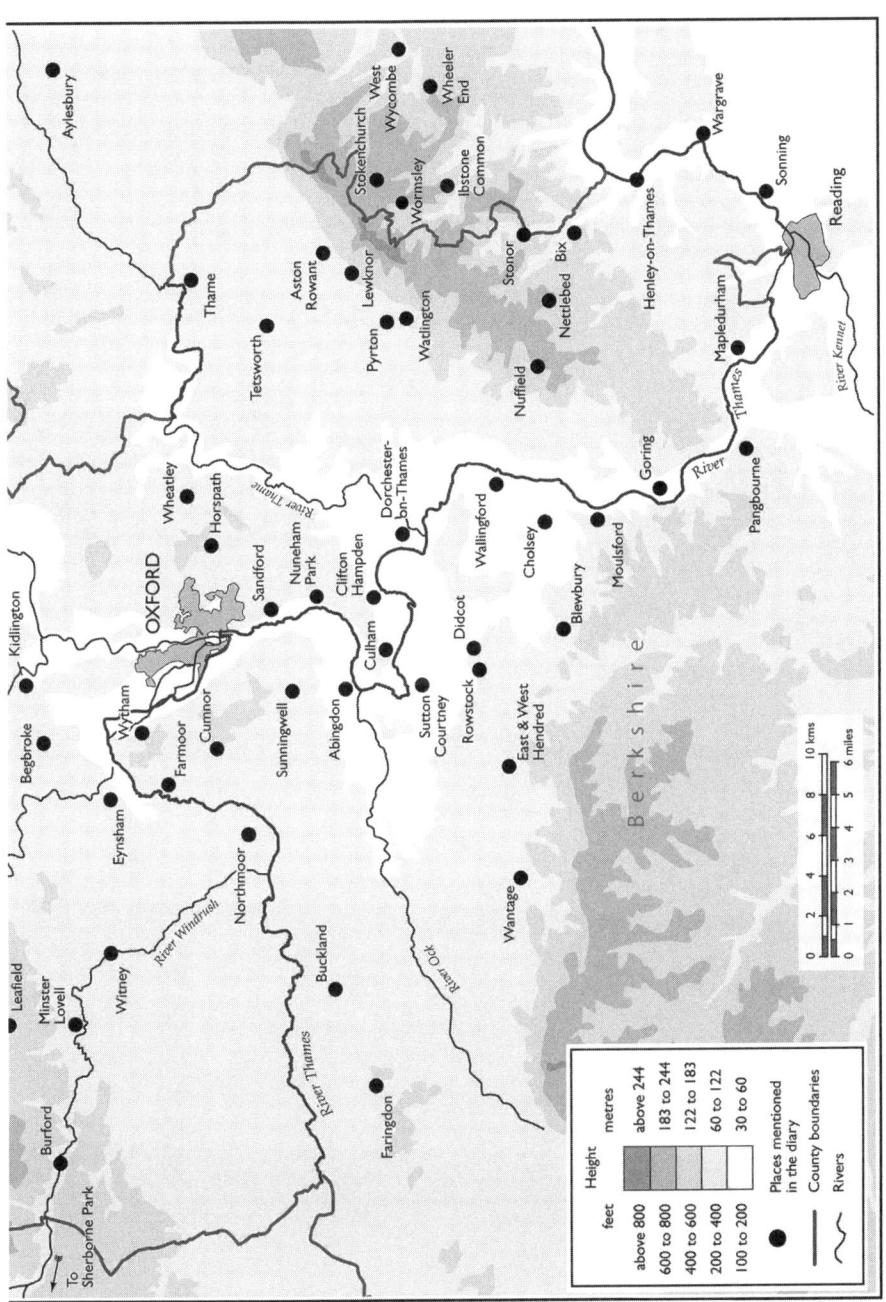

Map 3 The Oxfordshire Region
Places in Oxfordshire and the neighbouring counties visited by Madge and Robert Martin on their walking excursions.

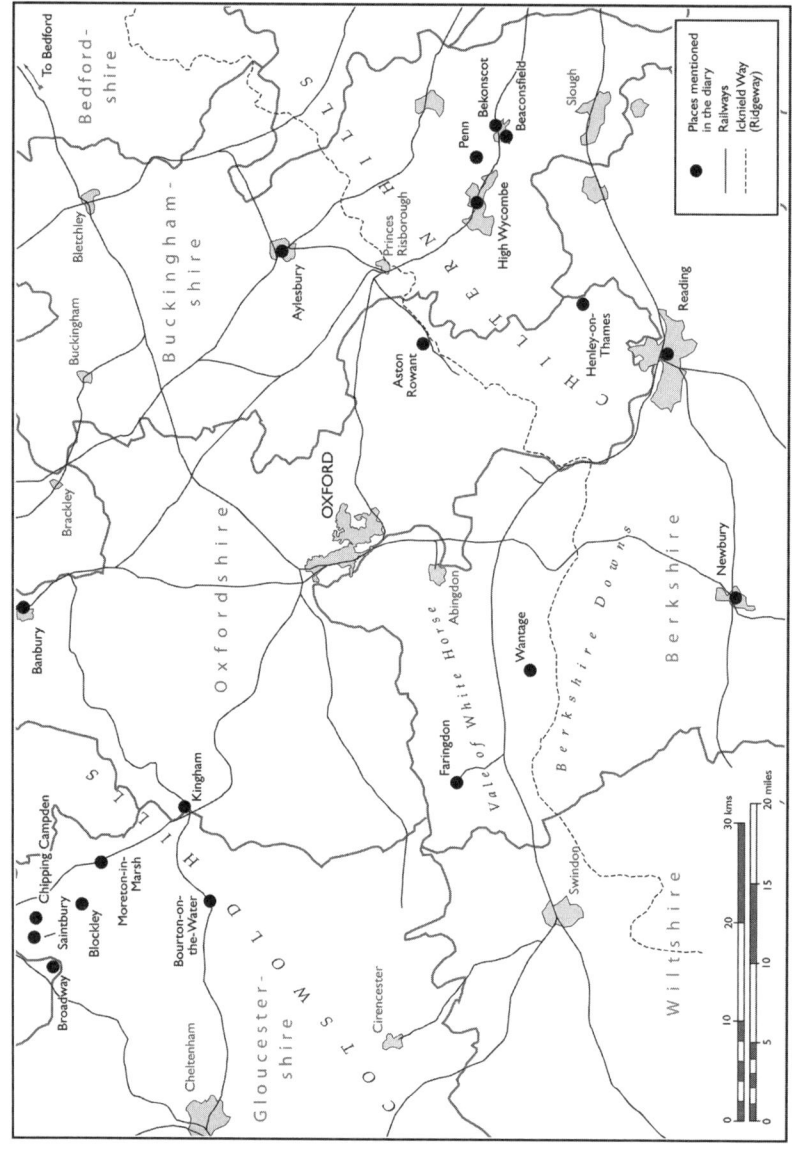

Map 4 Beyond Oxfordshire
Places beyond Map 3 visited by Madge and Robert Martin and the railway network on which they travelled.

1

From Peace to War

September 1938–September 1939

Madge Martin and her husband Robert were keen on holidays and took lots of them, commonly in April/May and perhaps twice in July through September – not to mention many day trips to London and excursions into the countryside near Oxford. During the first eight and a half months of 1938 they were away from Oxfordshire for some ten weeks, or about a quarter of the time. They spent much of the second half of the summer of 1938 on holiday, first three weeks in Scarborough, a longstanding annual event for them,[1] and later in Austria for almost a fortnight, where they did lots of walking and sightseeing and Madge tried out her still rather feeble German. This Continental holiday ended on Friday, 16 September, when the couple travelled from Paris to London, and then, in Madge's words, 'Back to Oxford on our old friend, the 7.40 [from Paddington], and very good dinner on it. Vera [Dyer] there waiting, and Danna [her mother-in-law], and beautiful home [at 1 Wellington Place, St Giles] and English tea, and bright lights and nice bath-room, and quiet bed-room, so I was not dispirited. Thank God for a lovely safe holiday.'

Saturday, 17 September. Back to Saturday morning shopping, but made holidayish by coffee with Vera at the Cadena.[2] I washed my hair in the afternoon, and lazily read, prolonging the holiday as much as possible. Vera came with us to the pictures at night, to see *Test Pilot* [starring Clark Gable,

---

1   Favoured holiday destinations were Brighton and Scarborough, but in the spring of 1938 they chose to spend a fortnight in Portmeirion, North Wales, the fashionable Italianate tourist resort and village on the coast of Snowdonia, designed and developed by Clough Williams-Ellis from the mid-1920s.
2   The Cadena Cafe was at 43–47 Cornmarket Street. It was one of a chain of upmarket coffee shops, most of them in south-west England.

Myrna Loy, Spencer Tracy, and Lionel Barrymore], which was very good [and a favourite among film-goers in 1938].

Sunday, 18 September. Back to the usual Oxford Sunday, or perhaps not *quite* usual, John [Hall] not being here. I heard from [his sister] Susie that he has *been* in Oxford from 6.30 last night to 10.30 this morning, and not come along as he said he would, if he returned to Oxford in the middle of his holiday, but had played badminton instead. Of course this has opened my eyes quite a bit, and may be a good thing in the end. I've been waiting for something to show me the way. Adrian Rushworth [the Church organist] to tea. He is all 'het up' about the experimental organ, being tried out today. To Church again with Vera, and to her house to supper.[3] The kitten is adored by all, and is very frisky.

Monday, 19 September. A busy morning, with much shopping, and then to the station with Vera to meet [sister] Nancy and Roger and Sally, two sweet children, Roger, now 5, Sally 2. They seemed at home at once. We went out again in the afternoon, visiting Woolworths [in Cornmarket Street] and other places of childish interest; then a huge tea. Robert and I and Vera went to see *South Riding*, the film from the book.[4] It was very good indeed. Nancy had seen it, so stayed to look after the children. We had cocktails and supper and chats.

Tuesday, 20 September. A rainy morning. It is a nuisance when we wanted fine weather for the children, however. We took them out in the morning, round the shops, and market, feeding rabbits, and buying things at Woolworths, and having ices at the Cadena. They are both very sweet, and attractive, and well brought up. Out again with Sally after tea. Marjorie took Roger out; they have made friends, as I hoped.[5] There was a momentous [Church] Council meeting at night about the new Compton organ which was passed *nem. con.* [without contradiction] for adoption, after a very plausible young

---

3   The Dyers ran The Turf public house, off Holywell Street.
4   The cast of this 1938 film included Edna Best, Ann Todd, and Ralph Richardson. It was based on the novel by Winifred Holtby, published posthumously in 1936.
5   Marjorie Matthews had been hired earlier this year as a maid. 'She is only 14,' Madge wrote on 2 February, 'and very timid, but I think will serve our purpose, and I mustn't expect too much.' At this point Madge is spelling her name 'Margery', but it is almost certain, from later entries and census data, that the correct spelling is 'Marjorie'.

man from the firm had talked persuasively.⁶ We had supper with Nance after, at the Snack Bar.⁷

Wednesday, 21 September. Shopping with the children, and again the rabbits, Woolworths and ices at the Cadena. I had a long, half apologetic, half facetious letter from John, which I answered in the afternoon – mine half reproachful, half informative (about the organ). Fräulein Hendewerk and Mr Jenkins came to quite a cheery tea, and the latter is getting quite chatty and pleasant.⁸ We all had a taxi to the Regal Cinema [in Cowley Road], and saw quite nice pictures, especially *Judge Hardy's Children* [the third film in the Andy Hardy series], with the marvellous Mickey Rooney.

---

6   The acquisition of a new organ was the first step in a major project of church renovation that was close to Robert's heart. The objective was to restore the Church's ancient Lady Chapel, which was almost entirely occupied and hidden by the large organ in place there since 1914, by first acquiring a new and much smaller organ. According to Martin, Rushworth, the organist, thought that this Compton Electrone organ 'had none of the disadvantages which were criticized in other models, and it could be purchased with less than it was hoped to gain from the sale of the old pipe-organ, which was eventually reconstructed in the Church of St Mary and St John in Cowley Road. The Electrone, though belittled by many musicians, sounded exactly the same as a real pipe-organ to the un-musical majority, and it was so cheap, and suitable to our purpose, that it is not surprising that its purchase was agreed upon at a special Church Meeting with only one dissentient.' (Martin, *Church and Parish of St Michael at the Northgate*, p. 179; and *Parish Magazine*, November 1938, pp. 3 and 10.)

The new organ was in place by the end of the following year, when Madge wrote (Saturday, 16 December 1939): 'I went to an organ-recital given by Mr Rushworth, on the new Compton organ, in Church, in the afternoon. I still don't think it a patch on the old one, but the spacious freed Lady Chapel fully compensates for the loss.' Her husband had already written about the change in the *Parish Magazine*, September 1939, p. 3: the Chapel 'now stands revealed. It is, of course, very worn and dirty, but already shows to the discerning eye how beautiful it will be when properly restored. It seems to have been one of the earliest parts of the Church' – thought to be fourteenth-century (its eleventh-century tower is the oldest surviving building in Oxford). After some understandable wartime delays, the Chapel was official reopened by the Bishop of Dorchester on 2 February 1941.

7   This eating place had been mentioned on 11 April 1938, when, after the cinema, she and Robert went 'to supper at the Snack Bar at 129 High Street, where we lived so happily for years. It was strange walking up the familiar dirty stairs.'

8   Ruth Hendewerk, a refugee, taught German to Madge, who thought highly of her. 'She is really a splendid person, I think, so brave and cheery in spite of all her worries' (26 May 1938) – 'one of the finest characters I know' (22 July 1938). Kenneth Jenkins was the new curate at St Michael's, where he had been ordained on Sunday, 24 July 1938. Madge was there: 'Quite an occasion, with Bishop Allen [Bishop of Dorchester], and important looking vestments and flowers and candles and all the lovely plate being impressive.' The Bishop was also Archdeacon of Oxford and often officiated in Oxford.

Thursday, 22 September. A very bright clear autumn morning. Nance and I took the children to the Meadows to see the barges, then for their ices at the Cadena. Marjorie-the-obliging took them out in the afternoon. Mrs Bryant called, and interrupted our peace. There was a Committee meeting at night, to arrange all the fascinating (?)[9] whist-drives for the season. Thank heaven, the working party has been abandoned for the time being. How I did hate that Tuesday's boredom. Home quite early to books and supper.

Friday, 23 September. Quite warm and sunny. Nancy decided to risk leaving the babes with Marjorie and Doris,[10] and come walking with us, so we just caught a Henley bus, by chasing it breathlessly, and got out at Nettlebed, from where we walked – to Stonor, first having lunch at the Stonor Arms, then on to Wormsley, the trees of the lovely Chiltern country looking so beautiful in the September sunshine. We had a tremendous walk, falling, eventually, into the Beacon Café for tea, tired out. Bus back, the children quite safe but dirty when we got back. Norman [Nancy's husband] suddenly arrived, earlier than expected. Nice for him to have a little longer.

Saturday, 24 September. I took Sally out shopping with me in the morning – a slow but nice expedition. I took her to the Cadena for an ice, and met Muriel [Smith] there. She had to be sensible (Muriel); even Sally's company prevented any foolishness, except panic-stricken talk about war preparations. Nancy and I had a quiet afternoon resting our poor feet after yesterday's walk, then went out after tea, before settling down to a peaceful evening with books – all four of us.

Sunday, 25 September. Poor wee Roger not feeling well today. He had to stay in bed. There was the annual Church Parade of the Oxford Fire Brigade and St John's Ambulance Corps, for the first time at St Michael's. There were 200 of them and they almost filled the Church alone, and looked and sang grandly. We watched them all march away with band and engine. What a

---

9 Madge disliked whist, but church society required her frequently to organize and participate in whist-drives. She attended some eight or nine evening whist-drives during the first eight months of 1938.

10 Doris Dandridge, a married woman born in 1904, had served as a maid with the Martins for about a decade. Her husband was a steel works labourer, but had other skills as well, for he was employed to redecorate parts of 1 Wellington Place while Madge and Robert were holidaying in Scarborough in 1939 (17 August). The Dandridges appear to have had no children. Their home was at 24 Paradise Square, a working-class neighbourhood about half a mile south of Wellington Place. We are grateful to Ann Stephenson for her research on both Doris Dandridge and Marjorie Matthews.

shame Roger didn't see them.[11] A quite peaceful afternoon – Marjorie out with Sally. Poor little Roger still in bed. Evensong at night. John was back and we exchanged meaning[ful] glances. A lot of rioting in the streets, and cries of 'Down with Chamberlain' and 'We want peace'.[12]

Monday, 26 September. Roger still not well, and we decided to call in the Doctor. I took Sally to Worcester [College] Gardens, and the Cadena, and shopping with Muriel. I love the fat little thing. Out again with her in the afternoon. She is very friendly with me, and seems to like me. Muriel came for a hasty cup of tea before returning home. A quiet evening, reading. The dread of a European war is over everything at the moment, and one just dare not think about it. The only talk is of Hitler, Czechoslovakia and Chamberlain. Please God, we shall not have war. We cannot contemplate it.

Tuesday, 27 September. Out with Sally shopping etc. The papers glaring with head-lines about Hitler's passionate speech last night. One can only go about doing one's ordinary daily duties, as thinking only dazes one just now. I had a headache, so stayed in, listening to the Queen launching the giant new liner, the *Queen Elizabeth*. She made a very nice speech.[13] Nancy out with Sally and Marjorie. Roger improving in leaps and bounds. We were to have had a peaceful evening, but were plunged into the depths of gloom by a panic-stricken phone call from Norman to Nancy, urging her to stay here out of the danger-zone, and the late news, and the Prime Minister's speech, were disquieting to a degree.

---

11   'A regular thrill to see the Church packed, with huge men singing,' wrote Robert. 'The congregation seemed quite remote. I preached what I thought was a stirring sermon on the Crisis etc.'
12   While there is little or no evidence of rioting, there were certainly vigorous and angry protests against Chamberlain's appeasement policies. At a 'crowded and enthusiastic meeting' at the Town Hall on Saturday night, the principles of collective security were reaffirmed and Britain's prospective 'betrayal' of Czechoslovakia and 'shameful surrender' condemned. The meeting was organized by anti-Tories and the principal speakers included Patrick Gordon Walker, Labour candidate for Oxford City, and Councillor Richard Crossman, both major figures in the post-war Labour Party. (*Oxford Mail*, 26 September 1938, p. 6.)
13   The launch of this ship, the largest in the world at 85,000 tons, was a major event, witnessed on Clydeside (it was estimated) by at least a quarter of a million people. The BBC made 'elaborate arrangements' to broadcast the ceremony, using fourteen microphones. The event was portrayed as 'symbolic of brave hopes for the future. … The launch of such a ship as the Queen Elizabeth would be hailed by the nation as a triumph of national achievement at any time; today it is all the more notable as a reminder that the world's greatest achievements are those of peace and not of strife.' Because of 'the international situation', the King was unable to attend as planned. (*The Times*, 26 September 1938, p. 9 and 27 September 1938, pp. 9 and 13.)

Wednesday, 28 September. Feeling awful after an almost sleepless night, worrying and worrying about the probability of war. It is too dreadful. Nance in the same plight. I had such a very busy morning, too, decorating the Church with Michaelmas daisies, meeting the Bleibens[14] for coffee and having Nita, Dick,[15] Phil and Mr Holland to lunch. Dick is in a terrible state of nerves, and is already planning to send Nita and Kit [their son, Christopher] here to stay if war breaks out. We had a mixed afternoon, going round the colleges and talking war-war-war! After they went Robert and I tried to get our gas masks, but have to go tomorrow instead. The news was slightly more hopeful in the evening. There is to be a meeting tomorrow between Hitler, Neville Chamberlain, Ciano, Mussolini and Daladier. Let us *pray* some good will come of this.

Thursday, 29 September, Michaelmas Day. I went to the services in Church in the morning and met Nancy for shopping afterwards. There seems a hush over everything, as if all the world is waiting to know its fate. Nance and I left the children with Marjorie in the afternoon, and had a soothing walk on Magdalen Island, looking lovely in the sunshine. Mr Jenkins to tea again. He is a pessimist over the war question. Robert and I went to the old Playhouse [nearby, on Woodstock Road] where we have seen such jolly light-hearted shows, and were fitted for gas masks. It really depressed me more than anything to see the patient ordinary crowd of men, women and children waiting to be fitted on with these hideous monstrosities [she drew a picture of one], just in the day's work.[16] Mrs Martin [i.e., Danna, as she is usually referred to later] had hers fitted on, too, by our nearest ARP (Air Raid Precautions) officer, Mr Bullock. She took it quite calmly. Nance and I both went to Evensong. John came in for a long talk afterwards. He was cheerful, hopeful, and hard as nails. Robert seemed depressed at night. The waiting for the news is awful.

---

14   Winifred and Peter Bleiben were a regular presence in the Martins' lives. While his given names were Thomas Eric, Madge always referred to him as Peter. He was vicar of Holy Trinity at Headington Quarry, some three miles east of Wellington Place, and lived with his wife in the vicarage there. Both he and Robert were Oxford-educated; they and their wives were all born between 1895 and 1903; neither couple had children; and their incomes were probably fairly similar. Madge considered Winifred to be a much more effective parson's wife than she was: see note to 15 October 1943, p. 230.
15   Madge's other sister, Nita, was married to Dick; they were visiting from London, where they lived.
16   *Oxford Mail*, 27 September 1938, p. 5; *Oxford Times*, 30 September 1938, p. 13.

Friday, 30 September. God be praised! The morning newspapers had the blessed word **PEACE** shouting out the glad tidings in huge letters. The relief is so great that one feels, as yet, a little numb. The Conference was successful. Let us hope it is a *lasting* peace. Robert went up to town to meet [his brother] Harry, and Nance and I shopped. Roger looks very pale still, and is inclined to be naughty in his convalescence. Nance also is washed out – no wonder. Vera's mother has had another attack, but seemed cheerful when I went in to see her. Nance and I had tea at the Bleibens, which was nice, and very cheery. We listened in to Neville Chamberlain's arrival home and the tumultuous welcome he received. It was thrilling. Norman had arrived home when we got back, and we listened again to more triumphant receptions, and nearly wept with joy and pride. We had a very peaceful, cheerful evening talking over our thankfulness and relief.[17]

Saturday, 1 October. Everyone happy and smiling, thinking what a fearful week-end it might have been. I had another busy morning, attending again to the flowers and the children at the same time, and shopping and having coffee and talking to Mrs Potter. I really have lots to do these days, but I rather like it. I took the children over to the Potters' in the afternoon to see the machines, which they loved and the whole house.[18] Nancy and Norman at the pictures, and after tea, Robert and I went, but the films were poor, so we left early, came back for Nancy and Norman, and all had supper at the snack bar, then looked in on the Junior Guild Dance.[19] We left Norman and Nance there.

---

17 Madge pasted on the adjoining page in her diary a press clipping of Chamberlain holding up the letter of agreement from Munich with the accompanying words, 'This bears Herr Hitler's name and mine'. Just over two years later, with the Blitz on London well under way, on 10 November 1940, after Chamberlain's death from cancer, she offered a favourable verdict on him. 'What a wonderful gentle-heroic person he was. If only he could have lived to see the Peace he tried to save for us.'
18 Mr and Mrs Potter, who lived at 29 St Giles, were active members of St Michael's congregation, where he was on the PCC, a Ruridecanal representative and one of the church-wardens during the 1930s and 1940s. From his home he ran the Potter Press and in 1934 obtained the contract to print the *Parish Magazine*. The machines that caused the children such delight were probably printing presses. (PAR/211/3/A1/3, April 1933, December 1934; *Parish Magazine*, January 1942. Barbara Tearle kindly did the research for this note.)
19 St Michael's Guild, established in the later nineteenth century, was the Church's recreational society, whose principal business by now was organizing whist-drives. Around 1923 a Junior Guild – that is, a youth club for both sexes – was set up, when Robert was Assistant Curate, and he and Madge were active in helping to run it, as Robert later recounted. 'They [speaking of himself and Madge] were both interested in acting, and it was found that the performance of a play with all the preparation involved and improvisation of costumes,

Sunday, 2 October. Our Dedication Festival of St Michael's was swamped by the Thanksgiving Services of today. Torrential rain in the morning, but it didn't keep many people away from Church, to shout their joy and thanks for the deliverance from the awful Peril that so nearly overtook us all. John came in for a chat (mostly with Norman) after the Service. The little family departed after tea. We shall never forget this visit of theirs. I shall miss them, as I always do my family, and especially Sally whom I love dearly. I went with Marjorie to Evensong, and *what* an Evensong! A crowded Church, full of people eager to be thankful, a wonderful sermon from Robert, and glad, grateful hymns. I wanted to weep for joy all today, and have never felt so strongly that there is a God, who hears our prayers. Let me remember this.

Monday, 3 October. Oh, so quiet, without the children, and Marjorie said 'ghastly'. But one gets round the shops with great speed, and there is something to be said for peaceful arm-chairs and the quiet reading of books and newspapers. Winifred Bleiben and I went up to the tailor in Summertown and arranged about winter suits – mine to be black, hers blue. Then I went to see Vera whose mother is much better. I had a headache so went to bed all the afternoon. It was a wild tempestuous night and we were to have gone to the pictures, but Vera came a bit late, and it was really too bad to go out, so we had a cosy evening before the fire, talking most about PEACE. Now 'Thank we all our God'!

Tuesday, 4 October. Howling gale doing much damage still raging, and very cold, too. Robert and I bought one another 'Peace presents'. He to me *Gone*

---

properties and scenery, was the very best way of keeping young people in touch with the Church, which was the avowed object of this Guild. The normal non-dramatic activities were games, talks, discussions and monthly dances, but nothing maintained the interest of the young members so much as the choice of a new play, the agonizing rehearsals and triumphant performances' (Martin, *Church and Parish of St Michael at the Northgate*, p. 144). Robert went on (pp. 144–5) to recount some of the history of the young people's productions during the 1920s and 1930s. Drama, broadly conceived, was, as Madge's diary attests, a vital component of the Martins' existence.

Robert concluded by observing (p. 146) that the Junior Guild 'acted as an entirely innocent and most successful marriage market. The members ranged from sixteen to about twenty-five in age, and the shyest youth or girl would soon find a congenial partner there, or, if not suited at first, some would change partners without the slightest ill-will, until they found the right one, and many happily married couples in Oxford today [the mid-1960s] are glad to recall how they first met each other at the Junior Guild, and were married at St Michael's.'

with the Wind, which will be lovely to possess,[20] and I to him *The King's Service* (Ian Hay). The anti-climax feeling is on me, in spite of all I promised to myself, but I suppose everyone will feel this to a certain extent. We went out to tea with Mrs Sever and her son. She has a nice flat in Woodstock Close but is not very nice herself, being North Country, self-interested, and a snob. The son was quite pleasant. I went with Robert to New College where they now have very gloomy lighting, then to the Parochial meeting about the Compton organ for which everyone except one voted. Robert and I had a snack-bar supper. I must go on saying '**PEACE-PEACE**' to myself.

Wednesday, 5 October. Still gales and heavy rainstorms, but bright sunshine in between the showers, like March. Shopping in the morning, and to see Vera. Her mother is 'up and doing' and looks better. We went out to tea with the notorious Joyce Blencowe and her fiancé Prince Mahmoud, a quiet tiny Malayan. They have been the talk of the town, and England, before other things pushed them into the back-ground. The mother and grandmother also there for a rather confusing tea-party. Joyce is a blonde and traditionally 'dumb' but pleasant.[21] Vera came with us later to the Snack Bar and very

---

20   She had already seen the film three times (and would see it at least twice again) and read Margaret Mitchell's novel, presumably a borrowed copy.
21   Joyce Blencowe, daughter of the owner of a tailoring business in St Clements, Oxford, was engaged to be married to Prince Mahmoud, a son of the late Sultan of Trengganu, Malaya and brother to the current Sultan. Both principals were aged 20; they were said to have met at a dance during his student days at Oxford. Such an irregular alliance had, understandably, attracted public notice – as well as initial opposition from the Prince's brother. The sole reference to the couple in *The Times* (17 September 1938, p. 12) relates to a charge of assault against the Prince by a photographer who had taken a picture of them walking together in High Street, Oxford. (The summons was dismissed.) They were married in Oxford the following spring (*Oxford Mail*, 1 June 1939, p. 1).

Madge was well acquainted with the Blencowe household, who were among St Michael's congregation, for on 25 November 1939 she went 'to have tea with Mrs Blencowe, and her elder daughter and mother. It was chiefly to see stacks of photographs of Joy[ce], the younger daughter who married a Malaysian prince and went to Malay recently. The elder daughter is as plain and intelligent as the other is pretty and stupid. I quite liked my tea and looking at snaps is a thing I adore.' The young couple were back in Oxford nine months later (19 August 1940). 'Robert and I went to tea in the afternoon with the Blencowes, and the Prince Mahmoud and his bride – a Blencowe before marriage. They very sweetly brought us home a present from Malay – some very pretty native coffee spoons. We were very touched. She showed us many of her beautiful silver things, all carved by the natives, also the lovely baby clothes she had made for her baby-to-be. We quite enjoyed ourselves.' Madge went to the christening of this baby, 'little Prince Andrew Clive', on Sunday, 24 November 1940. 'We wanted to know if the baby would be black or white. It is white!' (See also below, 17 November 1938 and 11 June 1942. Barbara Tearle kindly passed on to us relevant newspaper evidence.)

good pictures, *The Divorce of Lady X* [a romantic comedy with Laurence Olivier and Ralph Richardson, 1938], at the Super [Oxford Super Cinema in Magdalen Street].

Thursday, 6 October. I bought new shoes and stockings, which I begrudge, then went with Winifred to have a fitting of our costumes which should be nice. A sort of tired lethargy is upon me, and I am annoyed and realise that I should be full of happiness, but there is a worrying *un*happiness somewhere. I shouldn't be surprised if John had something to do with it – but how silly if this is so. I am not sure. Fräulein Hendewerk came in the afternoon and talked and talked somewhat depressingly, about the world situation. It wasn't a lesson, but she talked German for the most part. The first whist-drive at night – a military one.[22] I was bored and tired, instead of being glad to be peacefully playing whist. How wicked I am.

Friday, 7 October. A London day. Torrents of rain did not upset us, and we went up on the 10.10, rejoicing in being able to do this, in Peace-time. I did some shopping at Lafayette's, two jumpers (pink, and red), gloves from Robert. A taxi through the sloshing rain to the Palace to find the times of the film we wanted to see. A nice lunch at the Regent Palace Hotel, then the film *Flashbacks*, showing the growth of films, and some very funny old ones of darling Mary Pickford and Charlie Chaplin,[23] and historical events. A quick tea and short walk, then to *Pygmalion* [by George Bernard Shaw], with our Leslie Howard and a good girl, Wendy Hillier, as Eliza. It was *very* good. Home on the 7.40. John came in and stayed till nearly mid-night. We, or I, had my grievance out, and if not penitent, he was at least kind, and we parted friends for the millionth time. I expect I shall now lose that stupefied feeling, and recover my lost pounds.

Saturday, 8 October. A busy morning – Saturday morning shopping, as well as the Harvest decorations to do. Vera is still keeping at home, so Susie Hall helped me bedeck the altar with flame-coloured gladioli and lilies. She and Grace had coffee at Fullers [24 Cornmarket] with me after. We had a couple to tea. The man, a fat oldish clergyman who has taken over the Police Court Missions Secretaryship from Robert, and his youngish somewhat cockney wife. They left no impression! Vera called, and we went, in the stormy

---

22 In military whist each table represents a country and strives to capture the flags of other countries by the winning hands.
23 Years later, on 4 December 1942, she saw Chaplin in one of his silent films, *The Gold Rush*, 'brought up to date with dialogue by Charlie himself.... He really is *the* genius of the screen.'

wetness, to see *Jezebel* at the distant Regal [in Cowley Road]. It was not so good as I had hoped, but Bette Davis is always worth seeing, in a snake-like way. My mind has got all unravelled again, and calm.

Sunday, 9 October. I got up early for the 8 o'clock Holy Communion. Because of the wild rain and wind, there were very few there, for Harvest. Better weather later in the morning, and quite a good congregation. John in as of old, hard and brightly sardonic, but goodish company – I call it his Sunday mood. A peaceful afternoon, reading. A crowded Harvest Festival evensong. Vera came to Church, but I didn't go home with her. Her mother is still not well. A nice read.

Monday, 10 October. Quite a nice day – no rain, sunny and cheerful. We decided suddenly to walk, so took a bus to Enstone, on the Chipping Norton road, and walked to Great Tew for lunch. A lot of to-day's walk, unfortunately seemed to be on roads. Great Tew is lovely, and we had a nice sandwich lunch at a pub there. Then walked over fields, with splendid clear autumn landscapes to look at, eventually to Glympton, and on to the Oxford Road, tired and tea-less. However we had a very nice tea when we got back, at the Ritz, then picked up Vera and went to the Super for quite good pictures [*Bringing Up Baby*, starring Katharine Hepburn and Cary Grant, and *Un Carnet de Bal* [1937], with Marie Bell]. A very long programme and a late supper. I was quite exhausted after the long day.

Tuesday, 11 October. Great excitement in the morning, when our drawing-room chimney caught fire tremendously, with flames and dense smoke, so that we had to send for the Fire-Brigade. By the time they arrived, of course, it was all over. We had the sweep later when things had cooled off a bit. I had a last fitting with Winifred for my black costume, then went out with Vera shopping. I had a 'facial' in the afternoon, washed my hair in the evening, and Vera came to supper.

Wednesday, 12 October. Shopping, and later to buy material for a blouse, and dress, with Vera. A German lesson in the afternoon. Sometimes I despair at my slowness, but I *must* persist, and keep up my interest. Ruth stayed to tea as usual, and I had a busy evening sticking holiday snaps in to the book, 61 in all. Mrs Acton and her daughter Peggy called. The latter has always interested me ever since I saw her, ten years ago, as an adorable child with red gold plaits. Now she is a beauty, with her hair piled on top of her head, and with, still, her childlike untouched air. Just lovely. They return to India for another spell, tomorrow. Vera in to supper.

Thursday, 13 October. Wild warm wet weather. I'm tired of having my hair blown about the face and coming out of curl. I went along to Miss Boyce [a dressmaker, at 187 Southmoor Road, Walton Manor] to arrange about my blouse, and dress, and shopped with Vera later. We all went to tea with the Grays, who are so friendly, and give us such a hearty old-fashioned tea, which we always enjoy.[24] A whist-drive at night. I went with Vera. Quite a lot there.

Friday, 14 October. At last, a beautiful autumn day, with sunshine and pale blue skies. Shopping with Robert and coffee with Winifred, then shopping with Vera. I must walk miles in the mornings but I like it. I had to play hostess to a Jamaica Church Aid meeting, in Lincoln College. Bishop [Gerald Burton Allen] and Mrs Allen there, and the Bishop of Jamaica, to speak.[25] I felt quite important, and wore my best clothes! What a difference these make, and how silly that they should.[26] John came in at 9.15 and, alas, we had stormy words, about his superior attitude and cynical remarks, and parted in anger.

Saturday, 15 October. Another perfect autumn day. Shopping and meeting Muriel at the Cadena for coffee. She tried hard to be sensible but it always seems a struggle. She and the Potters came to tea in the afternoon. I felt, as usual, dazed by the end, with Mrs Potter's gabble, but they are friendly people. Muriel came out for a little shopping with me after. Then Vera came and we all had (for us) an unusual evening talking amicably and having supper. I had a trying-on of my newly arrived black costume. Quite a pleasant unperturbed evening.

Sunday, 16 October. To Church in warm wettish weather, and my black costume. I always insist on wearing new things straight away, whatever the weather. Muriel there. John came in after and was suddenly and

---

24 The Gray family lived at 189 Banbury Road and had been active members of St Michael's Church for many years; Mr A.D. Gray as secretary, clerk and treasurer of various committees; and Mrs Gray as a PCC member and Ruridecanal representative. (*Parish Magazine* April 1938, p. 10 and January 1942, p. 12; PAR/211/3/A1/3, April 1933 and April 1935.)

25 The Jamaica Church Aid Association, which many churches in Britain supported, provided aid for the Jamaican Church. Bishop Edmund W. Sara was Assistant Bishop of Jamaica from 1937 to 1939. After his resignation, he was appointed Assistant Bishop of Bath and Wells (*The Times*, 20 September 1965, p. 12).

26 'I felt proud of my beautiful Bun,' wrote Robert in his diary about Madge at the event. 'Auntie Bun' was how Priscilla Ramsey, Madge's niece (b. 1930), spoke of her (information courtesy Priscilla Ramsey, November 2017).

astonishingly nice, and went so far as to suggest us seeing a play together in London. I was quite staggered at this change. I shall *never* understand him! A calm afternoon reading, the calm broken with Muriel's appearance before she returned to London. She cannot keep sensible for long. Church at night and to Vera's for the usual nice supper and chat. Their kitten, Andy, is the apple of their eyes.

Monday, 17 October. A nice holiday day with warm sunny weather, so we decided to walk again. Train in the morning to Reading, then a beautiful walk back near the shining silver Thames, and amongst green and russet leaves, to Maple-Durham and then on to Pangbourne for a late but very nice cold lunch. We had meant to continue to Goring, but feeling a bit tired, we thought we would come home earlier. We had to change at Didcot where we had time to see the town, which is a most desolate and haphazard sort of place. We came back in the new speedy diesel-coach, and then went straight to the Scala [on Walton Street] for not-so-good films [*Le Puritain* and *Two's Company*], nice bacon and eggs supper at 8.30 and an early bed for me.

Tuesday, 18 October. The weather dull and rainy again. I had much shopping and a fitting at Miss Boyce's. I can't think why I like Walton Street, as it is really as awful as most of the other Oxford suburban roads, but I am quite fond of it. Perhaps because it has the Scala in it, a cinema I like, in spite of shabbiness and old films. Strange![27] I sat knitting a square most of the afternoon – to be sent towards making blankets for the Chinese refugees. We went to the 'Super' at night with Vera, and saw two quite good films, *Blockade* [with Henry Fonda, set in the Spanish Civil war] and *Romance à la carte* [an English comedy].

Wednesday, 19 October. Up to town with Vera. Lovely sunny warm weather and both full of beans, except for me having a cold. We went straight to C & A's, a big shop which has a large stock of clothes. Vera bought a coat and dress, both navy. We had to have a taxi to meet mother at the Corner House. She was very lively, and glad to meet us, looking quite nice, in black. We

---

27 The Scala, according to one authority, 'developed a highly successful policy of programming specialist and foreign films (the latter always in the original and subtitled, never dubbed), with mainstream and classic re-runs during university vacations' (Ian Meyrick, *Oxfordshire Cinemas* [Stroud: Tempus, 2007], p. 95). 'I hate some of the Oxford suburbs,' she declared on 1 August 1941; and later that year, on 2 December, she wrote that 'The Cowley Road is a most dreary place, but has a morbid fascination, just as, in a bigger way, the south London suburbs have.'

hurried through our meal in the Brasserie, then went to the 'New' theatre to see a Victorian play called *She Too Was Young* [by Hilda Vaughan, b. 1892; published 1938]. It was very sweet and charming, and unhurried, and we enjoyed it. We did some further shopping and had tea in the crowded Corner house, and *more* shopping, then parted from mother, and returned on the 7.45.

Thursday, 20 October. St Luke's summer is with us, with its warmth and mellow sunshine. Very lovely. I am sneezing my head off at the moment, and oozing at the eyes. A bad cold makes one feel so inferior. Shopping in the morning, and a rest all afternoon, then Mr Jenkins for tea. He is much less shy, now. We changed into evening clothes, and met at the George [an expensive restaurant on the corner of Cornmarket Street and George Street] for a lovely dinner, then to the opening of the new Playhouse in Beaumont Street. It was a lovely occasion, with hundreds of boiled shirts and elegant women. Irene Vanbrugh spoke the prologue and A.P. Herbert the witty opening address. It is a simple, but most tasteful little place, and has a beautiful bar and lounge, where we met the Bleibens in the interval. The play was *And So to Bed* [by James Bernard Fagan, 1924], which was splendidly acted and dressed, but seems a bit dated since we saw it some years ago. We enjoyed our evening enormously.[28]

---

28 'We Turn over a New Leaf' was the headline of the story on the theatre's opening in the *Oxford Mail*, 21 October 1938, p. 4. It was said to be 'the first theatre built in the country for the special purpose of repertory' and the building itself was highly praised. 'The whole of Oxford ought to say "Thank you" to Eric Dance for building this charming place. To build a repertory theatre at all is heroic, to build it in Oxford is super-human. The people of Oxford now have a chance to show that they are not quite so friendless in the arts of repertory as they have sometimes, sadly, represented.'

The *Oxford Times*, 21 October 1938, p. 14 was equally enthusiastic about this 'most important development in the history of repertory in Oxford'. It also thought that the new building was 'a complete answer to those who feared that architecturally it would clash with the dignified frontages of the old Beaumont street houses. The architectural style of the rest of the street has been admirably followed, and although its neighbours may still resent some inevitable disturbance when motorists leave the theatre, about which much was said when the proposal was first put forward, this will presumably be their only ground for complaint.'

The Playhouse, which was registered this week as a private company established to build a repertory theatre in Oxford (*Oxford Times*, 21 October 1938, p. 7), would become a central fixture in the Martins' social and cultural lives. Its history from 1938 until the end of the war is recounted in Don Chapman, *Oxford Playhouse: High and Low Drama in a University City* (Hatfield: University of Hertfordshire Press, 2008), chap. 7.

Friday, 21 October. This diary would seem very dull reading for anyone hoping to find anything exciting. Still sneezing. I had a fitting for a black dress at Miss Boyce's. She is a very cheerful soul. Robert out to lunch with Mr Jenkins at the celebrated Vincent's Club [a select men's club at 11a King Edward Street, off the High Street]. We went out to tea together, to the Eareys, a friendly youngish couple who live in Windmill Road [Headington]. Their pet recreation is darts, which they play every evening. They wanted us to stay and play, but we made polite excuses. John in for his usual Friday night chat. He will always be a small boy in my eyes, although 27. He wasn't so cynical this time, and quite nice.

Saturday, 22 October. In bed most of the day with a return of the old terrible migraine headaches. I don't often get them as bad these days. I got up at 6.30, and Vera came for supper. The head became almost unbearable when I went to bed.

Sunday, 23 October. The head still there, but somewhat modified. I got up to see John, and to talk politics. He is often politically minded on Sundays. We made arrangements for tomorrow, all being well. Robert is coming up, too. I went to bed again for the afternoon and had tea there, then got up. I did not go to Church, but to Vera's for supper. It did me good – the tea, and sandwiches, and chat.

Monday, 24 October. The last shreds of the headache vanished during the day. Robert and I up to town on the 10.10. Very foggy when we arrived but it cleared a bit, later. We got tickets at the 'Duchess' and walked about, loving London intensely, in its autumn loveliness. Lunch at the Regent Palace Hotel, then to Hampstead Heath by bus. It was glorious up there, with the russet leaves and misty views, and charming old houses. We both love exploring bits of London. Back for tea at the Corner House then to see [the historical pageant] *Sixty Glorious Years* at the Odeon, a lovely coloured sequence to *Victoria the Great* [1937]. We loved it. Alas, we had to part after this, and I met John at *his* favourite haunt, the Strand Corner House, a place I dislike. However, it was fun, meeting, though John is a somewhat solemn companion in his efforts to do the correct thing. Even the buying of a nosegay of roses becomes somewhat ponderous. Still we always get on very well in town. We went to the 'Duchess' and saw one of the best plays I've seen for a long time, *The Corn is Green* with Emlyn Williams and Sybil Thorndyke. Everything about it was excellent. Story, and especially the acting which seemed perfect. I went home, to Nancy's, by the old familiar tube, and found them there waiting up. Mother in bed with a cold. I slept in Roger's little room and experienced no ghosts there.

Tuesday, 25 October. Very foggy indeed. We had a quiet morning chatting round the fire. Mother's cold seemed to weigh her down somewhat. She had made my favourite seasoned pudding for lunch, which was delicious. Nance and I went to Nita's [6 Friars Avenue, N20] to tea and had a very pleasant sisterly tea talking away. Christopher [aged 9] came in from school and looked very well and was sensible. We left about 6.30, but were held up five times in the fog on the way back [to Nancy's], and eventually had to abandon the bus and walk the rest of the way. The sweet children were just off to bed, also mother with her cold, so we had a quiet evening all reading our books.

Wednesday, 26 October. The fog completely gone, and a lovely day to greet us. Sally, as usual, came in and chatted merrily whilst I had breakfast. I love her. Mother's cold a bit better, but she was in bed. Nita called for me, and we went off early to see the Changing of the Guard at Buckingham Palace. I just get thrilled to bits with this noble ceremony, and it was lovely in the sunshine. We wandered a bit afterwards round St James' Palace and saw the scarlet and silver Household Cavalry flashing by on their black horses, with plumes flying in the wind. London is a wonderful place, and I wish I could see more; I never have enough time. We had lunch at the Brasserie, then had an orgy of shop-gazing, and a cup of tea at the Regent Palace Hotel before going to the New Gallery to see the latest Ginger Rogers and Fred Astaire picture *Carefree*. We were just in the mood for it and thoroughly enjoyed its gaiety and nonsense and lovely dancing. A very nice day altogether. We parted at Piccadilly Circus, and I came home on the 7.40. So nice to be back amongst warm fires and comfy beds. I was very very tired.

Thursday, 27 October. Most of the morning was spent at the hairdresser's having a few curlers put in to help my wild hair through the winter. Nothing much during the rest of the day, and a whist drive (military) at night. I am trying a new hair-style after years of a rather meek wavy bob. It is now pushed back from the ears and piled up in curls. Most people seem to like it, and it certainly is a bit more interesting-looking and dignified. It is amusing how a simple thing like a new hair-do makes a difference to one's behaviour.

Friday, 28 October. Such quiet peaceful days, thank God, that it is difficult to remember much about them when they are gone. This morning, however, I went with Marjorie to her doctor's to try and see what was the cause of the pain she has been having, but we got no nearer and she is to have another examination at the Radcliffe [Infirmary, Woodstock Road]. The family solicitor came to lunch with his daughter – on business. Quite harmless people and dull. I met Winifred for tea at Fullers, and later Robert at the Ritz [Cinema in George Street], for a *very* good film, *The Boy from Barnardo's*. Freddie Bartholomew and Mickey Rooney. It was a most pleasing film in every way.

Saturday, 29 October. I have had such a lot of wretched headaches lately and today's was a particularly vile sort. I met Muriel at the Cadena in the morning. Fortunately, she chose to be reasonable. I rested all afternoon, and the head improved in time for the Gray family's visit to tea. Joyce is *the* most well-behaved child, and Mr and Mrs Gray are very friendly too. We played a card-game after tea. Robert gave me a most lovely necklace for a 'headache present'! John came in for quite a long chat. I think I have persuaded him to give up a lot of these odd secretarial jobs that are such a trial to him and take up so much of his spare time.

Sunday, 30 October. To Church with Muriel, still quite reasonable. John in, cheerful as usual and full of Sunday's music chat. I went to tea with Fräulein Hendewerk and her charming employer, Miss Bourdillon, and another woman, a student, I think. We sat and drank fragrant china tea in a candle lit room and most of the conversation seemed to be in whispers to match the atmosphere. It was nice, but a wee bit subdued, and I longed to shout out loud, and be boisterous. Church again at night, and to Vera's. She is fed up with her family life at the moment. No wonder – it must be dreary.

Monday, 31 October. A lovely mild day with blue skies and soft sunshine. Coffee with Muriel in the morning. She had gone all stupid again and unreasonable and rude. She can be an awful trial sometimes, and is so childish, considering her age and position. The Bleibens to tea in the afternoon. They are always nice to have, and we have much in common with them. We went to the pictures with Vera and Muriel in the evening, and saw two very nice ones, *Strange Boarders* [a thriller] and *Stolen Heaven* [two jewel thieves pose as musicians to elude the police]. It is nice for Robert not being so rushed off his feet this winter, and having more spare time.

Tuesday, 1 November, All Saints' Day. I went to the Holy Communion Service at 11.00. Then met Muriel at the Cadena. She was more normal again – how she varies. I cannot endure unreasonableness. I went up to tea, with her and her sister, and the small Tony who was just recovering from tonsillitis, but ate an enormous tea all the same. He is not a very attractive child, and too noisy and spoilt. I cannot like the father or mother either, always talking of the amount they spend on him. I saw Muriel on her bus, and came home, very cold. Vera came to supper and we cooked tomato things and made coffee, which we find difficult to do *really* well.

Wednesday, 2 November. I met Winifred [Bleiben] in the morning for a quick hot drink at Fullers. The *hours* I spend waiting for her in that place. She can be anything up to half-an-hour late. However she is always so pleasant and responsive and we enjoy meeting one another. Vera and I met later, to buy our whist-drive prizes for tomorrow. We got stools and baskets from the blind-shop,[29] and chickens and biscuits. I had a German lesson in the afternoon. I must try not to be so lazy about reading in between. Fräulein stayed to tea. We are going to the theatre together on Saturday. Robert and I went out after tea for a little shopping. Then I had a cosy evening, reading my good novel *There Goes the Queen*.[30]

Thursday, 3 November. Rather a muddled sort of morning. The drawing room was in the hands of the decorator, mending the fire-place tiles. Marjorie at the Radcliffe where they found it was appendix after all, and she must now wait for a bed. Mrs Bleiben in for a drink and chat, and then round to the room with Vera to arrange our prizes. I read some German in the afternoon. I really should do this, daily, but it is rather tedious. The whist-drive at night. Quite a crowded one (14 tables), and very successful. The prizes were much admired. Robert walked home with Mr Jenkins whose affaires are alarmingly disturbed by some female, at the moment. Our curates seem fated in this way.

---

29 The blind shop was probably at 4 Little Clarendon Street, the premises of the Blind Welfare Committee, which also had a basket workshop in Paradise Street.

30 This 1935 novel by Geoffrey Uther Ellis is a sprawling family saga, recounted over several decades from the later nineteenth century, of the seven sons of a wealthy and domineering London doctor. The 'Queen' in the title is a pleasure steamer that plied the Thames in the summer months; she ended her days painted gunmetal grey and was sent into conflict in the Great War and eventually sunk by Turkish fire. This is the sort of fiction, rooted in social realism and family relations, which particularly appealed to Madge. In her diary she rarely mentions the titles of the books she was reading, but each year she compiled a list of all the books she had read. Two of these years, 1939 and 1942, are reproduced as Appendix B. It seems that Madge virtually never read a book published before the 1920s. Of the almost 350 titles she read during the six years 1938–43, not a single one was a 'classic' written before the twentieth century. She had a particular taste for just-published novels. Madge makes occasional reference to borrowing books from libraries ('loving my latest book from the library', 27 March 1939) as well as receiving them as presents.

Friday, 4 November. A holiday for Robert. We didn't do anything very special for it, but had a pleasant morning pottering about the shops and wandering about a mild autumnal Oxford. *Very* nice. An uneventful afternoon. We are both rather worried about Mr Jenkins and hope that there is no truth in his distressing situation. We had tea out together, then to the pictures. We seem to have gone a lot lately, and both love them. One of these was quite good, *Vivacious Lady* (Ginger Rogers), the other very bad, *Star of the Circus*. Home to supper. John in, very amusing about politics, history, and affairs in general. He can be very entertaining when he feels like it.

Saturday, 5 November. Shopping in the morning as usual.[31] The weather so like summer that I strolled round the [University] Parks afterwards. The yellow leaves of the silver-birches against the intensely blue sky took one's breath away, so beautiful they looked. The sun was as warm as in June. We went to tea with a most intellectual, earnest but coyly gay person who was entertaining, in a haphazard 'sit-on-the-floor-and-let's-be-informal' way. Two other girls as well as ourselves. It was rather trying, as she talks toothily without stopping, in a bookish way, and turns a deaf ear on other people's conversation. We endured it as best we could, then escaped gladly. We dined together at the George, which was packed out, then joined Fräulein at the theatre, to see again *Victoria Regina* [by Laurence Housman, b. 1865]. It was spoiled by the incessant barrage of fireworks without, which drowned a lot of the dialogue. However, we enjoyed it; so did Ruth. We had to come home amidst explosions, and the remaining wisps of a tear-gas bomb, which had been thrown outside the theatre.[32]

Sunday, 6 November. Morning Service. The new shortened version was tried out. It certainly speeds up the Service, and is an improvement I think. The usual chat with John before lunch. He is cheerful at the moment. I read most of the afternoon. Church again at night. Good singing by the choir. To Vera's after. Always a nice cosy room there, and good fire.

---

31   Madge rarely mentioned what she bought while shopping most mornings. However, it is virtually certain that her purchases were mainly food and other standard household provisions. She did no cooking – until later in the war.

32   It was Guy Fawkes Day and 'The centre of Oxford was crowded as usual … but both the University Authorities and the police had taken stringent precautions against any disorder. The crowd, which was more or less confined to George-street, contained surprisingly few undergraduates … The usual barrage of fireworks enlivened the crowd for some hours, and motorists had great difficulty pushing their way through' (*Oxford Times*, 11 November 1938, p. 22). Her reference to tear gas may have been an exaggeration.

Monday, 7 November. A lovely holiday day for us, and up to town on the 10.10. We didn't see much of London this time, which is a pity really, but there were two films we wanted to see, so we just had time for a hasty lunch at the Regent Palace Hotel Grill, then to the Gaumont to see a very funny film *You Can't Take it With You*.[33] Just time for tea before going to the Empire to see the splendid, glittering and sad *Marie Antoinette*, with Norma Shearer acting very well, and Robert Morley magnificent as Louis XVI. We liked it very much. A little wander up Oxford Street to look at the shops, and home on the usual 7.40. We watched an eclipse of the moon, which was very clearly seen.

Tuesday, 8 November. Very cold again. Shopping as usual. We had a parson for lunch, who came to copy some registers. He was not so bad, but rather loud-voiced and bleating. However he didn't stay long. Louise Thomas came calling in the afternoon, looking very smart. She is here to organise some dancing, and to ask us to go and see it. What a temperamental and effusive person she is, so unlike Peggy. She stayed to tea.[34] All the first part of the evening I wrote Christmas cards, then Vera came to supper. We knitted squares for the Chinese blankets.

Wednesday, 9 November. Still very cold and miserable, and I felt the same for no reason at all. Robert and I did odd things in the town, in the morning, and I bought Christmas cards at Mowbrays [church publishers at 9 High Street], who have a very good selection. I had a German lesson in the afternoon. I wish I could speak better but most of the time seems to be spent listening to *her* speak. Ruth stayed to tea, and I went with Vera in the evening and saw a very nice sentimental film *The Shopworn Angel* with the fascinating Margaret Sullavan. It was just the sort we like. Home quite early, and a nice long read after supper.

Thursday, 10 November. I seem to be very irritable and depressed these last few days, and it is hard to snap out of it, once one gets like this. Marjorie had word from the Radcliffe that she has to go in, on Saturday, so I hope

---

33   This film, directed by Frank Capra, starred Jean Arthur and James Stewart. It won the Oscar for best film in 1938.
34   Louise Thomas (b. 1909) and Peggy Longfield (b. 1908) were friends and had invited the Martins for lunch at their cottage in Somerset on 4 October 1935. Madge portrayed them as 'bohemian' and good company. Louise was a choreographer and dancing teacher, and they both sometimes attended St Michael's Church in the 1930s. Louise was also author of a novel, *Everyday* (1935), published under the name of Elena Shayne. (We are indebted to Barbara Tearle for these findings.)

we get someone suitable to take her place, in the mornings. I shopped with Vera, and addressed another batch of cards in the afternoon, then went with Robert to tea with Mrs Bazett-Jones [12 Wentworth Road, Summertown] and her son. She is an acid-tongued old lady, with a soft spot for us – the son not too bad. A whist-drive (Church Officials v Guild) at night. I played with Robert, which was nice. Vera won 2nd prize, a bowl of hyacinths.

Friday, 11 November. Armistice Day. I always have to go far enough away, not to hear the maroons, for the two minutes Silence, so Vera and I found ourselves on the Abingdon Road this time, with only a milk-cart and a few people to share it. We went to the Communion Service after, and then shopped. I should have been able to concentrate more than ever this year, but couldn't. It is always like that. We went to the Bleibens for tea, but the visit was hurried as we had to dash off, by taxi, to the Dragon School [preparatory school, Bardwell Road, North Oxford], to see the boys perform *The Pirates of Penzance* [by Gilbert and Sullivan, 1879]. It was most amusing, and beautifully done, and we loved it. We sat with George Anderson [a visiting American clergyman] and a young Queen's undergraduate friend of his. Another taxi rush to a quite different show in the Taylorian, *The Castle of Perseverance*, a 14th century morality play which Louise Thomas had persuaded us to see, because she was arranging the dances.[35] We didn't loathe it, as we had feared, and indeed the acting and costumes were marvellous. We could only see one act, as I had to get back for John, who spent an hour of his time writing letters, but was easy to get on with again. He stayed till nearly 12.00.

Saturday, 12 November. Up to town for 'Muriel's day' on the 10.10. I have to go once every term. She met me in, and was frisky and full of 'girlish spirits'.[36] We did a bit of shop-gazing before lunch at the Regent Palace Hotel Grill. I successfully kept my temper even against her foolish prattles, though it is a job. She does try to lavish things on me, and I must try and feel grateful. We went to see *Elisabeth of Austria* at the Garrick, a very interesting, tragic, but somewhat heavy play. We quite liked it. Tea in the crowded Corner House

---

35 The Taylorian Institution for modern languages shares a nineteenth-century building, designed by Charles Robert Cockerell, on the corner of St Giles and Beaumont Street, with the Ashmolean Museum.
36 Muriel Smith, a schoolteacher working in London, was born and raised in Oxford; she was six years younger than Madge, and unmarried. They probably met at St Michael's Church in the 1920s.

and a walk through Bond Street and Oxford Street in the mild evening. She saw me on the 7.40 train home.

Sunday, 13 November. Armistice Sunday services. Church in the morning. Muriel was waiting for me to come out, and walked home with me. John in after. Sundayish. Doris [her longstanding maid] has hurt her hand badly on top of all our bustle, with Marjorie now in hospital. I went with Robert and Danna to a very dull service in the Sheldonian, stuffy, and uninspiring.[37] Church again at night and a packed service. Muriel and Vera there. The latter went off, huffily, as is often her wont. Mr Anderson preached a popular but somewhat obvious armistice sermon. To Vera's for supper and talk.

Monday, 14 November. A beautiful day. November at its loveliest, warm, slightly misty, but with a soft sun-light over everything. We took a bus to High Wycombe, and then walked up behind the town and through beechwoods carpeted with russet leaves to Penn, a delightful village on a ridge with wooded distances, and blue hills all round. We found a lovely antique shop where we had a bacon and egg lunch, bought Christmas cards and several small things, and continued our way to Beaconsfield, a lovely little friendly town. We went to see the marvellous model village there, Bekonscot [opened in 1929], which would delight Christopher and Roger with its many miniature attractions. It is even more attractive than the one at Bourton-on-the-Water. We took a slow train back to Oxford, had tea at the Cadena, home for a bath and change, then supper at the snack-bar, and to the Playhouse to see *Fanny's First Play*, which only strengthened my dislike for Bernard Shaw. Robert, too, was disappointed in it.

Tuesday, 15 November. Dark, cold and foggy, true November weather. I had my hair done, then shopped with Vera. In the afternoon, I went with Danna and Robert to a meeting, the Comrades' annual one, held in Blackhall.[38] Robert in the chair. It was quite interesting, but I feel out of sympathy with most of the people who go. Dons' wives etc., and snobs. However, it was not too bad. An evening in the home, doing odd jobs in the kitchen. Vera to supper. We chatted in the waiting room after.

---

37 The Sheldonian Theatre was and still is the University's central venue for ceremonial events. It was designed by Sir Christopher Wren and built in Broad Street in the 1660s.
38 This may have been Oxford's Fire Brigade Club.

Wednesday, 16 November. Shopping as usual in the morning. I went to see Marjorie in the Cronshaw ward at the Radcliffe in the afternoon [recovering from appendicitis]. She seemed to be progressing very well, and was cheerful, and at home there. Vera and I to the Regal at night for quite nice pictures. I don't think anything else happened as far as I remember.[39]

Thursday, 17 November. A very rushed sort of day. The usual shopping – and a lot of it to do. I always come home burdened down with parcels. I helped Doris get tea for the Blencowes, then went off to the Playhouse to hear a recital of songs by a very beautiful soprano [Maria Marova] (the voice – not the face!) and Bernard Naylor, John's Queen's organist and friend who is a rude but brilliant young man whom I dislike, on sight.[40] It was a good concert. I rushed back to greet the Blencowes. Mrs B., her mother, her daughter Joyce and her Siamese prince [actually Malayan]. The girl is blonde, and 'dumb', the prince silent as the grave, the mother chatty and the grandmother subdued. There was a whist-drive at night. Mr Jenkins' 'nurse' was there.

Friday, 18 November. I went round the shops with Robert, it is always so nice when he can spare time to come with me, and makes it feel holiday-ish.

---

39   This last sentence is an indication – many more would follow over the years – that Madge often wrote up her diary well after the actual events; sometimes the delay was as much as four or five days. On 5 January 1939 she remarked that 'these last days after Christmas are very lazy and hard to remember'; the following day 'my brain refuses to remember these same-ish days, and especially in the afternoons'. Her entry for Friday, 3 February 1939 began with the words, 'It is Tuesday [7 February], and I can't remember much about Friday.' 'How hard these days are to remember afterwards,' she wrote on Tuesday, 4 April; 'it is always thus when mother is here. I think it is because we are somewhat lazy.' Similarly, on 15 May 1939 'I can't remember much about the afternoon'. On Tuesday, 20 June she had 'A lot of diary to write up. It is Saturday now [the 24th].'

So, a particular day's events and feelings were not always fresh in her mind when she wrote. This is a feature of Madge's writing that comes up again and again. As she said during the war, on Tuesday, 14 April 1942, when writing on the following Sunday (and there were dozens of such remarks), she couldn't remember a lot about the day, for 'unless one does something out of the ordinary, there is nothing to hang on to, in the way of remembering'. She confronted this issue of a hazy memory some years later, on 2 October 1945, after returning home after a holiday in Somerset. 'As soon as I get back to Oxford I just can't seem to remember what I did except by a great effort. I don't know why, as the days are quite varied. It is also quite hard when I wake in the morning to remember what day it is, whereas when I'm on holiday I know exactly what I did every minute.'

40   Bernard Naylor (1907–1986) was an organist, conductor, composer of vocal and choral music and teacher who went on to have an international career (*The Times*, 23 May 1986, p. 14).

I had a perfectly free afternoon for a change, and scarcely knew what to do with it, so unusual was it. However, it was a short one, as we had an early tea and then I joined Robert at the Ritz and Vera, too, and we saw quite nice films, one a 'Jones' family one [*A Trip to Paris* with Loretta Young and David Niven] – they are always entertaining. Robert and I had supper together at the Snack Bar, but my head ached. John came in for one of his pleasant Friday chats.

Saturday, 19 November. In bed all this day with the headache, but got up at 7.00, and Vera came to supper.

Sunday, 20 November. The head better, but not well enough to go to Church. It was a very wet day, with torrents of rain from morning till evening. John came in after Church soaked to the skin. On these occasions he wears a fearful cap which everyone mocks at. A quiet reading afternoon. I didn't go to Church, but to Vera's for supper and scandal.

Monday, 21 November. Foggy, but rather nice. I went shopping, and then down to Miss Barrett's [37 Whitehouse Road, Grandpont], walking there and back, to arrange about a blue dress. I think I had a quiet afternoon knitting and attending to the last of my Christmas cards. Vera and I went to the Ritz at night and saw *Three Comrades* again. I had seen it before – very nice, but almost too sad.[41] Vera back to supper.

Tuesday, 22 November. I went up to town on the 10.10. A cold, sunny morning. The country looked lovely from the train, the buildings rose-pink in the mellow sunshine, and the leafless trees, all lacy against a pale blue sky. I do so love more and more the English country-side. I met mother and Nita at Paddington, and we went to the 'Woman's Fair' at Olympia and spent the whole day there. It was fascinating, miles of things to interest women, and there were thousands of them there! We saw a lovely show of 'fashions and glamour' in the afternoon, and saw the 'Queen of Beauty' crowned by [actresses] Margaret Rawlings and Zena Dare. We spent lots of money on gadgets and had lunch and tea there, and had loads of fun. We left at 7.00, tired and dirty and loaded with parcels. I came back on the 7.40 as usual.

Wednesday, 23 November. A tremendous gale over the country. If it weren't for thinking what a lot of damage was being done to life and property, it

---

41 This 1938 film was based on a story by Erich Maria Remarque and starred Margaret Sullavan, already praised by Madge, Robert Taylor, and Robert Young. The screenplay was by F. Scott Fitzgerald.

would be rather fun hearing the wind howl in fury against the windows, and lash the trees about like whips. I battled against the elements in the morning shopping, and in the afternoon, we went with Vera and Peter Bleiben to the only Rugby game we've seen this season – against Major Stanley's XV. A very good game, which Oxford won. We were sheltered from the blasts, and enjoyed it enormously.[42] Robert and I had tea with Peter and Winifred at the Clarendon [in Cornmarket Street], a good place to meet and talk. Vera came in for a quiet evening.

Thursday, 24 November. I had coffee with Winifred at Fullers [at 24–25 Cornmarket Street] in the morning, and we watched with interest certain activities from the window, of a certain young nurse who is causing such upheaval at St Michael's at present [with regard to the curate, Mr Jenkins's affections]. Shopping with Vera after. A very difficult German lesson in the afternoon, which tried me a lot, though it is nice to be getting something definitive done. Ruth stayed to tea as usual. A military whist-drive at night. Our table won a prize. Nurse M. was there looking soulfully across at her victim.

Friday, 25 November. A holiday for Robert and, alas, a headache for me, so that I had to stay in bed till the afternoon. My kind Robert did all the shopping and brought me violets and read to me and I got up about 2.30 and went, rather rashly, out Christmas shopping with him, then to tea at the L'Etoile D'Or [at 55 High Street] and to the pictures at the Regal, which were good – Ginger Rogers in *Having a Wonderful Time*,[43] but my head was bad and I could hardly enjoy it. John came in and talked rather gloomily. We were both feeling ill and tired so sympathised with one another.

Saturday, 26 November. The headache winging its way, so I was able to shop, and to meet Vera at the Cadena for coffee. In the afternoon I went with Doris to the Radcliffe to see Marjorie, who seemed very happy and says she never felt better in her life. I marvel at the cheerfulness of most of the patients who must, mostly, be very ill. John called for us, and we had a snatched dinner at the George, failing to get into the snack-bar, then joined Vera at the Playhouse to see *The Silver King* [by Henry Arthur Jones and Henry Herman, 1882], a melodrama which our grandmothers used to take

---

42 A photograph in the *Oxford Mail*, 24 November 1938, p. 6, shows spectators well bundled up.
43 The cast of this 1938 film also included Douglas Fairbanks Jr, Lucille Ball, Red Skelton, and Eve Arden, the latter three to go on to post-war television fame in the United States.

seriously, but which now causes hoots of mirth. The Bleibens were there, too.

Sunday, 27 November. Church in the fine morning. John in, talking very interestingly about the Victorian era, and taste in music and art. He can be so very pleasant. A perfectly lazy afternoon reading, and Church again at night. Mr Anderson sat with us. To Vera's after. Very nice as usual. I *do* get tired of writing a diary.[44]

Diary-fatigue was setting in for Madge (not for the first time) – this was hardly unusual: many other diarists had, at least occasionally, similar weary sentiments – and it often showed during the following winter months. Routine and repetitions loomed large. 'These January days are so much the same,' she wrote on the 19th. Tuesday, 14 March 1939 conveyed a typical mood: 'The days are so similar just now that it is hard to remember them when they are gone – blissfully peaceful. Just morning shopping, sewing and reading in the afternoon. In the evening Vera and I went to the Ritz to see a very pleasant family film *Four Daughters* [a musical drama, 1938]. Home to supper of my favourite beef-roll and more of *The rains came*.' Some entries are noticeably short. Her writing generally lacked zest – and there is little in the way of new reflections or new activities.

On many days Madge suffered from serious headaches, some of which sent her to bed for hours. 'How I hate having to lie in bed with headaches' (4 December). On 24 December 'The head kept me in bed *all* day, missing all the Christmas fun, of Christmas Eve, decorating the Church, receiving parcels, last minute shopping. Oh dear!' She cursed 'the miserable migraine'. On 12 January 1939 she was 'nursing a headache all day … I should have gone to a [St Michael's] Guild meeting, but nursed the headache instead.' On 6 February 'The headache returned with a vengeance, so I had to stay in bed till after lunch'; on 28 February she was 'In bed all day with a headache of the beastliest variety'; and on 7 March 'I had another bad headache most of the day. I quite get depressed when I have too many.' A bad headache kept her in bed most of 17 and 18 March: she had to miss an Oxford v. Cambridge sports event that she had planned to attend with Robert. 'I was very depressed about it all, but it couldn't be helped.' On 23 March she reported 'Headache … I am sick to death of them.' On 5 April she had a 'throbbing head. I get a little downcast sometimes about headaches. However, this one improved during the evening.'

Headaches were a serious and longstanding debility. They had surfaced when Madge was a teenager and persisted throughout her life. There was rarely a month when she was not laid low with a headache, sometimes a crippling one, for at least a

---

44   Her final line the following day was: *'Thank God for Peace.'*

day or two. Her earliest reports of a headache were on 3 April 1916 and 4 November 1916, when she was 16. On the first of these dates she also mentioned that her mother had been suffering a bad headache that lasted several days, for which a doctor was called twice, though to little effect. Much later, on 28 October 1929, when Madge was almost thirty, she consulted a specialist, Sir Farqhuar Buzzard (b. 1871), by then Regius Professor of Medicine at Oxford, 'who was one of the King's doctors. He told me that there was no cure for my headaches, and they would only go away when I was older. I was very annoyed to hear that.' Sometimes these headaches became less frequent and/or less acute. 'My headaches are really getting much less severe,' she wrote on 9 March 1931, 'whether this is due to old age, or to phenacetin tablets, I can't say.' Such optimism, unfortunately, could not be sustained, for lapses always occurred. On 17 January 1938 she had 'a fiendish headache which refused to move in spite of many tablets and doctorings'. On 8 June that year she was taking 'strong headache tablets'. On 25 May 1939 she again had 'a wretched migraine. They seem to be pretty regular now, but they are not so dreadful to bear as they were.' This was not an easy time: 'My headaches have been a great hindrance lately' (31 May 1939). A few years before, on 13 February 1933, she had asked in frustration about these headaches: 'Hell – Am I always to be thus?' Beside this question is an answer, written by her in red ink in 1982, when she was in her early eighties, 'Yes, always!'

Madge's writing tends to come most alive when she went to London for a day or took a longer holiday, as in April 1939, when she and Robert spent ten days in Somerset, and her writing sparkles with enthusiasm for the landscape and local walks. During one 15-mile walk (18 April) 'We climbed up and up to the moors, overlooking the calm milky sea on our right and the great vistas of woodland hills and moors on the left. Just as we had wished it to be. Down into beautiful Selworthy with its perfect Green set with old thatched cottages, and its exquisite Church. On to Porlock Weir for lunch in the courtyard of the "Ship". Very quaint and quiet.' The following day 'We set off again with joy in our hearts' and walked another fifteen miles. Holidays certainly energized Madge, and her happiness showed. 'How I love this kind of life spent in walking with Robert by the sea in the country,' she wrote on 20 April 1939 in Somerset. 'I hope my particular bit of Heaven will be like this.' A day trip to London (and there were many) was also uplifting: 'No-one loves London as we love it,' she once declared (20 February 1939). By contrast, daily life in Oxford during these months seems to have been largely devoid of sparkle, sometimes even engagement, though it was normally 'peaceful' (which she liked).[45] 'I don't care for excitements and rushing here and there' (3 June). People who talked too much were

---

45   'Oxford can be so very depressing at times,' she wrote on 28 May 1938. 'I always feel it mostly when I have been away from it, even for a day, and yet it is lovely. Perhaps it's the people who live in it. I don't know.'

liable to get on her nerves (e.g., 30 July 1939), and she did not tolerate well domestic tensions.[46]

The content of Madge's life in Oxford from the end of November 1938 until the late summer of 1939 is not strikingly different from that of her life during the two-and-a-half months recorded above. Excepting Sunday, she shopped almost every day, usually in the morning. She saw the same people again and again – Vera, John, Muriel, etc. Meeting one or two people for tea or coffee was standard fare. Her mother visited. The theatre and cinema continued to be major attractions: in 1938 she saw 32 plays and some 160 films – cinema programmes almost always comprised at least two films; during 1939 she saw 39 plays and 139 films. These numbers, especially for films, must seem extraordinary to later, TV-focused generations.[47] She also read a lot, probably on average a little more than one book a week (see Appendix B).

Madge reported virtually no conflict with her husband. Indeed, theirs would seem to have been a very happy marriage. 'Our wedding anniversary,' she wrote on 17 July 1939 – they had been married for twenty-two years. 'How happy and lucky I have been – surely the luckiest wife living.' 'No one could have such a husband as I have,' she had written on their anniversary day two years before. On several occasions she remarked on his thoughtfulness. 'How we just love being together,' she had observed a couple of months before (15 May). The diary is full of evidence of their affection for each other. On 20 March 1943, for example, she celebrated the day during the Great War when they had first met. 'My luckiest day – the [28th] anniversary of the day Robert and I met, he as a young officer billeted on our family, me as a school girl, in gym-dress and two plaits. What a very lucky and happy day for me it turned out to be.' 'I remember it *so* well,' she had written on 20 March the previous year. There were many other occasions when she wrote of their love and happiness together and the pleasure she took in his company. Nothing was said directly during these months regarding the absence of children (which by then was probably taken for granted).

---

46   A remark on Tuesday, 25 July 1939, 'domestic troubles press me greatly lately', is entirely unexplained. There is certainly no evidence of marital difficulties. Later, on 17 August, back home after holidaying happily with Robert in Scarborough, she wished 'I could be sensible about certain matters', but said no more (which suggests that she was disinclined to confide some thoughts to her diary). The one passage that could be related to this unhappiness appears in her diary for 3 July 1939. 'An upsetting quarrel between Doris and Marjorie burst upon me at tea-time. These two, I fear, will never get on for long. Their ages are so far apart [Doris was married and much older]; but it can't be allowed to continue as we pride ourselves on being a peaceable house.' For Madge, as later years of the diary show, the 'servant problem', in various guises, had sticking power.

47   Many of these films were not full-length features; they were commonly shown as parts of double bills. Some films she saw for the second time or more. It is impossible to discount the importance of the cinema in her life.

Madge had little to say about social deprivation in late-1930s England. A rare exception is her entry for 17 January 1939, when 'Jack Odlum came to tea. He is a poor unfortunate, smashed up in the war, having to eke out a living, selling water-softeners. Poor thing – he loathes it, and is so ill and unhappy. If only a good job could be found for him. He made us all feel guilty and fat and prosperous.'[48] She usually steered clear of the harsh, ugly facts of contemporary life, no doubt partly from circumstances (her rather sheltered social life), partly from disinclination. On 19 April 1938 'I went to see Mrs Busby in the afternoon. The poor old soul is ill.' (Madge visited Mrs Busby at least eight times in 1938 and fairly regularly for years thereafter. Otherwise her visits to the housebound were infrequent.) 'I can't get to like visiting people ill in bed, especially in rather poor houses.' During the six years 1938–43, when she, usually with Robert, went to London many times, she never ventured into the East End, though on one occasion while en route by bus to Greenwich she found 'It was interesting going through shabby South London' (28 January 1938).

It is hard to know exactly how Madge felt about religion or her role as the wife of a clergyman. One gets the impression that, for her, religion primarily involved duty and ceremony and personal consolation, and that deep questions about faith did not much concern her. Perhaps her religious feelings were rather lukewarm. She never spoke of theological issues. 'I wish I liked Sundays more,' she wrote on Sunday, 5 March 1939, 'but I am always glad when they are over.' 'I'm not as fond as I should be of Sundays' (20 March). On Good Friday in 1938 (15 April) she wrote of the 'Long, long service in the morning. I suppose if one is in the mood, one should like this as much as the Festal times.' She did speak well of these, and indeed had a taste for religious pageantry. She spent some time in church society, but not a lot. Once, after being shown round a church in Somerset by its vicar, she said that 'I find most parsons rather irritating' (23 April 1939).[49] An afternoon tea on 27 January, she complained, 'was too much of a St Michael's gathering to be much fun'. After one church meeting in Oxford that she and her husband attended – 'but didn't endure it to the end' (1 May 1939) – she wondered, 'Why does the Church of England attract such depressed people?' Parishioners she often found 'dull'; 'sometimes I get quite angry with the people there', she said after attending church on Sunday, 15 May 1938. 'I don't know why.'[50] Robert seems to have performed most of his clerical

---

48 Jack Odlum was the son of Dorothy and Drelincourt Odlum, both actors, who stayed with the Martins in 1936, and were said by Madge to be 'frightfully poor' (10 February 1936). Their son had been seriously wounded in France in the Great War; in 1939 he was living with his widowed mother in London. (We are indebted to Barbara Tearle for her research on this family.)
49 Years later, on 3 November 1943, she remarked on 'how funny-looking most of the clergy are'.
50 A rare exception to her usual sentiments was reported on 13 December 1938, when she went to 'the [St Michael's] Senior Guild's "hop" and had quite a good time dancing old

duties without her, and the spiritual matters that are sometimes mentioned in his diary are almost completely missing in hers.

Madge Martin was not a woman with large aspirations. 'I ask nothing more of life than plenty of sun with good health and happiness to enjoy it,' she once declared (3 June 1939). She had a fondness for life as 'a perpetual holiday' (3 June 1939). She liked peace and affability and reasonableness. She was strikingly weather-sensitive. Almost every day she wrote about the weather, and when it was sunny and, ideally, warm, her spirits were usually buoyed. On a page of her diary just before mid-June 1938 she drew a woman's figure with outstretched arms, looking up at a brilliant sun, with the words 'I am a sun-worshipper'. 'What heavenly days these are,' she wrote on 21 April 1939 in Somerset, 'and how lucky we have been so far.' Walks, especially in hilly landscapes, often of at least ten miles, along with films, plays, and quiet hours for reading, seem to have been her prime sources of satisfaction. Sometimes she saw herself as lazy – especially with regard to her laxness about her German lessons, or her fondness for casual reading. There are occasional – and in the early 1940s, more frequent – remarks of self-denigration. On 6 May 1939 she mentions 'an extremely nice' friend who was expected for the weekend – 'too good, really, for the likes of me, and one feels so unworthy all the time'. The following day another acquaintance came for tea: 'She is cheerful and competent and I am still rather shy with her. I wish I could chatter like that.'

One has an impression of Madge Martin as a somewhat self-effacing person. Nor was she fully satisfied with her manner of living. She was explicit about this on 19 July 1938. 'Rather depressed all day. And feeling that I am one of those fluffy useless wives with too much time for pleasure. This guilty feeling often crops up, and I plan to do all sorts of helpful things, but usually settle lazily down again, and do nothing about it.'[51] She never actually indicated what the 'helpful things' were that she had contemplated, though it is likely that they would have involved some

---

fashioned and vigorous dances, including the Lambeth Walk, with Mr Jenkins.' As for her and her sisters' religious upbringing, Madge recalled that 'We never seemed to go to Church, although our parents were nominally Church of England, but we had quite a sound religious training at school, and were occasionally sent to Sunday School.' She added later that 'I often wished that I could be "Chapel" myself, as the people there seemed to have all the fun … ' ('A Yorkshire Childhood', pp. 15 and 20).

51 Her New Year's resolution in 1938 (1 January) appears to have come to naught: 'I seem to have led the most lazy life since Christmas, with hours spent in very light reading before blazing fires. I really must begin to be a bit more useful and do some German or something.' During the first 250 days of the year, her church-related daytime tasks (e.g., addressing envelopes, decorating the altar) may have amounted to the equivalent of two days' work. In the evenings she went to a church event (including whist drives) on average twice a month.

kind of volunteering. She had no professional ambitions and did not need more money;[52] and she probably felt the need to do housework only occasionally.[53]

World affairs are almost invisible in Madge Martin's diary during the months after October 1938. It is as if the larger world had escaped her notice – or perhaps she just didn't want to have to think about it. There are no sustained reflections on public affairs and only a handful of brief references to political matters. She was glad to 'see out' 1938 'in peace' (31 December); on 29 January 1939 she 'read the depressing papers full of war news, earthquakes and flying refugees'; and on 16 March she reported that Ruth Hendewerk, her German teacher and a refugee, 'was very depressed about Hitler's newest outrage, the purloining of Czecho-Slovakia altogether. I wonder how much more he can get away with.' No doubt thoughts about the threat of war sometimes entered her mind – how could they not? 'Each year we love Spring[54] more and more,' she wrote on 12 April. 'With the world on the brink of disaster almost daily, it seems there must be many wondering how many more Springs they will see.' Thereafter in 1939 nothing appears in her diary about a broader world until she reports, with pleasure, the well-received tour of the United States and Canada by the King and Queen (10 and 22 June). Otherwise the public events of the day were never mentioned – aside from passing references to John Hall's conviction that 'we shall have war with Germany any day now, over this question of Danzig' (2 July); Winifred Bleiben's opinion given the following day 'that war is inevitable now'; 'a "black-out" practice' in Oxford (8 July); and an inspection on 13 July of ARP equipment and a parade of civil defence workers ('Robert gave a prayer').[55]

This aloofness would change shortly after Madge and Robert returned from their annual vacation in Scarborough (this was their thirteenth Scarborough holiday) on 17 August 1939. Within a week her diary ceased to be a document exclusively concerned with private matters – or, to put it differently, her life was suddenly confronted by disturbances that any British diarist was bound to have to acknowledge. No doubt she had thought about and talked with others in the preceding months about the threat of war, but if so her diary is almost entirely silent about

---

52 According to *Crockford's Clerical Directory* for 1941, Robert Martin had a gross annual income of £419 plus a house (though the Vicarage on Botley Road was actually let out). Since his private income during the Great War had been around £400 per year, it seems reasonable to estimate that his total yearly income from all sources at the start of the war was in the vicinity of £1,000. This would have allowed for a comfortable lifestyle.

53 On the afternoon of Friday, 15 April 1938 she 'bustled about polishing the drawing room furniture. I like doing these odd jobs when the maids are out' (usually both were not out at the same time).

54 Madge always capitalized 'Spring', the season she mentioned most often.

55 The opening of Oxford's ARP Centre on 13 July 1939 received full coverage in the press (*Oxford Mail*, 14 July 1939, p. 7). Robert was Honorary Chaplain to the Fire Brigade.

these experiences. Now war seemed imminent – and would soon loom darkly as a central reality of living.

Wednesday, 23 August. Another Crisis impending. Germany is to sign a non-aggression Pact with Russia, which is causing much consternation. I get so muddled about these things and don't understand half of what I read. I just hope and hope there is no war. We seem to be living in a nightmare age, meanwhile ordinary things must go on – shopping etc. which I did in the morning. All afternoon I sat in the garden, pasting in our Scarborough snap-shots, and in the evening I bought a new hat and jumper with Vera. Then we all went for a walk over Shotover and down into Horspath and back to Headington. A beautiful, serene, mellow evening with a flaming sunset. Vera back to supper. I had a 'phone call from Ruth Hendewerk, who had suddenly curtailed her holiday in Switzerland because of the crisis.

Thursday, 24 August. The 'war' news very grave, and everyone in exactly the same state of tension as last year at almost the exact time. It is so awful, and one's heart feels like a stone, and one's knees like jelly! It certainly doesn't look like Switzerland for us next week [where she and Robert were planning to holiday]. The usual morning. Ruth came to tea in the afternoon. Usually I am so pleased to be with her, but somehow today I didn't feel like it, much, and being a German exile, naturally the talk was of nothing but the threatening situation. I walked a little with her in the evening in the sad misty [University] Parks. I had a chat with Tom Morley at the Gate of the Drive, and he was so vital and interesting that I almost forgot my depression. A quiet evening reading.

Friday, 25 August. We thought we'd escape the war-bug and all the fears and talk, and as it was a warm, mellow day we took the train to Moreton-in-the-Marsh, and walked to Blockley for lunch. Lovely hilly Cotswold country, in hazy warm sunshine. Lunch at the Crown Inn at Blockley which is a pleasant sleepy little place, in a hollow of the hills. Over the fields to Chipping Campden after lunch. What a gem of a place. We lingered there and had tea and saw the beautiful old Church. Back to Oxford in the comic diesel coach at 7.30. Change – bath – supper, and a very nice visit from John, who is excited and rather gay, and has applied for the Auxiliary Air Force. These hectic times cheer him up!

Saturday, 26 August. The news much the same. All the world has its eyes on Poland and Hitler. I had a lot of shopping to do. My legs grew weak and the mouth dry at the signs of ARP activities, dimming of lights for traffic etc. I can't help feeling awfully scared and miserable. One war was enough for me. I met, with Vera. Nance, Norman and the two children in. It *is* a pity that Nance *again* comes under the shadow of war. However we seemed to manage to be hopeful and cheerful and had quite a nice day, chatting, sitting in the garden, wandering round the town after tea, supper and reading. The children are loves.

Sunday, 27 August. A day of Intercession for Peace all over the country. We had special prayers and two lovely sermons from Robert at morning and evening services. We sat in the garden most of the warm afternoon, trying to forget the tension. Norman returned to London in the evening. I went to the evening service with Vera, who felt rather ill after it had started, so I saw her home and returned again to Church. Home afterwards to a quiet reading evening.

Monday, 28 August. No news of any importance. The Cabinet is meeting and discussing terms. Everyone seems rather frighteningly calm and almost disinterested, I think. We went out with the children bus-riding and having ices in the morning. Nancy and I sun-bathed in the garden all afternoon, so hot and lovely. Nance and I out for a stroll after tea. A beautiful golden evening. A quiet evening reading.

Tuesday, 29 August. A glorious hot summer day, one of the loveliest of the year. We took the children out for the day. Train to Bourton-on-the-Water, with a nice change at Kingham where Roger could look at the trains. We had lunch at the fascinating Studio Café, full of curios for children. Then to see the model village [in Bourton-on-the-Water] which is fascinating. After that to the beautiful shallow little stream which runs through the village. The children paddled, and even Nance and I dangled our feet but hastily withdrew them, as the water was so icy. Back to tea at Kingham and home on a train again, after a glorious day which we all enjoyed.

Wednesday, 30 August. Still no decisive news in the papers. Hitler has replied to our suggestions, but so far no-one knows what. A strange frightening calm over everybody. Beautiful weather still. I took the children out with Nance in the morning. I adore Sally and Roger is very 'taking' too, though willful. We all went to the pictures after tea, and saw two very good films, *Boy Trouble* [a melodrama, 1939] and *The Spy in Black* with Conrad Veidt. Very thrilling and interesting. Poor Robert felt ill, and had to go early to bed.

Thursday, 31 August. Thank goodness, Robert felt better, so we thought we would go walking with Nance, though the day was misty and dull. I got my shopping done with Roger's company. Then we went off by train to the now familiar Chipping Campden, which is so lovely. Lunch there. Then a beautiful walk over hilly fields to Saintbury which has a beautiful little Church, and on to Broadway. We loved the walk in spite of drizzle and dullness – but the sun was so nearly out. Tea at Broadway, and bus home. The wireless was put on in the bus for the 'news bulletin' and all our happiness faded when we heard the gravest news to date, men in army and navy to report to their stations and all school children in London's danger area to start evacuating tomorrow. Surely only a miracle can save us this time from dreadful war. I try to seem brave, but my legs will wobble, and my heart thump. I pray that if it comes, I may be given courage.

Friday, 1 September. A nightmare-like day. We heard in the morning that Germany had already attacked Poland and bombed several towns, so that it means that we *must* go to war with them now. It all seems unbelievably horrible, and I shudder to think what will happen to us all. We spent a lot of time getting our windows prepared for a complete black-out. It gave us something definite to do, which was comforting. Ruth came to tea, poor thing, feeling as if she should be regarded as an enemy German. A hectic evening. Vera and John for supper, and then the other section of our family arrived by *taxi* from London, Nita, Richard and Kit, and Norman. It was completely bewildering at first, but Marjorie rallied round and Vera [worked] to get them supper and see to the beds, and we all settled down to a long chat. It is much better to have one's family around, though it means an end to our peaceful existence – for how long?

Saturday, 2 September. This is a night-mare life, waiting for news from the wireless, everybody *waiting* for the final word. Ordinary things must go on, fortunately, and Robert and I had much shopping to do – more black stuff for windows, a toy-cupboard for the waiting-room which has been converted into a sort of nursery, and much food. Physical exhaustion is helpful in these times. There was the Jamaica meeting in Lincoln College. I poured out tea for a small depressed group, and listened to a very vivid address by Bishop Sara. A nasty evening, only brightened by having my family round me, listening to scraps of information from a soul-less radio, and planning expenditure for 'the duration'. What a life!

Sunday, 3 September. The worst has now been declared. Since we have had no reply to Britain's final offer, we are now at *war with Germany*. It is all too horrible to contemplate and we dare not think of the horrors to come. I took the message round to Robert in the middle of morning Prayer, after we had heard it on the wireless. We expected it, but one always hopes till the end. Norman and Richard went off home before lunch. Nita and Nancy were very brave about it. It might have been such an ordinary Sunday except for our thoughts, and the busy streets full of soldiers. Nita, Vera and I went to Church at night and it cheered us up. John came to supper and also helped. Men are great comforts.

Robert later wrote about this memorable day in his book, *Church and Parish of St Michael at the Northgate*, p. 179: 'The service had begun when Mrs Martin hurried to the Church with a card bearing the Prime Minister's announcement "this country is at war with Germany". It was enlivened by a sketch of our arch-enemy receiving a bomb himself such as we all expected he would immediately have dropped on us. Gas attacks were expected at once, and for months all worshippers carried gas-masks, as did everyone else when venturing out-of-doors, though they mercifully never had to use them. After the announcement the service proceeded as usual but Bishop Sara of Jamaica who was preaching begged as many as possible to remain for the Holy Communion which a very large number did on that solemn morning.' 'Please God end the nightmare soon,' were among the words Robert wrote this day in his diary.

2

Prelude to Bloodshed
September 1939–May 1940

With the outbreak of war, 1 Wellington Place had to accommodate many more residents and Madge found that she had a lot more work to do. Along with her mother-in-law, both her married sisters and their three children were living in the house, and her two brothers-in-law frequently came down from London. So it was not unusual for nine or ten, even occasionally eleven people, to be sleeping under the same roof, albeit a house with lots of rooms for beds (four bedrooms plus a large attic). These were very different days from those of just a couple of months before, when the Martins were able to consume much of their lives as a quiet couple.

Monday, 4 September. These terrible days seem endless, but the sunshine cheers one in spite of overwhelming worries. Nita, Nance and I seem to have so much to do – housework, shopping, looking after the children, making curtains dark and covering lights – that we are dead tired at night, yet can't sleep in case we are awakened by air-raid sirens. We have to carry our gas-masks always now. The town is bristling with war activities, and soldiers marching off.[1] We were hard at work in the evening filling sand-bags which John had got for us, and he worked like a nigger, filling in some of our basement area window. He is very cheerful and a great help. We three women cannot concentrate on anything at all, and are hating our thoughts and apprehensions. A British liner [the *SS Athenia*] was torpedoed by a U-Boat today.[2]

---

1   The arrival in Oxford and district of nearly 10,000 government-sponsored evacuees from London was reported in detail in the *Oxford Times*, 8 September 1939, p. 6. In fact, this issue of the paper was (understandably) packed with war-related stories.
2   Among the 112 people killed were 28 Americans. Some 1,300 people were saved.

Tuesday, 5 September. A similar day to yesterday. Beautiful weather which seems a mockery, and makes the thought of war seem even more incredible. We did our jobs and went shopping, our gas-helmets accompanying us. A peaceful, sunny afternoon in the garden giving the children a little teaching in dictation and General Knowledge, as goodness knows how long they may have to be away from school. Out again with Nita after tea. Muriel turned up, looking very off in khaki skirt and various badges. She had a few hours' leave.[3] I fear I still find her exasperating. John in, also soothingly. A queer, queer life.

Wednesday, 6 September. Our first air-raid warning went off, this morning at 7.40. We took refuge in the kitchen, trembling and apprehensive. Mrs Martin is so slow at getting up that she is a source of great anxiety to me. The 'All-Clear' went at 9.00 without any bother. Afterwards, we learned that enemy-air-craft had reached the East Coast but were driven back without any damage having been done. How true this is, we don't know. Anyway, we thank God for *one* escape. It is horrible, this life of suspense – like a frightful dream. Shall we *ever* again live a happy, normal life? I pray God so. Muriel appeared as we were having breakfast, on her return to town. A beautiful day. We stayed at home in the garden all the morning. Nita and I shopped in the afternoon, and we went out with the restless children in the evening. Later I went with Vera to see how Marina's last kitten was getting on, at her cousin Ethel [Warland]'s in St John Street. Vera is a comfort and still cheerful. We all hate the nights and now I think we shall often be awakened by air-raid warnings. *What* an existence!

Thursday, 7 September. A much less depressed day than yesterday, partly because we were not disturbed by air-raid sirens, and were able to sleep last night. The day was gloriously warm and sunny, and that makes a difference. Nance and I shopped – there is much of this to do – and thought, war or no war, that we must have coffee, so went to the marvellously cheerful Cadena, which was thronged with young soldiers and others. Most cheering. Nita and I called on Ruth in the afternoon and found her with a friend. We sat in the garden and talked to them both for a bit. Poor Ruth is now known as an 'enemy alien'. She seemed pleased to see us. Robert and I had a long walk after tea, through the sun-drenched [University] Parks, and round the

---

3   These details suggest that Muriel had joined the Auxiliary Territorial Service (ATS), but all other evidence indicates that she was still a teacher whose school was evacuated from London. So Madge's description is puzzling.

huge new Marston estate, full of box-like houses, all pathetically ready for 'black-out'. It seems a lunatic world, to be at war *again* when things could be so lovely. What will be the end of it all?

Friday, 8 September. Such lovely weather – the best, really, this year. It makes things easier to bear, when one can sit and bask in the hot sunshine. I am more active now than I have been for years, doing more housework, more shopping, more planning, and so far I feel well, instead of worn out. We all, now, have good appetites. I believe this hectic life makes lots of people hungry. We all had ices at the Cadena which is the liveliest place in Oxford at present. We sat and basked all afternoon, then Robert and I had tea at the Cadena and did some shopping and a little walk Headington way. A perfectly beautiful evening, the warmest this year. Richard [Nita's husband] came down for the week-end full of cheer and chat. John looked in, too.

Saturday, 9 September. The beautiful weather continues, so does the dreamlike existence, and the lack of much war news. No-one seems to know what is happening or what *will* happen. We are just thankful that so far, we have been mercifully spared air-raids in England – but for how much longer? I took Sally out in the morning, whilst the others fixed up at St Philip and St James' School for the boys [in Leckford Road]. The Oxford cinemas open today [all cinemas had been forced to close during the first week of war], and Nita, Dick, Kit and Roger went, which made things more normal than ever. Robert and I had tea with Winifred and Peter [Bleiben] and heard of their adventures getting home from Switzerland. John came in to complete our 'dug-out'. A quiet evening, thank God.

Sunday, 10 September. Almost an ordinary Sunday, except for one or two things like everyone taking gas-masks to Church. Unbelievable life this, and the awful thing is that things haven't really started. All the dreadful part is to come. However, we can only be as cheerful as possible, and it isn't hard, as yet, with crowds of family, and nothing alarming, so far, happening. My dear John is planning now to get quickly into the Air Force.[4] I daren't think ahead about anything yet. Church, morning and evening. We have to turn

---

4   John was the assistant manager and secretary at the Church Army Press, 81 Temple Road, Cowley and also active in St Michael's Church, both as a member of the choir and the PCC and, from 1936, as the secretary-treasurer of the Church Hall, a post that he continued to fulfil from a distance after he joined the RAF (PAR211/3/A1/3, p. 268, and *Parish Magazine*, April 1938, p. 10).

out the lights before the end of the service to be 'blacked-out' so in future our evening service will be at 3.00p.m.

Monday, 11 September. I went round to Worcester College in the morning to see about joining a War Supply Depôt which Mrs Lys is organizing. I feel I shall be doing something, though shall feel like a fish-out-of-water amongst so many 'University' people.[5] Norman [Nancy's husband] arrived for the night to take Richard's place, as it were. He seems, like Dick, very cheerful. Robert and I went out shopping and to tea, and the pictures, *Stagecoach* [starring John Wayne, directed by Robert Ford, 1939], which was very good in its way. Funny to be at the cinema again. Lots of people, even at that early hour, all with gas-masks. A peaceful evening. It is like living on the edge of an unseen precipice, not knowing how deep it will be.

Tuesday, 12 September. Colder today, but still fine. The papers still very unsatisfactory, we hear only bits of news [censorship had been imposed]. Warsaw still holding out, and British soldiers now in France. I cannot bear to think of the slaughter of thousands to come *again*. Surely a good God will help us all, and make it short. Norman had to return to town. Poor Nance and Nita – how much harder it is for them than for me, and how brave and cheery they are. I don't think I could be, now, though I went through it all, in the last war. We took the children to the Cadena in the morning. Nance and I went shopping in the afternoon. Mrs Claringbold and her daughter, who called at tea-time, stayed to tea. Mrs C. is rather tryingly soulful.[6] A quiet evening reading. I feel more depressed again – my brain is beginning to work again.

Wednesday, 13 September. Damp and cold today, but the weather doesn't seem to matter at all now-a-days. We go about at present, wrapped in the

---

5 This depôt at Worcester College was officially run by the Central Hospital Supply Service, 'the organisation of which is largely undertaken by the wives of heads of colleges and other prominent members of the University' (*Oxford Mail*, 23 October 1941, p. 3). Mrs Lys started this depôt for the Central Hospital Supply Service of the Red Cross and Order of St John. (*Worcester College Record 1939–1944*, p. 7. This publication for alumni is held in the College Archives. We are indebted to the Archivist, Emma Goodman, for the information.) A few weeks earlier (21 June 1939) Madge had also mentioned her insecurity concerning University society. '[I] came home to dress up for the Vice-Chancellor's garden-party at Magdalen [College]. It was a very grand occasion, and the men looked marvellous in their various robes. P.G. Wodehouse was there, after taking his degree, and Lord Nuffield. We felt as though we didn't really "belong".'
6 Rosina Claringbold, wife of a linen draper, lived at 46 Hill View Road, off Botley Road, and was an active member of St Michael's Church.

peace of false security, but knowing that, almost for certain, worse will come. The usual shopping, with and without the children. We took the boys down to Doris' in the afternoon, and she gave them tea and afterwards took them to the pictures. Ruth came to tea – she is determinedly cheerful. A quiet evening again, with our books, and a fire. We have our dressing gowns and slippers to hand at night, always, in case of air-raid warnings – oh horrible thought!

Thursday, 14 September. Still colder, but fine. The days are so similar at present and we thank God that they *are*. Shopping in the morning. I looked after Sally, whilst Nance and Nita went to the pictures in the afternoon. Vera came to a quite peaceful tea, as the boys had theirs in the kitchen. She and I took Sally for a little walk after tea. Another quiet evening. A very strange life – no time for boredom.

Friday, 15 September. Another similar day. Cold again. Lots of shopping with Nita in the morning. The town is twice as crowded these days with east-end Londoners as well as our own people. What with prams, gas-masks and bus queues, it is difficult to move. Out again in the afternoon – rainy. We don't know what the weather is to be like these days – no weather reports. John in after supper, pessimistic, and solemn, but no-one is just *bored* now. We almost wish we could be.

Saturday, 16 September. Life still goes strangely on, to all intents and purposes calm and pleasant, like a sleeping lion. I took Roger and Sally to have their hair cut, and then joined Nita and Nance and Kit for 'Saturday treat' Cadena drinks. The rest of the day spent in more shopping, reading, knitting (bed-socks for wounded), upbraiding and listening to the children. The usual quiet reading evening. Without, in St Giles, everything terrifyingly pitch-black. We wouldn't *dare* go out alone at night. How awful it will be in the winter-time, when it gets dark at 4.30.[7] What long, long evenings.

Sunday, 17 September. A strange Sunday, except for morning service, which might have been a peace-time one without the special prayers, and the appearances of dozens of gas-masks – hateful things! John in after – he seems quite at ease with all my family except mother. All the others went to afternoon Evensong but I stayed with the sleeping Sally, then took her to

---

7   There is a vivid evocation of fear felt in the blackout in Dorothy Whipple's 1941 short story, 'One Dark Night' (reprinted in her *Every Good Deed and Other Stories* [London: Persephone Books, 2016], pp. 223–33).

meet them coming out of Church. Vera came back to tea, and we had much singing round the piano afterwards, till black-out time, when she went. Supper, and another quiet evening, knitting mostly this time.

Monday, 18 September. Rather busy in the morning, doing housework, and shopping with Sally. I took her round to Vera's. She is a dear little thing, and not a bit shy. Marjorie took her leave in the afternoon, to be ward-maid in a hospital. Lately she had been very unsatisfactory, so I wasn't sorry to lose her. I went round to Worcester College and helped make swabs with a few other people. A very meticulous and boring job, but if it helps, I don't mind.[8] Home thankfully to tea, and out again after with Robert. The war-news bad. One of our air-craft carriers sunk [the *Courageous*], and the Poles almost defeated. I can't realise anything yet much – it all seems so impossible to believe, to be at *war again* – frightful. God grant it may be short and the end worth fighting for.

Tuesday, 19 September. The usual war-time shopping morning – crowded shops – gas-mask collisions, dearer food, and Sally holding my hand, a dear little companion. Danna's friend, Elsie Le Merk came to lunch, she is Swiss, and quite pleasant and harmless. It was Robert's holiday, so he took Nance and me to the pictures in the afternoon – *Q Planes* [1939] very good, with Ralph Richardson [Laurence Olivier and Valerie Hobson] – very amusing and acting beautifully. We had tea at the Cadena, then a bit of shopping, before coming home to a few songs round the piano and supper and reading.

Wednesday, 20 September. Lovely autumnal weather, but we don't seem aware of the month, day, or year. We live in a sort of dream-world which seems quite a lot like our usual life, but has unfathomable depths and unseen pitfalls. Shopping in the morning with the family. We all went to tea at Vera's in the afternoon – a large party of six. They gave us a lovely tea and we all enjoyed ourselves. They do *not* take the war seriously and their attitude is half reassuring, half irritating. John looked in for a minute or two before supper. The usual evening, except for a contretemps between Robert and me – on the question of tinned salmon being wasted!

---

8   Several weeks later (7 November 1939) she wrote of this 'bandaging' being done 'in the now familiar high-up room in the Provost of Worcester's lodgings'.

Thursday, 21 September. News of a Czech rebellion, which is a bit heartening.[9] Norman here for his weekly visit. One likes him increasingly. I went round to Worcester College to roll swabs etc again. I loathe and detest all this intensely, and the women are such snobs, with the exception of Mrs Lys and a few others. To my horror, I am to be put in charge of a whole room once a week. Me! – who can't command respect from Sally. My only comfort is that I am not being entirely idle in wartime. I had tea with Mrs and Dr Lys, with three others. How lovely to escape home! John in for a long talk. What different people I know.

Friday, 22 September. Still the days of unreality drift on. The war-news almost nil, and the air of expectancy always with us. Lots of shopping – very difficult now. In the afternoon, I went off to my swab-making again. Only another person there, as well as the nurse, so it wasn't as bad as usual. Though I'm sure I shall never learn to love my bit of 'war-work'. I met Vera for tea, at the Ritz, and then we saw the pictures there, Jeanette MacDonald in [*Broadway*] *Serenade* – quite good. Dick had arrived for the week-end when I returned. This is the first time I had been out in the evening. It is most uncanny – like a dead city.

Saturday, 23 September. I had a headache most of the day – the first for a long time, thank goodness. Shopping, and the Cadena treat. I went to bed in the afternoon and the head improved. Out with Robert after tea, and a quiet evening after.

Sunday, 24 September. Another of these strange Sundays. I stayed at home in the morning, darning socks and writing letters, and scanning the rather non-committal depressing newspapers. John looked in, solemnly. Evensong in the afternoon. Dick, Nita, Kit and Roger went too. Quite a large congregation turned out at this funny hour [3pm]. A very un-Sunday-ish evening, reading etc. One just lives from day to day, and tries not to think about what horrors might be in store for us.

Monday, 25 September. Headachey all day, as the result of having eaten too much. In spite of anxieties and depressing news, our appetites remain

---

9   *The Times*, 21 September 1939, p. 8. This report of the revolts and their repression by the German authorities from the Ministry of Information was cast in optimistic terms for the British cause. 'The fact that this is not just a flash in the pan is shown by the unanimity of purpose, the tenacity and the discipline of the participants.' It was also claimed that the brutal repressive responses 'do not appear to have had the effect intended: the fight against superior forces and ruthless tyranny continue with courage and determination'.

enormous. It must be some nervous affliction! Shopping as usual, and in the afternoon making swabs again. I discovered that the woman who has been talking the most nonsense, and the biggest snob, is the wife of the Master of one of the Colleges – Mrs D--. I am astonished that one whose husband was Vice-Chancellor for many years should apparently be so stupid![10] Home for tea, a trot round with Robert and a quiet evening.

Tuesday, 26 September. A perfect autumn morning – clear blue skies with a hint of early morning mist, and a sharp nip in the air. I hurried over my shopping, then collected Nance and Nita and all the children, and we walked in the Christ Church Meadows, so tranquil and serene, with the towers of Oxford shining white in the sunshine. Impossible to believe in war, in such peaceful surroundings. The Botanical Gardens gay with Michaelmas daisies. A lovely morning. An afternoon 'swabbing' – not quite so tedious, as the people there were reasonable. Tea there. Shopping again with Nita after. A typical evening, and the blissful read, after our daily toil was done. I needn't feel guilty about having too easy a life, now.

Wednesday, 27 September. Clear, bright, cold weather which in ordinary times one could enjoy so much, but now doesn't seem to matter one way or the other. The ordinary shopping morning – there is much more of that to do, with ten people [in the house]. In the afternoon, all the family, including Danna, went on a horrible excursion to Mrs Storr's allotment to fetch Michaelmas daisies to decorate the Church tomorrow. Most of us hated to turn out, but couldn't help admiring the blue, still sky over Port Meadows. Robert, Nance and I went to the Electra [Electra Palace Cinema in Queen Street], after leaving Nita in charge of the others at a Cadena tea. The films were mixed, a Jones family one [*Everybody's Baby*], always good and a dreadful old one [*Viennese Nights*]. Home frozen and irritated. The last straw is the news that Warsaw has fallen, and that income tax is to be 7s 6d in the pound [i.e., approaching 40%]. This war is going to be simply terrible.

Thursday, 28 September. A busy morning. Nita and I decorated the Church with Michaelmas daisies for tomorrow, then had coffee with Nance, Vera and Sally. Vera and I bought some wooly material afterwards, for winter dresses. The boys started school in the afternoon – much to our joy. Nita

---

10 But see also below, 28 September. She was referring to Frederick Holmes Dudden, Master of Pembroke College and Vice-Chancellor of the University, 1929–32. Madge sometimes wanted to avoid naming names when rendering harsh judgements.

and I went to make swabs and quite liked it. There were more there and even Mrs D-- was quite kind. Beautiful weather. We met Christopher coming out of school. He was *not* pleased at this. The usual evening. The part we enjoy begins at 9.30, after the washing up! Lovely cups of tea and books.

Friday, 29 September. The beautiful weather continues. Ever since war started, we have had lovely weather, just when it matters least. Nance went off to be with Norman for the week-end. Sally and Roger, when told, didn't make a fuss at all, and were very good all day. Nita and I went to our swab-making in the afternoon – quite pleasant again. A busy evening, bathing the children and putting them to bed, having supper, washing up, and then listening to John's gloomy views of the war-situation. *Russia* and Germany are now to offer a Peace Treaty!

Saturday, 30 September. Another enormously busy day, mostly because Nance was not here to look after her two children. Glorious weather still. Out in the morning to the Cadena with Sally and Roger, Christopher at home with a newly-found school chum, a charming little boy called Derek. A fairly peaceful afternoon, knitting and chatting, and getting tea. We had to drag Sally round the shops after tea – an agonizing performance as there are so many people now, and the shops are so crowded. The usual evening bathing children, getting them to bed, getting supper, washing up, and the blissful but all too short rest before bed.

Sunday, 1 October. Although Sunday, and a so called 'day of rest' – this was another exhausting day. I certainly went to Church in the morning, which *was* a rest, but the rest of the day was spent mostly in washing the naughty Sally again and again, as she would be 'dirty' in the most awful and sickening meaning of the word. Vera came to tea. She certainly becomes more crotchety and bitter as she gets older. We took Roger for a walk in the [University] Parks. Then after bathing him, the usual evening, and well-earned rest at 9.30. We shall be glad when Nance returns to her two infants.

Monday, 2 October. Very cold, but beautiful – clear, calm and sunny. The usual morning, shopping, looking after Sally, fetching Roger from school, hastening Kit *to* school. Nita and I to Worcester College in the afternoon, busy with complicated clear bandages and flannel, and herring-boned. We really almost look forward to going now – what a difference to my early hatred of it. We know the people now, and their names, and they are quite pleasant, really. Nance had returned when we got back, thank heaven! I went with Vera to see about a frock for the winter. A perfect evening, serene and cold and, later, a brilliant moon. Why, *why – war*?

Tuesday, 3 October. The brilliance of the weather is amazing, but it is very cold and crisp. Shopping as usual, war-supplies also as usual. A visit to see Mrs Cottrell-Horser, who has been ill so long. What a lovely view from their eyrie.[11] The usual evening. Robert had been to town to meet Nick, and brought me some lovely honey-suckle perfume from Floris – not a bit *like* honey-suckle, but very beautifully like some unknown flower.

Wednesday, 4 October. Oh so cold. Shopping – always so much to do of this every day. We thought we would have a change for once, so instead of going to our War-Supplies Nita came with us (Robert and Nancy) for a cold but pleasing walk from Boars Hill to Cumnor Hill and Old Hinksey. It was nice in spite of RAF bombers zooming above us as a constant reminder of war. We had a nice tea at the Cadena, then to some amusing pictures – *Lucky Night* (Myrna Loy and Robert Taylor). It was a lovely holiday for us and we enjoyed it. One still *can* enjoy things in spite of the horrors in store, maybe, for all of us. Please God, may it end soon.

Thursday, 5 October. Suddenly much warmer, but showery, in between bright bursts of glowing sunshine. Shopping – with Nita and Sally after feeding swans in Worcester [College] Garden. War Supplies all afternoon. They said they missed us yesterday, and I really do think we are their quickest workers, 'though I says it!' We are still treated with faint patronage by the leaders, I think, though the workers themselves are pleasant for the most part. Nice to be home at 5.00 for the usual evening, which rarely varies, attending to the children, supping, washing up and reading. The nicest moment of the day is when we have our cups of tea, at 9.30p.m.

Friday, 6 October. Everyone waiting for Hitler's peace 'offers'. It is a pity if we can't [have] Peace when it is so touch and go.[12] Shopping. The food is not exactly getting short, but one can't get things as cheaply, and there are such crowds everywhere, that it is a misery to shop, especially at week-ends. Our War Depôt as usual – less and less alarming but we long for a change of work to do, from herring-boning 'many-tailed' bandages. Nita and I both

---

11   She and her husband usually appear in most following diary entries as Mr and Mrs Horser. They lived at 50 Cornmarket Street on an upper storey. They were both active members of St Michael's congregation; he as a member of the Vestry; and she as a regular flower arranger, until she became ill during 1939. The *Parish Magazine*, January 1940, p. 3 refers to her 'being on the road to recovery' but Madge's diary does not bear this out.
12   *The Times*, 7 October 1939, pp. 6–8, gave full coverage to Hitler's 'peace terms'. There was no chance that Britain would accept his proposal for a conference aimed at a general settlement of disputes among the European powers.

bought new hats after tea. Richard home for the weekend. John in for his usual Friday talk. What different things we now have to discuss.

Saturday, 7 October. A horrid headache, and a busy morning, decorating the Church with the help of Nance and Vera, for the Harvest Festival tomorrow. More shopping after. To bed all afternoon, then a walk with Robert to buy shoes. Marina had her family of four kittens last night. We kept one. It is very heart-breaking to see her look for the others.

Sunday, 8 October. Harvest Festival. Nance and I went in the morning and stayed for the mid-day Holy Communion. A lovely service altogether, music, decorations and a splendid encouraging sermon from Robert [partly about the war]. John in after. I took the two boys in the afternoon to Evensong, which was crowded. Vera came back to tea, and we had a grand 'singing round the piano', mostly Gilbert and Sullivan, with a sprinkling of hymns. Most heartening. Good old G & S is so English and soothing. Vera had to go home in the black-out. Nice supper and read. What different Sundays these are to normal ones. Well, I often wanted a change and now I have one with a vengeance.

Monday, 9 October. A very wet day all day – the first for a long time. We did no shopping, but wrote letters and sewed etc. The war Supplies Depôt again. Then tea with the Bleibens at the Moorish [139 High Street] – very cheering and cosy. A bit more shopping before splashing home for the usual evening. John came in at a ghastly late hour to 'read over' a very grim contribution to his old school 'mag' he had written, on 'my job' and very technical and terrible it was, not to mention long. He wanted my advice, but I could only suggest that he cut it down considerably, and even then it would still be frightful. Poor John!

Tuesday, 10 October. Beautiful and warm again and sunny. I took Sally down with me to Miss Barrett's for a fitting of a jade wool frock. Then went into the Meadows for a bit. How exquisite Oxford looks from the Broad Walk. The usual afternoon at Worcester. Then more shopping before the usual evening. The children dressed up and acted a peculiar play for our amusement. This *is* a strange, strange life. When shall we go to town again for a lovely day's fun, or see the lights of Paris,[13] or more impossible still, the

---

13 Here she placed an asterisk, with these words on the back of the page: 'March 1952. We have seen the lights of Paris again – unchanged – and had many lovely days' fun in London, but not as yet an Austrian mountain or "onion" church spire. We still hope to – and many

green slopes of an Austrian mountain and a red 'onion' church spire? Will it ever be – in this life again?

Wednesday, 11 October. Still warm and mellow. Shopping. War Supply in the afternoon. More shopping. Nita and Nance went to the pictures, and I saw to the children and gave them their baths after we had seen a rather trying 'film show' given by Derek [school friend of Christopher] on his new cinema. The films were about 1912 vintage and hardly discernible. The same sort of evening – supper and books. We shouldn't grumble if the war went on in this way, but I fear it may soon be anything but peaceful when we refuse Hitler's 'Peace' offer.

Thursday, 12 October. A holiday for us all, and a lovely change. We took the 10 o'clock bus (leaving Doris in charge) to a short way past Stokenchurch. The day was, at first, grey and misty, but at mid-day, it brightened into a blue and gold autumnal day. We walked through beautiful and typical Chiltern country – hills, woods and fields to Wheeler-end Common for a bread and cheese lunch at a pub, then through more lovely woods – the trees turning gold and russet – to the outskirts of High Wycombe, where we looked over the impressive new, white Russian-looking church – then to West Wycombe, where we climbed up to the sinister church on the hill which overlooks the charming village. We didn't like the church or the 18th century mausoleum [the Dashwood Mausoleum], though there are glorious views from the summit of wooded hills. A very welcome tea at 'Apple Orchard'. Then the bus back through the golden evening, after a beautiful holiday. If only we hadn't war, how lovely everything would be, or so we think. Actually, I seem to find much more cause for private grumblings and boredom in Peacetime. I think this extra busy life just leaves no time for thinking, but if it did, there would be *plenty* to worry about.

Friday, 13 October. Friday mornings are always awful now. Shopping is dreadful with the week-end hordes of people. The usual Worcester College bandaging afternoon. It is tiresome having to turn out, but we like it when we get there. Robert and I went to the pictures to see *Beau Geste* afterwards. I liked it very much in spite of it not having good notices. Gary Cooper is such a lamb. Out into the pouring rain and pitch black-ness, quite dangerous having to grope one's way home. John came in. He has been accepted for an Air Observer in the RAF, and is thrilled to bits. The awful horror of people

---

people go, as usual again – but we haven't yet.' Clearly, in later life Madge read through at least some of her diary from these years.

like my beloved young John's pleasure at the opportunity of being killed, is beyond bearing. I feel so fatalistic about all this war and so helpless, that I could be stonily cheerful at his news and excitement, but no-one knows how I shall miss him, and if anything happened to him, I should nearly break my heart. God grant that all this nightmare may soon pass, and keep our loved ones safe.

Saturday, 14 October. A dull dark damp depressing day, with bad war news of a sunk Battle-ship [the *Royal Oak* at Scapa Flow] – by U-Boats. One should be miserable all the time, but really one can't help finding pleasure still in the ordinary things of life – books, and new frocks and food and warm rooms and the society of one's own people. If only we can at least keep those – but who knows what our future will be? Ruth came to tea, bringing little gifts for the children. Poor thing, what an outcast she must feel, and to think there are thousands of Germans as fine and noble as she. The nights are the most depressing, when I have time to think of awful things – air-raids, danger, and the departure of my ewe-lamb, John. Thank God the day-time is too busy.

Sunday, 15 October. Unceasing rain all day – frightful. Church in the morning with Nita, and in the afternoon with Nance, the boys and Vera. John in for his usual after-Church chat. How many more times will he come again, I wonder? I dare not think. Vera in to tea – this seems a Sunday habit now. The usual Sunday evening, so different from what it used to be. There are aspects of this war that are quite pleasant, and which I should miss if it came to an end, strange as it may seem.

Monday, 16 October. A nice, misty but lovely-to-look-at October day after yesterday's rain. A typical Monday of this war-time existence – shopping in the morning, War Supplies in the afternoon, washing hair in the evening. We heard that an attempt to bomb the Forth Bridge by German air-craft has failed. This is the first raid on the British Isles. How many more, I wonder?

Tuesday, 17 October. A pouring wet day. Robert up to town to meet Nick for lunch, and to say goodbye to him. He and Joy sail for Nigeria tomorrow on a convoyed boat.[14] Nita and I had our shopping, and our bandages in

---

14   Leonard Nicholls, aged 49, was married to Joy, aged 27, his second wife. Madge always referred to him as 'Nick'. He, like Robert, served in the Bedfordshire Regiment in the Great War and was billeted with him at the Setterington's London home in 1915. In 1919 he matriculated at Lincoln College, where Robert was also studying. (We are grateful to Lindsay McCormack, the College Archivist, for helping us to make use of the records in her care, and

the afternoon. Still drenching rain. A Committee meeting at night, in the Vestry of the Church. They have fixed up three tentative whist-drives in the Shamrock Tea Rooms [6 and 8 St Michael's Street].[15] Home in blackness and rain to a nice warm house and supper and reading.

Wednesday, 18 October. We had heavy thunder in the night, and such vivid lightning that it penetrated even our two lots of curtains! Cold and dismal but no more rain today. A very usual day, with shopping and bandaging, and Nita and I went to the pictures early in the evening to see *Made for Each Other* [with James Stewart and Carole Lombard, 1939] which was quite good in a sentimental sort of way. Supper and reading. Nance stayed up to greet Norman, due to arrive on the 2.00*a.m.* train. We enjoy increasingly our War-Supplies work. Another instance of 'the clouds ye so much dread …'

Thursday, 19 October. The days are so much alike now, except for details. Norman was here today, having arrived very late, or rather early in the morning, at 3.00a.m. Nita and I did shopping, and our bandages, and after tea I met Robert at the 'Oxford' [the Oxford Super Cinema in Magdalen Street] to see a very Hollywood version of *The Man in the Iron Mask* [based loosely on a mid-nineteenth-century story by Alexandre Dumas]. Not very good. Kippers for supper, and the usual blissful tea, and read after.

Friday, 20 October. Very cold and bright, and the news not so bad. We have signed a Pact with Turkey, but just what that means exactly, I know not.[16] Loads of shopping in the morning as usual. Bandages in the afternoon. More girl students there to supervise. Out a little with Robert afterwards. Richard came for the week-end. Nice supper – spaghetti cheese. John in. Now that a parting from one another seems inevitable, these meetings are precious. Poor lamb – he is so eager about it all, like so many other young things who are sent to the slaughter. Please God, not my John amongst them.

---

also to Barbara Tearle.) Nick reappears in Madge's diary on several occasions in the early 1940s.
15   As Madge records later in the diary, Miss Hardman, who kept the Shamrock Tea Rooms, was a supporter of St Michael's Church. In November, she made rooms at the Shamrock available for church meetings, an arrangement that continued throughout the war (*Parish Magazine*, November 1939, p. 10).
16   Turkey, a participant in the Great War as part of the Ottoman Empire, on the side of Germany, managed to avoid fighting in the Second World War.

Saturday, 21 October. Frightfully cold, but beautiful. I shopped, then met Vera for coffee at the Cadena, and did more shopping. I had the first German lesson since June, in the afternoon, at Fräulein's, as there doesn't seem much room or quietness here. Afterwards we had tea with Mrs Acton and Peggy in Blandford Avenue [off Woodstock Road], after missing a bus and arriving there very late. However, it was quite a pleasant tea, and Peggy is the same sweet and beautiful girl as she was when I admired her in Church, when she was an adorable red-gold plaited little girl. We quite enjoyed it. The usual evening – supper and reading.

Sunday, 22 October. Very cold and misty. Church in the morning. John in after. He unbends quite a bit with Nita and Nance because he isn't snubbed, as he is when mother is here. I didn't go to Evensong in the afternoon, but had an early cup of tea, then went round to a PCC meeting in the Lady Chapel to discuss, mostly, the decorating and restoring of it.[17] It was a very long meeting, and we were very cold and tired when we got home, for a peaceful evening. Christopher has a bad cold and is causing his parents a bit of anxiety. Marina's new tabby kitten, two weeks old, is adorable, and looks as if he will be thoroughly spoilt by everyone.

Monday, 23 October. A holiday for Robert, and for the first time for nearly four months we went up to town in the good old way. It was lovely to be there again, and, except for many sand-bags, less shoppers, less traffic, many closed theatres, and plenty of soldiers, there wasn't much difference to be seen in our dear old London. We looked at the shops a bit. They are full of uniforms, gas-mask containers, 'siren-suits', etc. A lovely lunch at the Regent Palace Hotel. Then to see *French Without Tears*, the film of the play [a comedy with Ray Milland and Ellen Drew, based on a 1936 play by Terrence Rattigan], quite well done, though not *quite* as funny as it might have been. Home on the 6.05, very strange and dark, with only a dim blue light allowed in the carriages, not enough to read by. We brought home a nice supper from Lyons, and small gifts all round. Altogether a most enjoyable holiday, in spite of old Hitler and this abominable war.

Tuesday, 24 October. Back to a more or less normal, ordinary day, with the morning shopping, afternoon bandages, evening meal and sublime after-supper rest and read and kitten worship. If it only wasn't for the war, I

---

17   Robert later wrote of the importance he attached to this restoration. 'In these trying times it is good to have an assertion of dignity and beauty when so much cruelty and destruction is going on' (*Parish Magazine*, June 1940, p. 3).

should honestly be enjoying this life quite a lot. I always enjoy my family's company, and the busy sociable life leaves no time for moods – or (touchwood) many headaches. I even now like enormously the company of those 'university' women at the War Depôt, and find most of them very kind and friendly. Nita being there makes a lot of difference. Of *course*, I know the war has scarcely begun, and of *course* I'd give anything for Peace, but it is wonderful how one can find things to like under any circumstances.

Wednesday, 25 October. Cold and beautiful, sunny pale blue skies and a tang in the air. The war apparently has now 'officially' begun after eight weeks of – what? Skirmishes and suspense. The usual morning, except that Nita and I had a Cadena interval – very pleasant. Worcester [College] in the afternoon. The view from the high up old nursery where we work, is entrancing. From one window we look over the oldest buildings of the College and the tree tops of the garden, and from the other, blue distant hills, the lake, and green lawns. The trees are now a blaze of glory. I looked after the children whilst Nance and Nita went to the pictures. Christopher showed me his nicest side, and talked most entertainingly.

During the following several weeks some things remained much the same in Madge's life (shopping, films, plays, visits to the Cadena, standard domestic routines), while others changed. She continued with her afternoon war work at Worcester College, some of it strenuous. 'We are very busy working on more than a thousand yards of gauze for swabs,' she wrote on 3 November, 'and it is extremely tiring.' Usually she went with her sister, Nita, sometimes Nancy too. On 6 November 'Nance and I cut up the interminable gauze, and sewed, late'; three days later 'we had a pleasant afternoon in spite of the hated abdominal swabs'. On Thursday, 16 November 'we had a very hard afternoon's work. Mrs Dew said farewells. She has been in charge of the swab-making so far but sails home to Australia on Saturday.' Not all was sweetness and light at the war depôt. 'Much rebellion [20 November] amongst us workers against the Nazi-like new notices dotted about the depôt over the week-end, and the snobbish attitude of the heads of the depôt who seem to want the work done by a chosen few when it is wanted so badly.' On 23 November she reported that 'Nita and I were in charge of our swab department in the afternoon "Key women"! It was quite pleasant, but the afternoons are so short now that we seem to be no sooner started than 4 o'clock comes along, when we have to stop now, as our room cannot be "blacked out" properly.' Of course, their labour allowed ample opportunity for conversation. On 29 November she mentioned a 'few rather slandering souls there', and on 4 December she 'listened to the usual gossip which is certainly very amusing'. There was a pause in this work, from 13 December. 'The last afternoon at the War Depôt before "breaking up" for Christmas. There was an exhibition of our work in the magnificent drawing-room, and an extra nice tea in the library. Everyone very pleasant and full of good wishes.'

New facts of life were also mentioned. On 27 October, 'Butter is getting very scarce and we were only allowed ½lb each at Sainsburys [in High Street].' On Guy Fawkes Day fireworks for the children had to be set off indoors, because of the blackout. Then there were, for Madge, changes in her household. On 28 October 'Nita's late maid arrived to be my parlour-maid, for the time being, at least. She seems a very nice maid indeed.' Subsequent experience proved satisfactory: 'Helen is so nice to have after the rampaging Marjorie, and looks neat in her uniform' (13 November). No two minutes of silence were observed on Remembrance Day, but the following day, a Sunday, there was an armistice service at St Michael's 'with a very touching sermon from Robert which touched our hearts, and also our pockets for the sum of nearly £16'. Before the war Madge virtually never mentioned talks on the radio; now she did. 'The Queen spoke beautifully on the wireless to the women of England,' she wrote on 11 November; and the following evening 'Winston Churchill made a very amusing but provoking speech which I fear will infuriate the German rulers to immediate revenge.'[18]

One striking feature of most weeks in September/October is the absence of any mention of headaches. This only changed on 29 October, when she fell on her way to church and 'gave myself the first real headache of the war, which lasted for days'. She stayed in bed for almost all of the following two days; on 1 November she 'went to bed again for the afternoon and slept' – in the evening 'the headache [was] not quite good enough for reading'; and on 2 November 'The beastly head returned somewhat, but I got up and shopped, and Cadena'd, and "bandaged" in the afternoon, and it very gradually receded.' Then she seems to have been headache-free, or at least relatively so, for about a month – until 12 December, 'A beast of a headache all day', which subsided the following day. 'My birthday, and no headache!' on 20 December. 'Cheers!'

A key feature of the outbreak of war for Madge was the arrival in Oxford of her two sisters and their families, which had various implications. The day-to-day ones, involving concrete tasks and events, are clear and documented above. Then there were, for Madge, the deeper meanings and feelings, which she wrote of on

18   Churchill's humour was partly at the expense of Goering, 'who is one of the few Germans who has been having a pretty good time for the last few years'. His contempt for the enemy was overt: he spoke of 'these boastful and bullying Nazis [who] are looking with hungry eyes for some small countries in the west which they can trample down and loot', and imagined Hitler someday displaying 'the frenzy of a cornered maniac'. He concluded by referring to Hitlerism as 'this monstrous apparition' and the Nazi Party machine as a 'seething mass of criminality and corruption'. Robert thought the speech was 'fierce'. (Robert Rhodes James, ed., *Winston S. Churchill: His Complete Speeches, 1897–1963* [London: Chelsea House, 1974, 8 vols], vi, 6171–5.)

26 November. 'There are so many aspects of this war-life I lead that I love that sometimes the thought of going back to normal dismays me, though of course *everyone* wants Peace. I always knew I was fond of my family, but I never realised just *how* fond, till war came.' Earlier that month she spoke of the 'happiness I get from my sisters' company' (8 November). War, then, had strengthened her feelings about family connections, almost entirely positively.[19] 'I daren't think of the time when Nita goes,' she wrote on 11 December, 'I really dread the loss it will be.' But change there would be – after all, many of those who had fled London over three months earlier now felt they could safely return. There had been no air raids. Most fears had not been realized. Both Madge's sisters were planning to return to their homes after Christmas. 'I really am more sorry than I have been about anything for a long time,' she lamented on Sunday, 17 December. 'Having them both here, even with the pandemonium attached, has been a marvellous happiness to me … However, one must think of their husbands' loneliness.' (Madge's mother, though, who had been living elsewhere, arrived in Oxford on 19 December 1939 for a prolonged stay.)

Tuesday, 26 December. Alas I had a bad head, and stayed in bed till the evening, when I tottered up to go to the pantomime with all the family except Sally. A whole row of us [her mother included]. It was a *splendid* pantomime, 'Jack and the Beanstalk' [at the New Theatre], and we all adored it. Roger and Christopher thrilled to bits. My head unfortunately like a raging furnace.

Wednesday, 27 December. A miserable day. I was in bed till the evening – and Nita went.[20]

---

19   A rare exception was recorded on Sunday, 3 December 1939. 'Just sometimes this continual crowd of people gets me down – although I like quite a lot of it. There was, after tea, the first bit of friction since "the gathering of the clans", but we have done remarkably well, I think, considering various temperaments. The friction was over a bit of "peace and quiet" being insured for the drawing-room. Nancy was under the impression that the noisy ones were being cruelly banished, and gave a piece of her mind. I felt upset for a bit, as I have tried very hard not to lay down laws more than I can help in our once quiet house – but I sought refuge with Robert and soon cheered up. Nita was highly indignant at Nance. Ah me, Hitler causes lots of indirect trouble.' This was a weekend when both her brothers-in-law were also in residence (during the week they were normally in London), making for seven visitors at 1 Wellington Place.
20   Almost three months later, on Wednesday, 20 March 1940, just before Easter, Nita and her husband and son arrived at 1 Wellington Place to spend a week. 'We were overjoyed to see each other again, and spent a noisy, happy evening talking. Poor Robert didn't get much

Thursday, 28 December. The headache better, but I felt very washed out, as always after such beastly things. Snow today, everything looking lovely beneath a dove-grey sky. I adore snow. Mother, Nance and I shopped. Vera and Muriel at home. The former glum. A very lazy afternoon writing 'thank you' letters, and dozing. John came in to say goodbye before going off to his RAF Training Camp. I feel thankfully wooden-headed about it, thank Heaven, so far, and after a very sentimental farewell chat, was able to send him off with bright smiles, and not a tear. Right at the back of my wooden-ness there is a deep depression, but layers of resignation cover it for the moment. If I don't think too deeply ahead, I can manage, but one day I shall wake up to the fact that he has gone, and Nita has gone, and Nancy soon to go, also mother. I have been so happy this autumn. However, my darling Robert is my real happiness, and whilst I have him *nothing* matters.

Friday, 29 December. A heavenly day to look at – frosty and faintly pinkish, over the crisp snow – but very cold. My wooden feeling persists, and I can think of John away to Warrington, and Nita gone back home, with composure, but do not delve too deep into things. Shopping with mother in the snow. I went with Nance and the wee Sally to the Scala to see an old Shirley Temple film, *Curly Top*. Sally seemed to understand and enjoy it, and so did we. After tea I went to more pictures with mother, quite good ones. I do *not* like these ghost-days after Christmas. They should not exist, and this year they are specially hard to bear.[21]

Saturday, 30 December. Still snowy and beautiful. Lots of shopping as usual on Saturday morning. Richard appeared on a hurried visit to take all their belongings and some of Nancy's away, also our adorable kitten. My depression is beginning to rear its grey head, under the stony feeling, but having mother and Nance still here helps. I had tea at Fullers with Muriel, who never seems to improve in silliness. We met Nance and Vera at the Ritz, and saw that adorable pair Fred Astaire and Ginger Rogers again in the

---

reading done.' 'Like old times,' she remarked the following day, 'having Nita pop in after breakfast to see how things were. I think it would be ideal if she could always be here. But maybe it wouldn't – one never knows.'

21 Her meaning of 'ghost-days' had been revealed a year before (28 December 1938). 'These days after Christmas don't seem to belong to anywhere, just a vague interlude before the New Year.' But this year's transition from old year to New Year was more painful than usual. 'I am having rather a spell of headaches lately,' she wrote on 6 January 1940, 'ever since Christmas. It must be due to my deep-seated depression, which I try not to show. … How slowly the time goes now.'

lovely film *The Story of Mr and Mrs Vernon Castle* [1939; actually *The Story of Vernon and Irene Castle*].

Sunday, 31 December. Goodbye to 1939, and no-one will be sorry to see it go. May 1940 be an improvement. And yet what personal joys I have had – holidays, and especially having my family since the beginning of the war, and even the war-Depôt, which I hated at first, and the family Christmas. It was after Christmas that the dreary things happened, Nita going, and John, and next week Nancy and the children. Well, I still have everything to make me happy, and shouldn't murmur a *word* of complaint. We have much to be thankful for – so far, no bombs on English towns, and as yet not many casualties in France. Doubtless these dreadful things will all be stored up for the Spring, but we can only trust and hope and pray. I hope my John will be brought safely through the war, and that he may be happy in the Air Force, and that we may all see Peace next year.

Monday, 1 January 1940. Last year I started my diary with the hope that we should see 1939 through in Peace, but my hope was not granted, and we have been at war for four months. What will this year bring? One cannot think ahead, but please God, it *will* bring Peace to all the world.[22] A quiet New Year's Day – snow on the ground. Shopping with mother and Nance and the children, and coffee with them and Muriel, home on leave from her country school [in Devon] where she has been evacuated since the war. She was fairly sensible. Nance goes on Wednesday. Nita went last week. With what regret I see them go after such a happy autumn, but the husbands need them. A quiet evening. I had a mysterious card from John who had gone to an RAF Training Camp, saying he might be sent home on deferred service. I don't know how I feel about this.

Tuesday, 2 January. A holiday for Robert, and the most lovely wintry day imaginable, so we went for a walk from Boars Hill to Abingdon. The country looked wonderful under a crisp, sparkling cover of snow, and the softest of blue skies overhead, with a warm sun shining benignly. It was a lovely walk and we had a welcome lunch at the Queen's Hotel at Abingdon, then back to Oxford and a warm crumpet tea, before going on with Nance to the Ritz to see the best of the Andy Hardy films, I think, as yet, *Andy Hardy Gets Spring*

---

22 'God hears one's prayers,' she wrote on a slip of paper headed 'New Year's Day 1940', along with some biblical quotes of reassurance. Almost a fortnight later, on 14 January 1940, she asked herself: 'What personal suffering and anxiety am I to be let in for, before this war is over, I wonder? But I must thank God for his goodness.'

Fever [with Mickey Rooney]. No word yet about John. I do hope 'no news is good news'. Nancy's last night, alas.

Wednesday, 3 January. The coldest day yet – thick frost, and ringing pavements underfoot. Nance and I went shopping on her last morning and had coffee together. She is also sorry to go, as I am to see her and the children go, but she isn't as sorry as Nita was, as although she has been brave and happy-ish here, she didn't really love it so much as Nita, being of a more independent nature. Mother and I saw them off, and now the house is strangely quiet, but how soon one gets used to any change. It even seems normal now, though when mother goes, I dread to think of the dullness. I had a permanent wave in the afternoon, and they took away all my long curls, so that I nearly wept with dismay at my cropped modern appearance. We went to the Playhouse at night with Vera and Muriel to see *The Scarlet Pimpernel* [1934], which creaked badly. We were bored with its old-fashioned dialogue and situations, though we liked Dennis Price as the hero.[23] No word about John yet. Where *is* he?[24]

During the following four months the war sometimes vanishes from Madge's diary. Since these were the months of the 'phoney war', when combat involving Britons was close to non-existent except on the seas, it was not surprising that war was not front and centre in many people's minds. It certainly was not in Madge's. Her war-related remarks are almost all connected to the background circumstances of life, either hers or people she knew. The year began with one of the coldest winters on record – this brutal cold persisted until 19 February – and the consequences feature prominently in the diary. There was lots of sickness. People known to Madge were confined to their beds. 'I am very fed up with life at the moment,' she wrote on 22 January. 'Frigid cold, headaches, ill mothers – nothing is worth recording.' Her spirits were low in January and she even wondered 'if this will be my last diary' (the 16th). For five or six weeks her life seems to have been awash in gloom. Still, through the first quarter of the year, there continued to be lots of film-going and

---

23   Dennis Price (1915–1973) had been a member of the Oxford University Drama Society while at Worcester College. He was soon (March 1940) to join the Royal Artillery. The *Oxford Times*, 29 December 1939, p. 4 and 5 January 1940, p. 4, also liked his performance but was lukewarm about the production as a whole.

24   A letter from him two days later 'set my jittery nerves at rest. Nothing has happened to him. He is still at Warrington, and has started his training. I am glad for his sake – though the poor lamb is frozen with cold.'

occasional visits to the theatre.[25] (She almost never mentioned listening to the BBC for pleasure.)

On Monday, 8 January – 'Rationing starts today for butter, sugar, ham and bacon; meat is soon to be rationed'[26] – Madge returned to the War Depôt 'for the usual sewing, but how deadly dull it seems now without the sisters, and a depressed melancholy seems to have settled on it all.' On 23 January she made a rare reference to war news: 'horrible things in the papers – Nazi oppressions in Poland, destroyers sunk, Finns bombed. What will be the end of it all?' She expected worse to come, including German bombing in the spring (4 March). She did not think the war would soon be over (17 March). It was a stressful time. 'This war hanging over our heads is wearing everyone's nerves to shatters' (18 February). She tried to keep herself in check (20 February): 'I must not let myself become too nervy – these days I am in danger of doing so.'

Madge certainly did have a hand in the war effort. On 8 January she was making an 'Air-Force scarf', and four days later 'I knitted an Air-Force sock' on the train to London. And she did more. In February and March she attended a number of Lenten discussions on 'What we are fighting', one of which was given by her husband on the history of Germany (Thursday, 8 February). The following Thursday she heard 'a fascinating lecture given by Dr Maxwell Garnett [an authority on the League of Nations] on "What we are fighting for". He is a most attractive man and a very interesting talker. The room was crowded again.' The talk on 22 February was by 'a young statistic-loving, but not uninteresting man from Balliol'. On Thursday, 7 March she heard 'Dr Koeppler, a German, and a Magdalen professor talk on "What we are fighting against". He was most enthralling and comforting.'[27] She attended the last of these Guild discussions the following Thursday – all this testifying to (at the least) Madge's interest in trying to understand better the current state of European affairs and the conflict with Germany.

Her main contribution to the war continued to be her Red Cross work, especially at Worcester College preparing hospital supplies, which usually involved several afternoons a week, mainly bandaging. On 12 February 'we have a rush order for "surgeons'-mask" bandages', which were still being made weeks later (4 March). On 7 March 'I was all alone in the Bandaging Room in the afternoon, but I didn't

---

25 Unusually, one film prompted her to comment on a matter of social justice. On 11 March she saw a very 'solemn film, *The Stars Look Down*. It was wonderfully acted, and made us think very hard about the wretchedly dangerous lives miners lead.' This 1940 film was based on A.J. Cronin's novel of the same name about a north-east mining community. It was directed by Carol Reed and starred Michael Redgrave and Margaret Lockwood.

26 'How we used to look back on the last war's ration books with amused pity,' she added 'now here we are again! We are allowed ¼lb of butter and bacon a week each, and I think 12ozs of sugar. We must get used to the taste of margarine!'

27 H.F. Koeppler was co-author with Maxwell Garnett of the 1940 book, *A Lasting Peace ... With some chapters on the basis of German co-operation*.

mind at all. I "set up" foot amputation bandages. Why I don't faint at the very idea is surprising.' After a break over and following Easter, she was back at the Depôt 'making sample bandages to be sent up to a Red Cross Exhibition' (25 April).

These gatherings for war work, usually of only a handful of women, were the sole occasions when Madge regularly socialized with strangers, and class-consciousness was sometimes imbedded in her remarks. 'Mrs Lys is a great snob, I think, and too anxious to please the "right people"' (31 January). The afternoon of the following Friday, 2 February was unusual: 'dozens of unknown faces turned up for the inspection visit of Viscountess Falmouth and Lady [Gertrude] Bruce-Gardiner, both nice modest people. I had a chat with both. It seemed funny to have such crowds there, when usually there are such a few. Mrs Lys all excitement.'[28] On 19 February 'Mrs Lys came and had a few "gracious" words' with Madge and Miss Butler. 'She is too "sweety-sweety" to please many.' On 20 February only one other woman was at the Depôt. 'She is a talkative, amusing, but somewhat waspish Argentine with whom I imagine it is best to keep on the right side.' On 22 February she was again working only with Miss Butler: 'She is an intelligent and interesting woman and I just have no time to be shy there now.' On 28 February the War Depôt was 'a bit more interesting today as there were a few nice girl-students. I never thought they *could* be nice, but all the ones who come to the Depôt are.' Clearly, volunteering enlarged significantly Madge's social circle, even if she sometimes felt awkward.[29]

The main change at 1 Wellington Place (aside from her mother living there, and she was sometimes not in good health) involved domestic help. On 9 January 1940 Madge reported that 'we are without a second maid. Helen will not be returning, as she has been "called up". We must find another.' At the end of the month (31 January) Madge mentioned feeling tired at night 'as we have no maid to do the supper and washing up at present'. On 27 January she 'interviewed a pert and pretty perhaps-maid-to-be – but what can one gather from first impressions?' Perhaps things did work out, for a few days later, on 6 February, 'A new maid came, and she is pretty and smart, and seems cheerful and efficient. I do hope it will last. Her name is Rose Horne.' Rose in fact quickly won approval, especially considering that Doris was sick with the flu and away from work for almost four weeks from 8 February. On 13 February it was said that Rose 'is doing extremely well, *so far*'. On 19 February she was praised for a supper of 'enterprising savouries'; Madge thought she 'is a wonder with her nice little supper dishes, and I'm still touching wood about her' (24 February).

---

28   On 9 February, after she and Robert had tea with a young couple in his rooms at Trinity College, Madge wrote that 'She is modern and nice. They are very "country" so I don't suppose we shall see much of them now that she doesn't come to the Depôt any more.'
29   On 29 April at the Depôt 'the conversation, mostly by Mrs Dudden, was so "University" and "whose father was what" that I felt irritated for once. I feel so apart from all that.'

While Madge's Easter holidays did not start well[30] – she had 'a fearful headache' on Good Friday (22 March; it improved the next day) – she wrote with enthusiasm about Easter Sunday and Monday.

Sunday, 24 March. A joyful Easter Day, though as I hadn't realized Lent so much this year, and especially Holy Week, I didn't feel the relief and happiness of the religious side of the day so much, nor did I deserve to do so. Nita and I got up for the 8 o'clock Holy Communion, and Vera was there too. We looked at our Easter-egg gifts after breakfast – nearly like a small Christmas.[31] Morning Service with Nita, Vera and Muriel, and John in, like the good old days, beer and all. To my joy he seconded the idea of a walk with me in the afternoon, and called for me at 3.00. We went the Lake Street [New Hinksey] to Boars Hill walk, which was very muddy but we loved it. He did most of the talking, and told me a lot about his camp and his life there and his ambitions. I like to visualize it all. More and more I realize that he is almost strictly unimaginative and practical, and my exact opposite, but we do enjoy one another's company so much in spite of it. He came back to tea, then I went to Evensong with mother and the girls. Very festal – and the first real Evensong since war started. Thank God for a happy Easter.

Monday, 25 March. A beautiful sunny warm morning for our Easter holiday. We coaxed mother to come with us on our excursion, and all of us set off by bus to High Wycombe. Birds and Spring flowers and sunshine all the way. We did the walk from High Wycombe to Penn, and mother kept up with us bravely in spite of steep hills and slippery paths through glorious woods, and with beautiful blue horizons. When we got to Penn, we found our little café had closed, so had to walk on to the fashionable and crowded 'Crown' where, after a long long wait amidst rather horrid sporting people, we got sandwiches and coffee. Down after lunch to Beaconsfield, and then to see 'Bekonscot', the beautiful little model village, which also was crowded.

---

30   A few days earlier there was a bright moment, for on 20 March Madge received a 'Greetings Telegram' from Robert, which read: 'TWENTY FIVE YEARS LOVE DARLING'. She added the notation that this was 'the day Robert and I met in 1915'.

31   On an attached page she made a list of these 'Easter presents' and their givers. Robert gave her nail polish, perfume, a brooch, and 'four little rabbits. Mother – scarlet geranium, buttonhole. Nita and Dick – rock-plants, peppermint creams. John – hydrangea plant. Vera – cami-knickers. Muriel – cami-knickers. Rose – yellow tulips. Susie – green posy and hankie.' (Cami-knickers, a one-piece woman's undergarment, combine camisole and knickers.) Exchanging presents on special occasions was *de rigueur* in Madge's social circle.

Christopher loved it. The day clouded over and grew cold there, and we were glad to get tea in the town. Robert and I explored the real old Beaconsfield before catching trains back home. John came in to say goodbye before going back to Padgate [Camp, near Warrington]. This is a dreadful wrench always and after a pleasant talk, gradually it got spoiled by my compassionate pity for certain aspects of his life, annoying him very much, so that he shouted in anger and misunderstanding, and reduced me to misery. Why do I bother to pity him when he is so self-sufficient? What a pity. So sad an ending to his leave, but I do mean so well and he doesn't seem to understand what pity and sympathy really mean.

Tuesday, 26 March. A wet miserable day – cold, rainy and windy. The worst combination. Nita and I had fittings for our Spring suits. I rang up John and sent him away with a cheerful, practical memory of me. In the afternoon we went to the Ritz to see *Gulliver's Travels* again [1939, animated]. I liked it more this time and the others liked it, too. The vestry meeting at night in the Morrell Hall[32] – not too long – and we were able to be home to supper. In spite of John going, I feel less wretched tonight.[33]

Wednesday, 27 March. Very cold again, but sunny and cheerful. I had still my long-standing headache. A fortnight old now – but it wasn't unbearable. Much shopping in the morning with the family and coffee with Muriel who is still nerve-racking. After tea, all the family departed – mother, too. This is the first time that we haven't had some of my people here, since August, and the house seemed strangely quiet. I wonder if I shall be very depressed? I think I am growing used to goodbyes. Robert and I went to the snack-bar for supper. Then joined Vera and Muriel at the Playhouse to see *Hay Fever* [by Noel Coward, 1924], which was great fun again. Home early to a quiet home.

Thursday, 28 March. Still very cold and brilliant. I was alone in my shopping for the first time in months. I went all wild and extravagant, and bought a cheap black swagger coat, a grey jumper and cardigan to match. Coffee with

---

32 Morrell Hall, in Victoria Court, belonged to the parish of St Mary Magdalene, which it was now sharing with St Michael's. St Michael's' Church Hall, in Shoe Lane, had been taken over in later 1939 by the Army.

33 Later this week, on Friday, 29 March, 'A curt sort of letter from John kept me awake against my common-sense.' But the next week brought a happier gesture. On 6 April 'I had a lovely surprise in the morning, in the way of a present from John – a little powder compact with the RAF badge on it. This brightened my whole day, of course, and I wrote to thank him.'

Muriel in the Cadena. David Calcutt, the cynic of the Junior Guild, now in the Army, joined us. He always rather interests me, and seems to like airing his young lordly ideas. A quiet afternoon and evening. Vera and Muriel came to supper and Marina had her kittens – three tabbies.

As usual, the Martins' April holiday was a red-letter occasion for Madge. This year it was to be in Cornwall. On Monday, 8 April ('At last, the longed-for day of the holidays') they went by train to Looe, where they were to spend ten days based at the Rock Towers Hotel. They did a great deal of walking[34] and some sightseeing, and Madge confessed that she had 'fallen in love with Cornwall' (14 and 17 April). 'So hard to realise that the world is fiercely at war,' she remarked after a day of walking around Fowey and Polperro (10 April). During the three weeks following Cornwall she enjoyed four days in London, savouring some of its attractions. She then spent a few afternoons in Oxford at the War Depôt[35] but did not mention the war directly until 10 May – 'The war has now begun in grim earnest.' This proved, undeniably, to be true.

---

34 Long walks by now had many devotees in England, including some of Oxford's undergraduates. (Mark Mazower, *What You Did Not Tell: A Russian Past and the Journey Home* [New York: Other Press, 2017], pp. 304–5.)
35 On Wednesday, 24 April 'I went to the Depôt for the first time since the holidays. How depleted it is nowadays. Even the amusing but scandal-mongering Mrs Howe has gone back to London.' The mood there was different on 8 May. 'I went to the War Depôt in the afternoon, and it was quite gay, with six chatty people, so I enjoyed it.'

3

In Danger

May 1940–September 1940[1]

Monday, 13 May. These are dismal days to write about really – what will be the end of us all? The Germans are sweeping through Holland and Belgium and each newspaper and radio news brings fresh stories of their successes. It is hard to raise a smile at all these days. We did not have a Whit-Monday walk, as usual – the Bank Holiday had been called off, and most of the shops were open. People were asked not to travel unless they must. Vera and I went to the Holy Communion Service at 11.00, then joined Muriel and mother at the Cadena, which was as usual the only cheerful place in Oxford at the moment. We sat in the warm sunshine all the afternoon, and in the evening went to the pictures to see a good film, *The Old Maid* [1939, adapted from the 1924 Edith Wharton novella and starring Bette Davis and Miriam Hopkins].

Tuesday, 14 May. The news continues to be simply awful, with Holland practically over-run and more German advances. Their parachutists seem a great and terrifying menace. It is like living in a nightmare all the time, but with the certainty that worse is almost sure to come. Lovely, lovely weather – too ridiculous really. Shopping, and the Cadena with Muriel – more sunning in the garden, and shopping for new shoes. Ruth came to tea – poor dear. What she must be feeling like. If all Germans were like her ––. Mother, Vera and I went to *The Pirates of Penzance* and *Trial by Jury* at night. Now these Gilbert and Sullivan operas are *real* antidotes to the war news.

Wednesday, 15 May. Warm and thundery. The news also thundery. Threats of massed bombing attacks, invasions by parachutists etc. Really – who

---

1 The sense of immediacy in Madge's writing during these months suggests that, as at the beginning of the war, she did not usually wait long to compose her entries.

would be alive to-day? Mother and I seem particularly cowardly and apprehensive and must try and pull ourselves together. What must it be like in Belgium? Poor Holland has had to give in. The War Depôt in the afternoon. More depressing conversation, and thunder crashing overhead. The only nice thing that happened in the day was two nice letters from John which I answered after tea. I had arranged to meet Winifred for this at Fullers [i.e., tea] but she never turned up. Not unusual.

Thursday, 16 May. Really horrid days these except for the perfect weather which increases the sense of madness. Shopping – I suppose. It is hard to remember these days. The War Depôt in the afternoon, when I got my [Red Cross] badge at long last. A new member, a Mrs Allen, is very nice to me and friendly. Mother and I had a stroll through the [University] Parks after tea. The river was as blue as a cornflower and the sun shone on such a bitterly peaceful scene. We had a talk to the Guild from a Mr Harvey on 'The Religion of National Socialism' which was terrifying but fascinating. I pray for courage to face whatever may be in store.

Friday, 17 May. Such lovely, lovely weather, so we decided to have a day in the country in spite of the war. I had a headache which fortunately soon cleared up. The 10.20 train to Reading and a bus to within a mile of Sonning, which proved to be one of the loveliest villages we've seen, beautiful to a degree and full of glorious old houses. We walked along the river which was sparkling like blue aquamarine and banked with sweet smelling may, and flowing between yellow fields of buttercups. Nothing to show of war, except the unceasing roar of 'planes. Lunch on a hotel lawn at Wargrave, so lovely, then a road walk to Henley, but it was a very beautiful road. Such blue dim distances, heavy chest-nut blooms, singing birds, and warm scented air. May at its most perfect. Tea in Henley which never impresses me, though it is beautifully situated. Back by bus to Oxford. A hurried change and Snack-Bar supper. Then to *Ruddigore* [by Gilbert and Sullivan, 1887] which still isn't quite a favourite of mine, though we love all the G & S operas dearly.

Saturday, 18 May. The morning news bad again – how our hearts sink when we read of these German successes. Please God – help the Allies. Coffee with Muriel and shopping with her and mother. Basking in the garden in the afternoon with the familiar bombing RAF planes roaring away in the blue sky. Robert and I to Miss Bourdillon's farewell 'At Home' in Barnett House.[2] In the evening we went to see *The Two Bouquets* [by Eleanor and Herbert Farjeon, 1936] at the Playhouse, quite an amusing Victorian operetta.

Sunday, 19 May. The flawless weather continues, everybody notices how especially lovely the country is looking, just as if they are just appreciating it for the first time now they are not sure they will see another Spring. We sat in the garden all morning, Muriel too, a *very* peculiar person she is, never knowing what she wants and always aggrieved. A rather awful bumptious parson to lunch – Mr Davies, and Susie to tea, cheery and chatty as usual. Church at night. We listened to the new Prime Minister, Winston Churchill's speech at night. He was much graver than usual.[3]

Monday, 20 May. One must remark about the weather which is so remarkable in its perfection, and the only beautiful thing in a wicked world. One lives and dies (inside) on the news and anything bad sends us shuddering through the day and anything good lightens us up a bit. I met Winifred for coffee and shopping. It is a comfort to chat with a similar frightened soul. The War Depôt in the afternoon. Much nicer now that there are more. We went to the pictures at night and saw *Babes in Arms* with Mickey Rooney and Judy Garland. It was very good. I had a very nice letter from John.

Tuesday, 21 May. I wonder if we shall ever look back on these May days, so mockingly lovely as to weather, and thank God that things are better now, or else envy even the misery of them compared to future bigger miseries. It looks as though only a miracle can save us from losing this terrible war against Nazi-ism, now. The Germans are getting nearer and nearer the French coast, and we shall be the next victims of their assault. I have no heart to write about these times, and I am so ashamed of my cowardice and

---

2   Barnett House Institution for Social and Economic Studies, located in 1940 at the corner of Beaumont Street and St John's Street, conducted social research. Miss A.F.C. Bourdillon had edited their *A Survey of the Social Services in the Oxford District, I, Economics and Government of a Changing Area* (Oxford: Oxford University Press, 1938). She moved to Nuffield College.
3   This was Churchill's first broadcast since becoming Prime Minister on 10 May. He spoke of this being 'a solemn hour for the life of our country, of our Empire, of our Allies, and, above all, of the cause of Freedom'. He acknowledged the remarkable successes of the German invasion of France; and while some of his words were encouraging, he did not wish 'to disguise the gravity of the hour'. He anticipated that the might of the enemy would soon be turned against Britain: 'we are ready to face it; to endure it; and to retaliate against it'. (*Complete Speeches*, vi, 6221–3.)

lack of trust in God's goodness. I do pray for more courage and faith, and long that my prayers will be granted in spite of the dreadful news. Mother and I went to *Patience* [by Gilbert and Sullivan, 1881] for which we had seats. It comforted us to see the crowds of laughing people. Surely Hitler cannot destroy the spirit of our English people – it cannot be.

Wednesday, 22 May. For the first time for days we had grey skies and very drenching rain, but everyone was very glad as we felt that even bad weather might help the Allies' cause. I went to the War Intercession Service at 12.00 and got great comfort from it – the prayers were so strengthening but I'm ashamed that I go only when things have got so bad. The War Depôt in the afternoon, with everyone in a more cheerful mood, since the last news was that the French had recaptured Arras. I had tea at the Cadena with Winifred – we get on well, and are much alike, with our jittery nerves and too vivid imaginations. I went out shopping later with mother, and then we did a bit of weeding which was very soothing. The news bulletin not too disquieting, and everyone determined, it seems, to win this war, however black things seem at present, fighting, as the French and British Armies are, with their backs to the wall. God give us all courage and strength to see it through.

Thursday, 23 May. So far, the most depressing day, I think, since the war started, though we shall certainly have to face far worse. We heard that the Germans had got through to Boulogne – now there is nothing to stop them bombing England as much as they wish. We had to go to the Guild Whist-Drive and Dance at night, almost unable to face the prospect, but it seems that this family is far more nervous than anyone else, and St Michael's people behaved as though it were a peace-time meeting, which cheered us up in spite of everything. I actually won a prize. The nights are hard to bear.

Friday, 24 May. In the morning one feels braver. It is as the day goes on that the spirits sink lower and lower. The news much about the same in the morning. What a fearful fight must be going on over in France. Surely we must win *eventually*. We couldn't let the Nazis dominate us, they are so unspeakable. Mother and I tired after bad nights, but she is very cheerful, when we had expected her to be very hot and bothered. We went to rather mediocre pictures at night, then heard the King's grave but inspiring speech over the wireless at night. He told us to put our trust in God and keep a smile, so we must try.[4]

---

4   Madge was keen on royalty and always wrote respectfully of members of the royal family. On 20 January 1936, after learning of the King's death, she wrote that 'Everyone

Saturday, 25 May. I had a headache most of the day, but no wonder – everyone must be feeling tense and fearful just now. Shopping in the morning. I rested some of the afternoon, then went to tea with Mr and Mrs Allen who have rooms in Canterbury Road [off Banbury Road]. She comes to the bandaging room, and is very friendly. He is very nice, also. We all went to *The Mikado* [by Gilbert and Sullivan, 1885] at night and enjoyed it enormously in spite of all our thoughts. We are not to be told very much war news for a few days. Perhaps the Allies have a plan.

Sunday, 26 May. This was the day of National Prayer, and the people seemed to respond wonderfully, as far, anyway, as Oxford went. Our Church was packed in the morning, and Susie and I went to the Service in the Town Hall [in St Aldate's] in the afternoon, which was also packed. We sang hymns enough to raise the roof, and listened to heartening prayers by the Bishop of Dorchester. Susie came home to tea with me. She is a very unselfish and on the whole, cheerful girl. To Church again in the evening. Another crowd, and a splendid collection for the Red Cross. We must all try to be confident in God's goodness.[5]

---

loved him, and everyone must feel as I do, sad at heart, and lost without such a wonderful and wise ruler.' But there was consolation in the thought of his successor: 'The Prince of Wales has always been a hero of mine and I hope he will make a fine king.' Robert attended George V's funeral at Windsor and gave 'glowing accounts' of it (28 January 1936). On a page adjoining her diary for 2 November 1938, Madge had attached a newspaper photograph of 'Princess Alexandra, daughter of the Duke and Duchess of Kent'; such clippings were almost always an indication of her enthusiasm for the subject portrayed, whether human or scenic. Years earlier, on 7 July 1929, she had reported a disagreement with John Hall concerning thanksgiving services that day for the King's recovery from illness: while she was 'stirred' and impressed, he, she complained, 'is rather a socialistic person, and wasn't thrilled about the Services'.

Understandably, Madge and other fervent royalists were ill at ease with the developments at court in 1936 – or at least their outcome. On the back of her diary page for 14 and 15 September 1939, she pasted a picture of the ex-King, Edward VIII, and wrote underneath: 'After nearly three years exile, the Duke and Duchess of Windsor have returned to England. The Duke is to have a war appointment. So nice to have him back.' (He was in fact a serious headache for the British government, which succeeded in shunting him off to the Bahamas.) Just before Edward's abdication she had expressed the 'hope above all that we do not lose our wonderful king' (5 December 1936). 'A black day for England,' she wrote five days later. 'All seems to fade away except the fact that … our beloved King Edward VIII abdicated and gave up the throne … I feel almost broken hearted as I have always adored him.'

5   The congregations at church this Sunday were large, and some 2,500 people gathered at the Town Hall for a special ceremony, which included the singing of 'Onward Christian Soldiers' (*Oxford Times*, 31 May 1940, p. 9).

Monday, 27 May. The news just gets steadily worse, and I really don't know what keeps us going except the will to win, though I personally can only see a miracle doing that for us. It poured with rain off and on, and was very warm. I went to the Depôt in the afternoon and made the familiar foot bandages. Crowds there now. Ruth was at tea when I got home. Then we went to the pictures and saw a very good film about American politics, *Mr. Smith Goes to Washington* [with Jean Arthur and James Stewart].

Tuesday, 28 May. The worst news *ever* to-day. The King of the Belgians has capitulated to the Germans without a word of warning to the Allies. This dreadful blow is so shattering that we can't really believe it. The Allies now are faced with the most dreadful peril of being cut off on three sides and not being able to get away at all. Oh – what awful times these are. Shall we *ever* be happy again, or free of the German peril? I was called to the Depôt to cut out pillow-cases, and was rather relieved to have something definite to do. The evening papers simply awful to read. I wrote to John, interviewed a prospective new maid, and washed my hair.

Wednesday, 29 May. I sleep badly these days, and feel very queer during the day, but we go on hoping for better news. The papers now full of stories about our troops, and the French fighting to escape back to England through terrible German onslaughts. The act of the Belgian King has encircled them and made escape a most perilous thing. The days are got through somehow, in sadness and apprehension. Shopping, War Depôt, with intervals for listening to the news and reading the papers.

Thursday, 30 May. I had a fiendish head all day after another bad night, but for the moment our jitteriness is quenched, as we know now that we have lost the first big battle for the North Coast of France. We are now anxiously watching the fate of our escaping Army, many of whom are wearily limping home. Heaven knows what the casualty list will be like when it comes. I went to bed all afternoon, and after tea Vera appeared after a long interval, and we had a little walk round the [University] Parks. Vera is amazingly unconcerned about the war.

Friday, 31 May. A lovely summer day. What a wonderful month May has been – in weather. My head much better so we took sandwiches, and went to Iffley by bus, then along the towing-path to Abingdon. Such peace along the blue river, and through the fields filled with marguerites and buttercups – how *can* there be war when such beauty exists? We had our lunch by the river-side and went on our way, but had to turn back as the towing path ceased near Abingdon. We became bogged and I lost my gas-mask but eventually we tottered into Abingdon for a glorious cup of tea and rest. Home on top of a bus, and a quiet evening.

Saturday, 1 June. Beautiful weather, and our hearts a *wee* bit lighter, as we hear of more and more of our men from Flanders coming back safely. The Germans, though they have had a terrific victory, have not had their hearts' desire – to annihilate the whole of our British Expeditionary Force there. Now they are intact, four-fifths of them, to meet the enemy later. I had to have coffee with Muriel who really seems to get more and more extraordinary. Robert and I went to Cowley Road to get another gas-mask for me. I lost my other one somewhere on the walk yesterday. Mother and I went to tea with Susie, after I had visited Mrs Horser in her hot stuffy eyrie. She is sitting up now.[6] It was funny at the Halls without John, but we enjoyed it.

Sunday, 2 June. To Church in the glorious summer morning. We sat out in the garden all the afternoon reading the Sunday papers which are full of the stories of our rescued BEF men who are being taken away from the bombarded Dunkirk in all sorts of strange vessels as well as by our Navy, whilst the RAF protect them as well as they can. A wonderful display of courage by all. Mother, Danna and I went to a Concert in aid of the Finnish Relief in Balliol Hall. May Harrison played the violin most beautifully, and Astra Desmond sang gloriously. All the music was Finnish. May Harrison had rung us up beforehand, but hadn't time to look us up.[7] Evensong afterwards.

Monday, 3 June. Another headache. I get a lot these days – it must be the stress of worry and the uncertainty of horrors to come. The weather has been magnificent for weeks now, with only one or two lapses. Shopping with mother – she is being quite splendid these days. My head too bad for the Depôt so I went to rest all afternoon. A letter from John – he sounds very contented. Vera came, and instead of the pictures we had a combined bus ride and walk, from Pullen's Lane [at the top of Headington Hill]. A beautiful evening.

---

6   Madge had visited her a few weeks before (Saturday, 16 March 1940). 'I went to see Mrs Cottrell-Horser in the afternoon. How poor old Mr Horser keeps cheerful with his wretched sort of life I can't think – an invalid wife in a stuffy room, hundreds of stairs to climb, and long evenings with her. He is very cheerful, and I like him.'
7   For more about May Harrison, see below, 7 March and 23–24 October 1943, pp. 212, 231.

Tuesday, 4 June. This lovely summer weather is such a mockery, but makes things easier to bear. Mother and I shopped, then went to Kenneth Jenkins' wedding in our Church. He looked quite splendid in his Squadron-Leader's uniform, and she was very attractive in full white array with two 'blue' bridesmaids. There was a sumptuous repast at the Randolph [Hotel, Beaumont Street]. We sat and guzzled at a small table, with Adrian Rushworth, and got dazed on champagne. A much more cheerful reception than most. Well, I hope that things go well with both of them, but knowing him … !⁸ We slept off the effects of the champagne in the garden, and in the evening went to the Scala to see two good old films. June Martin was at home when we returned. She has a Forestry job at Woodstock, and I expect we shall see a lot of her. She is a nice simple, hearty girl.⁹

Wednesday, 5 June. In the heat, mother and I went down to the Cattle Market [Oxpens], which is always fun, with its crowds and animals. We came back laden with fruit and vegetables and plants, all very cheap. The War Depôt in the afternoon – very hot indeed in that high sunny room. A quiet evening writing letters. The Germans have started a new offensive against Paris. Oh, don't let them get into our adored and beautiful Paris, our favourite city.¹⁰

Thursday, 6 June. Whenever have we *had* such a summer to taunt us with thoughts of how lovely everything could be if only there wasn't this constant fear of being completely wiped out before we may ever see another. Shopping as usual. The Depôt in the afternoon terribly hot again. Vera, mother and I went [on] the Port Meadow, Godstow, Wytham walk, in the clear, hot evening – very beautiful it was. Mother is getting to be quite a good walker.

Friday, 7 June. Surely the hottest day for years. We decided that it was much too boiling for walking, so we went on the river, taking sandwiches for lunch. We stayed there from 11.30 to 5.30, enjoying the green sylvan peace of it, the lapping of the shining water, the pure blue of the sky between the willow

---

8   On the outbreak of war Rev. Jenkins had volunteered as a Chaplain to the Royal Air Force and Robert was without a curate for a year (Martin, *Church and Parish of St Michael at the Northgate*, p. 180). Jenkins married Joy Towell. Madge appears to have reservations (unexplained) about him as a husband.
9   June Martin, in her early twenties, was the daughter of Robert's eldest brother, Harry. She was a member of the Women's Land Army.
10   Four years later on 5 June 1944, on re-reading her diary for the same day in 1940, Madge added: 'PS. The Allies have just entered Rome!' Then she appears to have written the words, 'Sucks to the Italians.' This expression of derision seems strange coming from Madge; perhaps it testifies to the widespread British disdain for Italians.

branches, and the brown, naked young things disporting themselves whilst they may, for who knows how long they have. We had tea at Timm's Boat House,[11] then drifted lazily back. Everything green and clear and silent. The heat made us all languid and we rested all evening. The Allies are holding the Germans fairly well, so far, in the new big battle. I wonder – I wonder – how it will all end.

Saturday, 8 June. Still very hot, and thundery. I had to meet Muriel for coffee at the Cadena. She was quite too awful and never introduced me to the chatting friends she was with, so that the conversation flowed over me. She sat in the garden after, looking and behaving like a stuffed fish. She bores and irritates me more than anyone I know. I sat sunning myself all afternoon – with thunder-clouds hovering. June Martin brought a friend over from Woodstock and we had supper at the snack-bar, then joined mother at the theatre to see Robert Donat in [George Bernard Shaw's] *The Devil's Disciple*. He was most charming.

Sunday, 9 June. Still beautiful, but thundery. To Church with the simply infuriating Muriel to whom I just was impelled to give 'a piece of my mind' so awfully bad mannered and unreasonable has she become lately, even more than usual. She never seems satisfied with anything. She went off in a huff which wasn't surprising. We sun-bathed all the afternoon, and June strolled in for tea. I think she will just come when she can and feel at home. We didn't go to Church, as a thunder-storm hovered about, but it never developed. Vera looked in to chat.

Monday, 10 June. There was such a darkness over the land in the morning. The sun shone through like an evil white eye. It looked like a tremendous thunderstorm approaching, or an eclipse, or the end of the world. However, this blackness and weird horror also disappeared, leaving fresh blue skies. The war news is horrible, and Italy has now taken the opportunity to join Germany just when France is in its extremity. The whole world is revolted by this dastardly act. After the War Depôt and shopping, I wrote to John, then washed my hair.

Tuesday, 11 June. The weather gradually cooling off – but no rain yet. Shopping as usual. To tea with Vera in the afternoon. They always give us a *grand* tea, and all talk at once. Vera came back with us to supper. June

---

11 Thomas Tims had a boat-building works and boathouses. The boathouse at Bardwell Road, North Oxford, provided refreshments.

also came over from Woodstock. Then we all went to the pictures to see a bloodcurdling film about Red Indians *Drums Along the Mohawk* [starring Claudette Colbert and Henry Fonda and based on the 1936 novel of the same title by William D. Edmonds].

Wednesday, 12 June. These days are dreadful in a way, though we, personally, are still untouched, but the Germans creep nearer and nearer Paris each day, and [we] are appealing frantically to America for help. Mother and I go through all sorts of moods – mostly desperate – but one can't feel desperate *all* the time, and we still enjoy certain things like shop-gazing and especially our small garden, which sheds a comforting peace over us every time we look at it. The War Depôt in the afternoon as usual and a quiet evening. The Germans at Senlis.

Thursday, 13 June. The weather continues perfect but the news gets just steadily worse. The Germans have taken 6000 of our prisoners, and are nearly *in* our beloved Paris. I wonder if ever we shall look back on this from happier days and pity ourselves for living in such a time, though we, ourselves have much to be thankful for. My darling Robert is with me – not at the war like the last time. Mrs Booth came to tea after the War Depôt – she is very friendly but almost too sympathetic. She came to New College with us. We had another War Talk from Councillor Watts on 'How to make a good Peace'. How ironic at this time. He was very good though.

Friday, 14 June. Although the news was very bad, we decided to go into the country, as that always soothes us for the time being. We took an Abingdon bus after doing lots of shopping, and walked along to Sutton Courtney where we had lunch by the river-side after ginger-beer at the local pub. A very hot walk to Culham and Clifton Hampden – fortunately, I love the hot sun and had a big shady hat. Tea in a very picturesque but filthy cottage – the tea, and lettuce was good, though. A hot walk again to the Dorchester Road and home on a bus, and beastly news – the Germans actually in the gates of Paris. *Oh Hell!*

Saturday, 15 June. I hate writing of these grim days which in an ordinary way could be so lovely. Not for years have we had such a perfect early summer – but how can we enjoy it? Shopping, basking in the garden in the afternoon, an unexpected and nice letter from John, Pam[12] over from Woodstock to tea. We looked at shops after tea, then saw two old films *Wings of the*

---

12   Possibly June Martin's sister, Pamela Cowper.

Morning [1937] and *Cardinal Richelieu* [1935]. The first very good. Pam in for supper.

Sunday, 16 June. The weather threatening to break up at last. We do need rain very badly. The day of intercession for France. I went in the morning, and was moved to tears by the Marseillaise played softly on the organ. Pam for tea again and Church again at night.

Monday, 17 June. This day *quite* the blackest of the war, and we can hardly have a blacker. France has laid down her arms and ceased hostilities. Well, well. I suppose we are not all *that* surprised. What will happen now – shall we fight on alone, in Britain? Oh, what an outlook, but may we conquer in the end against these so far invincible foes. The Depôt ladies are horrified at the news, but still confident in the end. I had tea with an equally horrified Winifred, then went to the Headington Cinema to see the beautiful Griffith Jones [b. 1909] in *Young Man's Fancy.*

Tuesday, 18 June. The weather is simply amazing – no sign of a break. The spirits not so down today, either; it is wonderful how soon the human body recovers from shocks, and it is as well, as we shall have greater ones yet, I fear, to face. Shopping in the morning. I toasted my legs in the afternoon. I am trying to get them brown so that I needn't wear stockings, which are so expensive. We all went, even Danna, to the pictures to see a most moving but harrowing film, *Pastor Hall*, which made us resolved to try and fight to the end, so awful is the German oppression.[13]

Wednesday, 19 June. Still glorious weather, and still waiting to hear Hitler and Mussolini's so called 'Peace' terms to the French, who seem still to be fighting. I had a great to-do with Doris in the morning and had the first cross words with her in 13 years, but she asked for it. Both of us, I think, felt wretched after, but she complained of not getting enough to eat here, which is sheer nonsense. I was in a boiling rage. The War Depôt in the afternoon. More and more I like Mrs Dudden. We went out after tea and to an exhibition of Bernard Gotch's drawings.[14] This life is so like and yet so unlike our normal.

---

13 The film was based on the 1939 play of the same title by Ernst Toller, and was inspired by the recent life of Pastor Martin Niemöller, who was imprisoned in Dachau for criticizing the Nazis.
14 Robert also wrote of Gotch at this time (*Parish Magazine*, July 1940, p. 3): 'Mr Bernard Gotch [b. 1876], the talented local artist, whose picture of Ship Street in the Church is one of our great treasures, has now completed a companion picture of the Broad Street houses. The

Thursday, 20 June. The air-raids on Britain have already begun, but I expect we shall have them much more seriously soon, together with invasion attempts. Oh, how I pray that we shall be in the end, victorious, but I cannot see how on earth it will be achieved with a so much smaller Air Force, and no allies now. We all live for the moment, only. The War Depôt is very calming and I should really miss it now, although I curse having to turn out so soon after lunch. The women there are so unflurried. Vera came in the evening. We walked up and down North Oxford a bit, and she returned to supper.

Friday, 21 June. Our holiday day of the week. It was dull in the morning and rather cold, but we took the 10.50 to Didcot and walked from that dismal little place to Blewbury. The day by now had become beautiful again. Blewbury is an enchanting village of thatched cottages and 'roses – roses all the way'. We lunched at the Treble House, a nice old place but a poor lunch. We skirted the foot of the downs to Cholsey, through hot corn fields, lovely down-land country, wide blue skies and larks in the fields. Beautiful. Train back to Oxford, tea at the Cadena, then the pictures – mother joined us – *Raffles* [starring David Niven and Olivia de Havilland] quite good. June to supper.

Saturday, 22 June. Quite a lot of rain at last, how the country needs it. Saturday morning Mrs Bourne stayed to lunch. We actually had a fire, the day was so chilly, and I read some movie magazines by it all afternoon. I went to New College after mother and I had looked round the shops. I wonder very much in what circumstance, if any, we shall be there again? Will there *be* any Autumn term? And if so shall we be alive to see it? What a life!

Sunday, 23 June. Lots more rain, nearly all day. Much needed. Church in the morning. Last Sunday we prayed for France. Now they are having to submit to the most shameful German terms. Can this be an obscure answer to prayers? It may well be. A quiet afternoon – knitting and reading. Then Church again at night. More people come these days. An instinctive longing for reassurance against these nightmare days.

Vicar has undertaken to purchase this on behalf of the Church, as it is essential that, even in wartime, the beauties of our ancient Parish should be recorded.' Robert was concerned, in part, to preserve a record of ancient houses that at this time were threatened with demolition (Martin, *Church and Parish of St Michael at the Northgate*, pp. 176–8). The cost of this watercolour was ten guineas; Robert appealed for donations and was later able to say that it had been purchased (*Parish Magazine*, August 1940, p. 3), though the money needed was still coming in.

Monday, 24 June. Nice weather again, and warm. Not much more news – we are awaiting the Blitz-Krieg on England. The French Colonies refuse to give in and mean to fight on. No-one knows what will happen to the French Fleet. Shopping in the morning. War Depôt in the afternoon. The Playhouse at night – Vera too. We saw *Yellow Sands* [by Eden and Adelaide Philpotts] again which remains a splendid play and was very well acted indeed. A real tonic.[15]

Tuesday, 25 June. We were awakened at 1.00a.m. by the air-raid siren, the first warning since September. It is a horribly sinister sound, makes one dither all over. We huddled together in the basement kitchen for 50 minutes, when the blissfully welcome 'all clear' sounded, and we went back to bed, but not much sleep for me. However, in the morning we felt well enough for a 'jaunt' into the country – mother came with us. We took the bus to Tetsworth and walked over rather ordinary fields, and prettyish lanes, to Lewknor and then to the Lambert Arms [in Aston Rowant] for a hearty lunch. We left mother in the hotel lounge and walked up the hill above the Icknield way. Lovely views of blue distances, and honeysuckle for me to gather, on the sunny downland. Back to the hotel for tea, then the bus back home, passing lorry loads of cheery Canadian troops, who give a most reassuring atmosphere. Just as I was going to bed at 11.30, the air-raid siren went again, and this time we were in our 'bolt-hole' for four hours and heard distant bombs and guns. This is a very ghastly time to live in.

Wednesday, 26 June. To bed at 3.30a.m., after the 'All clear' sirens had wailed their welcome message. Although keyed-up to a degree, I fell asleep extremely soundly. The bombs had dropped only about 12 miles away. So they *can* get to Oxford! – or in the vicinity. They were obviously after the air-grounds here. I went to have a fitting of two summer frocks in the morning. The Depôt in the afternoon, the new curate-to-be to tea. We like the little we have seen of him. Vera came round shopping with me after tea and stayed to chat.

Thursday, 27 June. We were allowed a peaceful night, which was a blessing and made us feel more like human beings, though other parts of England had raiders. Shopping in the morning, the Depôt in the afternoon, a youth from Sainsburys to tea, extremely well-mannered and nice. A call from a very sweet person, Miss Egerton, at the unusual hour of 6.00. She is a

---

15 The *Oxford Times*, 28 June 1940, p. 4, spoke of this 'excellent production' as 'the best of all antidotes to war weariness'.

violin teacher and seems a dear. I went to see the Cottrell-Horsers then, who always give me a good welcome, up in their incredibly stuffy room with the magnificent view. June came to supper, and shampooed my hair and set it for me. She is an obliging girl.

Friday, 28 June. Yet another undisturbed night, praise be, but I don't sleep at all well, waiting for possible sirens. Lots of shopping, and a fitting of one foul frock and one nice one. I rested all afternoon, but couldn't sleep. Mother and I went to the pictures after tea and saw *Swanee River* [with Don Ameche, Andrea Leeds, and Al Jolson] quite a good coloured film. We all hate the lovely calm moon-lit nights, so good for bombing.

Saturday, 29 June. I don't think I ever remember such a beautiful summer, as far as weather goes. What does it all mean? Perhaps it is to teach us to appreciate the lovely things even more than ever. The usual busy shopping Saturday morning and a sun-bath in the garden all afternoon. Our iron railings have gone to help feed the guns as so many others have. It improves the look of places enormously and perhaps we shall be a less suspicious nation if we ever live through what is coming.[16] We all went to see *Wee Willie Winkie* (Shirley Temple) at the Scala. We'd seen it before, but always love her films.

Sunday, 30 June. More perfect weather, and the newspapers full of the imminent onslaught of Britain, by air, sea and land. One feels quite helpless

---

16   This appeal from the Ministry of Supply for iron railings is discussed in Malcolm Graham, *Oxfordshire at War* (Stroud: Alan Sutton, 1994), pp. 134–5; it was first publicized in a letter from the Mayor (*Oxford Times*, 5 July 1940, p. 6). In it the Mayor reported that Mr W.A. Daft, an architect, who had been asked to organize a collection, was working with a number of builders 'who are prepared to remove railings and make good the walls or other foundations of the railings without cost to the householder'. He had started 'on the North Oxford Estate of St John's College [which included Wellington Place], where the residents, with very few exceptions, have patriotically presented their railings, which are being rapidly removed'. The iron railings around St Michael's Churchyard were also being taken down and, according to Robert, whose thinking was much like Madge's, 'Many people consider that the appearance of a building is much improved by the removal of railings from around it, and it has been found that this does not lead to trespassing or desecration as some would fear. We have arranged, however, for the beautiful wrought-iron gate and railings to the north of the Tower to be left as they are … All the back of the Church will still be enclosed for safety, while the front is thrown open for beauty, and for the help of our country in its hour of need.' (*Parish Magazine*, July 1940, p. 3.) Elsewhere others also approved of these removals of iron railings: Peter Thorsheim, *Waste into Weapons: Recycling in Britain during the Second World War* (New York: Cambridge University Press, 2015), pp. 165–8. Removals were later made compulsory and met with much protest (Graham, *Oxfordshire at War*, p. 135).

about it, and can only pray for bravery and endurance. I'm quite terrified of being unequal to the strain and being cowardly, but I ask God for help. Mrs Booth called for me, and we went to Church together. Another basking afternoon, and Church again at night. The airplanes fly unceasingly all night long, and we await the siren with loathing.

Monday, 1 July. Week after week of gloriously warm weather such as I never remember before. Rain is so much wanted, and we nearly forget what it is like, in spite of having a little of it last week. Hitler's 'Blitzkreig' on Britain is supposed to start officially any day now, and he has promised his people to dictate Peace from London on August 15th. He has been able, so far, to keep all his other threats. Will *this* one come off? One fears, and can only pray. Shopping in the morning, bandage-making in the afternoon, and the Playhouse at night to see a very amusing little play, *Lovers' Leap* [by Philip Johnson, c. 1935].

Tuesday, 2 July. Thank God for every quiet night, and safe awakening to more sunny days. We shopped in the morning and at 1.15 Robert and I had our weekly excursion – a bus to Rowstock on the Newbury Road, then a very pleasant walk through East and West Hendred by hot cornfields, red with poppies. The villages are lovely in this district. We ended up at Wantage for tea, then a bus home. We met mother and then went on to the Regal Cinema to see an extraordinary but very interesting film, *The Earl of Chicago* [starring Robert Montgomery]. A rather terse letter from John. He must be overworking, I fear.

Wednesday, 3 July. A little rain in the night, but not enough to do much good. I couldn't sleep, imagining gun-fire and bombing in the distance, but again, thank God, the siren never went to jerk us from our beds. A usual day of shopping, bandaging, shopping again after tea, and a quiet evening. This is a very strange life, like living on the edge of a cliff, waiting either for a puff of wind to send us over, or a rescue party to bring us back to safety.[17]

Thursday, 4 July. We heard that the British had taken possession of most of the French Fleet, which had been signed away by Pétain's government to the Germans. Unfortunately, some of the French admirals refused to give in without fighting, obeying orders, and the British had to engage them in

---

17 'Madge had the first headache for a long time,' according to her husband this day. In his diary he often mentioned her headaches when she, in her diary for the same day, had also written of them.

battle, sinking some and crippling others. A simply terrible thing to have to do, but the only choice, as Germany, in spite of promises not to use the ships against us, would never have kept those promises, we know only too well. We had a demonstration of how to use a stirrup pump, in the evening and most of Wellington Place met in Miss Harcourt's garden for it. May we never have to use it for the incendiary bomb it is meant for.[18]

Friday, 5 July. Another good night – thank God. Lovely sunny weather *still*. The papers now full of the French Fleet business. Oh, how complicated things are getting – and how can it end, and *when*? Shopping. Ruth to tea. Poor Ruth, in a hard new house-keeping job, threatened any time with internment [as an enemy alien], cut off from her family, tired out and depressed, but uncomplaining. There are Germans *and* Germans. A nice Intercession Service in Church. A quiet evening.

Saturday, 6 July. Shopping as usual with mother. Mr and Mrs Allen to tea in the afternoon, quite a nice couple. June also to tea – she bought me a very nice book of Edmund Dulac's pictures, which pleased me enormously. We all went out to dinner at the George for a treat, then to the pictures to see *Judge Hardy and Son*, which was a very good addition to the series [it was the eighth in the Andy Hardy series].

Sunday, 7 July. The weather has broken up a bit, but we welcome rain for many reasons. Danna's 81st birthday. Harry came over from town for the afternoon and evening and to spend the night. I cannot get over my fear of him, born in 1916 [when she first met him], though he is quite pleasant now, and anxious to please.[19] June came over, too, from Woodstock. A rather boring afternoon, chatting. Everyone turned out for Church at night, to Danna's joy. The evening after supper, was got through somehow, with games and talking.

Monday, 8 July. Harry returned to town at 10.00, thanks be, though why I should be scared of him, I don't know. Robert was even more pleased to get normal again than I. Shopping in the morning, the Depôt in the afternoon,

---

18   'Quite a large jolly party in Miss Harcourt's garden,' according to Robert – 'but rather cold.' This is probably Miss Vernon-Harcourt who lived at 4 Wellington Place.
19   Harry Martin 'still petrifies me', Madge had written on 7 July 1939. Harry, five years older than Robert, was, like his brother, a graduate of Lincoln College. He was also a former international badminton player, Richmond Herald, and a Fellow of the Society of Antiquaries. He was sufficiently prominent to be accorded an obituary in *The Times* (13 August 1942, p. 7). Our thanks to Barbara Tearle for her research on Harry Martin.

and to the Playhouse at night to see a rather crude Emlyn Williams written ten years ago, *A Murder Has Been Arranged*. Not up to the usual Playhouse standard.[20]

Tuesday, 9 July. Once again we are being lulled into a sense of false security, having had no air-raid warnings in two weeks. However, we are truly thankful for every night's respite. We didn't go for our usual walk today as it was rather wild and stormy. We had a nice surprise in the afternoon in a visit from Paul and Kay Harper who came over from Winchester on business. We really are always very glad to see them, and get on well with them. He is still a great favourite with us, and we like her too, 'golden' haired and nervy though she is. We met[21] the nice new curate [Malcolm Pearce], too, after we had had tea with Kay and Paul at the Cadena, and he showed us over his rooms [at no. 11] in Ship Street. He seems a very pleasant young man. A quiet evening. I had one of the very nicest letters from John.

Wednesday, 10 July. A very rainy day. I should think the wettest this year, and everyone was glad to see it. There was a thunderstorm at mid-day and we had to wait in Church where Danna, Robert and I had been at a War Intercession service, an hour or more till we could get home in a taxi. I didn't go to the Depôt in the afternoon, in case the thunder returned. We went to the Scala at night, but the films [*Heart of the North* and *Newsboys' Home*] were not so good.

Thursday, 11 July. Still rainy and rather cold. The usual morning, the Depôt in the afternoon, always cheery, this. The pictures again in the evening. Our fascinating Rex Harrison in an amusing spy film, *Ten Days in Paris*. Time just goes on in a sort of waking-dream way of waiting for something awful to happen.

Friday, 12 July. I can't remember much about this day except that it rained nearly all the time. I expect we shopped in the morning, and I know I went out in it in the afternoon. I love shopping sometimes, especially when I am buying small presents, as I was this time. Ruth came to tea again, then on to the Intercession Service with me. Mother made raspberry jam, and it turned out most successfully.

20 'A silly thing, neither macabre nor interesting,' according to Robert's diary.
21 She actually wrote 'might'. This is a rare instance where a word makes no sense and we have replaced it with one that does.

Saturday, 13 July. Shopping as usual. Tea is the latest thing to be rationed, and there was great joy when we managed to get a little extra from our kind grocer. We are only allowed 2ozs a week each, and I am such a tea-fiend. June came for the week-end, and Tony Fryer and a friend came from their RASC Camp at Witney to tea. Nice Yorkshire lads, both. We showed them John's Gardens [St John's College Gardens] and the Church, then left them to go to the Scala to see a very funny Jessie Matthews' film, *Climbing High*. June had been to see Rex Harrison's film on her own.

Sunday, 14 July. Church in the morning. I was very tired and sleepy after a bad wakeful night jittering and fancying bombs and guns. I *am* a coward. I went to bed in the afternoon and actually slept a little. Church again at night. June rather shrewdly comes in slacks, so that she cannot be dragged to Church against her will. There was a splendid speech by the Prime Minister on the wireless.[22]

Monday, 15 July. Raining now and then on St Swithin's Day, but who cares now?[23] And at one time, weather was one of the most discussed things in England. Do we care now that July is turning out to be the usual wet dreary month? No – we rather welcome storms, as being perhaps a set-back for Hitler's invasion. A usual morning, a Depôt afternoon, and the *Playhouse Revue* in the evening which we thought quite brilliant on the whole. They [the Oxford Repertory Players] are a talented lot.[24]

Tuesday, 16 July. Hot and airless and tiring. Shopping. I felt snappy and rather hysterical all day. Why? Perhaps because of thunder in the air. I had another nice letter from John which I promptly answered. He might get leave soon – he seems to long for it. So do I, except that it makes the parting so awful after. Mother and I went to the Regal at night and saw a very good

22 Churchill's powerful speech included words that must have inspired Madge and many others. 'I stand at the head of a Government representing all Parties in the State – all creeds, all classes, every recognizable section of opinion. We are ranged beneath the Crown of our ancient monarchy. We are supported by a free Parliament and a free Press … This is no war of chieftains or of princes, of dynasties or national ambition: it is a war of people and of causes. … This is a War of the Unknown Warriors; but let us all strive without failing in faith or in duty, and the dark curse of Hitler will be lifted from our age.' (*Complete Speeches*, vi, 6250.)
23 A piece of folklore held that the weather on this feast day would persist for another 40 days.
24 These players had 'a constant struggle to keep going', according to the *Oxford Times*, 19 July 1940, p. 4, but when this humorous *Revue* was staged the theatre was nearly full.

programme, *The Shop Around the Corner*, with dear James Stewart and Margaret Sullavan, and fascinating Barry Barnes in *The Midas Touch*.

Wednesday, 17 July. Our wedding anniversary – and no headache! So after exchanging presents, an Elizabeth Arden lipstick and Yardley's Bond Street perfume from Robert to me, and a lighter and chocolate from me to him, and money from the mothers, we went up to town on the 8.40. We hadn't been for ages and were delighted to be there. London seems much less war-conscious than Oxford and though quiet, very gay. We went to the Royal Academy, which was a delight, as always, then lunch at the 'Troc' [Trocadero] – only one meat course allowed now! Then instead of our usual pictures, to a very funny and grand review, *Up and Doing*, with Leslie Henson, Binnie Hale, Stanley Holloway and Cyril Ritchard. We loved it and laughed like anything. Just the sort of thing one wants in war-time, and Leslie Henson is as funny as he was in the *last* war! We gazed round a bit afterwards, then a snack at Paddington before getting the 7.40 home.

Thursday, 18 July. Shopping as usual. The Depôt also as usual in the afternoon. We are to have three weeks' holiday starting next week. In the evening we were shown over the new Baptist College which we have watched being built from our windows, for months. It is a beautiful place and we enjoyed looking round.[25] Robert had his first ARP lecture at 8.00 [in Pusey House].

Friday, 19 July. We had a disturbed night, thinking that loud explosions we heard at 4.00a.m. were bombs, and we got up, mother and I. We learned after that it was from a big fire at the Aerated Water Company's works, where there *were* explosions.[26] I got a headache in consequence. I had an exciting card from John to say he had got leave this week-end and would be here tomorrow. I have very mixed feelings about this, as, though I love seeing him, yet the parting after makes me miserable all over again, just when I've got used to being without him. Still I am *not* ungrateful. Vera and I to the Super to see a strange, but well-acted film, *Of Mice and Men* [based on John Steinbeck's 1937 novella].

---

25   Regent's Park College in Pusey Street provided postgraduate instruction in theology. Its students were members of the University.
26   Householders near the flames were evacuated, with coats flung over their night attire. 'Several explosions occurred which threw burning wood scores of feet into the air and made people all over Oxford think that an air raid was in progress.' (*Oxford Times*, 19 July 1940, p. 10.) On 12 July, in preparation for possible raids, Robert had 'pasted some more strips on the windows in the morning' to reduce the risk of the glass splintering.

Saturday, 20 July. A fiendish headache. It *would* come just when I wanted to feel particularly well. I have been so free for a long time. John rang up very early and came to see me at 11.30. It was glorious to see him again and he looks much fatter and very fit. It is lovely to see his thin cheeks all filled out, and his narrow shoulders broad. We had a joyous reunion and talked and talked. I retired to bed for the afternoon, but the headache wouldn't go. We went to the Ritz after tea and saw *We Are Not Alone*, a very good film [based on the 1937 novel by James Hilton]. John came to supper and stayed till 10.30 – just like old times, bless his ginger-head.

Sunday, 21 July. Still, the head, blast it! Church in the morning. How nice to see John in the choir again. I pray that one day everything will be back to normal, and that he might be there for good, but a happier man, as he is now. I think he is happier than he's ever been, in the RAF. I rested in the afternoon and the head was a wee bit easier when I got up. June gave me scalp-massage – she is a kind girl, I think, in spite of a hard manner, and boyish clothes. John came back to supper and stayed talking. The war has brought us more closely together than ever before, and petty disagreements are out of the question now we are faced with the possibility of a future without one another. He talks, as other young soldiers do, rather too enthusiastically of death and glory, not caring about the agony he may be inflicting on me by the very mention of it. My heart feels sometimes broken by horror and despair, then at other times my trust in God's mercies upholds me – but what I should do if any of my loved ones died before me, I don't know. I'm rather afraid I should fall completely by the wayside, without caring, and without faith. I'm not a very good sort of person, and as weak as water, much too dependent on others. What ever will become of me?

Monday, 22 July. Miserable day. Mother went up to stay and help at Nita's for a bit, as Richard is still ill and needs a lot of attention. John returned to Scotland. He came in to say goodbye and I managed to send him away with smiles, thank God – heaven knows how, as I was quite devastated really, as I felt I should be. If only I could think he would come through this war safely, I would gladly say goodbye for years if need be. I haven't been so heartbroken for years, but had to pull myself together to entertain young Mr Pearce [the new curate] and a coy friend of his, to tea ['Rather "pansy" we thought,' said her husband of the friend]. Then out with dear Robert who is the most understanding person in the world. Vera and I to the pictures, and she home to supper. How I hate the war that takes my adored Johnnie away. I *hate* it.

Tuesday, 23 July. A walking day. The weather was hot and cloudy but fine. We took the 10.15 bus to Minster Lovell. For the first time, we had to show our identification cards which were twice examined by armed soldiers on the bus. We walked from M. Lovell to Charlbury, having lunch at an Inn at Leafield. Quite a pleasant but unremarkable 'field' walk. It is good to get into the country, and nothing soothes us more. We returned by train from Charlbury, and had a quiet reading evening after tea at the Cadena. I feel extraordinarily cheerful now, so surprisingly soon after being so extra down-in-the-dumps. It is a great relief to be calm again. Thank God for it.

Wednesday, 24 July. Such dull depressing weather. Letter from mother. Richard is still having to have great attention and Nita must be glad of mother's help. I miss her, especially for shopping and chatting to. The last Depôt afternoon for five weeks. I shall miss the calming talk there, and must find something more to do. How strange it is to have liked that so much, after dreading it nearly a year ago. Robert and I had supper out, then joined Vera at the Playhouse for the second version of the *Revue* which had Nellie Wallace in it, and wasn't as good as the first, but quite fun.[27]

Thursday, 25 July. Rainy weather now, as is always in July. It is funny shopping without mother. I went to the Holy Communion at 11.00, but didn't feel very 'like it'. I answered a letter from John in the afternoon. He is all brisked up and newly fortified after his leave, and not at all unstrung as I was when he first returned. Vera and I to Headington Cinema at night to see an old Deanna Durbin film [*First Love*] which wasn't as good as some. We got caught in heavy rain coming out.

Friday, 26 July. Better weather but not hot yet. Shopping as usual. To Mrs Busby's new house in Albert Street [no. 5, in Jericho] with Robert in the afternoon. It must be nice to have sunshine after living in such a dark hole [at 3 Saunders Yard, off Broad Street] for so many years. I chatted a little with Mrs Jimenez and [her daughter] Natalia in the garden before tea. Mrs J. is so very nice; they both are – in fact *all* are really. I hope they don't have to go away if Spain comes into this hellish war.[28] The Intercession Service at night, then I washed my hair.

---

27 Nellie Wallace (1870–1948) was a well-known music hall star, actress, comedian, and dancer.
28 On 22 November 1939 she had written of 'the nice Spanish people next door', that is, at 2 Wellington Place, which is attached to no. 1. Alberto Jimenez Fraud (1883–1964) was a liberal educationalist, and Director of the Residencia de Estudiante in Madrid 1910–37,

Saturday, 27 July. Very rainy and thundery. I helped write marriage certificates in the Vestry with Robert and Mr Pearce, then shopped in the cold cold rain. I went to see Mrs Horser in her stuffy room in the afternoon, Mr Horser wasn't there, which was a pity, as he is not so querulous (?). June and her friend Jean to tea. I get very tired of their everlasting trousers, shirts, and ties, and dislike the manner-less Jean so far but really like June very much. Robert and I went to the pictures to see a macabre and American film, *The Tower of London* [with Basil Rathbone, Boris Karloff and Vincent Price]. I got a headache and went to bed earlier than usual.

Sunday, 28 July. A nicer day in the weather line, for ages. Church in the morning, an Intercession Service in the Town Hall in the afternoon at which nice Lord Elton spoke, though rather gloomily.[29] June to tea, she is very helpful and washes up and things. Church again at night, then to Vera's to supper for the first time for many weeks. Quite like old times to be coming home in the black-out.

Monday, 29 July. Letters from John and mother. She seems to be enjoying the change, in town. An ordinary morning. We had heard guns and bombs in the night. I wish I could have a more courageous body, but it seems to act before the brain can get courageous to combat the fear of noise and destruction. Miss Spurling came to tea. She is quite a nice old lady, from the Depôt, full of calmness and humour, and having known very interesting people in her time.[30] Vera and I went to the Playhouse Revue again at night. Very good as usual. June came over but went to the pictures.

---

before leaving Spain and going into exile in September 1936. He settled in Oxford, where he was a lecturer in Spanish. He and his wife spent the rest of their lives in England. We are grateful to Barbara Tearle for this information.

29   Godfrey Elton (b. 1892), a historian, 'sincere Christian' (*The Times*, 19 April 1973, p. 20), peer since 1934, former fellow of Queen's College and now Secretary of the Rhodes Trust, is reported to have said that 'If we seize this opportunity of regeneration through suffering, we may indeed hope to save not only ourselves, but the world for a new and clean age.' He highlighted the role of education in this Christian revival. (*Oxford Times*, 2 August 1940, p. 7.) See also below, 24 March 1941, p. 126.

30   On 14 December 1940, Madge read of the death of 'one of our nicest Depôt ladies, Miss Spurling. We shall miss her quiet, pleasant company very much. Everyone liked her immensely.' She was found dead in her flat in Linkside Avenue on 13 December (*Oxford Times*, 20 December 1940). Her obituary charts her career as a history teacher, headmistress and then warden of training colleges in Manchester and London (*Cheshire Chronicle*, 21 December 1940).

Tuesday, 30 July. What a queer summer. Ordinarily we should be at Scarborough now, loving all of it. It is hard to dwell on those things, but please God, next year may bring it all back. My usual trot round the shops. In the afternoon I called on Mrs (Darcy) Dalton. She is quite nice in a talkative sort of way and has done up their flat most beautifully, in [nearby] St Michael's Street. We had tea with the Bleibens, but he is so grave and harried now, that we didn't enjoy the meeting as much as usual. Robert and I went to see *Gas-light* [starring Anton Walbrook and Diana Wynyard, and based on Patrick Hamilton's 1938 play], a good film, at night.

Wednesday, 31 July. The warmest day this month, I think. I had a headache which fortunately disappeared quite soon. A holiday so we had a walking day. A bus to Enstone, then over rather rough fields to Chadlington for lunch. Lovely gently hilly and wooded country, with cornfields creamy looking against the hazy blue sky. Bread and cheese at a spot-less pub in Chadlington, then on to Spelsbury and Charlbury. Almost too hot for comfort, but very lovely. If only we could get away from the noise of 'planes everywhere.[31] Back by train from Charlbury and a bad tea at the dirty hope-less North-Gate Tea Rooms – a rest, bath and quiet evening.

Thursday, 1 August. What will August bring – horror and desolation, inactivity, or new hope? Hitler promised his people Peace by August 15th and he likes to keep his word – sometimes. We shall see. Beautiful weather again – oh, that we were at Scarborough, having our daily round at Peasholm and our nightly visit to the Spa. When shall we be there again? Miss Butler and her mother to tea – one of those confusing teas when there are two conversations going. I do like the cheerful Miss Butler. Vera called, and we sat in the [University] Parks for a little under a tree in the slanting sunshine. Then she came back for supper. Robert had had amusing experiences at his ARP dealing with a mock incendiary bomb.

Friday, 2 August. Gloriously hot sunshine again, so that I am able to bask in my little garden which is so pretty this year. I get very wearied trying to think of meals, and food is getting so expensive. I sat toasting myself all afternoon, then Ruth came to tea. She has a wonderful character, and all her sorrows seem to have made it still finer. I think Doris resents having to wait on a German, as she always flings on the thickest chunks of bread and doesn't bother to make things dainty at all for her. What a pity, when she

---

31   There were over two dozen airfields in the county: Robin J. Brooks, *Oxfordshire Airfields in the Second World War* (Newbury: Countryside Books, 2001).

is about the best and most-to-be-admired person I know. The Intercession Service at night with Vera.

Saturday, 3 August. Very hot weather. I love it though I don't think it is very good for one. Lots of shopping. Basking in the sunshine in the afternoon. I love this, too, but again, in spite of sun-glasses, I get sun glare headaches from it. June came to tea, and we all went to the pictures, which weren't bad – Sonja Henjie [in *Everything Happens at Night*] who is a dream on skates but nothing much off.

Sunday, 4 August. One of the hottest days of the year. I did odd jobs in the morning – washed my hair, ironed dresses, weeded the garden. We had had a 'phone call from Nita last night, saying that Richard feels miraculously better, and has been sent home from hospital, so could they come here on Tuesday for a week, bringing mother back with them. Great joy! Basking in the afternoon. Church at night then to Vera's. I have got a very sneezy cold which makes me feel hot and bothered. A boilingly hot night.

Monday, 5 August. A strange 'Bank Holiday' with the shops all open as usual and no trippers about, and we in Oxford instead of Scarborough. My wretched cold very annoying but it will take its time, doubtless. Still very hot and thundery. Shopping. Resting in the garden and indoors. I am having a lazy holiday from the Depôt. June to tea. She and I went shopping afterwards. Then she went to the pictures. I went after supper to Ruth's to take her some knitting and to sit with her in her pleasant room at the top of her new house where she works. Very pleasant except that I was so full of cold that I could scarcely speak.

Tuesday, 6 August. A busy morning getting in food for the family. Beautiful weather. Surely this summer has been, except for July perhaps, the best for decades. Mother, Nita, Richard and Kit came at 3.30 – Dick surprisingly well considering his very bad illness, though he doesn't look himself yet by any means. We talked and laughed and had large meals in the family way, lovely and carefree it seems in spite of the war. We all went to the Playhouse at night. The Revue was as good as ever, and one gets very fond of the company. Late to bed.

Wednesday, 7 August. More lovely weather. Shopping with the family, Cadena etc. Nita and I sat in the garden most of the afternoon. Richard and Kit on the river. Richard should have been resting but does *anything* to please the boy. It is a tragedy, though beautiful too, in a way. I gave Nita a 'facial' which rested her – she badly needs a rest. She came out glowing and pretty from it. To the pictures at night – Deanna Durbin in *It's a Date*, which wasn't up to her early ones, but good.

Thursday, 8 August. Warm still, but cloudier. Richard not so well today – we think he did too much yesterday. Shopping in the morning. It always reminds me now of the autumn when all the family was here. A quiet afternoon. In the evening we went to the pictures – mother, Nita, Kit and me. Richard rested at home, Robert at his ARP lecture. Not a bad film – one *Remember the Night* [starring Barbara Stanwyck and Fred MacMurray].

Friday, 9 August. We had to get up at 6.00 to get the doctor for Richard who had his bad pain again. The doctor gave him morphia. It *is* a shame to have this fiendish kidney disease, and it must be so painful. Dr McMichael is always so sweet and reassuring. It is very depressing for Nita *and* Richard. In the afternoon Robert and I went for a little walk from Wootton, back to Woodstock, a very pretty hill way, with cornfields on every side. Tea at Woodstock – we saw June on her way back from her tree-felling.

Saturday, 10 August. Richard better today, but in bed till after tea. He seems to love Dr McMichael as we all do. I met Muriel for coffee at the Cadena. She has a holiday and for once wasn't quite so irritating as usual. She and Vera met Robert, mother and me at the theatre at night to see the Revue *Nine o'clock Sharp*, which was very amusing in parts, but which we didn't enjoy as much as our Playhouse ones.[32] Much colder weather, though very sunny still.

Sunday, 11 August. Church in the morning with Nita and Muriel. All the Scouts and Guides there. Very cold suddenly. A quiet afternoon. Richard much better and up to lunch. Church again at night. Christopher very busy all day making a tiny model battle-ship – he is awfully good at these things.

Monday, 12 August. Lovely again today. We really have had a most lovely summer. Lots of shopping with mother and Nita and coffee at the Cadena with Muriel. We went for a walk, all except Richard and mother and Danna, in the afternoon. Vera joined us. We walked up from Cumnor Foot over to Boars Hill – beautiful views all round of sun-lit cornfields and distant misty hills. Boars Hill is beautiful with its sandy ways and fir trees. We came

---

[32] According to the *Oxford Times*, 9 August 1940, p. 4, this revue at the New Theatre in George Street 'had a great run in London, but one feels that, like the bored "Non-Stop Nudes" in the sketch, the whole company must have grown rather tired of the show, and find it difficult to put into it the verve which made it go with such a swing in the West End'.

back for tea and pictures at the Ritz. Divine Fred Astaire in a very excellent musical, *Broadway Melody of 1940*. Robert had to go patrolling the streets for culprits of 'black-outs'.

Tuesday, 13 August. Tuesday usually means a letter from John. He is in his last weeks now, in Scotland; then gets moved to a Station somewhere, perhaps quite near here. All went shopping and Cadena-ing, where we, of course, ran into Muriel. She is amiable just now, as she is seeing quite a lot of us. A quiet afternoon writing letters and reading. A little stroll in the [University] Parks after tea with Nita and a chat on a sunny seat. Early supper, then we all went to the last of the Playhouse revues. Vera and Muriel there, too. Not quite as good as it might have been, but very enjoyable as usual. The nights are getting very dark, alas!

Wednesday, 14 August. Rather a dull, damp morning, but we determined to take no notice of it, and have our planned walk, and to reward us, after lunch it came out hot and sunny. Nita came with Robert and me. A bus to Wootton turn, then a hilly corn-fieldy walk to Middle-Barton which wasn't as nice a village as June had led us to believe. We had a welcome bread and cheese lunch at a pub there then walked the seven miles back to Woodstock, which was glorious in the warmth, along a long wide straight lane, with the yellow cornfields all round. Tired after 14 miles and ready for a welcome tea at the 'Roof Tree'. Mother, Richard and Kit had been to the pictures. An evening singing old favourites and reading.

Thursday, 15 August. Lovely and hot again. I think this must have been a very uneventful and quiet day, as I don't remember much about it, even after three days only. I think we all shopped and Cadena'd, with Muriel and sat in the hot sunny garden all afternoon. The RAF is doing simply wonderfully against the German massed air-raids which occur every day now. They have brought down over 400 in six days as against our losses of 90 odd. If only we can keep up this 'ratio'.[33] We all went round the rather dreary (I always think) but cool and beautiful Christ Church meadows after tea. Robert had to go through the gas test tonight at his ARP.[34]

---

33 Madge, of course, was simply repeating what she had heard on the news or read in the press. The German losses were in fact much smaller (Michael Korda, *With Wings Like Eagles: A History of the Battle of Britain* [New York: HarperCollins, 2009], pp. 172–3 and 201–2). Still, the British defence had indeed been highly effective and Fighter Command had performed well.

34 Robert went 'with Pearce to the Gas Chamber in Cowley Road. I didn't risk smelling it.'

Friday, 16 August. Wonderful weather continuing. Yesterday was supposed to be the date on which Hitler was to proclaim his victorious peace from Buckingham Palace, instead of which the Air Force had their record 'bag' of planes. Let me hope and pray that this is a good omen. Shopping, coffee at the Cadena, all of us with Muriel. In the afternoon 300 New Zealand Troops arrived to see the sights of Oxford. Robert took a batch round, and Kit went with him. Nita and I, thrilled by the bronzed, handsome and friendly men, followed and tracked them all afternoon, which was enormous fun. We both have a real hero-worship for almost anything in uniform! – and these were particularly attractive.[35] Ruth came to tea, and after seeing the 'Anzaco' off, we had a quiet evening.

Saturday, 17 August. Nita, Richard and Kit departed on the 10.20 train. We like having them so much, and I think Nita and I are particularly happy to be together. Mother seems, however, much more cheery when she is here alone. I think she likes a bit of peace nowadays. The usual morning. It was the hottest day this year, I should imagine, though we have to guess these things, now the weather cannot be mentioned in the papers. Many districts in Oxfordshire had been bombed last evening, but the Air Force continues to bring their planes down in great numbers. It was such a lovely day that in the afternoon we went up to Boars Hill again and took Muriel. We walked through the grounds of Ripon Hall which are beautiful – great fir-trees in a deep ravine surrounding a dark swimming-pool. The view from the terrace is magnificent. We walked through Jarne's Mound gardens and had a most excellent tea at 'Ebor', which is run by a rather busy-body St Michael's devotee. To the pictures at night [*Vigil in the Night*, with Carol Lombard and Brian Ahearne]. Very, very hot and not very good.

---

35 Robert wrote this day: '300 New Zealand soldiers arrived at the YMCA and I gladly took a party of about 50 of them over my usual route. A large audience to posture before but naturally not so appreciative as giggling women. ... We saw them going away after tea, officers and men chatting with us together quite happily – not *my* way at all (snob).' The *Oxford Mail* (p. 1) the following day featured two photographs of these New Zealanders: one of a moment in Robert's guided tour for them of the University (around twenty were in the picture) – he was pointing to a site of interest; and one of two of the soldiers admiring a seated member of the ATS, all smiles, with the accompanying words, 'Colleges were not the only attractions during yesterday's visit of the New Zealanders to Oxford.' This was an early example of Britain playing the gracious host to troops from the Commonwealth, whose support was highly valued, especially, perhaps, at this time of acute peril, well before American engagement in the war. The expressions of mutual appreciation between New Zealand and historic Oxford were highlighted in the *Oxford Times*, 17 August 1940, p. 3.

'What a lot of diary to write up,' Madge observed the next day. 'Five days. Why is it such a horrid bore, writing up back days?' Doris was on holiday for a week 'so mother and I helping with the house-work and quite enjoying it'. By now a new second maid was in employment (a fact not previously reported), for she added that 'Gladys is a very sensible and intelligent person and we get on very well, with no fuss or irritation.' Madge's volunteer work continued, and on 22 August she went to tea with Mrs Holmes-Dudden. 'She is one of the War Depôt people I like most, so entertaining and ruthless and kind all at once. Her husband is Master of Pembroke. How come I to be asked out to such *grand* homes? This much has the Depôt done for me. It is surprising how very sweet really important people are. ... Life is funny.' The war entered Madge's diary in a different form on 28 August, when she noted 'a procession in the evening in aid of the "Fighter" which Oxford is giving. ... Quite an impressive parade ... We were thrilled.' This was one of the first major public events to promote war savings (over £5,000 were subscribed to this fund)[36] – and there would be many more during the following four years.

German raids on Britain were now well under way, and Madge mentioned these threats from the air. On Friday, 23 August she was in London, which 'had been bombed in the early hours – the suburbs – and the papers were full of news of the bombarding of the Kentish coast-towns. However, all was serene and cheerful as far as we could see.' The following day she reported that 'The mass air-raids have started again in earnest' and, writing from Oxford on 25 August, 'German planes disturbed us at night, and guns.' The next day she was 'Tired after a late and restless night. These "lone-raid" air attacks are the latest worry, and are so wide-spread all over the country. ... More gun-fire, or bombs, at night. We sat in the kitchen for a time "in case". I hate the chug-chug of the bombers.' On 27 August she said that she and her mother 'always feel very sleepy in the mornings after rather wakeful nights trying to detect German bomber planes amongst those which fly constantly.'

While the Martins were unable to enjoy their usual Scarborough holiday this summer, they did not allow themselves to be entirely confined to Oxfordshire. On Friday, 30 August they headed off for a week of walking and sightseeing in Derbyshire. This holiday differed from others they had taken in two respects. First, the threat of war could not be ignored. Planes were often overhead; warning sirens were heard routinely at night; a few bomb-blasts were heard; and an alert the first night required them to spend time in the basement of their Matlock hotel. On 30 August in their bedroom 'I lay miserably awake, hearing the German plane circling round and distant explosions, till 4.00a.m. when the "all clear" sounded.' Since they liked neither Matlock nor the hotel ('raffish, dirty, noisy'), the next day they looked elsewhere for accommodation and found a tiny cottage for rent at a farm on nearby

---

36   *Oxford Times*, 23 August 1940, p. 3 and 30 August 1940, p. 3.

Riber Hill. This was not up to their usual standards – but they took it. 'Mrs Marsden, the owner, was so nice and welcoming and homely that in spite of, for us, incredible "roughing" as to bedroom, toilet, etc., we decided to come up [from the town], so fetched our luggage and settled in our minute bedroom where the bed took almost every inch of space.' Madge liked 'the sounds of farm life' (31 August). 'The food here is really very fine', but 'a honeymoon couple spent the night in the other too near bedroom' (1 September). An 'overwhelmingly typical North-Country miner appeared to sleep in the stair-room, and chatted for hours' (2 September). 'He is so straight from the stage,' she remarked the next day, 'that we couldn't believe him to be real, but he is a real good sort – my father would have liked him.' They enjoyed most of the walking in countryside with 'great wooded heights and deep gorges, so very like Austria, but the villages and stone walls are very like my native Yorkshire' (3 September), and spent a day at Chatsworth (4 September). It was a 'very novel holiday', she declared (4 September).

On Saturday, 7 September there were 'Fond farewells to Mrs Marsden, who gave us butter and eggs. We were sorry to leave the country and the fresh air, but glad to be getting back to cleanliness and civilisation. ... Home about 4.30. The house looked amazingly clean and spacious after Sunnyside Farm. We went out shopping after tea, then a glorious bath for me. Robert and I had supper at the Snack-Bar. Oxford is absolutely packed out. Nice to lie on a soft bed with clean sheets again.'

4

Battlegrounds

September 1940–May 1941

On their way back from holiday on 7 September 1940, Madge and Robert 'saw the result of German bombs at Birmingham'. War activity was being seen and heard virtually daily. But these incidents were just a warm-up to what was to come, from the second week in September.

Sunday, 8 September. A day of National Prayer. There was a terrible air-raid on London last night, and hundreds killed and injured. Hitler is determined to try and bring this war to a quick end by bombing people to bits. I wonder how long human endurance will stand it. I am worried about Nita and Nancy in London and fear they must be having a terrible time. We can't expect Oxford to be left alone for ever and I wonder how I shall stick it? Church in the morning with Mrs Booth, June in, for tea. She is a cheerful person to have around. Church at night, then to Vera's for supper.

Monday, 9 September. Very cold suddenly. More stories of awful raids in London. Their planes seem to have penetrated right to the centre – flying very high in the dark. I shopped. Marina's kitten went to its new home – I shall miss it. The War Depôt in the afternoon. I went along with a young doctor's wife, Mrs Mills. She is very nice and shy-ish. We are now making pneumonia jackets [a flannel garment for the upper body]. It was pleasant to see all the friendly placid faces again and I was welcomed. How different from a year ago, when I hated it so. There was an air-raid warning at 6.00 but it only lasted half an hour. Vera came to supper. The newest maid arrived – a young fresh-looking little girl, Winifred Walker. I wonder how she'll turn out. I am somewhat disillusioned now.[1]

Tuesday, 10 September. The raids in London make terrible reading in the mornings' papers, which are usually very late.[2] I think constantly of Nita and Nancy, who must be having a terrible time. Shopping in the morning and afternoon. A quiet evening washing my hair and writing a lot of letters. The Prime Minister spoke on the wireless. The Germans are ready for a big invasion. Buckingham Palace has been badly damaged by a time bomb. Luckily the King and Queen were not in residence.[3]

Thursday, 12 September. The weather rather wild and stormy. We pray for high winds to beat the Channel up against the threatened Invasion. Oxford is full of East-end refugees – whole families with nothing left of their homes but the clothes they wear; 7,000 of them, but they are very cheerful.[4] I

---

1   We assume that Madge had been dissatisfied with at least one of her recent maids, but she wrote nothing of these matters in her diary.
2   Later that year, on the morning of Monday, 9 December, there were no papers at all in Oxford as a consequence of the previous night's blitz on London.
3   At this point the diary becomes muddled, albeit briefly. At the end of this entry she wrote, 'Sorry – all this was Wednesday!' And her entry under Wednesday's date is brief and mechanistic.
4   A Report from the WVS (Women's Voluntary Services) indicated that some 6,000 official evacuees were received at the Oxford station, about half of whom were to be billeted in the city itself. Looking after them was a major undertaking. 'The Town Hall was given over to the unaccompanied school children of whom there were between 500 and 600. The staff of the Town Hall, for all purposes, was supplied entirely by the WVS and the Red Cross, who were on duty day and night in the body of the Hall. The WVS also staffed and catered for the evacuees at the Holyoak Hall in Headington, where there were about 230 evacuees, namely, mothers, children and old people.' Then 'Unofficial refugees began to stream into Oxford about 9 September and were housed in a large Cinema just outside the City [the Majestic on Botley Road]. ... Numbers became so large that the whole of the Cinema had to be taken over with a certain number of paid staff. The WVS sent between 30 and 40 helpers each day and about 6 to 8 were on duty every night.' (RVS Archive & Heritage Collection, Narrative Report for Oxford City, September 1940.)
    Newspaper and other reports disclosed the struggles to accommodate the thousands of evacuees who surged into the city during these weeks, and temporary billets were found in Rhodes House, the headquarters of the Rhodes Trust, and numerous colleges, among them Christ Church, Balliol, University, Merton, St Hilda's, Wadham, and Lady Margaret Hall (*Oxford Times*, 27 September 1940, pp. 6 and 10; 4 October, pp. 7 and 12; and 11 October, p. 8; and Norman Longmate, *How We Lived Then: A History of Everyday Life during the Second World War* [London: Pimlico, 2002; first published 1971], p. 206). Some 112 women and children were sheltered for ten days at Rhodes House, whose Warden at the time later recalled the emergency. The evacuees – 'all humble folk' – 'had been expected during the

shopped and went down to Miss Barrett's to see about a blue jacket. The War Depôt in the afternoon. I wrote to the morose John when I got back. Vera came to supper.

Friday, 13 September. We half expected the German invasion to start on this sinister date [i.e., a Friday the 13th] – but no, though most people seem to think that it is very imminent. Shopping – which is more difficult than ever with the refugees in thousands about the streets. A lazy afternoon on the whole. The war Intercession Service at night with Vera. Buckingham Palace was bombed again today. The King and Queen were there, but unharmed. The Germans seem to be trying to get them to leave London. It is all frightful.

Saturday, 14 September. Shopping, and at 1 o'clock I went on my first canteen shift till 3.00. Mrs Booth introduced me to the St Giles' one – just round the corner. My job was mostly cooking sausages and fried eggs which was simple but tiring after a time. As usual, at anywhere for the first time, I rather disliked it, but I know by experience that one usually gets to enjoy things more when accustomed to everything and everybody. Very tired after it, but I shall get less so, I expect.[5] We went to the Playhouse with Vera at night to see *Fresh Fields*, a rather dated 1933 play of Ivor Novello's.

---

day, but they did not arrive until late on a black, streaming September night in 1940, after travelling from early morning with little food or warmth. I shall never forget the uncomplaining patience of young and old. Uprooted from their homes and hurriedly dispatched into the unknown, they cannot have been a happy band of pilgrims when at last Oxford greeted them with a relentless downpour, but they endured all with stoicism not unmingled with humour.' His wife took the lead in helping to organize a makeshift dormitory; arrangements for feeding also had to be made. Virtually no damage was done by the children to the building's interior. 'When the time came for departure to permanent billets throughout Oxford, there was a touching little ceremony. The mothers, none of them well off, collected a little sum of money to be given to an Oxford charity by way of thanks for shelter and care.' (Sir Carleton Allen, 'The Rhodes Scholars and Oxford 1931–52', in Lord Elton, ed., *The First Fifty Years of the Rhodes Trust and the Rhodes Scholarships 1903–1953* [Oxford: Basil Blackwell, 1955], pp. 167–8.)

5   Canteens were being set up in many cities, mainly to cater for people who in the daytime were away from home, such as civil defence workers, evacuees, and war workers. The WVS report cited indicated that 'The Mobile Canteen was just finished in time to be of use during this emergency and has already been called six times by the Local Authorities.' (RVS Archive & Heritage Collection, Narrative Report for Oxford City, September 1940.) Months later, in March 1941, canteens continued to be busy sources of welfare in wartime. 'A good many new evacuees have been coming into Oxford during the last month, a direct result of bombing in London and elsewhere. The Mobile Canteen has twice been called out by the Evacuation Officer to meet a train load of mothers and young children at the station. We supplied them with tea and biscuits and a great deal of milk for the children before they were taken on by

Sunday, 15 September. There was a great mass attack in day-light on London and the coast today, but our marvellous RAF brought down 185 of their planes, 130 of which were bombers. If only this always happens after such attacks! The Invasion still is expected, but the weather is getting rather wild, and windy, which is a great blessing, and which may hamper them. I do worry about Nita and Nancy in the midst of such frightfulness. Church in the morning, June to tea. Church at night, and supper with Vera.

Monday, 16 September. Very rainy almost all day – the first rain for weeks – and it was very welcome. The wind also got up strongly. We pray for tempests on the sea, so that the enemy may be foiled. Robert and I were wildly extravagant and went out and bought a lovely new gas cooker and boiler [costing £16 15s, according to Robert] and an electric kettle. Are we mad? The Depôt in the afternoon and a quiet evening. Vera to supper. We are both knitting socks.

Tuesday, 17 September. The news is always the horrible same. Bombs on London, many buildings destroyed, 'some casualties', which means hundreds. Our RAF bomb military targets in German. All so senseless and murderous. Shopping as usual. Difficult amongst the new hordes of refugees – poor things. The Canteen from 1.00 to 3.30. Very strange people there – and I don't like the atmosphere – but fortunately I'm too busy cooking to get involved in their awful vulgar brawls. I went to see Mrs Maclagan's baby after tea. He is very like her. The husband is an extraordinary taciturn and languid person. Very tired, and glad of an arm-chair after a busy day.

Wednesday, 18 September. We are glad to have early gales blowing wildly and, we hope, holding back the invasion indefinitely. London bombed again. Three large shops, Bourne and Hollingsworth, Lewis' and Evans, badly bombed. Poor London – what will be left of her? Shopping as usual, the Depôt in the afternoon, a fitting for a blue coat straight after. Then the pictures with Robert and Vera, *Dr Cyclops* [a science fiction horror film] – not too bad, in rather a crude way.

Thursday, 19 September. A wild stormy day, but we decided, after much debating, to go off on a holiday whatever the weather. Also the grey skies and tempestuous winds were welcomed. We took the 11.20 bus to Thame, looked at the lovely old Church, and had lunch at the Spread Eagle which

bus to a rest centre in the county.' (RVS Archive & Heritage Collection, Oxford City Narrative Report, March 1941.)

was filled to overflowing with guests in search of quiet. We had a funny little walk through the nearby fields. We passed some bomb craters, and were held up at one point by a red notice attended by RE's saying 'Danger – unexploded bombs'. We faded swiftly away, in case they blew up. We went to the Headington Cinema on our way home. Not a bad programme [*Laugh It Off* and *Secret Journey*].

Friday, 20 September. Shopping as usual I suppose. In the afternoon I stuck net on the bath-room and sun-parlour windows. It was a most horrible job, as Robert, who had tried it himself, warned me. One has to slosh water on the window and thump hard with a wet cloth to make it stick. It is supposed to make splinters less likely to fly far, but one would almost as soon *be* splintered. The war Intercession Service at night, with Vera. She came back to supper.

Saturday, 21 September. Lovely weather again. The news much about the same. London bombed again. I do wonder how much longer they can stand it. Shopping in the morning. I did some personal shopping in the afternoon – Jumpers – for a new suit, and went to see Mrs Horser in her stuffy and smelly little top attic room. I am so sorry for poor *Mr* Horser having to live with such a poor fractious old bed-ridden soul. I went alone to see a good but gloomy film, *The Grapes of Wrath* [directed by John Ford and based on John Steinbeck's 1939 novel].

Sunday, 22 September. I had one of my old headaches, and stayed at home all day, and in bed for quite a lot of it. Thank heaven – I am really much better than I used to be.

Monday, 23 September. Lovely weather again. The headache much improved, so I was able to shop and go to the Depôt in the afternoon. We had a phone call from Nancy after tea. The poor things have had such a horrible time, and now incendiary bombs to cope with, that they are coming down here, for a *second* evacuation, tomorrow. I hope and *pray* that they find peace here. Robert and I went out to dinner, and to *Autumn Crocus* [by Dodie Smith, 1931] at the Playhouse, which they did most beautifully.

Tuesday, 24 September. A very busy morning shopping for the family. I went to meet Nance and the children who came at 2.20, the train not being so very late. Nance was very brave and cheerful, but obviously badly shaken after her awful experiences. The children seemed quite unaffected by it all, but pale and tired after such bad nights. It was nice to see them. They had lunch and tea, and we listened to the tales of horror they had to tell. How

Nance stuck it so long is amazing. We had a meeting of the Guild at night. The children and Nancy so glad to get into proper beds after so many nights in the dug-out.

Wednesday, 25 September. Heavenly weather, but very very cold. We had a really reminiscent morning – exactly like last September – shopping, and the Cadena with the children. I went to the Depôt in the afternoon, and in the evening Robert and I saw Shirley Temple in *The Blue Bird*. We liked it very much, though Shirley is growing up so fast now. There were distant bombs before bed-time to startle Nancy again. I hope and *pray* that things keep quiet here.

Thursday, 26 September. Still very sunny and cold. I have got a cold and cannot speak much. I seem liable now to catching bad throats. Shopping, and the Cadena with Nancy. I hope she gets rested – she is very plucky. There was the Depôt anniversary 'At Home' in the afternoon. I went to sew, first, then all the 'bandaging room' went down to a very sumptuous tea, and to see a display of our work. Crowds there and all very gay. I do enjoy it all there now. Our 'room' is such a nice collection of people. Nance and I helped with marriage registers afterwards. Harry came down for the night. Nance joins me in my 'regards' for him.

Friday, 27 September. A vile head – I should be thankful that I don't get so many [now] – but on the other hand they seem worse after a long interval. I shopped with Nance and went to bed in the afternoon. Up after tea. We heard bombs at 8.00p.m. which fell on Boars Hill, and the siren went after. We fetched the children down and eventually had supper in the kitchen. The 'all clear' at 9.30. A queer life, this.

Saturday, 28 September. The head raging away like anything, but I went with Nance and the children and Mrs Booth to Church to decorate the Church with Michaelmas daisies. Vera came too. Mrs Booth was very confusing and bustling. We had coffee at Fullers after. I went to bed again for the afternoon. Then the headache went. June came to tea, and Nance and I went round the *very* seething town shop-gazing but the crowds were too awful to bear. June stayed to supper.

Sunday, 29 September. Frightfully cold and dismal. Nance and I to Church. As usual on Festivals, I had no voice with which to sing the lovely hymns. The Church looked lovely with its daisies. There was a warning at tea-time again so we had tea down in the kitchen. Only about half an hour again. Vera and I to Church at night – very dark now coming home. Nita rang up and asked if we could have Christopher to stay, as he has such bad nights, so of course we are very glad to have him.

Monday, 30 September. Still very cold. Out shopping as usual. Christopher arrived – very forlorn and quiet, but he recovered gradually as the day went on. We had a quiet afternoon, but a warning again at tea-time for the usual half-hour. I went out after the 'all clear' to buy a new hat to wear with my new suit. Nancy and Vera came to help choose. Nothing else I think.

Tuesday, 1 October. Shopping with Nance. Norman arrived for the night – he is always cheerful. Christopher more himself today. I went to the Depôt in the afternoon, calming and quiet. Mother arrived at 6.00, so we are more crowded than ever. She is sleeping in the waiting room.[6] I am afraid she is very nervous about the war still, and doesn't sleep well. Unfortunately, we had a warning at 3.30a.m., for about ¾ of an hour. We all got up and came down into the kitchen, and made cups of tea. The 'all clear' is a lovely sound.

Wednesday, 2 October. All a bit sleepy after our broken night. The usual busy shopping morning, and coffee at the Cadena to refresh us. I went to the Depôt in the afternoon. This life is almost a replica of last year's, except that Nita isn't here. However she rang up and told us that she and Dick are coming for a week, on Saturday. I had a bit of trouble with Kit in the evening over rudeness to Winnie, but he soon forgot his 'telling off' and seemed to bear me no grudge.

Thursday, 3 October. A very rainy day – we have had so few that we feel quite interested to see rain. Shopping as usual for our immense party. I feel somewhat headachey, so didn't go to the Depôt. There was the Guild Whist-Drive and social at night to open the 'Season'. I wonder if air-raids on Oxford will put a stop to these soon. Much as I loathe whist, I would put up with endless such evenings rather than raids. This one wasn't so bad. Mother came – even facing the dark wet 'black-out'.

Friday, 4 October. Another very rainy day. Much shopping in the morning. Mother is very apprehensive about everything, and still doesn't sleep. Robert joined us all at the Cadena, and he and I took the boys to the pictures at the Scala in the afternoon. *The Drum* [1938 British adventure film based on the 1937 novel by A.E.W. Mason] which Kit had seen three times, but enjoyed

---

6   In his diary for this day, Robert also remarked on her arrival: 'so we are now ten in this house by night and eleven by day. No room for evacuees!' This latter remark was undoubtedly an expression of relief that 1 Wellington Place would not be asked to take in strangers.

again. Roger liked it too. It is a fine film. The other, very amusing too, *Hold My Hand* [1938 British musical comedy]. We played vingt-et-un [blackjack] round the dining-room table at night. Quite fun.

Saturday, 5 October. A very busy morning, shopping, decorating the Church for Harvest with a rather meagre collection of flowers and fruit – real war offerings. Nita and Dick arrived for lunch, for a week. It is amazing how cheerful these brave Londoners are. We are an enormous party now. Nita and Dick sleep out, however, and have breakfast at Mr Pearce's boarding house in Beaumont Street [at no. 18], which simplifies things. We had much talk and shopped, and in the evening went to the Playhouse to see *Ambrose Apple John's Adventure* [by Walter Hackett] which was very good. Mother is the only member of the family who doesn't seem to be enjoying the crowds. Bombs in the night – quite close.

Sunday, 6 October. Dismal weather – rainy and cold. Nita, Nance and I went to the Harvest Festival Morning Service. I got my voice partially back so I could sing some of the hymns. We went again at night, with mother this time. She hates the black-out. It is like old times – the family being here and I like it, on the whole.

Monday, 7 October. Still wild weather. I hope it puts the Invasion further off. The usual shopping with some of the family, and the Cadena. It was a very sunny afternoon, and suddenly warm, so lots of us went for a walk in the [University] Parks and round by Mesopotamia [a narrow island between two channels of the River Cherwell] – lovely. In the evening some of us went to see quite a good film *Lillian Russell* [with Alice Faye in the title role]. No time for anything much these days – exactly like last year. We like our cups of tea after supper.

Tuesday, 8 October. Shopping in the morning. Nita and Richard very unsettled as to know what to do with Christopher's schooling. He may possibly go to school here. Nita came with me to the Depôt, where Mrs Lys and Mrs McGregor greeted her very warmly. It was lovely to have her there again. I wrote to John in the sanctuary of the study. Norman suddenly appeared, so now the family really *is* complete. Nita, Dick, mother, Robert and I went to the Playhouse again to see *Quiet Wedding* [a 1938 comedy by Esther McCracken] which was great fun.

Wednesday, 9 October. Frightfully wild and stormy, but beautiful. The usual morning shopping and Cadena-ing – this diary must read identically with last year's at this time. The Depôt in the afternoon – a bit of peace, not that I

1   Madge Martin on holiday in Kitzbühel, 1937, age 37

2 (above) Danna Martin, July 1940, with her two sons living in England, Harry Martin (left) and Robert Martin (right)

3 (below) Doris Dandridge, the Martins' principal servant, with Marina, the cat

4   (above) Nita Holland and Nancy Barrett with their families in the University Parks, 1940
Nita Holland is on the left; Nancy Barrett on the right; Nita's husband, Richard (Dick) Holland, in the centre. (Nancy's husband, Norman Barrett, is absent.) The children, from top to bottom, are Christopher (Kit) Holland, Sally Barrett, and Roger Barrett

5   (below) Nick and Joy Nicholls, 1937
Nick was a longstanding friend of the Martins – since 1915. The Nicholls' marriage did not last.

6 John Hall and Madge Martin at Eynsham station, March 1936

7   (above) Robert Martin, in May 1942, showing Oxford to visiting members of the RAF. Robert was seen as something of an authority on local history. (See also Madge's diary for 16 August 1940.) (Courtesy of *Oxford Mail*)

8   (below, left) Ruth Hendewerk, 1937. Ruth Hendewerk was a refugee from Germany and much admired by Madge Martin

9   (below, right) Mrs Setterington in the garden, 1944. Edith Setterington, Madge Martin's mother, had been a widow since 1933

10–13 Drawings in her diary, by Madge Martin
10 (above, left) Nazi girl, Feldkirch, Austria, September 1938. 'The town all decked out with red, white and black Nazi banners,' Madge wrote on Tuesday, 13 September 1938. 'Very fine they looked indeed, in honour of the contingents returning from Nuremburg'
11 (above, right) Scarlett O'Hara, in *Gone with the Wind* (3–4 January 1938). It was one of her favourite books and films
12 (below, left) 'Untame-able hair!' (3 August 1939) 'I waste an awful lot of time trying to manage my hair which is long, dry and very wild. It irks me!'
13 (below, right) 'Robert's new table' (28 January 1938), given to him by Madge for his birthday

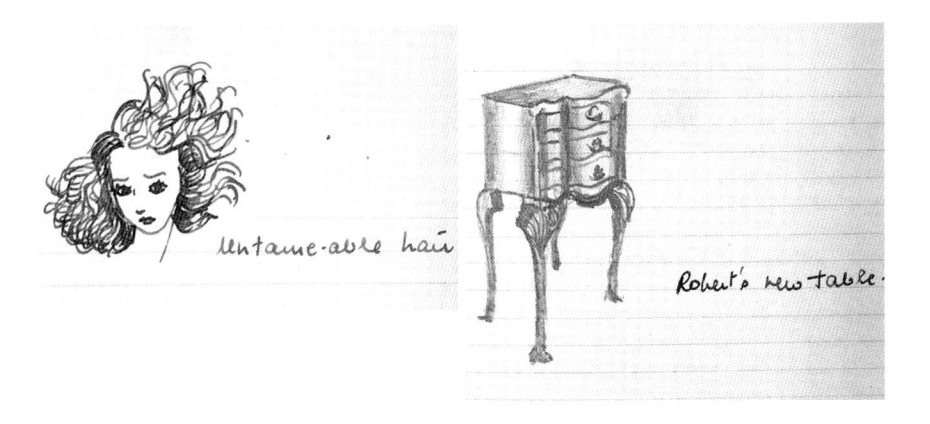

14 (above) Red Cross volunteers at Worcester College, 1942
Madge is sitting on the left, her sister Nancy on the right. Mrs Booth is sitting between them

15 (below) Cadena Café, 44–46 Cornmarket Street (*Courtesy of Oxfordshire County Council – Oxfordshire History Centre*)
The Cadena Café was a favourite place for Madge Martin to socialize. See diary for 17 September 1938 and many later entries

16   Rubber salvage, 1942 (©Imperial War Museum (D 8933))
A woman and her two children at a salvage exhibition in Oxford in 1942 look at a large display panel about rubber. See also the first footnote to the diary entry for 8 January 1943

mind the pandemonium. I rather like it. I went with Vera to the Intercession Service and lecture last night.⁷ Very cold and dark. Norman and Nance had been to the pictures.

Thursday, 10 October. Roger started school again – at St Philip and St James, so things are even more like last year than ever now. Christopher may be going to Southfield [in Barracks Lane, East Oxford], as he is getting no education at his school in London, and the air-raid shelter existence is very bad for him. A typical morning. I played truant from the War Depôt as I had the Whist-Drive to go to at night. Nance and I took Sally round Magdalen Island – beautiful in its riotous autumn colouring. The whist-drive at night. Vera and I had to wrestle with the refreshments, so didn't play ourselves. Mother and Nita went.

Friday, 11 October. A perfect autumn day, so Nita, Dick, Christopher, Nancy, Robert and I had a day's walking. A bus to Farmoor, then over rather flat country to Northmoor for a good lunch of bread and cheese at the pub. Robert saw his farmer tenant there [regarding Parish glebe land]. The rest of the walk was prettier and hillier, ending up on Cumnor Hill. We got the bus at Third Acre Rise. Mother came with Robert and me to the Ritz to see *Rebecca*. Robert hadn't seen it before and was very impressed. We had a very amusing singing evening at 9.00. Mr Pearce [the musically accomplished new curate] came and helped by playing very well and supplying a useful tenor. Great fun.

Saturday, 12 October. Another lovely day. The whole party had coffee as usual. Nita and Dick had to go back to 'the front line' after lunch, leaving Kit with us whilst they make enquiries about his school. We were all so sorry for them having to go back to all that horror, danger and noise. We took the children to Shotover in the afternoon where they ran about happily. Nance and I went to New College at night where we were rested and soothed by the exquisite singing. I wondered where I should be, when I went last to New College, at this time.⁸

Sunday, 13 October. Church in the morning. Mrs Booth there, and also Mrs Elliot, who has come back from London, and will start again at the Depôt. She was there till Christmas but finds Queen's Gate too 'hot'. We listened in

---

7   Robert gave his first lecture on 'The History of Freedom' the previous Wednesday evening, apparently at St Michael's Church.
8   Madge is referring, albeit clumsily, to her diary entry on 22 June 1940, p. 89.

to the first broadcast speech of Princess Elizabeth in the Children's Hour. She spoke beautifully. Church again at night. The servant problem is annoying me just now. Doris has given notice, and has no apparent reason except that as usual she cannot get on with Winnie, the house-maid. I refuse to get hot and bothered about it.[9]

Monday, 14 October. Very difficult days to remember. This was a very wet and tiresome one. Shopping as usual, and I suppose the Cadena. Very dark and gloomy in the afternoon. I wrote to John at night, but was interrupted by sensational happenings. The boys were encouraged to go out on the roof from Winnie's bed-room in the black-out. Winnie lied like a trooper and swore innocence about it all, till caught red-handed. Nance flew into an understandable rage, and I had nothing left but to give the girl notice. Then a terrible scene with Christopher followed. *He* was caught trying to escape altogether with a packed suit-case and 5 shillings in his pocket, having left the traditional dramatic note on the dressing-table. He is so unused to scoldings that he 'can't take it'. Robert had to talk to him, and gradually things quietened down, but what an upheaval in our quiet home![10]

Tuesday, 15 October. The usual morning, shopping etc. The War Depôt in the afternoon, sane, cheerful, and comforting. Robert, Mother and I to the Playhouse at night to see *Love from a Stranger* [1936, by Frank Vosper, and based on a 1924 short story by Agatha Christie] which was very good, but not so thrilling as the [1937] film. Torrents of rain. We had supper at the snack-bar first.

Wednesday, 16 October. I should write this diary daily instead of letting it drift on for days, as it is so hard to remember each day's doings. Nance and I went down to the Food Control office where her family and Christopher were registered permanently [for ration cards] in Oxford. The Depôt again. Dr Armstrong's wife is a new member and very nice. What a pleasant, intelligent lot they are – all of them. Norman came for a couple of nights. There was a warning at 8.00 to 9.30, and bombs in the outskirts. We had to give supper to Elsie Harris and Dudley Buttrum [both members of St Michael's

---

9   While Madge employed at least one daily maid during most of the years of this edited diary, Doris Dandridge for the longest period, these women are almost always in the background in her writing. Few if any details were revealed about their behaviour and personalities. The entry for the following day is a rare exception.
10 'A fierce disturbance in our happy home,' was Robert's reflection on this 'fearful row'. He and his wife valued a 'placid' existence, a word both used in a positive sense.

congregation and actors] who were here at the time, also another young soldier who only got a cock-tail.

Thursday, 17 October. Shopping and Cadena-ing. Norman and Nancy went off walking together. I spurned the Depôt again, as I went to tea at Vera's. It was a nice rest and as usual they gave me a lovely tea. She and I and Robert went to the Ritz for a fairly amusing film [*The Doctor Takes a Wife*, with Loretta Young and Ray Milland]. A lovely harvest moon, bright orange like a lantern. Christopher started at St Clement Dane's School [a London grammar school], which is with 'Southfield' for the war.

Friday, 18 October. Very tired and somewhat low-spirited today. Sometimes everything becomes too much for me – the crowds at home, the crowds shopping, the untidiness of our peaceful home and the interfering attitude of the two mothers. But these moods don't last long, and I do realize how much I have to be thankful for.[11] Lots of shopping for the weekend. Nance and I and Sally went to see Mrs Busby in the cold afternoon. A quiet evening. I helped Kit with his French. He is very quick.

Saturday, 19 October. Lovely warmth and sunshine. Shopping. The crowds are fearful and shopping on Saturday is a torture.[12] There was a rush on silk stockings, as we hear that after December 2nd no-one will be allowed to sell them. We are starting sacrificing years after the German women. Let us hope we can catch up on them! We all went to the pictures at the Regal, Cowley Road, in the afternoon, except Sally. We saw Mickey Rooney in *Young Tom Edison* which was good, but not *quite* as good as one expected. We had a nice tea at a café opposite, then home through the crowds. A very nice letter from my John.

Sunday, 20 October. As warm as summer. Church with Nancy in the morning, and she and I went with Robert to the Majestic Cinema where he

---

11 She revisited her negative mood a few weeks later (13 November 1940): 'Sometimes the constant arguments and confusion and interference which ruffle what was a peaceful house just are too much for me, and so it was this evening.'
12 '*What* crowds,' she wrote just before Christmas, on Monday, 23 December. 'The shops seem quite empty after the ravening horde of Oxford's swollen population has been at work in them.' On Saturday, 28 December 'the shops [were] exhausted and empty, and the people exhausted too.' Oxford's population at this time was probably a little over 100,000, perhaps as much as 110,000. A post-war estimate put the peak wartime population at some 20,000 over the pre-war norm, and this was one of those peak times (*Oxford Times*, 11 May 1945, p. 6).

took a short service for the refugees from the East-End, who are there.[13] It was uphill work shouting hymns above the racket there.[14] The poor things herd together in that dark stuffy hall with just a mattress and their few possessions round them. What a lot we have to be thankful for here in *Oxford*, and please God, we shall never be in the same plight. Norman here again for the night. I went to Church alone.

Tuesday, 22 October. Beautiful today, and as warm as Summer. (Just now – Thursday, 12.15 – the siren went, and I am now writing this in our basement. Poor Robert is conducting a wedding, and mother is out alone shopping.) The Depôt in the afternoon. Then I met Robert and we went out to tea with a very nice woman, Mrs Wreford-Brown, who has a *most* lovely house in Bartlemas Lane [East Oxford]. Everything so charming and gracious. Oxford looked glorious, coming home, in the smoky sunset. Mother, Robert and I went to the Playhouse, after a snack at the snack-bar, to see a rather silly farce, *Baa-Baa Black Sheep* [by Ian Hay and P.G. Wodehouse, 1930]. The Bleibens were with us.[15]

Thursday, 24 October. Cold but beautiful and sunny. We were busy moving beds and things 'against' the crowd for the week-end, then out with Nance and Sally. The warning I wrote about [on 22 October] went off at 12.20 – only for a short time. I went to a glorious concert in the Sheldonian with Miss Walker from the Depôt. It was the London Philharmonic Orchestra conducted by Malcolm Sargent. I didn't notice the very expensive and uncomfortable seats, listening to Haydn, Smetana, Brahms, Beethoven and Tchaikovsky. It was beautiful, and I felt most exhilarated. A military Whist-Drive at night. Not bad, but my head ached.

---

13   Around 700 people were still being put up in this cinema's bleak conditions (RVS Archive & Heritage Collection, Oxford Narrative Report, October 1940). It had opened in 1930 in Botley Road as a skating rink and was later converted to cinema use, seating 1,900. 'Up to 5,000 [evacuees] passed through the building' and tons of straw had to be purchased to fill mattresses (Meyrick, *Oxfordshire Cinemas*, p. 106).
14   Robert got little pleasure from this event. 'I had the dreaded Service for the "Evacuees". It was pretty bad. They were few, scattered over the enormous place and quite apathetic. T.A.R. [Rushworth, the Church organist] made the piano ring, the boys sang and I shouted. Glad to get it over at 3.30.'
15   The *Oxford Times*, 25 October 1940, p. 4, admitted that 'To the serious playgoer the piece could only be regarded as of slight theatrical significance, but the players managed to get the utmost out of their story. … Altogether the show is a mirthful tonic that should prove acceptable in these anxious days.'

Friday, 25 October. A holiday for me and Robert. Lovely weather but very cold. The 10 o'clock bus to the Lambert Arms [in Aston Rowant], then a typical Chiltern walk – Ibstone Common, Stokenchurch, West Wycombe. The trees were glorious in wild flaming colours of every russet, gold, yellow and orange, and the hills were blue and clear-cut. Marvellous. A bus back after tea at the Apple Orchard at West Wycombe. Nita and Dick came till Sunday, and Norman had already arrived. Much chatter round the supper-table. A warning for an hour or so after supper, but no bombs.

Saturday, 26 October. Shopping with hordes of family. Muriel home for the week-end.[16] We had coffee with her. Nita and I, Vera and Muriel went to the Elsie Harris–Dudley Buttrum wedding in the afternoon [at St Michael at the North Gate]. More shopping, then New College with Nita which soothed my headache away altogether. Very, very cold. A quiet evening, in spite of a five-hour warning from 7.00 to 12.30. All was quiet except for the German 'planes overhead – a nasty noise.

Sunday, 27 October. Church in the sharp cold, with Nita, Nance and Muriel. Nita and Dick had to go after lunch. God keep them safe till next time. Christopher doesn't seem to mind much whether they come or go. Church again at night with Vera only. Very cold and dark coming home. Fancy another winter of black-out!

Monday, 28 October. Freezingly cold. Quite a spot of housework to do, as Doris is working alone now, and doing very well, with our help. I met Muriel at the Cadena for coffee. Then she had to go – a fortunately short visit, this time. Nancy, Sally and I went up to Christopher's school, Southfield, to see an exhibition in their gymnasium of war souvenirs. Very cold and rather dull. Nancy, Robert and I went to the Ritz to see *The Mortal Storm*, a very good film version of the novel.[17]

Tuesday, 29 October. Still frightfully cold. Shopping and coffee at Elliston's [in Magdalen Street] for a change from the Cadena. Nancy came to the Depôt

---

16 Muriel had been moving about a lot in 1940. On 2 May Madge reported that she was returning to her London school 'after her months of evacuation'; some four months later (25 August) she was going back to 'her evacuation village in Devon'.
17 The author of this 1937 novel was Phyllis Bottome. The cast in the 1940 film included James Stewart, Margaret Sullavan, Robert Young, Frank Morgan, and Robert Stack. Unusually, it was an anti-Nazi Hollywood film released well before the entry of the United States into the war.

with me in the afternoon. The women there are so optimistic[18] – even about the newest phase of the war, the invasion of Greece by Italy. What is the world coming to these days? Mother, Robert and I went to the Playhouse to see *Berkeley Square* [by John Balderston, 1926] which was most charmingly done, and very touching. There were bombs again whilst we were there, but no siren.[19]

Wednesday, 30 October. The coldest and darkest day we've had this autumn. Quite painful to be out shopping. We were glad of hot drinks, at 11. The Depôt again, then an evening spent in polishing the silver. Doris took the boys to the theatre.

Friday, 1 November. Busy about the house in the morning, and shopping for the great crowd. In the afternoon Ruth came for her birthday tea-party which we made quite festive with candles and crackers and her small heap of presents on her plate. She was quite overcome and was nearly in tears. It was lovely to see her enjoy it so. Poor dear – she must be so lonely, and she has such a hard life. Norman, Dick and Nita arrived in the evening, so we had a full life.

Saturday, 2 November. Lots of us – shopping, Cadena. Everyone except me went to the pictures in the afternoon. I stayed and read *Alice in Wonderland* to Roger and Sally. June came in for tea. I felt very put out, for some reason. I think it was a little matter of not being invited with the others to have a drink at the Lamb and Flag [in St Giles], but I shouldn't let these things worry me, as slights are never intended. I expect I was tired, but I recovered later and we all played cards till a late supper.

Sunday, 3 November. Pouring torrents of rain all day. I gave Church a miss, and walked with Nita, Dick and Christopher to Magdalen Deer Park, in the rain. It was beautiful even in these conditions, all softly coloured in the blue rainy light. Nita and Dick had to go after lunch again – back to the bombs and guns. I read quietly at home in the afternoon and didn't hear the bombs which fell at Kidlington. Church at night in a taxi and back the same way. Drenchingly wet, but it was a good thing for raids, as we heard that London had its first raid-less night for weeks.

---

18   She wrote in a similar vein the following Tuesday, 5 November: Nancy 'came with me to the Depôt in the afternoon, and we were soothed by the pleasant chatter of the pleasant women there'.
19   Madge later mentioned six air-raid warnings between 15 and 30 November, and there may well have been more.

Wednesday, 6 November. Such wet weather day after day. Shopping as usual with Nancy and Sally. Mother usually goes off by herself. I had a permanent wave at Elliston's in the afternoon. Quite comfortable and luxurious, and a nice man to do it, but it seems too loose a wave to last long.[20] Tony [Robert's brother Edward's son] came for a couple of nights. He is on leave, and is now a 2nd Lieutenant in the West Kents. He is fortunately much thinner, and not so ineffectual, but just the same Tony as he was at 10 years old. June came over for supper. Mother and Nancy at the Playhouse.

Thursday, 7 November. I had a headache, so stayed in bed till 11.00, when it lifted a little and I went out with mother. I had to go to the Depôt in the afternoon, headache or no, as I was in charge there. We are making children's nightdresses, which I loathe, but they look sweet when finished. A quiet evening. Tony went to the whist-drive with Robert.

Madge touched upon several issues during the weeks following November 1940. She sometimes felt exhausted (7 and 28 December). She was kept very busy, rushing about to get things done in a now much more populous household. 'This house is very like an hotel,' she said on 30 December. On Saturday, 11 January twelve people sat down to tea at her house. 'We certainly do work hard these days – maids-of-all-work' (7 December); Doris may have been Madge's only regular paid help for several months. Domestic tasks had become much more demanding. 'Just lately I feel my nerves getting frayed with so much shopping, talk, noise, crowds, and a longing for solitude,' she remarked on 6 February – and she was not given to inordinate complaining. 'This time of the year is always hard to endure, even without a war, so it is not surprising that nerves should be strung-up, I suppose, when there are war-time conditions to put up with, too. But I *will* try not to become bad-tempered and harassed.' Robert spent at least a few evenings fire-watching. While air-raid warnings were frequent for a while, they receded in January; and of course there was alarming news of the destruction inflicted on London in later 1940. On 31 December she referred to 'this horrible senseless war', and she sometimes had to

---

20   On Friday, 23 June 1939 she had a more satisfactory experience with a hairdresser. 'I had my hair "permed" in the afternoon so it should remain curly now in spite of the rain. It was a very comfortable process, machineless, the "Zotos" [brand] method.' Still, hair remained for her something of a trial (3 August 1939): 'I waste an awful lot of time trying to manage my hair, which is long, dry and very wild. It irks me!' On 18 August 1941 she tried something new: 'I went to the hairdressers all afternoon and came out with a new "up-swept" hair-do which I think rather formal, but anything for a change!' See also below, 25 July 1941 and 2 October 1943, p. 147 and 229n.

struggle to sustain hope. 'If I thought we couldn't win this ghastly war,' she wrote on 2 March 1941, 'I should feel inclined to throw all up – and sometimes one wonders how we *shall* win it.' On 8 January 1941 she had a personal encounter with wartime death: 'We went to tea with the Harbers at the Cadena, and afterwards to choose a silver salver for the Lady Chapel to the memory of their son, killed at Dunkirk, poor things.'[21]

Austerity and restrictions on supplies of provisions became prominent from the end of 1940. On 20 November 1940 Madge was finding that 'Many things are almost impossible to get now – cheese, chocolate, biscuits, onions, lemons – but none of these are really essential, except cheese, which one can get sometimes.'[22] A week later she declared shopping 'increasingly difficult now – almost every other thing one asks for is unobtainable'. Some days were 'almost meat-less' (1 January 1941). 'One feels triumphant', she said on 10 January, 'when one manages to get such ordinary things as marmalade, biscuits and oranges,' and the following day she was thrilled to come home with a 7 pound jar of marmalade. In the first week of March she reported shopping problems 'getting serious' (3 March) – shopping, she said three days later, was 'hellishly difficult' – vegetables replacing meat for the main course (also 6 March), and on 7 March 'an exhausting morning shopping, trying to find suitable things for supper etc., and having to stand in queues for it'. A few weeks earlier she had tried to be stoical (30 January): 'one is grateful for small mercies these days, such as no bombs, and warm fires, and the luxury of an egg'.

The winter of 1940–1 was not a pleasant one. For one thing, there was a lot of illness at 1 Wellington Place, including the common cold and flu. Madge's mother was intermittently sick. On 21 December young Christopher came down with chicken pox, which later spread to three other permanent or sometime residents – Sally, Roger, and most severely, their father Norman, who, on 6 January 1941, 'suddenly appeared at 11.30 full of chicken-pox'. 'Poor Norman has to be in bed for a week, also the children' (7 January); two days later 'The chicken-pox invalids slowly progressing, though Norman has got it very badly.' This mini-epidemic lasted about a month. Then, on 8 February, Madge took sick and was confined to her bed for most of the rest of that month, with flu and migraines and 'neuritis in the knee' (19 February) and perhaps more. She also mentioned 'sleepless nights' (18 February). 'I haven't been able to eat anything at all for a fortnight – just drinks' (21 February). She was sufficiently unwell that she wrote little in her diary until March. All this is a reminder of the prevalence and persistence of ill-health in the early 1940s.

---

21   Captain Harber's name was the first on the Church's Roll of Honour. He was the eldest son of Mr and Mrs Harber of Beverley, Cumnor Hill, 'who have been faithful friends of St Michael's since their coming to Oxford in 1938'. (*Parish Magazine* July 1940, p. 3.)
22   The references in this paragraph offer rare disclosures of the items commonly sought after during Madge's almost daily outings to shop.

Saturday, 8 March, 1941. Lots of us went off to our usual Cadena coffee interlude, then broke up into shopping parties. It is nice to have Nita here – she is refreshing and cool. She and Nance went to the pictures in the afternoon, mother and I took Sally to Worcester [College] Gardens, which is starred with early Spring flowers. After tea Robert, mother and I went to *The Great Profile* a crazy John Barrymore film. When I got back, Nita and Nance had been busy making my favourite jam tarts as a surprise for me, which pleased me greatly. I heard at last from John, who is now a Sergeant and expects to begin a new course, in Scotland, at any minute. Thank God – it isn't foreign service. Air alert at 9.00 but over quite early.

Sunday, 9 March. I still didn't go to Church because I always want to see as much of Nita as possible on her alternative week-ends, so we all went round the [University] Parks which I think are very dull but conveniently near. Very cold but many signs of Spring. Nita and Dick went back on the 2.15 bus as usual. London had had a bad air attack again after a lull of quite a time. A cosy afternoon with nice new film magazines. Vera in, in the evening.

Monday, 10 March. A quietish sort of day – still very cold. Shopping and the Cadena in the morning. Nance, Sally and I went up by bus to the tailor in South Parade [Summertown] to arrange about a tweed coat, whilst one can still *get* good tweeds. We walked back via Park Town, which is fascinating but rather sombre. The usual huge tea-party – nine cups to pour tea for, always, and to refill: Robert, Danna, mother, Nance, Maud,[23] Christopher, Roger, Sally and me. Was there ever a time when Robert and I were alone? I washed my unsatisfactory hair at night, and helped Robert in addressing envelopes.[24]

Tuesday, 11 March. Bitterly cold weather and snow on the ground when we woke. Shopping as usual. Nance and I got a bit of pork, which was a treat in these days. I meant to go to the Depôt this week, but it would be foolish to face that cold airy room whilst it is so freezing.[25] Robert and I went to the Playhouse at night and saw Bernard Shaw's *Mrs Warren's Profession* which was fun, but heartless. The dresses were 1902 which made it all the more

---

23 For Maud Pead, see below, pp. 149–50.
24 This is a fairly rare instance of Madge recording that she helped her husband with Church business – though not unprecedented: on Monday, 11 April 1938 'I addressed envelopes, all afternoon, invitations to the Easter Vestry meeting.'
25 Madge had spent little if any time at the Red Cross Depôt since December, when she had been working on a rush order for 1,000 jaw bandages (11 and 18 December).

amusing. There was an 'alert' from 8.15 to 12.30. These perfect moon-lit nights are the dangerous ones.

Wednesday, 12 March. It was so bleak and cold that we didn't go out at all till after tea, when we shopped a bit, and hurried in, breathless after facing the north wind. We had another alert at 8.30 – and later in the evening, quite loud bombs, two lots; so we brought the children down to the basement [their normal refuge from prospective bombs]. However, there were no more, and the 'all clear' went just at mid-night. The thunderous noise of bombs is quite alarming, even when some distance away. What can it be like at close quarters?

Thursday, 13 March. Shopping. In the afternoon – quite a treat – mother and I went to Vera's to tea. Lovely and warm and, as always, a glorious tea. Vera and I and the children went to the lecture in Church.[26] An alert at night again – a long one, till 3.30a.m.

Friday, 14 March. A most heavenly real Spring day, with warm sunshine and an entirely new feeling everywhere. I went out with Robert in the afternoon. A bus to Rose Hill, then a walk through to Cowley village – what enormous new estates there are everywhere. We looked into the new and beautiful St Luke's Church whilst we were up there. It is really lovely, spacious, and all of one style.[27] We had tea at the 'Moorish' then saw a dismal film at the Oxford, *The Long Voyage Home* [directed by John Ford and starring John Wayne and set at the beginning of the Second World War]. Another alert at night till 2.00a.m.

Saturday, 15 March. Not so warm, but still beautiful. Much shopping. In the afternoon I went out with Vera, first to Olive Whittaker's wedding [at St Michael at the North Gate] – rather a grand one – then a good shop-gaze, and tea at the Moorish. The Cadena just packed out. Harry, Diana and June had come over from Woodstock and took us, Robert and I, back to the Marlborough Arms where Harry and Diana are staying, for a lovely dinner. Harry was quite nice this time and I wasn't so afraid of him. Diana brought us home. What nice girls they all are. Two 'alerts'.

---

26 Robert identified this as 'the Third Lantern Lecture' ("the age of strife") – good congregation and collection'.
27 This Church, on Cowley Road, was opened in 1938 to serve the growing population in the area. It is now home to the Oxfordshire History Centre.

Sunday, 16 March. To Church with Nance and Diana, who came over from Woodstock in her little car. I hadn't been for weeks, and it is nearly mid-lent. Harry and the two girls came over to tea. There is always rather confusion when any Martins get together in any numbers, and Robert is almost gladder than anybody to get back to normal. Vera came in after tea and we listened in to *H.M.S. Pinafore* [by Gilbert and Sullivan, 1878], I'm afraid, instead of going to Church. Yet another alert, but a short one.

Monday, 17 March. After the lovely weather, it was very cold and dreary today, and no joy to be out. Mother and I went up to the Regal in the afternoon to see a pleasant little film, *Christmas in July* [a comedy directed by Preston Sturges and based on his 1931 play *A Cup of Coffee*] and had tea at the Fulbrook Farm Café [Cowley Road]. A quiet evening, with actually, I believe, no alert.

Tuesday, 18 March. Lovely sunshine, blue skies, warmth and every sign of Spring. I suppose we shopped, but really every morning is so like every other, that it is hard to remember them, even when writing the very next day. I had a very nice letter from John, who is in Prestwick again, doing hush-hush work as an air-gunner/wireless operator. I returned to the Depôt after a long interval. The same un-harassed atmosphere, and they welcomed me warmly back. Robert, Nance and I went to the Playhouse to see a very good little domestic comedy, *The Dominant Sex* [by Michael Egan, 1935]. Two alerts at night, the all clear at 5.40a.m.

Wednesday, 19 March. Rather tired after the broken night, and I had a bit of a head. Mother also very tired – she cannot sleep and is very nervous. Shopping – the Depôt in the afternoon, and a walk with Nance in the golden evening round the [Christ Church] Meadows and Merton Street. Oxford at its best, with quietness and mellow old buildings. Why should there be *war*? Two more alerts at night, but the 'all clear' about 12.00.

Thursday, 20 March. Peerless Spring weather – sharp frost in the morning, silvering the grass and trees, but growing warmer as the day goes on. Mother quiet and depressed – these broken nights distress her so. The usual morning. I was so sleepy that I went to bed in the afternoon. A military Whist-Drive for mid-Lent at night. Robert, mother, Vera and I made up a four. I think it cheered mother up.

Friday, 21 March. A holiday for Robert and me, and we actually got in a walk, as the morning lived up to its 'first day of Spring' name. Bus to Stokenchurch, then a beautiful walk through familiar and typical Chiltern country. Lunch at the 'Apple Orchard' at West Wycombe. It was a meatless day, but they did us very well. We continued our walk to High Wycombe for tea, and then the 4.30 bus back to Oxford. There had been a tremendous tea-party in our absence, including John Byron of the Playhouse Company[28] and Molly Heanley, a friend of Nancy's. Nita and Dick here.

Saturday, 22 March. A miserable dark and damp day. All the family here, but Norman returned in the afternoon. I went out with Nita, Roger and Sally to enquire about dancing lessons for Sally, but I hadn't much success this time. However, I shall persist in my enquiries, as she really has talent. We had coffee at Boswell House Cafeteria, then extravagantly bought records. I actually bought a Bing Crosby one. What would John say? Out again in the afternoon to buy grey material for a coat for mother – at least she bought it. We went to the Scala – lots of us, at night, to see one of the best *Hardy* films [*Out West with the Hardys*, starring Mickey Rooney and Judy Garland].

Sunday, 23 March. Still cold and damp, so we had a lazy morning listening to the new records. One is a lovely one – *The Bartered Bride* overture [by Bedrich Smetana]. Nita and Dick went back in the afternoon, and I wrote to Miss Cline in Philadelphia.[29] In the evening mother, Vera and I went to Church which was packed for the National Day of Prayer. No alerts for three days!

Monday, 24 March. Not so cold, but damp and disappointingly wintry. A nondescript sort of day on the whole with the usual sort of morning, except for a fleeting visit from Nancy's friend, Molly Heanley, on her way back to Ludlow. I can't remember a thing about the afternoon – and this is only Wednesday. Oh yes, I have got the day all wrong, as it wasn't very usual. Mother, Nancy and I had lunch as guests at a Ladies' Rotary Guest Lunch at which [historian] Lord Elton spoke, very well, on the new Social Order.[30]

---

28   John Byron (1912–1995), a former ballet dancer, acted with the Playhouse Company 1941–5, had a season at Stratford in 1944 and later appeared in films and on television. (*The Stage*, 7 December 1995, p. 36.)
29   'The talkative but friendly' Mrs and Miss Cline took tea with Madge on 18 July 1939. Miss Cline was one of Madge's regular correspondents, sending her film magazines monthly from Philadelphia (12 January 1942).
30   Lord Elton's speech covered a broad canvas. He emphasized the importance of 'spiritual regeneration', without which 'it was no use talking about new social orders ... To think in terms of the material always spelt doom.' (He regretted, though, the plight of the middle class, faced with very high taxes.) 'The new social order must be both Christian and democratic and there must be enough people in key positions who were Christians to dominate an

The lunch was at the Randolph. There was a Parish Church Council meeting at night at the 'Shamrock', after which Robert and I had a lovely dinner at the 'George'.

Tuesday, 25 March. Shopping, and a visit to Miss Barrett's to arrange about a blue frock for me and a grey 'swagger' coat for mother. The Depôt in the afternoon, and at night mother came with Robert and me to the Playhouse to see *The Letter* [by Somerset Maugham, 1927] which was quite well done.

Wednesday, 26 March. Spring-like again, and all the buds bursting out in hopeful green in North Oxford where we went up to Bateman's [tailor at 213 Banbury Road in Summertown] to see about a tweed coat for me. I am being very extravagant lately about clothes, but they say that soon it will be impossible to buy anything at a reasonable price, and then only very shoddy things, so I am trying to buy clothes and shoes whilst I can. Nance and I went to the Scala in the afternoon to see an old but good film, *Three Comrades* [1938]. There was an 'alert' whilst we were there – for two hours. A busy evening washing my hair and cleaning silver.

Thursday, 27 March. Shopping, the Depôt in the afternoon. Miss Walker, a cheerful Scottish lady, is going to enquire about rooms at St Ives for us after Easter. Nonsense, we shall not really ever go away – surely the Germans will be invading by then, or some new terrible phase of the war will have started. We are being warned again strongly to carry gas-masks. Well, we shall see. The lantern lecture at night – very good.

Friday, 28 March. A typical Spring day, sunny and then cloudy, but very hopeful. Christopher went home for the Easter holidays, very excited inwardly, though outwardly unmoved. The afternoon was pleasant, so Robert, mother, Nancy, Sally and I went on a bus to Sandford and walked back by the river to Iffley. Very soothing, except for the constant droning of our huge bombers, practising from Abingdon. Mother, Robert and I had a very restful tea at the Moorish, then went to the Oxford for two soothing and sweet films, *Laddie* [based on a novel by Gene Stratton-Porter] and *You*

---

influence on the new age.' He was not unaware of the impact of war on social relations. 'The new social order would be based, he hoped, on the new friendliness which the air war had brought about, and that new friendliness, working in with the new enforced simplicity, would shape a good deal of the social landscape of the new age.' Class divisions, then, were likely to erode. He also foresaw a post-war continuation of many of the welfare provisions of wartime, and citizens, he said, 'must also expect, in the future, a much more controlled society.' (*Oxford Times*, 28 March 1941, p. 7.)

Will Remember [with Robert Morley and Emlyn Williams]. Altogether a 'soothing' sort of day.

Saturday, 29 March. Icily cold again and sunless, but nothing can prevent Spring in the air. Everything seems more hopeful – even the war news. Jugo-Slavia defying Germany by refusing to sign a pact with them which would have made them just one other country under Hitler's ruling. The Allies doing well in their Eastern Campaigns. If only we can quell the U-boats which threaten our shipping so. However, we should gradually, with American help.[31] Vera and I had tea together at Kemp Hall [Cafeteria, Broad Street], and then I hurried home to get warm.

In early April 1941 the London Philharmonic Orchestra returned to Oxford for a week and Madge went to its performances on four consecutive days, 2 to 5 April. The music every evening was 'simply beautiful'; on the last day she and Nancy 'were spell-bound as usual. The theatre has been packed for it this week – very encouraging. How we loved it.'[32] During the war major orchestras toured widely, playing in many towns where classical music was not standard fare, and, as diarists and others in these places testified, they were almost always enthusiastically received.

These tours (some London theatres toured, too) were another way of helping to maintain morale in wartime – and this happened to be a time when the war news was discouraging. The news 'gets worse, and we have all our work cut out to be cheerful. Thank God for the solace of books and warm fires' (9 April). Madge was feeling (10 April) that, while matters seemed grim, 'we must hope that things will be better one day. We have had to bear such depressing news so often.'

Monday, 14 April, Easter Monday. A damp miserable morning and afternoon. We had intended taking the children to Woodstock but when we went to the bus station, we couldn't get on a bus – the crowds were awful – and so, failing also to get into the pictures, we took a bus, in the wind and rain, to

---

31   She was much less sanguine ten days later (8 April). 'The war-news, after being more encouraging of late, is now awful, with the Germans successfully invading Greece and Jugo-Slavia, and we being pushed out of Libya after struggling so hard there against the Italians. Oh dear. What *will* be the outcome of it all?'
32   By contrast, on 4 April Madge and Robert also went 'to an exhibition of modern art in the Ashmolean. We were not impressed.' Two days later a version of *Romeo and Juliet* on the wireless 'was beautiful'.

Thame. A bus ride is always nice, even in dismal weather, and the children loved it. We looked over the lovely Church and had a most sumptuous tea at the 'Spread Eagle', then home, in the surprisingly sunny blue evening. The country looked heavenly with its fresh green leaves and blue distances.

Tuesday, 15 April. Perfect Spring weather again which cheers one up a lot in spite of dismal war news. Shopping, and a long chat with Mrs Booth, I think – or was it Wednesday? All days are so similar. Mother and I and the children went to Vera's to tea and it was a great treat for everyone. Christopher returned from his holidays – in long trousers. It seems a pity that he has to go into them at only 12 years of age, but what he wants, he has. Still, he looks very nice in them. Vera and I went to the Easter Vestry meeting in Church – not many there. Afterwards Robert and I had a wartime dinner (two courses) at the George, as we usually do after long meetings. An alert again at night, and the 'all clear' at 4.20a.m.

Wednesday, 16 April. More lovely weather, but most of the day shopping, and in the afternoon I took Sally to Worcester and St John's [Colleges'] Gardens. She looks a real little school-girl now, with her hair tied back and a navy blazer over her kilt – very sweet. Robert and I to the Ritz, after having tea together at the Kemp Hall Cafeteria. A rather good Techni-coloured film, *North-West Mounted Police*, with nice Gary Cooper ambling through it. Another short alert at night, but over before midnight. London had its worst raid since war started, so Nancy didn't escape after all. How frightful is this war.

Thursday, 17 April. Wonderful weather, and the trees just bursting into bloom. Shopping and down to Miss Barrett's with mother to have her grey coat fitted. Doris took the children home to tea with her, very kindly, and mother and I went to the Electra to see *Strike up the Band* which I had missed when having 'flu. It was a grand picture, and Mickey Rooney and Judy Garland both were wonderful. We had a quiet tea at the Moorish, then home to read about poor London's terrible raid in the West-End. Vera came and stayed to supper and Nancy returned at 8.15, having had a lovely time in spite of last night's 'Blitz'.

Friday, 18 April. Very April-like, rainy dismal weather again. Shopping with Nance and mother and coffee. I wrote to John in the afternoon, then went up to Linton Road [North Oxford] for tea with Miss Walker who works at the Depôt with me, and who is awfully nice. She is an aunt of Dr Macbeth. Her sister and the doctor's mother there. They have a *most* lovely house, which she showed me, and a glorious garden all bursting into greenery. But what am *I* doing these days, associating with all these grand people? I feel very second-rate in comparison. The Depôt has led to all this. Anyway, it has taught me that the 'aristocracy' of Oxford is not to be feared and scorned – at least those members I meet at the Depôt aren't.[33] Mother, Vera, Robert and I went to the theatre to see *On Approval* [by Frederick Lonsdale, 1926] at the theatre. A *very* good amusing play with a most attractive cast of four – Barry K. Barnes, Diana Churchill, Roland Culver and Cathleen Nesbitt.

Saturday, 19 April. More gloom and cold in the morning, but brightening up later. Frenzied shopping and in the afternoon, packing, more shopping after tea. A bitter bitter disappointment in the evening in the shape of a wire from John saying that he has ten days' leave from *Monday* when we go away, to Friday, May 2nd when we come back. I almost cannot bear it, but must hope against hope that I see him soon. It is three months since I did, and may be another three till I do.

Sunday, 20 April. Church in the morning with Nancy. Rather an anti-climax sort of service after Easter Sunday. A real April day with soft blue skies emerging from showers. London had another bad raid last night, and they say now that she is at last beginning to show her scars – poor darling London. Rather a depressed sort of day, as strangely enough it always is, just before going away. It all seems so unreal somehow that we should be going to the sea in the midst of such horrors. Vera in at night. We didn't go to Church.

Monday, 21 April. I got up hopefully at 7.00, when John's train was expected to arrive, but alas he never came, and we had to leave for our holiday without seeing him at all. This is the second time we have been unlucky in both getting holidays at the same time. We said goodbye to the family – we shan't see mother for some time, as she goes to Yorkshire on Thursday for a long stay [with relatives]. We had an immensely long journey to St Ives, from 9.55a.m. to 9.30p.m., through Bristol where we saw quite a lot of raid damage even from the train, in the way of wrecked houses, and stores, and

---

33   This was not the first time that Madge had disclosed her status sensitivity. On 24 January 1941 she had tea with Mrs Maclagan and Mrs Dudden, whom 'I like very much', and went on to say that 'The Maclagans are leaving Oxford, so we shall say goodbye to this rather unreal acquaintance. She is very nice too, but they move in a different "strata" of society, so we couldn't ever really become friends.' Madge may also have felt occasional self-doubts about her cultural tastes, for on 21 January she had gone to see Ibsen's *Hedda Gabler*, 'which was very good, and not half as alarmingly high-brow as we feared'.

a church. At Plymouth only smashed windows were to be seen. The lovely country became rather grim after Truro, as we expected, but we needn't walk inland. Very thankful to reach St Ives at last in the dusk, and have a hot meal at the quite nice hotel.

The Martins stayed in St Ives for a week and a half, during which there were several alerts, followed by all-clears. Their travels included a visit to Penzance (23 April), which 'has been bombed, and we saw three wrecked buildings and many shattered windows'. Saturday, 26 April marked the beginning of St Ives' War Weapons Week: crowds 'swarmed the streets' and Madge and Robert watched 'the procession of soldiers, Home Guard etc. – quite thrilling'.[34] She, unfortunately, was suffering from a 'vile' headache during the next four days, which kept her in bed a lot. 'Sometimes, really, I feel very old and withered.' (She was 41.) Their last full day in Cornwall (Friday, 2 May) was more successful: good weather, an improving head. 'I shall hate to leave the sea beyond words, and the Spring walks with the celandines, violets and primroses in the hedges – and the freshness of the air. If only one could have one's real *fill* of all this, but there is never enough time.' The Martins returned home by train the following day, on 3 May, and passed through Plymouth, where 'The devastation since we came through before is terrible.' They were greeted at Oxford by loved ones, there was 'much chatter', and 'Robert plunged straight into work. Two alerts during the night.' Madge now found herself 'even busier about the house' for her mother was no longer there to help out (5 May).

Tuesday, 6 May. This day was noticeable for the fact that we managed to buy three pounds of *oranges*, the first seen for months. Great triumph and joy. Shopping in the morning, to the Depôt in the afternoon. Nance came too. We are in the drawing room now, and like it, I think even more, and the view is nearly as nice.[35] I had tea with Mrs Bleiben at Kemp Hall and we

---

34   War Weapons Weeks, which were almost universal in British towns, including Oxford, were designed to promote war savings. On Sunday, 1 December 1940 Madge had written about 'a great procession for War Weapons Week in St Giles in the afternoon … Soldiers, bands and guns – very exciting.' These fund-raising weeks were to become fixtures of wartime life.
35   Madge had worked at the Depôt on 'the last day before the Easter holidays', 2 April, and reported that 'We have to say goodbye to the lovely room at the top of the house at Worcester [College], where we have worked for 18 months. They are moving us down to the drawing room after the holiday. No more lovely view of the lake, and the tree-tops.'

enthusiastically talked over our respective holidays. She is always nice to be with. Robert, Vera and I to the Ritz after to see *Escape* [set in pre-war Nazi Germany] which was quite good in a ponderous way. Another alert at night.

Wednesday, 7 May. So dismally cold for May. A very trying morning shopping. The shops are really beginning to look depleted now. The Depôt in the afternoon with Nance. Letter writing at night. An alert I think, as usual.

Thursday, 8 May. This cold weather just goes on and on. Shopping – Depôt in the afternoon. Norman came in the evening, and he and Nance went to the pictures whilst I stayed and bathed the children. Another alert.

Friday, 9 May. The air is so clear and fresh now in the mornings. We have 'double summer time' so that it is two hours earlier than it says by the clock. It seems the best time of the day now, with all the sunshine.[36] Nance, Norman, Robert and I had a nice walk in the morning. We took the bus to Wheatley, and walked all the way home, over Shotover Hill, where the distances and light were beautiful, and then old Headington and Mesopotamia, a pleasant seven mile amble. Robert and I went to see two good films at the Scala in the afternoon,[37] and in the evening went to the Snack Bar for supper, and on to the theatre to see our beloved Jack Buchanan [Scottish actor and producer, b. 1890] in a very amusing comedy thriller, *The Body Was Well Nourished* [by Frank Launder]. He is as charming and gay as ever he was. Wonderful!

Saturday, 10 May. The weather gradually improving, getting a wee bit sunnier and warmer. Lots of shopping – problem shopping! In the afternoon we took Sally and Roger and two little friends, Jean and Michael [Warland], Vera's cousin's children, who live in Pusey Street, to the Scouts' Rally and Display on the Rugger Ground. There were hundreds of Scouts, Cubs, Sea Scouts, etc. there, Christopher amongst them. The new Chief Scout, Lord Somers [since January 1941], reviewed them and spoke. It was quite a good

---

36 Double Summer Time was implemented in 1941–5, starting in April and ending in August. Clocks were put two hours ahead of GMT, thereby giving less sunlight in the very early morning when most adults were still asleep and more in the evening when most people were likely still to be active. The objective was to reduce the need for artificial light and the energy required to produce it by adjusting clock time to conform better to the rhythms of normal working days. With the clock now two hours ahead of standard time, Madge, not an early riser, could more readily enjoy a day's full sunshine.
37 *The Ship Around the Corner*, with Margaret Sullavan and James Stewart, and *Inspector Hornleigh on Holiday*, with Gordon Harker and Alistair Sim.

show.[38] We had the two little friends to tea after. A quiet evening here, but London had a big raid, and we brought down 33 enemy planes – the record for one night so far.

Sunday, 11 May. Much warmer at last. Nance and I did a lot of mending in the morning, and a lazy afternoon reading the belated Sunday papers which were very late in coming down after yesterday's big raid.[39] To Church in the evening with Vera, but it always takes me some time to get 'au fait' with Church matters after a holiday, and the services, especially then, seem to mean very little to me. Robert and I both slept through an alert but awoke for the 'all clear' at 4.30a.m. This is the first siren which hasn't awakened me, except for one on our first night in St Ives.

---

38   It was described in glowing detail in the *Oxford Mail*, 14 May 1941, p. 4.
39   As things turned out, this was to be the last major air raid on London until 1944. Germany redirected the bulk of its armed forces for war to the East against the Soviet Union.

5

Matters New, Matters Old

May 1941–September 1941

Thursday, 22 May, Ascension Day. The beating of the bounds after the Holy Communion which Nita and I attended. Roger, Dick, Nancy, Nita and I followed round the usual familiar boundary of St Michael's parish,[1] but I had to leave the procession halfway through to go to the dentist. I was going round dutifully to the Depôt after lunch but Nita and Dick seized me on the way and lured me off to the pictures instead, which was naughty but nice. The picture very good, *Arise, My Love* [a romantic comedy starring Claudette Colbert and Ray Milland]. A quiet evening except for sounds of turmoil above when Christopher got into hot water and was chastised by his parents!

Friday, 23 May. In spite of rather gloomy looking weather, Nita, Dick, Kit, Robert and I had a very good excursion, and were rewarded by the day turning out quite fine later. Bus to Boars Hill, and down through the pretty Sunningwell to Abingdon for lunch. We were very lucky to see the King and Queen and the princesses driving through on their way to visit an aerodrome. The King was in Air-Force uniform, and the Queen looked

---

1 The annual custom of beating the bounds was celebrated by Robert in his 'Vicar's Letter' in the June issue of the *Parish Magazine* (p. 1). 'I am happy that we are even able to "beat the bounds" of the Parish and maintain the traditional meal of fellowship that concludes this age-old custom by which each year we record once more the little plot of England which is our own St Michael's responsibility to God. May next Ascensiontide see us "beating the bounds" in Peace, or at least still strong in Liberty, Fellowship and Love.' Details concerning the procession are found in his 1961 pamphlet, *Beating the Bounds of the Parish of St Michael at the North Gate, Oxford* (held in the OHC). See also below, 14 May 1942, pp. 171–2. Robert had a high regard for ceremony and longstanding traditions. 'Is it the English way?' was an important question to him on church matters. (Martin, *Church and Parish of St Michael at the Northgate*, pp. 158–9.)

beautiful in similar blue, and the princesses too. It was a real thrill.[2] A very expensive and rather dull lunch at the Queen's Hotel, then we continued our walk, along the river and on the outskirts of Nuneham Park, which was perfectly lovely country – lakes of misty blue-bells in the fresh green woods. A small dog attached herself to us and followed us for miles, and we had to leave her at a police-house on our way back, on the London Road, where we luckily caught a bus. Just time to wash and change and have a snack before going with Dick and Nita to Milham Ford School to see the girls do *The Gondoliers* [by Gilbert and Sullivan, 1889]. It was quite a good performance in its way, but the school alone was worth the journey out. It is the best I have yet seen – simply superb, very modern and huge and beautifully designed [opened in 1939, between Harberton Mead and Marston Road].[3] Norman had arrived for his 33rd birthday. An alert at night.

Saturday, 24 May. Cold and wet and utterly foul all day. Out with Dick and Nita to the Cadena in the morning. Joy Nicholls [wife of 'Nick'] suddenly appeared out of the blue in the afternoon. Fancy coming home from peaceful Nigeria to war-ridden England! But she seems glad to be here in spite of London's blitzes which greeted her.[4] Norman, Nance, Robert and I went to the Playhouse at 5.30 to see Eden Philpotts' *The Runaways* [1928]. Pleasantly unexciting.

Sunday, 25 May. Still terribly cold and wet. When are we to get any warm weather. I went alone to Church but didn't seem to enjoy it. Everyone very down-cast at the news of the sinking of the world's largest battle-ship, *HMS Hood*, with all her crew. This war is dreadful, and is going so well for the

---

2   This Bomber Command Aerodrome was not identified in the press, which was the usual practice. However, 'News of the Royal visit had circulated through the towns adjoining the station and the roads and streets were thronged with people who gave the King and Queen a hearty reception.' (*Oxford Mail*, 24 May 1941, p. 4.) The Court Circular for 23 May stated only that 'The King and Queen, attended by Lady Hyde and Wing Commander Edward Fielden, visited Royal Air Force Aerodromes of the Bomber Command today.' (*The Times*, 24 May 1941, p. 6.)
3   Images of these fine buildings may be found at www.headington.org.uk/history/schools/milham_ford.pdf From 2004 the buildings were occupied by the School of Health Care of Oxford Brookes University.
4   Her estranged husband appeared later and more prominently in the Martins' lives: see below, 26–29 May, 2–4 July, and 7 August 1942, pp. 174–5, 181–3, 188.

powerful Germans so far.[5] A lazy afternoon, all sitting round the fire and getting stupid. Nita and Dick went back after tea, taking both kittens with them. We shall miss the darlings. To Church with Vera in the evening.

Monday, 26 May. This month is more like April than May, with its fitful showers and bursts of sunshine. I did a bit of spring-cleaning in the morning – hard and dirty work. Letter-writing in the afternoon, and at 4.30 I went with the children and Norman and Nance to Rosaire's Circus at Grandpont. It was a very good one, and the atmosphere was just right – the 'big top', ponies, spangles, trapeze acts, lions and a very pukka [i.e., excellent, authentic] Ring Master. There were some wonderfully clever performances and we all enjoyed it enormously.[6]

Tuesday, 27 May. In spite of stormy-looking skies, we decided to go out walking, so with rain-coats and sandwiches we set off. Nance came too. The familiar 10 o'clock bus to Tetsworth, and a pleasant though showery walk across very wet fields to Pyrton, where we had lunch in a small Inn. We heard there, over the wireless, the news that the *Bismarck*, the German battleship which sunk the *Hood*, has been sunk herself. We could not help rejoicing over this bit of grim retribution. We went on to Watlington where the rain became heavy, so after waiting an hour in this dismal place, looking at the undistinguished Church, we gladly took the bus back to Oxford to hot baths for the feet and a wash. Robert and I went to the George for dinner, and then to the Playhouse to see a good 'thriller', *The Fourth Wall* [1928, by A.A. Milne].

Wednesday, 28 May. A bit better, as to weather, but, like last year at this time, when we were evacuating our soldiers from Dunkirk, the news is depressing. It looks as if there will be yet *another* evacuation – of Crete, this time. I am tired of reading the story of successful withdrawals. Shopping, then the Depôt. Nance and I went to *The Mikado* at night – just the same as ever. These operas will, I am sure, endure forever, permanent reminders of a happier age. A packed theatre of Gilbert and Sullivan enthusiasts.

---

5   Five days before she had noted that 'The Germans are now invading Crete by para-chute and air-troops. There are great battles going on. I wonder if, as usual, they will succeed by sheer numbers. I expect so – they seem absolutely unbeatable, so far.'
6   This circus – advertised as Jean's Regal Circus – was billed as 'the greatest aggregation of Anglo-American circus talent ever seen in this city'. It was held in Tuckwell's Field, White House Road, off Abingdon Road. (*Oxford Times*, 23 May 1941, p. 7.)

These were rather gloomy days. On 30 May 'Nancy and I felt quite fed up with the war, shopping, people, food – everything. We did a bit of spring-cleaning in the afternoon, of my bedroom, and as usual the hard work cheered us up a wee bit.' 'We think that physical labour is most soothing' (2 June). Alerts were being sounded fairly regularly around midnight (3 June), and the weather was frequently disappointing. As for Whit Sunday, 1 June, it 'always fails to thrill though it is important I suppose'.

Saturday, 7 June. For once a lovely warm summer morning – a pleasure to be out in short-sleeved frock, shopping, and even, later, basking in the garden. It was still so nice in the afternoon that we took the children to Boars Hill, getting off at Sunningwell Turn and walking up through buttercup fields to the hill, where the children played about on Foxcombe Hill Common. Marvellous up there, with the distant blue hills to gaze at. We had a grand tea at the funny little Ebor Café which is run by a St Michael's admirer. Lovely hot scones and cakes. We just got home in time to dodge a thunderstorm. Change. Then Robert took us out to dinner at the George for Nancy's birthday treat tomorrow. We had a lovely, though very expensive, meal. Their menu is pathetically depleted, but we enjoyed it very much and had glasses of sherry.

Sunday, 8 June. The thunderstorm upset the weather again and most of the day was stormy and showery. Nancy's birthday. She got money from almost everyone, as now that we have to give coupons for clothes, no-one can give them as presents. To Church with her in the morning and a lazy afternoon. The sun came out in the evening, and Vera called, so we funked Church and went for a walk over the [University] Parks, which looked lovely with the lush green grass, and the hawthorn hedges in bloom.

Monday, 9 June. I never remember such a dreary summer in all my life. We should be basking in the garden and on the river now, not watching the rain pour down ceaselessly all day. Nance and I were hard at work all day spring-cleaning the drawing room, and were filthy and exhausted by 3.45 when we fell into baths. It all looks and smells lovely though. We went, as a relaxation, to see *Kipps* at the Super [adaptation of the H.G. Wells novel]. It was a beautiful film and Michael Redgrave was really wonderful as Kipps – we 'fell for him'. So nice to see such a very tip-top picture – they come so rarely.

The following afternoon she started spring-cleaning Robert's study, 'a great task', and the day after she went with Nancy and Norman to see the Anglo-Polish Ballet at the New Theatre. On Thursday, 12 June there was a whist-drive in the evening – 'so dull playing cards in daylight'.

Friday, 13 June. A holiday for Robert, so we went off with sandwiches. A very early start, 9.30 bus to Moulsford. We were taken across the river there by a kind man in a punt, as the ferry wasn't working. Robert left his map behind in the punt, so we had to do the rest of the walk 'blind'. The weather was dull at first, and the country too, but both improved, and both became lovely. We walked to Bix through most beautiful country, wooded and hilly, with rhododendron bushes flaming in the woods, and the hills blue in the distance. It was a long hot walk and we were very tired when we reached Bix. We sat on the grass there till a Henley bus picked us up, to take us to a glorious tea there, and then a comfortable return journey to Oxford. Nita and Richard came for the week-end. The usual long chat after supper. An alert at night.

Saturday, 14 June. Cold as ever. Shopping, and coffee at Kemp Hall with the family and a friend of Nita's and Anne's, Marian Slocombe, who is an amusing, large person, in Oxford to make enquiries about St Edward's School [boarding school on the Woodstock Road] for her equally large son. Nita, Vera and I went again to see *Kipps* in the afternoon. A quiet evening.

Sunday, 15 June. At last the weather changed and became hot and sunny. Nita, Nance and I took Sally over the [University] Parks and back through Marston in the morning. Then I dressed up in my new blue frock and flowery hat and went to Max Russell's wedding at 1.30. Robert and I went on to the reception which was most sumptuous and as good as pre-war. It really was very fine, and we enjoyed it.[7] Bob Russell was very easy to talk to

---

7   Robert officiated at the wedding. The Russell family were parishioners, former tenants of St Michael's Vicarage, Botley Road, and currently living at 6, Ship Street. Max, a clerk, was the assistant organist at St Michael's Church. His mother had proposed the formation of the Junior Guild in the 1920s and was in charge of advertisements for the *Parish Magazine*. His father, Harry Russell, was manciple or butler at Lincoln College. (*Parish Magazine*, July 1941, p. 13; Martin, *Church and Parish of St Michael at the Northgate*, p. 144; *Oxford Times*, 15 May

– next to me. Sleepy after unaccustomed wine and rich foods, but woke up in time to go to Evensong with Vera.

Monday, 16 June. Wonderfully hot – really summer at last. We spent most of the day in the garden, browning in the sun, and nearly complaining of the *heat* for a change. So strange to see the blue skies and to feel the sun on our faces.

Tuesday, 17 June. How lovely to have it really hot – we have waited so long for it. It is a pleasure to move lazily about in the heat, with no stockings and a warmth seeping into one's soul. Shopping, and basking in the garden till I had to go to the dentist to have a tooth filled. I had forgotten how unpleasant this can be.[8] We went out to supper and to the Playhouse at night, but were not too impressed by the play which, though amusing enough, was not worthy of their talents – *Spring Tide*.[9] Home in the sunset – at 10.00p.m!

Wednesday, 18 June. Still hot and lovely. Shopping – and hunting round for presents for Sally's birthday. The toy-shops are sadly depleted. We got her a garden-chair of her *own*, and a book. I succumbed to the temptation to cut the Depôt, and sat and baked in the garden. Then up to tea with the Grays, which is always nice. They are so genuine, especially Mrs Gray, and even in war-time gave us their usual splendid tea. Such a hot day – how nice to record it after so much beastliness. I wish we could get some good war-news to match.

Thursday, 19 June. Warmer than ever, and every bit of house-work an effort, but not a grumble! Shopping. Norman here just in time for Sally's birthday. I went to the Depôt, then Robert and I gave the Harbers tea at the Moorish. We just cannot have people here now. I was nurse-maid to the children whilst Norman and Nance went out. I was very indulgent, letting them play with the hose in the garden and have leisurely baths etc. They are sweet sometimes.

Friday, 20 June. Sally's 5th birthday – she is a little girl now, no longer a baby. She had lots of presents. We gave her a book, and a garden-chair for

---

1953, p. 14.) We are grateful to Barbara Tearle and Lindsay McCormack, Lincoln College Archivist, for research on this family.
8   'I had a tooth stopped at 4.30,' she wrote the following Monday, 23 June. 'Not so bad as I feared.'
9   This comedy was by George Billam and J.B. Priestley. The *Oxford Times*, 20 June 1941, p. 7, judged it a 'light farce and provides quite good entertainment for those who are not too exacting'.

herself – a miniature one. Robert and I took our holiday. It was a very hot and perfect day. A train to Reading – how it reminded us of happy trips up to London. I simply daren't go now to see the damage to our beloved places, but I think I must sometime. We walked along the towing-path from Reading to Sonning. It was rather hot and dull at first, but became beautiful near perfect little Sonning. We had a very expensive, but absolutely pre-war in its luxury, lunch at the 'White Hart' which was full of rich refugees from London (I suppose). The whole village was a bower of roses and June flowers, cascading over the beautiful houses. A real picture of England at her best. We walked on to Henley through most lovely wooded and down-land country. A welcome tea before catching the 4.15 back to Oxford. Very very hot and wonderful. We all went to the 'Friends of the OUDS' production of *Much Ado About Nothing* in New College Gardens. Anne Buttrum (née Elsie Harris) played Beatrice quite well.[10] A perfect evening for it – and light right up to midnight.

Saturday, 21 June. Even hotter today. We were out buying cool things to eat – salads – it is awful having no fruit to finish with. Coffee with Susie [sister of John] who is very thin but looks better, I think. The whole afternoon in the garden, but we just had to come in and have cool baths – it was too much. The children in bathing costumes. Too hot to sleep really, but we adore it. We have so little real warmth in England. We heard that poor Jamie Reid died today. Poor Celia!

While Madge's existence might seem to have permitted lots of leisure, this was not the way she necessarily saw things. 'Life is one long rush,' she wrote on Monday, 23 June, 'and it always seems to be bed-time before one has done anything.' The following day was made up of (in chronological order), spring-cleaning, shopping, work at the Depôt, tea with the Bleibens in the [Oxford] Union Gardens ('they had only hot buttered toast to offer us in the heat'), dinner with Robert at the Moorish, and a play, *Dear Brutus* by J.M. Barrie (1917), starring John Gielgud, in the evening. On Wednesday she and Nancy went to Sally's school, 'where there was a medical examination – the babies are sweet'; and that afternoon at the Depôt 'I took snaps of some of our room (the bandaging) – I hope they come out. Nance took me to see *Back Street*, a nice sentimental film with Charles Boyer, the romantic, and homely Margaret Sullavan.' On a separate page, and rather casually, she recorded, without

---

10 The *Oxford Times*, 27 June 1941, p. 5 thought she acted the part of Beatrice 'with spirit and her entrances and exits were striking'. (Was this damning with faint praise?)

elaboration, an event of some importance: 'The Germans attacking Russia now – and after that – Invasion for us?' On Sunday, 29 June she attended Church with her sisters: 'It is a lovely feeling, sometimes to be all three together like that.'

Monday, 30 June. Back to great heat again. I spent an exhausting morning scrubbing the bed-room carpet, then relaxed in the garden for the afternoon till Robert took Nancy and me out to a luxurious tea at Fullers, where we had delicious fruit sundaes, then on to the Bernard Gotch exhibition in Peckwater Quad [Christ Church]. There were some lovely things, and I long to have one [see above, 19 June 1940, p. 88]. I washed my hair at night. Great excitement next door over the wedding [see 2 July].

Tuesday, 1 July. Still very hot. It is lovely to have day after day of it. Shopping in the morning, the Depôt in the afternoon – strawberries for tea! Robert and I had dinner at the Moorish in the evening, then met Nance at the Playhouse to see *The Lilies of the Field* [a comedy by John Hastings Turner, 1923], which was great fun.

Wednesday, 2 July. I think the hottest day this year. Great excitement next door. Natalia's wedding day, and hosts of people rushing up and down the Drive all day with flowers and gifts. She was married to a handsome Naval lieutenant, first at a Registry Office, then by Robert at 4.00 in the afternoon in New College Chapel. We all went, of course. A marvellous wedding with crowds of guests. Natalia radiant in white tulle. The reception in New College Cloisters – very crowded and hot, and smart.[11] Robert and I and Vera went to the theatre to see *The Dancing Years* [by Ivor Novello] at night. We had seen it before, at Drury Lane, but adored it again. Lovely music and sentimental story, and a fine cast with all the London stars, including Ivor Novello. We loved it all.

Thursday, 3 July. Well, the weather is making up for lost time – day after day of lovely sunshine and heat. I had a bit of a head after yesterday's lovely day, but most of the day I rested in the garden, and by the evening it had nearly gone.

Friday, 4 July. This is the anniversary of the day that I said 'yes' when my darling asked me to marry him [in 1917]. How lucky was that day for me.

---

11 Senorita Natalia Jimenez was married to Mr John Stucley, the son of a baronet. Their wedding photograph, from the *Oxford Mail*, 3 July 1941, p. 3, was pasted in Madge's diary.

It was too hot for walking, so Robert went up to town to see the damage, and I had a quiet day in the garden, then went to the pictures with Nance after tea to see quite a pleasant film, *The Tree of Liberty* [starring Cary Grant and based on the 1939 novel with the same title by Elizabeth Page]. Robert came back, astonished to find so much of London untouched by bombs, except round St Paul's, so I must go sometime. He brought me home some cami-knickers for which he had sacrificed 3 of his own coupons – bless him. Ruth was in to supper. I'm so glad that she still comes. An 'alert' at 3.15a.m., the first for three weeks.

Saturday, 5 July. The fine weather spell now three weeks long. It is so lovely to wake with the sunshine glittering on the leaves of the apple tree and the sky a cloudless blue. It makes everything seem like a holiday, in spite of the war. We spent most of the day, when our shopping was done, in the garden. Norman came until Tuesday. Nance, Sally and I went round to old Mrs Busby's, just before tea. I had just written to John, when I heard from him by wire that he expects to be home tomorrow. Well, well. It is six months exactly since our last meeting. I wonder if he is changed.

Sunday, 6 July. Broilingly hot. I stayed at home all day in case John arrived, as he did when we were about to start supper. The Air-Force has not changed him at all except to fatten him out a bit and roughen slightly his appearance. He stayed to supper, and for his usual chat, which we were able to continue as though only six hours had elapsed since his last visit, not six months. He is just the same faithful, reliable, boyish dear Ginger of old, and nothing can alter our steadfast and wonderful friendship. It is good but rather unsettling to see him again.

Monday, 7 July. Extremely hot still. Wonderful days full of sunshine, and moonlight nights, warm and lovely. Danna's 82nd birthday.[12] She is getting frail now, but enjoyed her favourite cherry pie for her birthday lunch – cherries are, unfortunately, 3s 6d a pound! Nance and Norman on the river all day till 7.00. John came for the afternoon and stayed for tea after accompanying me to fetch Sally from school. I must not get *sad* when he goes, as I am really quite happy and peaceful in a negative way, as regards him, when

---

12 Although Danna, Robert's mother, is mentioned only intermittently in Madge's diary from 1938 to 1941, she was in fact by now a permanent resident at 1 Wellington Place. When the September 1939 Register was compiled, the Martin residence in Bedford at 50 Adelaide Square was unoccupied. Madge's mother moved about, sometimes staying in Oxford, at other times elsewhere, including Yorkshire, where her sisters lived, and London.

he is away – happier really, as dear though he is, he unsettles me and I feel vaguely depressed when he isn't here, whereas his letters content me, in his long absences – so I must remember [this] when his fourteen days' leave are ended. There was a lecture on fire-fighting in the evening at [nearby] Regent's [Park] College. We went, and the two boys who were thrilled.

Tuesday, 8 July. I must mention the weather, as it makes such cheerful reading, all this sunshine and warmth, in its third unbroken week. John came at 11.00 for a long talk. Even though I don't understand all he talks about – wireless, gunnery, machines – I like to listen, and he is so keen. How different from his boredom at the Church Army Press [where, pre-war, he was assistant manager]. The Depôt in the afternoon after a final visit to the dentist. We spent a lot of time in the evening filling in our new ration books – oh so complicated. Norman returned to London. Another alert at 2.00a.m. till 4.10a.m.

Wednesday, 9 July. Still hot and lovely. A pleasure to wake up each morning. There is nothing better for the morale than a long stretch of fine weather. Shopping, and in the afternoon John came for a nice chat, then walked up with me to Mrs Eliot's in the Banbury Road, where I met Robert for tea. Mrs Eliot is very nice indeed and we enjoyed it. Home to supper and then to the Playhouse to see *Murder on the Second Floor* [by Frank Vosper, 1929] which they did very well indeed.

Thursday, 10 July. In spite of the continuing fine weather, I felt rather bad-tempered in the morning, perhaps at the prospect of an impending visit from Harry [Robert's brother], always a terrifying prospect for me. John looked in before lunch, which soothed me down, as also did the Depôt in the afternoon. He also came in at night for a lovely long heart-to-heart talk. Very hot at night again.

Friday, 11 July. Hotter than ever I think. Shopping with Nance and a strawberry ice for elevenses – quite a good one, too, for war-time. Robert and I saw Nance off with the children for her stay in town with Nita. It will be quiet whilst they are gone. Robert actually went bathing at Parson's Pleasure[13] after, and I sat in the garden. Mrs Parker came and chatted a bit. Robert and I went to the pictures after tea. Then John came in for quite a

---

13 Parson's Pleasure was in the University Parks at the south-east corner. It was a secluded area for men-only nude bathing on the River Cherwell.

traditional Friday evening visit. There was a terrific thunderstorm from 5.30 to 7.30, but we missed the worst of it – in the pictures.

Saturday, 12 July. The heat was overpowering today. John came in to mend the washer on the hose in the garden. He always does things thoroughly. I sat adding more brown to my legs in the afternoon. Harry and June arrived for tea, and we later went over to Woodstock and gave them dinner at the Bear, after having cock-tails in her funny old barn where she lives by herself. We had had a heavy thunderstorm after tea and I got a headache, but enjoyed my potent cock-tail and dinner. The 9.20 bus home.

Sunday, 13 July. Cooler and cloudier after the thunder. I went to Church in the morning. It seemed quite natural to see John's ginger head in the choir and to hear his flute-like alto, also to have him round after the service in his usual gloomy mood. He hasn't changed really and never will. We had another storm in the afternoon which eventually cleared the air. Church again at night with Vera and John in to supper and more cheerful talk than in the morning.

Monday, 14 July. I felt rather ill all day and somewhat depressed, partly because the hot sunny weather I love has gone at last. The rain, one hears, was much wanted, but I love the sun, especially when it is blazingly hot. John came in the afternoon but Christopher monopolized most of his time. Miss Walker, the canny and kind, came to tea and seemed to enjoy herself. She is very entertaining. Kenneth Jenkins [former curate at St Michael's] and his nice wife followed. He is going East soon. Robert and I both exhausted by party manners after that. We rearranged his study which has a new soft green carpet.

Tuesday, 15 July. St Swithin's Day, and torrents of rain most of the day![14] I know that rain is needed, but I do miss my lovely hot sunshine. These stormy grey skies are awful. Shopping. John in before – and after – lunch. It is rather alarming how soon the old Oxford influence creeps over him. I am almost, in fact, quite as happy in a placid way when he isn't here. It unsettles me, but at the same time I can't have *enough* of his company. He can be dull – and then the nicest and most understanding of friends, very tantalizing! Robert and I had a nice dinner at the George, then went to the Playhouse to see *The Wind and the Rain* [by New Zealander, Merton Hodge, 1934] which

---

14   See note to 15 July 1940, p. 95.

I liked much more than the first time. Strangely enough, John and his party (sister, cousin, aunt) had the adjoining seats – very nice.

Wednesday, 16 July. More dismal weather and cold, too. I was up early to see Christopher off to school. Shopping, and busy about the house in the morning. John in for the afternoon. The waiting room has a dour feeling, but we manage to triumph over it sometimes if not always. Only two more days left now. God keep him safe and happy. Mrs Booth to tea – oh so talkative but friendly. We took Vera out to the Snack-Bar to supper, then to see *The Philadelphia Story* at the Ritz. Sophisticated, amusing and slightly mad, but well done.[15]

Thursday, 17 July. Our wedding anniversary, and we spent it by going up to town. I haven't been since last August and had not wanted to, as I thought that the sight of my beloved London devastated by bombs would depress me too much, but I was wrong. We went up on the 8.55 and got in at 10.30. We had a good look from the bus, and by walking round our familiar haunts, at the many horrid gaps and ruins, but it was all so much less knocked about than I feared, and gave me the impression of cheerful unchangeableness. I felt sad and angry at the scars, but not horrified as I had feared.[16] We did some shopping, and went to the Royal Academy, and after trying seven different places for lunch (such crowds there were)[17] we finally had it at a new place to us, 'A la Broche' in Jermyn Street. It was a very good and cheerful place with excellent food. We went on to the Odeon to see Leslie Howard's new film, *Pimpernel Smith*, which was very good indeed. Back to Oxford on the 6.05 after a surprisingly happy day in spite of our dear London's scars and general shabbiness. John in for a rancorous talk about the upper and lower classes, which always turns me into a great defender of the aristocracy as against his virtuous poor.

---

15 The cast of this highly successful film included Gary Grant, Katharine Hepburn, and James Stewart, who won an Academy Award for his performance.
16 Madge was more impressed by the damage in London a few weeks later (7 August): 'Poor Park Lane – all its lovely houses wrecked – heart-breaking – and chunks of Bond Street missing, windows out, spattered shrapnel marks and bomb splinters everywhere. Still London carries on cheerfully, just the same.' Later still, on 22 August, she, Muriel, and Vera rode 'on top of a bus to St Paul's, to see for ourselves the damage to the City by bombs. It is an indescribable scene – the Cathedral standing, enormous and serene and apparently unhurt (though we know it has two great bomb-holes) amidst scenes of utter desolation; great areas of offices, shops and factories either completely demolished or else shells only. ... I'm glad I've seen this most awe-inspiring sight.'
17 On 7 August in London there were 'great queues everywhere for food, even at 11.30a.m.'

Friday, 18 July. St Swithin's Day has a lot to answer for! Rain for most of the day. Dreary shopping in the morning and a pleasanter visit from John, though his leave is now beginning to wear thin at the edges, and I shall definitely be relieved when he goes, much as I look forward to seeing him again. But I feel the old horrible restlessness creep over me and I am still the same fool about him in the end, so I almost look forward to my placid existence when only his letters come. Strange![18] Nita and Richard came in the evening for a fortnight. I am so glad they will be here to take me right out of prison (as this John-ish life really is).

Saturday, 19 July. The day turned from sunshine and blue skies to torrents of rain again. John in, in the morning. He goes tomorrow morning early and proposes coming in to see me at a god-less hour. It seems that he makes a great convenience of me. How *sad* and foolish things are, and how much I expect; *too* much, of him, and always have. He is only a most ordinary individual, my John and a very priggish one, but with all his faults ––.

Sunday, 20 July. For the very first time since knowing John, nearly 18 years in all, I was glad to see him go. He only barely looked in on his way to the station, and I walked with him a little way, and broke my resolve, I am ashamed to say, of 'no recriminations', but he has treated his old friend in the same casual way which has always marred our acquaintance from time to time. I didn't mean to complain but he certainly has made a convenience of me, and his queer times of coming here, this leave, and I as usual have been foolish enough to accommodate him. Poor boy – he means well, but I really shouldn't expect so much of him. Our parting was almost acrimonious, alas, and I feel somewhat guilty, as his job is hazardous and if anything happens to him of whom I am rashly fond, I shall wish with all my heart that I had spoiled him, whatever the cost, to the last minute. So God preserve him.

Monday, 21 July. The weather beginning to cheer up again. It is nice having Nita and Dick here – just at the right time too. I shopped with them, and wrote letters in the afternoon. Then Robert and I went to see a really beautiful

---

18 'I really am much happier with John away,' she wrote a few days later, on 28 July, 'much as I love seeing him. The absent John, with my thoughts of him (not always true to life) and his solemn letters, gives me more pleasure than the reality. I am, I suppose, a romantic and idealist.' See Appendix A for an attempt at a fuller discussion of John Hall and Madge's peculiar relationship with him.

coloured film, *The Thief of Bagdad*, which we enjoyed very much. The others had seen it in the afternoon. It was the best Techni-color film we've seen.[19]

Tuesday, 22 July. A lovely day, and Robert's holiday, so the four grown-ups went off walking. A bus to Wallingford, then along Grim's Dyke to Nuffield, where we ate our nice sandwich lunch. The country looked lovely in the splendid July day – the cornfields yellowing under the blue sky, and the distant blue rolling country falling away all round. We got a bus from Bix into Henley for tea, and another one home. Baths, fish and chipped potatoes for supper, and then we 'sung' through all *Iolanthe*.

Wednesday, 23 July. Warm and sunny again – so nice to have the warmth back. Busy with housework and shopping in the morning, the Depôt in the afternoon. In the evening Nita and Dick treated us to dinner at the Moorish, then the Playhouse, *The Shining Hour* [by Keith Winter, 1934] a rather too melodramatic but enjoyable play. We all like it quite well, except Richard, who is a little more critical.

Thursday, 24 July. Very warm and lovely again. The usual morning shopping, and the last Depôt afternoon before our long holiday. We all had that schoolgirl breaking-up feeling, though none of us young, alas! We had tea in the garden – very festive! I was tired and not too well-feeling afterwards. Nita and Dick were on the river so I went round to Vera's for a nice rest and chat, and when I returned, Nita had cooked a lovely supper. She is very thoughtful and kind.

Friday, 25 July. I had a permanent wave at 9.30 and as usual hated the immediate results, but as usual I suppose I shall get over it, and like it more as it loses its fuzzy unmanageableness. I had tea with Mrs Bleiben – a hurried one – at Fullers, then met Robert at the 'Super' to see *Major Barbara*, which was witty in the best Bernard Shaw way, but rather tiring to listen to. A very thundery evening. Nita had again prepared dinner.

Saturday, 26 July. A letter from John – quite a nice one and as apologetic and affectionate as he can be when he knows that a Censor will read it. All letters from Ireland are censored of course. Torrents of rain all day, with some thunder. Nita and I started making lemon marmalade in the afternoon with some lemons just acquired, an almost forgotten fruit.

---

19   The film won three Academy Awards, for cinematography, art direction, and special effects.

War events at this time made few appearances in the diary. An exception was the entry for 1 August: 'The Russians are still doing wonders in holding the Germans. If only ––' On 25 August 'There was a parade of tanks in St Giles, with the Oxfordshire and Buckinghamshire band, … which intrigued the children.' Although Madge almost certainly listened regularly to the news on the radio, she hardly ever mentioned it. A rare reference to wartime culture appeared in her diary for Sunday, 17 August. 'We listened to Gracie Fields doing a farewell concert to the Troops before returning to America. I am beginning to see, too late, the charm of her robust personality.'

As in most families, food was more and more on people's minds. 'A singing evening', Madge wrote on Saturday, 2 August, 'after a glorious supper of bacon, mushrooms, tomatoes and fried potatoes – absolutely pre-war!' Looking ahead, though, she anticipated further austerity. 'When milk is rationed in the autumn,' she remarked on 18 August, 'I should think morning coffees will be curtailed or cut out altogether.' (Months later, on 3 March 1942, she noted that at the much-visited Cadena 'now one has to help oneself to coffee as there are no more waitresses'.) During the first half of August 1941 Madge's life was notably less busy, for the Depôt was on holiday and, more importantly, her home was much less active, for her sisters and their families were all away from Oxford for almost a fortnight, and her mother was still in Yorkshire.

Sunday, 3 August. Alas! Nita and Dick had to go after lunch, taking Christopher with them. I was very sorry to part with Nita and Dick, but Christopher has been very trying lately and seems so rude just now, and ungracious. Perhaps he will improve later. His parents' presence certainly does seem to have the worst effect on him. He tries to show off. I read luxuriously in the strangely quiet drawing room all afternoon. Although I love the quiet, I'm sure I should get tired of it in time. Vera came at night. We chatted during church-time, I'm afraid.

Tuesday, 5 August. Such cold wet weather – very gloomy. I spent the morning and afternoon cleaning 'mother's' bedroom which looks and smells very nice now. The results of a real spring-cleaning are always worth the tiredness and dirt which fade away after a hot bath. To the Playhouse in the evening after dinner at the George. A very absorbing but unfinished and somewhat morbid play, *Somebody Knows* [by John Van Druten, 1932].

Wednesday, 6 August. Such quiet mornings. Not much shopping to do and the house is so tidy that there is not much house-work either. It is nice to have quite a lot of leisure. Vera and I went to the pictures soon after tea. Quite an amusing film, *That Uncertain Feeling,* fun to see, but easy to forget [a woman has a case of incurable hiccups]. I went to Vera's to supper after. Everyone out but us. The pub was closed, as so many have to do often these days for lack of beer.[20] It seemed quite uncanny. I enjoyed being there – like old times.

On Sunday, 10 August Madge went to Church: 'I hate going alone and am always bored then. I can quite see how important it is to have friends and relations to share in everything one does. I am a very sociable, dependent person.'[21] There was one new visitor, on 12 August, a young cousin, Kenneth Denton (b. 1915), the son of Madge's mother's sister Lina, who spent a 48-hours leave in Oxford. He 'has joined the Non-Combatants' Corps and is stationed at Swindon. He is a cheerful typical Yorkshire lad, very amenable, but oh so laconic – strangely enough very fond of music and quite a good pianist.' In the evening they 'sang lots of Church music till a late hour', after they had seen the film *Love on the Dole,*[22] had supper at the Snack-Bar and been taken by Robert 'to the back of the theatre, where we saw the show from the "flies"'.[23] Doris was on holiday for a while and Maud, her temporary replacement, was much praised by Madge for 'doing wonders, I must say – she knows how to work' (8 August; also 9 August). 'Maudie still doing Doris' work very thoroughly [11 August]. In fact she goes out of her way to *find* work and all the kitchen and scullery in an awful muddle. I can lead the life of a lady whilst she slaves away, but nothing will stop her.' On 14 August Maudie was 'scrubbing away day after day, hour after hour'; and two days later Madge spoke of her as 'Maud, the efficient', who 'even cooks our supper for us. She is spoiling us.'[24] On 15 August 'Nancy and

---

20   She again found The Turf closed because of 'not enough drinks' on 1 July 1942.
21   This need did not go away: 'I need companionship more than ever just now,' she wrote on 15 September 1943. She occasionally acknowledged her dependence on Robert. On the night of 4 December 1941 she was in London without him and stayed at Nita's house: 'I couldn't sleep without my husband,' she wrote. And the following day: 'I never enjoy London so much with anyone as him.'
22   Starring Deborah Kerr and Clifford Evans, set in Salford, and based on Walter Greenwood's 1932 novel.
23   The 'flies' was the space above the front of the stage. This incident further testifies to Robert being very much 'in' with Oxford's theatrical society.
24   Maud Pead made her first appearance in Madge's diary on 16 November 1939: 'When we got home we found Maud Pead ensconced. She is after a job in Oxford, and we all pray she doesn't get it.' The following day she wrote of 'Maudie to lunch. What a poor tiresome creature she is.' And a little over a fortnight later, on 5 December, 'Maudie turned up,' reported Madge, 'alarmingly for tea. She is after a job in Little Clarendon Street.' This alarm was revived a year

the children returned from their holiday at tea-time. We shall soon get used to having a crowd again, but the short spell of peace has been lovely. Still, we are very, very lucky in our "evacuees". This, too, was a period when Madge's headaches were less frequent and less severe.

Madge wrote only occasionally about her neighbours. One instance was on 19 August, when she had Mrs Harcourt from 3 Wellington Place to tea. She was 'Cool, immaculate, self-possessed, everything I'm not. Those sort of people simply petrify me into dreadful shyness which now takes the form of inane chatter. She is a typical Indian Army "Colonel's lady", with much mentioning of titled people and major-generals! Still, I mustn't judge on short knowing. Look how I grew to love the Red Cross Depôt.' Later that year, on 30 November, Madge and Nancy were invited to tea with Mrs Harcourt. 'We had dreaded this, as we are secretly terrified of her immaculate appearance and manner, but she was surprisingly nice and friendly and had a nice friend. Their house is smaller than this, but has more "atmosphere" and is beautifully furnished.' Then there was her refugee friend, Ruth Hendewerk, with whom she had tea on 27 August 'in her room at the top of the house in the Woodstock Road. She is a truly great and good person, and always makes one feel so second-rate.'

On 3 September she voiced a sentiment that many others must have shared. 'Glorious warmth for the second anniversary of this blasted war. Still, we have *so much* to be thankful for after two years, considering what ghastly things have taken place during it.' After 'a really perfect excursion' that afternoon to the Chilterns in the Bleibens' car – 'an unexpected treat' – in the evening she 'went to a service in Church to commemorate the outbreak of war'.[25]

later (17 December 1940): 'Maudie arrived at last. She has been threatening for ages. She is to have a room, eventually, in Kingston Road. Horror for Danna and all of us.' Five days later Maud 'arrived in Oxford for the "duration" probably. She is Danna's Muriel, but even more tiresome. We must try and be patient with her.'
Madge's altered and now, in August 1941, positive view of Maud is unexplained; and nothing is said anywhere in the diary to indicate Maud's background, though it is clear that she was a cousin of Danna's and had been living at Danna's house in Bedford as a 24-year-old at the time of the 1901 census. Maud, mid-war, was in her mid-sixties. She was to remain in Oxford for the rest of the war and would soon become a disruptive presence in the Martin household and a source of much distress: see below, the sentence immediately prior to 17 September 1942. (We are indebted to Barbara Tearle for helping us to establish Maud's identity.)
25   She marked the following Sunday, 7 September, as 'the fifth day of National Prayer we have had since the war started'. It was a 'crowded service'. Almost a fortnight earlier (Monday, 25 August) there had been a very visible military display near Wellington Place: 'There was a parade of tanks in St Giles, with the Oxfordshire and Buckinghamshire band, in the morning, which intrigued the children.'

Tuesday, 9 September. Robert not well today. He had pains in the night and sickness later on, so we had the doctor. Unfortunately Dr McMichael is away, but his nice young 'locum' came. He thought it might be appendicitis and called in Dr Whitlock, who is a marvellously cheery, reassuring person, and didn't seem to think it was anything very serious, perhaps a chill, perhaps a touch of rheumatism – very mysterious but hopeful and we were all very thankful indeed, and Robert went on feeling better and better, but stayed in bed the rest of the day. Norman came for his bit of weekly leave.

Wednesday, 10 September. Thank God – Robert better today. It must surely have been a chill. Anyway, I cannot be too thankful that it is not as serious as it seemed yesterday. I had quite given up all hope of our [imminent] holiday. Lots of shopping for our last morning, as always, settling last minute things, and packing in the afternoon. In the evening mother returned from Yorkshire, and the rest of the time was spent in greetings and exchanging all the news, her and ours. She seems very cheery and looks much better than when she went away. I hope we all settle down nicely for the winter months – our complete 'evacuation' family – and that everything goes smoothly.

Thursday, 11 September. Actually – the holiday at last, and such a wonder being able to go, after Tuesday's scare. I do hope my Robert gets rested and soothed by his holiday – me, too, though I don't feel in the need of much soothing. My nerves are pretty good, better than after the trouble-some and cold winter. We said goodbye to the family and the wee kitten, and went north on the 10.30 train. Three changes, at Bletchley, Preston and Oxenholme, for Windermere. The train was very full, but we didn't do so badly and managed to get lunch and tea on the way. A very dull and ugly journey as far as Preston. Then, how different. In a golden evening our beloved Lake District slowly unfurled itself – and at Windermere a lovely sunset arranged a spectacular show for our benefit. The only snag was that our heavy luggage, with all our walking kit, didn't turn up, and we had to leave the station in a car with another passenger for Hawkshead without it. We were whirled through miles of beautiful country in the twilight and arrived at Ohmcroft Farm before dark. We were given a very nice hot supper, and have very comfortable rooms to ourselves. Given the weather and good health, all should be grand.

Friday, 12 September. A fine day. We were still without our luggage and had to arrange for a carrier to bring it, if found. We could not do much walking in our town clothes and my high-heeled shoes, so decided to go over to our well-loved Keswick. We took the 10.10 bus from Hawkshead, which appears to be an enchanting little town. Changed buses at Ambleside – all the towns are very crowded, and great queues form for the buses. We drove through the familiar and exquisitely lovely country – Rydal, Grasmere, Thirlmere and into Keswick where we had lunch at our own Royal Oak in the company of two friendly and chatty women. Almost everyone seems friendly and merry here except the café people who have so many people to deal with that they get above themselves, as in other evacuation areas.[26] We did our familiar and ever-lovely drive by bus to Seatoller. Everything looked just the same as we remembered it, only more vividly lovely. We walked a little way up the hill beyond the village, then back to Keswick, to sit for ¾ of an hour in another bus queue, to Ambleside. We must try and avoid buses. A quick tea there, then back to peaceful little Hawkshead for supper. We were feeling very depressed at our luggage still not arriving, when to our joy it actually *did*. We were so thankful, and now should be really happy.

This Cumbrian holiday did not disappoint. She and Robert walked a lot, often admired fine views, travelled twice on steamers on Lake Windermere, enjoyed good meals, and did some sightseeing. Kendal she found 'is a thriving busy town, with all the modern shops, but it retains a dignified old personality as well' (19 September). Not all was to her taste: Coniston 'is quite awful and depressing' (15 September); the following day 'we had to go to Ulverston to get our emergency ration cards' – a town she found '*vile*'. On 17 September they received 'Letters and parcels from home. We did a bit of answering.' (They also had 'a lot of letters' waiting for them on the 23rd.) During one walk (20 September), they took a short-cut across private property. 'I don't feel happy, trespassing. I haven't got a bold appearance or spirit for it.' The next day they 'watched one of the clever sheep-dogs bring in sheep and cows.' Unfortunately, the last full day away (24 September) was marred by a nasty

---

26   Evacuation is a major theme in our *Wartime Cumbria, 1939–1945: Aspects of Life and Work* (Cumberland and Westmorland Antiquarian and Archaeological Society, 2017). The peak time for evacuees in many 'reception areas' was around mid-1941. Later their numbers declined. According to Oxford City's WVS in September 1941, 'Oxford is certainly much emptier than it was three or four months ago and during August a good many of the evacuated secondary school children went home for the holidays' (RVS Archive & Heritage Collection, Oxford City Report, September 1941). It was said months later, in May 1943, that 'The evacuated population of Oxford continues to decrease' (RVS Archive & Heritage Collection, Oxford City Report, May 1943). This decline was by then the norm; many if not most evacuees were back at home.

headache; and the journey home the following day was 'long, hot and very tiring and I loathed it'. Still, she declared it 'a *lovely* holiday – quite perfect in every way'.

Friday, 26 September. Back to all the normal things again – the family, house-work, shopping – and very pleasant on the whole, too, to return to, even after such a really perfect holiday as ours. It was nice, too, to go to the pictures after tea after so much unsophistication. There are so many nice things in the world, and so different – reading, walking, chatting to family and friends, watching children grow up, quietness – and noisiness – theatres, shops, solitude, warm fires, comfy beds, friends, letters, food. It could be a lovely life, if we had peace and contentment of spirit always.

6

A Mixture of Frailties
October 1941–June 1942

Almost every life in wartime Britain was governed by routine – at least most of the time, barring emergencies. There was the rhythm of the ordinary week (Sunday was important and distinctive to most people but in different ways) along with the daily predictability of work, whether paid or unpaid, for the great majority of people. Madge Martin more than once used the word 'monotony' to describe the repetitions in her life. Often, for her, one day was much like any other. On 9 December 1941 she wrote of 'Another nondescript sort of day,' and said little more. Weather, shopping, coffee with a friend, working at the Depôt in the afternoon, a walk (almost always with other people), the cinema or the theatre in the evening: these come up again and again, and did not change much from later 1941.

We are now altering somewhat our editorial approach for the rest of this book. First, we omit entries that say little or nothing *unexpected* about Madge's life in Oxford. This means that most of the films and plays that Madge attended are not mentioned. If a sentence or two in an otherwise unremarkable diary entry offers some new information, we have placed this information elsewhere, usually in a footnote or commentary, as in previous chapters. Second, our selections are mainly of entries that say something new, either about the war, or public life in Oxford, or Madge's relations with others. In contrast to previous chapters, there are fewer pages of chronologically consecutive entries, as there were, for example, in Chapters 1 and 3 and most of the first half of Chapter 4. More of the entries that follow are not connected to several preceding or succeeding days of the diary. The selections from October 1941 on tend to be snapshots of briefer periods of time and not so much moving pictures of recorded time, as Madge's life developed over a period of weeks.[1]

---

1   In later 1941, the three children were regular residents at 1 Wellington Place, as were Madge's mother and mother-in-law. Her two sisters were often there as well, especially Nancy; and one or both brothers-in-law sometimes appeared on weekends.

Thursday, 16 October, 1941. A very tiring day with not much leisure. Out in the blustering weather shopping in the morning,[2] standing all afternoon cutting up slings for wounded Russians all afternoon. Then to tea with Miss Blay, youngish, smart and friendly in a rather superficial way; then almost straight to a semi-partners' whist-drive, exhausting and boring. When we got home, we found that Marjory Fryer had arrived, in great trouble as her soldier husband had been brought to Littlemore Mental hospital, with a severe breakdown, and she came to us for shelter, poor dear.[3]

Friday, 17 October. Very tired and a bit headachey after yesterday's tiring energy. Marjory seemed brave and cheerful in spite of her troubles, and came out coffee-ing with us, and in the afternoon she went to Littlemore to see her husband and found him very depressed in that miserable place. Robert and I went to the pictures as it was supposed to be our holiday. In the evening, Nita and Richard arrived, the vanguard of our week-end tribe of guests!

Saturday, 18 October. Round the town with part of the hosts [i.e., crowds of people] – and coffee at Kemp Hall. I had a headache and went to bed to nurse it in the afternoon. After tea, Nita, Nance and I went up to the tailors, Nita to be fitted, and I to collect my dark blue suit, which is very nice.[4] Anne and Jim arrived at 8.00 and we had a huge party for supper. Anne is very large, now, and grey, but exactly the same extraordinary person as she ever was, Jim, the nicest of men, handsome, courteous, talented and humble. We had songs, but they weren't such fun as with the family only.

Sunday, 19 October. Such a tiring day. I couldn't go to Church but had a walk with Anne, Jim, Nita, Dick and the three children round Magdalen, and the Meadows. A fairly quiet afternoon – Nita and Dick gone, the children at Sunday school, Marjory at the hospital, and mother in bed. Nancy doing

---

2 She actually linked this shopping to 'the afternoon', clearly a slip of the pen, which we have corrected. Such obvious errors are rare in her writing.
3 Marjory Fryer was a friend from Yeadon in Yorkshire and had been a bridesmaid at Madge's wedding in 1917 (*Hendon and Finchley Times*, 20 July 1917, p. 8). In her memoir Madge spells her name as 'Margery'. (This is a name she seemed to spell in various ways, which we have changed to 'Marjory'.)
4 New clothes were increasingly hard to get. On 10 October she had visited 'the dressmakers to arrange about my one winter dress – one *can* only have one, no coupons for more. This is to be bright scarlet, to cheer up a miserable period of war.'

washing, so I was alone with Anne and Jim and was able to listen in peace. I went with them to Boars Hill in the somewhat dark and wild evening, as Anne was eager to see it, but it didn't look its best in the twilight. Vera was at home when I returned, and sympathised with the upheaval. She helped to get supper. Norman, by this time, had arrived! Fortunately Anne and Jim have meals and sleep at the Oxenford [private hotel, 13 to 17 Magdalen Street]. A 'chatty' evening. Robert in his sanctuary.

Monday, 20 October. Simply beautiful weather with brilliant sunshine. These few days are simply overwhelmed by Cissie [this must be Anne, and written as 'Ciss' or 'Cissy' later], who dominates every minute one is with her, and I was with her a great deal – shopping, coffee-ing, and in the afternoon walking round Worcester [College] Gardens and having tea at Fullers. She seems utterly dazed by our crowded household, and funked coming in after supper. We were all rather pleased as we were worn out. After months of quiet, we had an 'alert' at night, but a short one.

Tuesday, 21 October. Still perfectly beautiful weather. Out with some of the family and the unquenchable Ciss. I can see the bewildered child under all the silly boasting, so I don't mind her as much as some do, though I find her very tiring indeed. Nance and I were glad of a peaceful afternoon at the Depôt. All is agog against the Duchess of Kent's visit tomorrow.[5] I went to the theatre at night with Vera and Cissy (a queer mixture) to see *The Doctor's Dilemma*. It was absolutely brilliant – marvellous acting, wonderfully stimulating dialogue, and Vivien Leigh looking a dream in 1908 costumes.

Wednesday, 22 October. Such wonderful weather, but very cold. We had coffee at the Cadena, Nancy, Marjory, Cissy and I. Cissy really is quite impossible and I just couldn't do with her, she tires me out completely, with her complacency and conceit. I was really glad to see her go after lunch. Nance and I went round to the Depôt, which was all agog. Lots of people turned up, all immaculate in white, to see the Duchess of Kent, who arrived at 4.00 to inspect our work. She is quite beautiful and very gracious. She walked round and actually had a word with *me*. My knees knocked like a school-girl. It was a thrill for all of us.[6] We hurried back to entertain Julian

---

5   A week before Madge had written that 'We hear that the Duchess of Kent is to visit us next Wednesday. I cannot help but be thrilled at this news, though I have to appear unmoved like the other members of the Depôt.'
6   It was reported that the Central Hospital Supply Service at Worcester College, which was headed by Lady Gertrude Bruce-Gardner, 'is largely undertaken by the wives of

D'Albie for tea, from the Playhouse. He was charming indeed and we all liked him.[7]

Thursday, 23 October. Still very cold, but sunny. Doris in a great rage about something, which always blackens the atmosphere. Coffee, shopping. Nance and I went to a symphony concert in the afternoon – the London Symphony Orchestra with Sir Henry Wood, and Cyril Smith playing divinely on the piano. It was beautiful, but I think I liked the Malcolm Sargent concerts more. I went in the evening to see Ginger Rogers in *Kitty Foyle*, with Vera. She (Ginger) was wonderfully good in a good film.

After two somewhat stale weeks, which included some black moods[8] and little new testimony, Madge's diary-writing recovered a degree of descriptive vigour.

Thursday, 6 November. My mind is getting bemused lately. I just cannot concentrate on anything, even when I try to say my prayers at night, I fall asleep. It must be the busy household and many small activities. Now I remember, we had lunch with Mrs Scott, a very nice lady, kind and polite. She gave us a glorious lunch at the Randolph, which was a great treat for us. John [on

---

heads of colleges and other prominent members of the University'. (*Oxford Mail*, 23 October 1941, p. 3.)
7   Julian D'Albie (1892–1978) had a long career from the 1920s as an actor on the London and provincial stage, on radio, and in films and television. He acted in, and was in charge of, the Playhouse Company during 1941. (Chapman, *Oxford Playhouse*, p. 123; *The Times*, 12 April 1978, p. 19.)
8   'I am feeling exceedingly bad-tempered, depressed and sorry for myself', she wrote on 27 October, 'but nothing helps these fits, which are few and far between, except time.' On the following day, 'My black mood of depression [is] still on me, and everything seems wrong at the moment, but there is no real excuse for it.' She thought there was 'Nothing like activity for black moods.' In her last diary entry for 1936, she had acknowledged her moodiness. 'Alas, I don't improve in tempestuous outbursts from time to time, and depths of depression, and the other extreme of rapture and happiness. ... I seem too old to change now and it seems to be *me*.' Occasionally dark moods had different dimensions. Much later, on 7 July 1945, she wrote that 'Sometimes, especially lately, the devil seems to enter me, and I feel really wicked, as I did at tea-time. I went tramping up the Woodstock Road to walk my cross-ness off, then called on Mrs Busby and Ruth, who always set me an example of contentment, which makes me ashamed, but a mood like this isn't easily thrown off. So much unadulterated sweetness is alien to me, and I can sympathize with mother's furious exasperation, though realizing that we are both wrong to mind.'

leave] in again in the afternoon, and we went to a whist-drive at night. Mrs Fryer came for a week, and a good thing she did, as Marjory was taken ill in the night – our latest worry.

Friday, 7 November. We are all very concerned about Marjory, who has had slight haemorrhage (she has TB), and it is a double tragedy with her husband in the mental home. However, we are thankful Mrs Fryer is here to look after her, and they are both very cheerful. Shopping. John in after lunch – he spent most of the afternoon getting morse on the wireless, a real busman's holiday! He and Susie and Nancy came with us to the Playhouse to see *Spring Meeting* [by M.J. Farrell and John Perry, 1941] – quite amusing.

Saturday, 8 November. Such a beautiful day, but icily cold. Marjory had had two or three attacks in the night, poor thing, but Dr McMichael doesn't sound too grave about it. I dashed about during the morning. John looked in, and in the afternoon lots of us went up to the Dragon School to see *Patience* [by Gilbert and Sullivan, 1881], marvellously done as usual. Vera looked in after tea. There are *nine* women, one way and another, at present in this house [Robert was the only man].[9]

Sunday, 9 November. Remembrance Day – for the 11th. Nancy and I went to Church and took Sally to see Roger and Christopher in the parade of Cubs and Scout Church Parade. It was very cold again, and I didn't go out again. John came in after Evensong, very depressed, as in pre-war days, with the choir until he cheered up with a spot of whiskey and a long talk, as in days of yore. Things never change with us and we have known one another 18 years this month!

Monday, 10 November. Rainy and milder. Shopping. Marjory seems much better, and I think she will be able to return home with Mrs Fryer next week. They are both exceeding cheery exuberant people, but the house is really very overcrowded and everyone is getting a bit nervy with so many contrasting personalities. John came in the afternoon – his cheerfulness is lasting still and we reminisced over old diaries and Rugby cards. John's memories are marvellous. In the evening, Robert, Nance and I went to the theatre to see the International Ballet. It was very good, and we liked especially the *Prince Igor*, *Fête Bohème*, and *Endymion*. Ballet is so very unworldly, somehow, and pure.

---

9   A week later, on 15 November, she wrote of 'this enormous family and its trials'.

This was a month when tension was rife in this extended family. On 13 November Madge recounted an incident of conflict. 'I took the children along to a lantern lecture in Church at night on 50 years of London, which went on far too long but had interesting bits. Danna was very exasperating about me bringing them home, but I was allowed to at last, very late, after waiting for a non-existent taxi. I wonder how long it will be before I burst out against this atmosphere of clashing personalities.' And there was more. On Sunday, 16 November 'Doris had the morning "off" so we were all very busy about the house in the morning. Another rancorous argument at lunch, mostly between mother and Nancy. I get very fed up sometimes, but mother is really the culprit – she is so very fierce.' On 25 November there was 'A very unpleasant supper, with Robert and I the silent on-lookers of a heated discussion on naughty children. The atmosphere very strained, and relations cool.' Madge had been very glad to have her sister, Nita, arrive from London on 20 November: 'It is a comfort to have confidantes in such a household.' Losing control of one's own house, even to loved ones, must certainly have been – at least sometimes – aggravating. Some of Madge's irritation probably stemmed from being on the receiving end of unsolicited advice: weeks later, on 10 January 1942, she admitted to some resentment at 'not being able to run my own home, however badly, without the comments and kindly-meant advice of so many others. But I must try to hide my annoyance … ' Her relations with her mother were, it seems, rather hot and cold: on 15 January 1942 'Mother upset my cheerful feelings by working herself into a rage about nothing at lunch-time.'

During these weeks Madge mentioned a variety of wartime issues. In late October Aid to Russia Week was being observed in Oxford 'and the Red Flag is flying on Carfax Tower. Strange things happen in this war' (31 October).[10] Another detail concerned dress (17 November): 'What a good thing turbans are the fashion these days. They do keep the hair nice and tidy.' At the Depôt on 19 November 'Nance at last got her badge like mine.' Madge saw the film *49th Parallel* on 21 November and declared it 'a *perfect* propaganda film and exciting, too.' The next day Oxford was as usual on a wartime Saturday 'packed with people, and it was a nightmare to be in it. … the town was like an ant heap'. Given the 'gloomy sulks' at home (26 November), 'it is a relief to get out of the house on any pretext. Nance and I went to the Depôt in the afternoon where arguments and discussions are always conducted in a friendly way.' Wartime volunteering was one way to escape domestic tribulations. Still, war brought all sorts of strains. On the very crowded train back from London on 28 November, she and Robert 'had to sit in the corridor after Reading, but rather enjoyed gazing out on the darkened country instead of huddling together in a stuffy carriage'.

---

10 British aid for Russia had suddenly found numerous supporters in Oxford. (*Oxford Times*, 24 October 1941, p. 8.)

The following day, 29 November, a Saturday, after shopping 'the whole family went to the Communal Kitchen in New Inn Hall Street, so save us from worrying about what to get for lunch. It was a rather interesting experience, and we got a very good hot lunch, and frightfully cheap – grown-ups a shilling, for meat, vegetables, pudding, roll, and a cup of tea, and children 4d!' This was Madge's first – and perhaps only – exposure to a highly successful wartime innovation, the British Restaurant, known in Oxford as 'Municipal Restaurants': this one, in a Baptist Church, had opened on 14 July 1941.[11] As for Christmas shopping, usually a big deal, the need now to use coupons was enforcing austerity (1 December), and shops in London, she observed, 'never wrap parcels up now, so everyone looks most queer carrying their things for all the world to see' (4 December).

With 1941 winding down, Madge celebrated her 42nd birthday on 20 December, 'and I can really feel now that I am no longer young, mostly because I cannot get terribly excited about it'. The next day, a Sunday, 'I had an immense queue of people to knit socks after Robert's appeal,[12] and Nancy and I were busy packing parcels of

---

11   *Oxford Mail*, 15 July 1941, p. 3. Over 160 people had a meal at this restaurant on the opening day (*Oxford Times*, 18 July 1941, p. 5). It was the third such restaurant to be established in Oxford; by 1943 there were nine (*Kelly's Directory of Oxford, 1943*, p. 509). On 1 December 1943 Robert took 'Lunch alone in the Communal Restaurant in the Assembly room. Not bad "Cottage pie" and marmalade pudding for about 1s 4d.' (The work of these restaurants is summarized in Graham, *Oxfordshire at War*, pp. 145–6.)

These Municipal/British Restaurants were designed to provide a nourishing, hot, two- or three-course midday meal for a shilling or less. Service was usually cafeteria-style (something of an innovation); no ration cards were needed; and many of the serving and clean-up staff were volunteers, commonly members of the WVS. The cooks were normally paid. The people most likely to benefit from these catering services included evacuees, men and women working at a distance from home, and those unable to afford commercial restaurants (which meant most Britons). The Municipal Restaurant in New Inn Hall Street that Madge visited was very busy: almost 500 people were eating there daily, though the dining hall was small (*Oxford Times*, 24 October 1941, p. 5), and queues were normal (*Oxford Mail*, 7 August 1941, p. 2). A speaker at one official opening hoped that 'if people meet more at meals it might go even further in the direction of stimulating the kind of community spirit which we need for fighting this war' (*Oxford Times*, 17 January 1941, p. 7). Municipal Restaurants in Oxford were making a profit in 1941 and there was widespread satisfaction with their operation (*Oxford Times*, 19 December 1941, p. 5).

12   Knitting was a notably prevalent form of women's work, in peace and even more so in war, and knitting for various worthy wartime causes was one of the most common volunteer activities. The county's WVS reported in December 1943 that 'We are knitting 1,500lbs of wool for the forces. Almost every village in Oxfordshire is taking part. We are also knitting vests for the Occupied Countries.' (RVS Archive & Heritage Collection, County Report, December 1943.)

There was a group of knitters at St Michael's at the North Gate (*Parish Magazine*, July 1941, p. 10) and, partly because of Madge, the Church was closely connected with the city's Red Cross. In the *Parish Magazine* for February 1940 (p. 3), Robert reported that 'Mrs Martin

wool up for the knitters after supper.' The following day, 22 December, 'Everyone very busy – dashing about with Christmas trees, and parcels, for Christmas in spite of silly old Hitler.'

———

Wednesday, 24 December. Christmas Eve – the busiest day in all the whole year. We rushed through our house-work, then decorated the Altar and Chancel of the Church with ever-greens and two miniature Christmas trees. It looked lovely. Last minute shopping and packing up for the rest of the day. Nita and Dick and Norman all arrived one by one, and we were all complete by supper-time, and soon after we brought down all our presents. No-one would have thought that there was a war on at all to see the piles and piles of brightly covered packages. We have no pillow-cases to spare, so had to put them out in individual heaps. Most exciting.

Thursday, 25 December. Up for the 8 o'clock Communion Service with Nita – absolutely pitch black. The Church beautiful and mysterious.[13] Home to a long and very happy day. It took us until tea-time to open our parcels one after another, in order of age. So some of us had to wait till after lunch. To the morning Service with Nita, Dick, Vera and Muriel, singing our hearts out in Christmas hymns. Then home to a beautiful lunch of turkey and Christmas pudding, in spite of Hitler. I opened my wonderful presents

would be glad to hear from any lady who would like to receive wool for knitting comforts,' and during the following three years the magazine contained numerous references to the acquisition and distribution of wool and the knitting of garments, some of which mentioned Madge as the key organizer. It was announced in September 1940 (*Parish Magazine*, p. 10) that there was a Red Cross box in the Church for contributions to the POW comforts fund. In May 1941 (*Parish Magazine*, p. 10) St Michael's conveyed its thanks to the congregation for knitted garments for the Forces, and Robert added that 'Knitting wool is naturally now expensive, and so further gifts of money will be very useful, in order that ladies who wish to help may be supplied with the necessary materials. The Red Cross Supply Depôt at Worcester College is extremely grateful for all the help received.' At the Depôt on 25 March 1942, Madge had had 'a busy afternoon packing wool up to send to my sub-Depôt knitters'. In his history of St Michael's (p. 180), Robert said that many women who were members of the Church – and others – were organized by his wife, and 'provided enormous quantities of knitted scarves, socks, gloves and Balaclava helmets, through the Red Cross Society, for the troops'.
13 These were the elements of religion that particularly moved Madge. Later, on Sunday, 1 March 1942, she attended Church in the morning 'and enjoyed the Benedicite as I always do in Lent, with its vivid words conjuring up beautiful pictures of all things wonderful in the world'.

in the afternoon[14] – also Robert and mother and Danna. Then a party tea with lighted tree and crackers. Maudie there too. An evening of games and charades, and at last a little quiet read. One of the happiest days for years. We are very lucky to be all together.

Friday, 26 December. Another rather busy day, as we let Doris have the day off – therefore having to do the housework and the cooking, which kept us running about all morning. We had a cosy early tea in the kitchen. Then all dressed up for the pantomime. I wore Robert's superb sparkling ear-rings with my ancient but still pretty black lace and satin 'semi-evening' and they looked lovely. There were twelve of us – all the family (except Norman who had to go back yesterday), also Vera, Muriel and Ruth. It was *Aladdin* and most lavish and splendid in every way. We loved it, and all felt well and very happy for it.

As 1941 wound down, Madge was busier than she expected to be, for Doris did not show up for work, a fact that was mentioned in every diary entry between 29 December and 4 January.[15] 'We quite like doing our own work,' Madge remarked on 29 December, 'for a time, at least, and get through it with the minimum fuss.' She expressed similar feelings the following day: 'apart from being extra busy, we didn't mind at all [Doris being away] – everything goes so smoothly and economically'. Madge was 'very busy again' on New Year's Eve – and also reflected on the past 'wicked year'. She recognized that 'it might have been worse, especially for lucky people like we are, in Oxford. What will next year bring? The Americans are now in the war with a vengeance, whether for better or worse we don't yet know. The Japanese are doing fiendishly well as yet.' The following day, the first of 1942, she was fatalistic. 'I have ceased to wonder what the New Year will bring. It is no use worrying or speculating about things – only to hope is best.'

---

14   On a separate page she listed presents she received from eighteen sources, both individuals and couples (such as her sisters and their husbands). Gift-giving in this family was a well-developed custom. If most of the other people then residing at 1 Wellington Place received a similar number of presents, it is understandable that opening them consumed a good chunk of the day.
15   Doris did come back – on 5 January; Madge offered no explanation as to her absence. She did, though, suggest a certain lack of enthusiasm for Doris in remarking on 1 January that, without her, 'food is cooked as well, if not better, and the work gets done, not too badly'. However, housework had a downside: 'One feels very grubby at the end of the day in spite of constant washings' (2 January 1942).

A key fact about Madge's writing in 1942 was that she was unable to buy her usual printed diary with a limited space allotted to each day – 'the war, of course. So now I have this exercise book instead, and it might be better as I can spread myself on the days with much to say about, or cut it down to a mere word or two' (1 January). Five days later, after a little experience with the new style of book, she remained optimistic. 'This sort of diary is rather fun. One can spread oneself as much as one wants.'[16] And occasionally she did, writing more expansively than she had before.

Wednesday, 7 January, 1942. I rushed round my work quickly, as John came at 10.30, in a most cheerful mood for a chat. He is bringing a friend in this evening for a sandwich supper. He is a young Canadian and a member of his crew, and is returning with him tomorrow. His (John's) cheerfulness made me so, too. I have bought with the Christmas money he gave me the variations of the theme by Paganini – three glorious records – the piano played by Rachmaninoff and the orchestra, the Philadelphia Philharmonic, with [conductor Leopold] Stowkowski. They are most lovely things. John brought Susie and his young Canadian air-gunner – his second wireless operator of the crew he is working in at present. He turned out to be a darling – young, fair and shy; but he seemed to enjoy the homely evening of chatter and sandwiches, mince-pies and sherry, and so did John and Susie. We were glad to have them all, and to know they were enjoying it too. The young thing's name is Kenneth Nelson.

Friday, 23 January. Torrents of rain, sweeping away the snow in the streets, but making a sea of grey slush in the less frequented places, like Wellington Place. Nance and I struggled out shopping, holding fast to one another. After lunch there was a nightmare-like row between mother, Nance and I – mostly mother against us. If I ever do assert my authority in any way, mother takes affront and bursts into tears. She said some very bitter things to Nance, who was the only one who was *not* reduced, in the end, to tears. I succumbed, with great shame, and spent the rest of the afternoon very miserably in an icy bed-room. I am in a hole – whether to be weak and silent as mistress of this house, or strong and ruthless. One hurts me, the other mother, Danna and Maud. Anyway, *this* is a miserable state of affairs!

---

16 She revisited this advantage of greater freedom the following year, when her diary was written in two exercise books (1 January and 1 August 1943).

Fortunately, Dick and Nita came for the week-end in the evening and so we had to put on an appearance of unconcern, though I, for one, felt awful.

Saturday, 24 January. How nice it would be to be wafted away from this troubled world to a place of utter beauty and serenity and purity, like this mountain-scene [an alpine photograph was attached], instead of this day of rapid thaw and running streets, and a feeling of cold depression. No use to say that we are lucky compared with the poor tormented people ruined by the war. It doesn't make one less depressed, rather more, as one feels one hasn't even the *excuse* to feel so. Out with Nita, Nance, Sally and the grim silence of mother, who showed no sign of thawing herself, like the weather. Miss Hardman of the Shamrock Tea Rooms gave us lovely coffee there, when we called with some wool. She is a dear. I went shopping for Robert's birthday at Blackwells and Parkers [bookshops in Broad Street]. Most of the family at the pictures. We had gramophone records in the evening to fill in the silences!

Sunday, 25 January. We didn't go to Church, as it was Nita's birthday, and we didn't feel very 'Churchy'. The feelings still extremely strained with mother who doesn't seem to be able to forgive and forget easily. Nita and Dick went in the afternoon. Nance not feeling so well, so she went to bed. I sat and read all afternoon. To Church in the evening with Vera, but I just cannot feel uplifted by Mr Pearce's sermons.[17]

Wednesday, 28 January. Robert's birthday [he was 47]. He seemed to like all his presents, bless him, though mine, anyway, were rather war-time meek ones – books, a book-token, gloves and a cock-tail glass. He had two funerals to take (a jolly way of spending a birthday), so we couldn't have a whole day's fling. However, we did go to the pictures in the afternoon, to see a nice 'Andy Hardy' film, and had dinner, after Robert had taken his evening service, at the George – roast chicken!

17 On Sunday, 14 December 1941, Madge had endured 'a dreary hell-fire sermon from Mr Pearce', Robert's curate; and on Sunday, 11 January 1942 she skipped the evening service because she 'couldn't face the cold again for Church and one of Mr Pearce's too, too orthodox sermons'. Her husband's public speaking, by contrast, met with her approval. On 27 January she reported that Robert suddenly had to do the New College broadcast instead of the usual chaplain, who was laid up. 'It was a thrill to hear him, and the service came over very well.' Years earlier, on Armistice Sunday 1930 (9 November), she said that 'Robert preached a marvellous sermon and reduced me to tears, in spite of the new splendour of my black winter coat with skunk collar.'

Thursday, 29 January. Such weather – sleet, rain, wind, snow, and icy coldness in turn. Ugh. Not much doing all day. I was to have had tea with Susie, but she was not well enough – she seems to get cold on cold. We went to a semi-partners' whist-drive in the Morrell Hall, which was icily cold, with its heating system not functioning, and one bar of an electric fire to 'heat' it. No-one took off their coats! But at least the atmosphere was pleasant and friendly.

Friday, 30 January. Torrents of rain most of the day. The usual morning shopping. In the afternoon two members of the Playhouse came to tea. They were dripping from top to toe, but didn't seem to mind having to turn out – Winifred Evans and Norah Nicholson, who play the 'not so young' parts, always marvellously, and who are almost the most important of the whole lot. They are great friends and don't seem to mind the question as to who gets the better part every week. We – and they – both enjoyed their visit immensely and they were sweet to the children, who regarded them with stage-struck awe, and brought autograph albums for them to sign. We hurried off after they had gone, to the Playhouse itself to see *They Knew What They Wanted* [by Sidney Howard, 1924]. Pamela Brown, again, was very good in it, also the Austrian, Frederick Richter (b. 1894). Mother came with us.

Saturday, 31 January. Everyone will be glad to see January go. It has been a bitter month, with bitter war news in keeping, except for the news from Russia where the Germans are being continually pushed back. But everywhere else, especially in the Far-East, the situation is very bad. Mr Churchill tells us not to expect anything *but* very bad news for months to come, so we must try and be patient.[18] Anyway, our big cities have not had to suffer big 'blitzes' this winter, which is a great blessing. Shopping. I did a small 1941 fashion plate for Robert's lecture, on Monday, in the afternoon. I could only think of trousers and a turban. June came from Henley, and took me out to supper at a snack-bar. The food was bad, but it was kind of her to think of it. She is a nice independent, sunny-tempered young thing.

Sunday, 1 February. Just as the first lot of thick snow had all thawed away, we awoke to find a fresh fall – almost as thick. I felt lazy, and stayed at home all day. June here to lunch, but left soon after. I fear I am getting a bit slack about Church-going but this is always a rather uninteresting time in the way

18   Said in the House of Commons, 27 January 1942. (*Complete Speeches*, vi, 6554–5 and 6570–1.)

of services and music, and Mr Pearce's sermons are the dullest I ever heard, though he is quite nice himself. Anyway, I played truant today, and read, wrote letters and generally relaxed.

Friday, 13 February. Shopping in the morning and in the afternoon. I ran into Vera, also out shopping, and we continued together. Very cold again and snowing a bit. We watched the kilted Cameron Highlanders marching up and down St Giles to the swirl of the bagpipes [a part of Oxford's 'Warship Week' savings campaign] – very fascinating but somewhat monotonous after a time. Mother, Robert and I went to the Playhouse to see *Tovarich* [by Jacques Deval and Robert Sherwood, 1936], which was pleasing, but everything at the moment pales beside the Ballet.[19] This was a black day for our part in this war, when three mighty German battle-ships managed to escape from their bases [in the Bay of Biscay] after being bottled up there for months or even nearly years. They sailed up the Straits of Dover in a fog and though attacked by our RAF got safely away [to home ports]. Everyone more disgusted than almost anything that has gone wrong before – and almost all has gone wrong that could so far![20] I was worried about John, who is with Coastal Command, but, thank God, he sent me a wire on Saturday to say all was well.

Saturday, 14 February. We all got lovely Valentines – mine from Robert was a most exquisite little real Victorian one. June came in the afternoon, and in the evening I took her to the Ballet, for a belated Christmas present. They did the charming *Les Patineurs* and *Giselle*. The second act of this I liked much more, though as a ballet it isn't so appealing as some because of its early Victorian miming and uninspired music. *But* what I did love was Margot Fonteyn's loveliness and grace, as Giselle, and Robert Helpmann's romantically picturesque and tragic Albrecht. His dancing was superb, too. In fact for him and the Ballet all round, I got a return, lost for many years, of that *utter* thrill and whole hearted enjoyment of the theatre. I thought

---

19   The Sadler's Wells Ballet, with Margot Fonteyn and Robert Helpmann, was performing at the New Theatre for six nights and two matinees starting Monday, 9 February. Madge had already been three times this week. 'How I love ballet,' she wrote on 11 February.

20   As the *Oxford Mail*, 14 February 1942, p. 2, editorialized, the three warships confined in Brest 'were supposed to have been pounded out of action, but now they are back again in Germany for repairs which will enable them to take to the sea with other formidable ships of the still considerable German fleet'. The escape was seen as 'a missed opportunity at sea on our side'. It was also widely seen as a national embarrassment, showing British forces in a bad light.

that I was too old to feel that half-melancholy, half-rapturous feeling again, but perhaps it is my swan-song, and I must settle down to old-age now. However, thank goodness I'm not yet quite decrepit.

Sunday, 15 February. To Church in the morning – very cold again. No sermon, but a vaguely pleasant but enormously long Pastoral letter from the Bishop, about the Diocese being 400 years old. I suppose this is important, but seems rather a fuss to make about nothing, under the present circumstances.[21] I wrote to John in the afternoon. We heard on the 6 o'clock news that Singapore had fallen to the Japanese. Really, this news coming on the top of that of the escape of the three German battleships is enough to depress even the most optimistic. The Prime Minister gave a speech at 9 o'clock. I feel sorry for all the responsibilities, criticism, and disappointments he has to bear.[22]

Sunday, 22 February. Doris had a day off, so we were all busy in the morning, tired in the afternoon, and relaxed in the evening. I didn't go to Church, as I felt I could not bear with a Lenten Sermon by Mr Pearce, who is gloomy enough even at festive times, goodness knows.

Monday, 23 February. The morning was darkened by the threat of a dentist's visit, but when I actually went it wasn't bad at all. It never is! Mother heard from Leeds that Auntie Blanche [her mother's sister, b. 1870] is gravely ill, and not expected to recover. Of course, this is a terrible blow for mother, as she is her favourite sister and she has always stayed with her and Celia [her daughter, b. 1900]. She is going up there on Friday. I can see that soon I shall be left high and dry, as all my 'evacuees' are thinking of departing in turn – Nance and the children after Easter, to be with Norman, Christopher back to his own parents, and mother to Yorkshire, but not, I hope, for long. For nearly every reason, I shall *hate* them going. Robert and I went to the Scala in the evening for goodish films [*Vivacious Lady*, with Ginger Rogers and James Stewart, and *Trouble Chaser*, with Granville Owen and Buster Keaton].

---

21   Mr Pearce, the curate, read it out, which took half an hour according to Robert.
22   *Complete Speeches*, vi, 6583–7. This marked probably the lowest point in the war for public morale, and patience with Churchill's government was weakening in some circles. The Prime Minister, while acknowledging recent setbacks (albeit rather briefly), took pains to emphasize the larger picture and favourable long-term prospects. 'We must remember that we are no longer alone. We are in the midst of great company. Three-quarters of the human race are now moving with us. The whole future of mankind may depend upon our action and upon our conduct. So far we have not failed. We shall not fail now' (p. 6587).

Tuesday, 24 February. Nancy up to town in the morning to see about the house she and Norman hope to share, for the duration. Mother and I were in all morning, busying ourselves about the house – out shopping in the afternoon – and in all evening. It makes quite a big difference not having Nance here. The children are very good, but full of irrepressible spirits which makes getting them to bed very exhausting.

Wednesday, 25 February. Still a very bitter wind, but more sunshine. A busy shopping morning. This points scheme for rationing soap and cleaning things, not to mention the other rationed goods, makes shopping a most wearisome affair. I think we just stayed indoors most of the rest of the afternoon and evening.

Thursday, 26 February. I over-tired myself, in a foolish way, cleaning windows, shopping etc., so started myself a headache. I had a quiet afternoon, snoozing in a middle-aged way. I gave the children baths at night, and did a bit of cooking for supper. In fact a suspiciously 'house-wife-ish' sort of day. It doesn't really suit me; and I'm not very good at it.

The following day Madge's mother left for Yorkshire and Nancy arrived – for a short stay. 'I shall be glad of the distraction of house-work,' Madge mused on 2 March, 'when Nancy and the children have gone, to help me from getting too lonely.' The war had brought the sisters closer together. 'I *shall* miss her so much,' Madge said of Nancy on 10 March. 'She has become so much nearer to me, in the last year, and we get on very well, as indeed we all three sisters do, and even living together for so long doesn't seem to have spoiled things.' It was the weather that got her down. On 5 March she and Nancy 'went to see a coloured picture, all about enormously rich people, dressed in exotic clothes, living a life of utter luxury in Miami [*Moon Over Miami*]. It was ridiculous, but how we loved the colours, sunshine, silks and furs – pink blondes – and blue sea. We came out into a blizzard, and laughed bitterly!'

Nancy and her children returned to London from 1 Wellington Place on 13 March – 'It will leave a great blank, them going. The only thing I shall enjoy to a minor degree will be the gradual tidiness again of our home.' Christopher was the only Londoner who remained with her, and his parents took him home on 23 March, in 'a car so laden with the accumulated possessions of two years' evacuation, that it could scarcely start'. 'I miss Nancy and mother very much when I am washing up after supper!' (15 March) While a quiet house would have its merits, she acknowledged, there was (she feared) a lot to lose in fun and stimulating company.[23]

Tuesday, 17 March. Lovely mild Spring weather, showery, but how lovely after the bitter unbending winter. Another busy morning. The Depôt in the afternoon. I felt for the first time since the very early days a faint hostility towards this collection of very 'correct' women. I must have been feeling particularly plebeian, as usually I admire them all so much and feel happy and at home with them. I expect it was just a 'mood'. Another evening at home. John [on leave] just looked in for a few minutes before his madrigal society. He soon gets immersed in his old Oxford activities.

Thursday, 26 March. Colder today but brilliantly sunny again. Shopping. The last Depôt afternoon before 'breaking up' for the Easter holidays, and the customary gala tea – brown scones with honey and cakes with cream, and a holiday atmosphere. The Provost is always brought in on these occasions – like a lamb to the slaughter. I went with Vera to the lantern lecture in Church on 'The Reformation'. I can never get very thrilled about Martin Luther, somehow.

Saturday, 4 April. The usual busy Easter Saturday, decorating the Church, or part of it, the altar and Sanctuary and Lady Chapel is my sphere. There were quite a lot of lovely Spring flowers in spite of the frightful prices of them, and the scarcity – mostly daffodils. It looked almost as beautiful as usual. The town is always more crowded on Easter Saturday than at any other time, and the queues for chocolates, cigarettes, and the cinema were enormous. Robert still very busy on his 'ye olde Englyshe printing' for the Church wardens' accounts.[24]

Sunday, 5 April, EASTER SUNDAY. Double-Summer time began today, so really Robert got up at 4.30a.m. by the real time, and I at 5.30. The mornings are darker of course, but later on the daylight lasts till nearly mid-night. I was up for the 8.00 Holy Communion with Vera. Then breakfast, Easter

---

23 Nancy and her children returned to Oxford for a while in the summer of 1944, in search of refuge from Germany's flying bombs (pilotless planes or doodlebugs), the V–1 missiles.
24 On Tuesday, 31 March he had also been doing 'his Parish Accounts in his lovely old English printing', which can be seen in the parish accounts (OHC, PAR211/4/F1/8). Different parish officials wrote up a fair copy of the accounts each year, vying with each other in their calligraphy.

cards, and Easter eggs, though of course now there are no chocolate ones. Robert gave me much-needed chocolates, though, in mine [her present], and stockings, equally welcome.[25] I gave him a tie, and a tin of asparagus, a real luxury now-a-days, and 2s 7½d for a tiny tin instead of 9½d! [So the price had more than tripled.] I had chocolate from Vera, too, a precious ¼lb [of] tea and two handkerchiefs (one coupon!). Muriel gave me toothpaste and brush. Most odd, but it really is difficult to find any little thing to give people, now when everything is rationed. Church in the morning and evening. Joyous hymns and music, and everything as festive as possible under the rather gloomy war circumstances.

Tuesday, 7 April. Sudden storms of rain and flashes of sunshine – really April weather. Shopping after the Easter lull. I had a chat with Mr Pearce, who came whilst Robert was out. I found him much more human and likeable than I thought and not such a frighteningly composed person [as] I had thought.[26] I polished furniture with vigour in the afternoon and went to the Easter Vestry Meeting at night [in Morrell Hall] with Vera. Since the war, St Michael's folks seem much more cheerful somehow. It must be the feeling of drawing together in the face of adversity, and it gives one a much warmer and friendlier atmosphere.

Friday, 24 April. Robert's holiday – he was busy on his beautiful church model, which is now in the sun-parlour.[27] It is a lovely plasticine model of St Michael's which he is building at every stage, each stage being photographed

---

25 As supplies of stockings plummeted, their value greatly increased, as did the importance of holding on to older ones. She had spent part of the afternoon of 15 January 1941 mending stockings; and later this month, on 21 April 1942, she was 'mending horrible stockings all the afternoon, but every laddered one is treasured these days, to the last'. Later still, on 22 April 1943, she spent 'An afternoon mending decrepit stockings, but every pair is now treasured fondly.'

26 She praised him again on Friday, 17 April, when she went 'to Mr Pearce's concert. He had a small triumph with his women's choir, violinist and soprano soloist. He really inspired those untrained women to sing quite well, as if they loved it.' According to Robert, the Rev. H.M. Pearce was an ARCM and 'an accomplished musician', and he praised him for organizing this choral society (Martin, *Church and Parish of St Michael at the Northgate*, p. 182). On 21 March 1942 Madge had remarked on the therapeutic value of singing: 'Singing is a wonderful cure for the blues or bad temper.'

27 Robert was constructing a scale model of St Michael's Church with the help of the choirboys and others who were attending his classes on church architecture 'in order that the boys may not only learn well but enjoy themselves'. (*Parish Magazine*, October 1941, pp. 10, 12.)

before he continues with the next. We went to the pictures after tea, and laughed till it hurt at Will Hay in *The Black Sheep of Whitehall*.

Saturday, 25 April. Very cold but fine. Shopping. June appeared very early, and it is very nice to have her but she is a somewhat disturbing element, as all visitors are, and one has to abandon all pretence of work and go where they go. I went through the Saturday crowds with her, shopping. Oxford is awful on Saturdays. We went to the Ballet together in the evening and saw *The Gods Go A'Begging*, *Lac des Cygnes* (scene two), which was beautiful, I thought, and *Facade*, which we both dislike. I wish they would leave it out of their programme.

Sunday, 26 April. I meant to do packing, but listened to gramophone records instead – June again! Mrs Harcourt [from 3 Wellington Place] looked in, of course immaculately dressed and caught me in my shabbiest and oldest clothes, as I meant to pack. Why am I always caught off my guard with her? Maddening. I really did pack in the afternoon. Vera came in the evening. No Church.

Two days later she and Robert were off for their customary spring holiday – this one based in Tenby, Wales. Maud had come to 1 Wellington Place to look after Danna in their absence.

Wednesday, 13 May. A day getting straight again, shopping, unpacking, catching up with my knitting depôt, and generally trying to get back into routine. Vera came to supper, which was nice. She seems to be resigned to her awful half-time war job at the St Clement's 'Co-op'.

Thursday, 14 May. I can't settle down properly yet, and hate work for the moment. I think it best not to do much when one feels like that, as it would only be done badly. There was the 'Beating of the Bounds' today, after the Services. I went to the Holy Communion at 10.30, and left the 'beaters' to do some shopping, but caught up with them for the nice salad, rolls and beer meal, usually at Lincoln [College], but since the war at the 'Roebuck' in Market Street, where, in spite of shortage of drink and everything, they produced a nice little meal. Vera and I went to the Service in the evening.[28]

Tuesday, 19 May. Shopping in the morning, the Depôt in the afternoon. Mrs Booth was there; otherwise I find the atmosphere there a bit dreary these days – there seems a certain lethargy on it. Robert and I to see Ginger Rogers in *Bachelor Mother* at night. I love her, and David Niven too, who was in it also. A nice film.

Wednesday, 20 May. Robert went up for a day in town with Nick, and I had a quiet domestic sort of time at home, except to go to the Depôt and look in at Maudie, who is to go to a sort of 'rest home' to nurse her bad knee. I scrubbed a bedroom carpet in the evening. Susie called with some knitting, and for a short chat. Robert back at 2.00a.m.

Thursday, 21 May. Showery and depressing weather. Shopping, Depôt, and a Ruridecanal Conference meeting at night. The speakers were rather more interesting than usual. Otherwise it was as deadly dull as ever.

Friday, 22 May. Lots of showers again, but I believe that it is welcome rain. A busy morning shopping and cleaning silver. Some people from the theatre came to tea – and Mrs Kelly, a brisk and somewhat self-satisfied woman. A quiet evening at home, cooking and so forth.

Saturday, 23 May. A busy day, it seemed. Church Whitsuntide decorating in the morning, with Muriel, home for the week-end, and Vera. Lovely white and red flowers, lilac, narcissus, lilies of the valley, and red tulips. Muriel to tea in the afternoon. Then I went to the station to meet Pansy, who has

---

28 'May our next Ascension-Day ceremony conclude once more within the hospitable walls' of Lincoln College, Robert wrote this year (*Parish Magazine*, June 1942, p. 3). Such traditions were important to him. On Ascension Day in 1943, 3 June, there was 'quite a large crowd for the beating of the bounds, and the traditional meal of beer and salad things', which was again given at the Roebuck Inn in Market Street, courtesy of the proprietor, Mr W. Harvey. During the war Lincoln College served as a nurses' residence (Martin, *Church and Parish of St Michael at the Northgate*, pp. 186–7), a not uncommon transformation of an Oxford building previously for men only. The WVS took a special interest in supporting the ATS companies in a city where women had previously not been catered to. 'We have made innumerable pairs of curtains for their hostels and in February we were able to get washed all the bedspreads of one unit, which is stationed in a college where there are no facilities for washing or drying large articles.' (RVS Archive & Heritage Collection, Oxford City Narrative Report, February 1943.)

special leave to come over from Dublin to see Danna.[29] She must be one of the truly good people in the world, and works hard for the [Oxford] Group movement, which of course means everything to her, so that she wants to pass her happiness on to others, which ordinary people like Robert and I find disturbing. In spite of this, she is so loving to others that one must love her too. If this feeling could be universal, without the embarrassment attached, what a wonderful world it would be.[30]

Sunday, 24 May (Whitsunday), Empire Day. To Church with Panny and Muriel. Whitsuntide hymns seem very dull compared with Easter.[31] Sunday lunch of lamb, asparagus, and rhubarb tart, and much theological conversation, in which I, naturally, feel somewhat at sea, though it's my own fault I do. My brain feels especially stupid on these occasions. Panny went out for the afternoon, so I had my usual Sunday read of the papers with their book reviews and amusement news. Church again at night with Vera and Muriel.

---

29   The British Government imposed severe restrictions on the inflow of people from the neutral (and suspect) Republic of Ireland. Mary Pansy Telford – also known as Panny – was Robert's younger sister and Danna's last child, born in Worthing on 16 April 1896, after Danna was widowed. She was a bridesmaid at Robert and Madge's wedding (and then named 'Miss Pansy Martin'), and was married herself in Kensington, London on 9 August 1920 to David Cecil Telford (born 1893), an Irishman. He, a chartered accountant in Dublin, was active in the Oxford Group, as was she, and in 1960 was ordained as a Minister in the Church of Ireland. They had three daughters, none of whom played a role in Madge's diary at this time (though one was mentioned in 1938: see below, the footnote to 2 October 1943, p. 229). Our main source for his life is an obituary in the *Irish Times*, 7 April 1967, p. 9; Barbara Tearle very kindly did most of this research concerning the Telford family.
30   The Oxford Group, inspired by the American evangelist Frank Buchman in the early 1930s, called on individuals, in pursuit of spiritual renewal, to surrender their lives to God's plan, or 'guidance', for their lives. It favoured open displays of personal faith, and it championed the need for moral re-armament, highlighting the imperatives of absolute honesty, absolute purity, absolute unselfishness, and absolute love. Such absolutist thinking was not to the taste of Madge and Robert. Nor were they crusaders or exponents of confessions in public; most members of the Group were both.
   The Telfords had visited the Martins on 28 March 1938 and stayed overnight, and according to Madge, 'Robert and I were both dreading their visit as we know the sickening way "Groupists" go at one, and try to "change" one,' though on that occasion, she added, 'it all turned out much more pleasantly than we thought'. At a Martin family gathering in Bedford on 19 May 1939, before Madge and Robert left for home 'came a ghastly time when Panny made poor Robert read aloud from a "Group" book'. On 16 January 1940 David Telford visited Oxford for lunch and tea: 'He is rather nice, in spite of his "putting off" Groupy ways.'
31   On Whit Sunday the previous year (1 June), she had written that it 'always fails to thrill, though it is important I suppose'.

Monday, 25 May (Whit Monday). Why are Bank Holidays often so awful as to weather? This one was one of the worst, except for the morning when it didn't actually rain. Panny and I walked up to see Maud in the home. I find it a bit difficult to follow her 'Group' reasonings about problems like Maud. She doesn't take the obvious 'Good Samaritan' view as to her future well-fare, as I should have supposed, but is quite willing to see her cast out into the street if that is the guidance.[32] Robert and I had tea with the Bleibens at their home. It was very pleasant in spite of the down-pour coming, and going. I'm glad, though, that I don't have to live in their gloomy house [Headington Quarry vicarage on Quarry Road].

Tuesday, 26 May. Panny went up to town to see a Group play, and dragged Robert up too, but he followed later. She (Panny) is so good and sincere that everyone finds it hard to refuse her persistent efforts to be interested in the Group movement. I didn't go as I had a lot to do at home, shopping and Depôt. Nick [Leonard Nicholls] suddenly appeared after tea – we had expected him later. It was rather fun for me, as he took me out to the Playhouse and to supper at the Randolph after. I did not feel quite so shy with him as usual, and quite enjoyed my evening. The Playhouse did *Sweeney Todd*, a melodrama [by George D. Pitt] which didn't seem quite so much fun as the others they did. Nick told me a lot about himself and his unfortunate second marriage [to Joy] at supper. He certainly doesn't seem to have much happiness with wives, and he is such a likeable person. Panny and Robert returned home at mid-night. I feel rather a dull sort of person when they are all together.

Wednesday, 27 May. My life is utterly confused when I cannot go on in my usual solitary routine way, especially when people so unusual and disturbing as Panny and Nick come, though Panny is so good, and helps in such a wonderfully efficient way.[33] Nick trailed round the shops in a dog-like way,

---

32 Such a person's suffering would presumably have been attributed to her failure to surrender herself to God. By contrast, those subject to divine guidance can live happily and without fear. As one handbook put it, 'Not only is our to-day in God's keeping but our to-morrow; we have surrendered that to Him, too, so why fear whatever we think to-morrow must bring us as a logical sequence of to-day's events? Fear of the future, whether it be to-morrow or old age, means that we do not trust God's guidance. Our faith in the future is the infallible test of our faith in Him.' (*What Is the Oxford Group?* [London: Oxford University Press, 1933], pp. 67–8, by an author identified as 'The Layman with a Notebook'.)
33 Panny 'really helps me a lot with my housework and tries not to be a nuisance successfully,' Madge remarked on 2 June, 'though I find her attitude of "relentless love" rather wearing'.

and had coffee with us. He is very impatient with rationing and the lack of luxuries he has begun to expect, but he is so funny about it that he makes us all laugh helplessly at his fury. The Depôt in the afternoon – a relief in a way to do something ordinary and 'routine'. We all went as Nick's guests to *The Gondoliers* at night. The D'Oyly Carte Opera Company is beginning to look very much 'over military age', poor dears, but sing very well. We meant to give them a rest this year, as we seem to have seen them so often in late years, and we don't want to become so tired of them that we never want to see them again. Nick came back to supper.

Thursday, 28 May. The weather is too depressing – showery and windy and dull. I met Vera in the morning and she helped me buy a pair of shoes, for which I had to beg 5 coupons from Robert. We had our new [ration] books this week, and only have 60 coupons for 14 months! I rested in the afternoon as I felt very tired, after late nights, and continually having to be on the 'qui-vive' [on the alert]. Robert and I went to a whist-drive at night, and had supper at the George. Panny and Nick were there finishing their dinner, and stayed all through ours. We sang songs when we came in – exhausting but great fun.

Friday, 29 May. Robert and Nick went off walking, but Panny and I couldn't face the idea of a showery, cold day tramping over the Chilterns, so we did a lot of shopping together, and I did odd things in the afternoon, ready for my weekend in London with Nita. I shall be so glad to go where I can feel more equal, somehow. Nick came in for supper and a hectic singing evening. Panny and I retired at mid-night, but the others, including June, who had come over for the night, went on till 3.30a.m., solemnly going through song-books alphabetically, so that I, in the bed-room directly overhead, nearly went mad, knowing just where they had got to in the books. Nick had to be supported back to his hotel [the Randolph] by Robert and June, who were slightly more sober. I felt very hot and bothered as I knew I had to be up in good time for a day in town tomorrow with June, but thank goodness, these hectic times are rare.

The following morning, according to Madge, 'I felt weary and headachey, but June, one of the culprits of the night before, looked as fresh as a daisy – it might have been *me* with the hangover!' They went together on a train to London. 'June insisted on travelling 1st class with a 3rd class ticket, and again *I* was the one who had to pay the extra, though I had protested, and she, not being in the carriage at the time, escaped the ticket-collector's clutches.' The outing was not unusual for London, and certainly busy: shopping, lunch at June's club, a visit to the National Gallery, tea, a snack at the Corner House bar, Sadler's Wells in the evening, and finally, for Madge, a bus to Barnet and Nita's house, where she was to stay for two nights. The next afternoon, a Sunday, they 'all went to Nancy's via Old Muswell Hill and East Finchley and beautiful Bishops Avenue. Nancy's new house (half of a nice little house) is in a most charming suburb, much more attractive than the old house, and they have a very pretty garden. It was lovely seeing all my family again, and the children, who of course seem doubly attractive and nice, not having them actually with one all the time.' On Monday she had 'a crashing headache until after lunch'; and then she and Nita met Nancy at Golders Green and 'went by bus into town, down the old familiar Finchley Road, whose old houses are now often ruined or spattered by "enemy action"'. Then they enjoyed lunch, another viewing of the film *How Green Was My Valley*, tea, and a visit to the Royal Academy, concluding with, for Madge, a train in the evening back to Oxford.

Wednesday, 3 June. These are horrid hectic days, Robert and I think, with no peace and order – people coming or threatening to come, no long reading evenings or peaceful meals and silent tranquility. I even wish that John's leave [he was then in Oxford] hadn't fallen into the midst of it all, though his visits are rather a rest from the strife. I am very busy with Depôt work too, trying to make people knit up pounds of wool. Harry came to supper and to spend the night. I was glad of the excuse of a large meal to prepare whilst the Martins got into a huddle and talked of themselves and theirs to the exclusion of everything else. Harry still makes me feel the dullest and most silent of people, though he is so much nicer really himself.

Thursday, 4 June. A very hectic hot feverish morning, so much to do in the catering line, and the Depôt as well. I felt quite frantic and quite resented Panny's advice 'not to worry about anything'. She is certainly one of the 'Marys' of this life, I a 'Martha'. At last both Panny and Harry went after lunch. Panny returns on Saturday, but, I hope, for the week-end only. I love her very much, but cannot go on too long in this routine-less way. John looked in after tea. Then I had dinner with Robert at the George and went to Magdalen Grove, where Vera joined us, to see the enchanting *Midsummer Night's Dream* against a perfect background, in perfect weather, and charmingly done. We all loved it.

Friday, 5 June. This should have been a holiday day, but I was so busy with dealing with wool, handling bales of hot khaki warm wool and writing notes about it, that I had to stay at home. Robert worked on his model. It was a very hot day indeed – but I love it. We went to see *Blood and Sand* [starring Tyrone Power and Linda Darnell] a good film with wonderful Technicolour Spanish atmosphere. June stayed the night. John came in for the traditional Friday night visit. The evenings now are light till nearly mid-night.

Saturday, 6 June. A very hot day again. I shopped as usual in the morning and did the flowers for the war-memorial window. I dealt again with bundles of hot wool in the afternoon and sat a bit in the garden, getting very hot and shiny. Even the evening seemed hot and flustered, with odd things to do. June, who had been at Stratford-on-Avon for the day, returned to spend the night, and Panny returned from London also, late, bringing back a 'Group' friend who was sleeping at another friend's house but having meals here.

Sunday, 7 June. Headachey in the morning, but I went to Church with Panny and her friend Phyllis Brown, who is thin and nervy, and rather refined, but not terrifying. She stayed all the rest of the day. John came in for a fleeting visit after morning service. Panny and I had the Holy Communion with Danna in the study in the afternoon. Robert took the service. Church again at night and a chat after supper with Mrs Jiminez, who came in. She is a beautiful person.

Monday, 8 June. Very cold again and cloudy – most annoying. I love the sun and warmth. I had coffee with Panny and her two friends, Phyllis and Kristy Morrison, at the Cadena, then did some shopping. John in for the afternoon. He does so soon become part of his Oxford back-ground. Robert and I went to the pictures after tea to see *Dr Jekyll and Mr Hyde* [with Spencer Tracy, Ingrid Bergman and Lana Turner], which was very well done, and very horrific. Supper with Panny and Phyllis Brown here and a few 'Brains Trust' questions after.[34]

Tuesday, 9 June. Departure of Panny and her friend. I love Panny but how nice it will be to get back into a peaceful unworried routine again. I had a fitting for a summer-frock in the morning, though it is perishingly cold now. I looked in at the Depôt but didn't stay to work in case people came to me about wool. I went with Vera after tea to the Scala to see Ginger Rogers and

---

34 The BBC's 'Brains Trust' was a vastly popular wartime question-and-answer programme, of a broadly intellectual, or at least questioning, character. Its panel comprised regular members and celebrity guests. Its question-and-answer format was widely imitated by associations and clubs around the nation.

Ronald Colman in rather a silly film, *Lucky Partners*. Nice to come home for a peaceful supper and, nicer still, a quiet read à deux.[35]

Wednesday, 10 June. Oh so cold – like March. Shopping, I suppose, and the Depôt in the afternoon. I don't seem to enjoy it very much now. I suppose, however nice most of the people are there, one gets tired of seeing them so often, and having done the same sort of work for nearly three years is a bit monotonous. Ruth appeared for tea and stayed chatting for quite a time. John came in after supper for a nice understanding chat.

Thursday, 11 June. Still icily cold. Out shopping and for a fitting of the flowery summer frock which will get worn, I suppose, one day.[36] Robert and I went to tea with the Blencowe family, ostensibly to see the new baby princess.[37] These Oxford people always give one marvellous teas. I went with Susie and John at 8.00 to a concert of motets in which he was singing – very beautiful in an austere way, but I don't enjoy so many of the same period things all at once. John seems, this leave, to have got right back to his pre-war existence and is changed by his RAF life much less than I thought, or it seems so on this leave. However, he is much easier to get on with – older, I suppose. He came in for a chat after the concert.

Wednesday, 17 June. I felt the familiar divided feeling of depression and relief which accompanies John's return to his Squadron, but as I write this, this evening, I already feel calmed and settled and no longer depressed. The Depôt in the afternoon. Evidently I'm not the only one there who feels disgruntled with the air of slackness which has crept into it of late, and the lack of real efficiency. In fact Miss Walker and I had a look at the 'munitions for women' exhibition in St Giles with half an idea of doing that instead of Red

---

35 'Nice quiet evenings we have now,' she wrote four days later, on 13 June, 'with two chairs and two books.' Madge was an early (by age three) and enthusiastic reader. 'I didn't really enjoy parties much, neither my own, or my friends, and would much rather have been reading.' ('A Yorkshire Childhood', pp. 1, 15, and 31.)
36 'I wore my new frock defiantly for Church in the morning,' she wrote on the following Sunday, 14 June, 'but was half frozen in spite of the sunshine.'
37 Robert baptized the new baby princess Afzan Joy Elizabeth on 27 September 1942. For an account of the Blencowes and Prince Mahmoud, see Chapter 1, p. 25.

Cross work, but I think it would be too strenuous and almost impossible to do it regularly and look after our houses too.[38]

---

38 There was a large notice in the *Oxford Times*, 12 June 1942, p. 7, inviting women 'To Make the Weapons for Attack!' The case was clear. 'The war is moving to its climax. In the next few months every war-factory in Britain must *pour out* weapons for attack. Every woman in the country can help, directly or indirectly, in this great arms drive. War-factories in this district have 2,000 full-time women's jobs to be filled at once, and thousands of part-time jobs as well. … Welding, turning, stitching, machine-operating, assembling, and inspection are the main types of work open now. You sit down to some of these jobs.' Further details were available at the War Work Exhibition in St Giles that Madge visited. It was stressed that part-time work would allow a woman to 'still keep your home running smoothly'. New nurseries were being planned to help women with children, though it was acknowledged that many mothers would need to get assistance with child-care from neighbours and friends. Those women interested in volunteering as 'an official Child-minder' were invited to call in at the Public Health Department on Paradise Street. This is all further evidence of the strenuous efforts being made in 1942 to utilize effectively the labour power of women.

7

Better Times?

June 1942–December 1942

Tuesday, 23 June. Beautiful golden sunshine to greet one again. Out shopping, and a little sun-basking. The Depôt in the afternoon. We all sat in the beautiful formal garden, fragrant with pinks and roses. It was quite a joy to work there. All the Depôt women from the other rooms there too. It is funny to be the youngest of a community. I find I feel rather dull there sometimes – they are all so intellectual. I stained the boards of the big top bedroom in the evening, a back-breaking business.

Wednesday, 24 June. Robert and I both feel rather ill, after, we think, a large and too rich 'welsh rarebit' for supper last night. It was nice at the time, though! I didn't go to the Depôt, but rested in the garden and felt better by tea-time, though cross. Maud is an absolutely infuriating person to have constantly around, and seems to find great joy in saying horrible things.[1] We escaped to the pictures after tea to see *Lydia*, which I rather liked. It was a sort of inferior *Carnet de Bal* [1937], but interesting, though Merle Oberon [b. 1911] is now not very attractive. There was an alert at 2.00a.m. for an hour or so. One forgets what a terrifying sound the siren is till one hears it again after such long months of silence.

Thursday, 25 June. Rather dreary weather again, but no rain. Shopping. The Depôt in the afternoon. Everyone is either knitting there, or marking the garments, ready for the big Prisoners of War parcel that is to be sent off. We all work together at present, so are getting to know some of the people from the other rooms. Robert and I went up to Headington for the Bleibens' out-of-doors missionary Festival, in which they are joined by other churches in

---

1   This is the 'helper' on whom Madge had lavished praise the previous August. She does not indicate exactly how Maud Pead was being disruptive. See also below, footnote 18, p. 190.

the Deanery. There was an out-of-door play which was not so bad, but took ages with long waits in between the acts. Crowds there. Home from Green Road. Headington Quarry village is a most strange place.[2]

Friday, 26 June. We had another lovely day's walking, taking the coach to somewhere past Burford (Sherborne), and having a most lovely Cotswold walk all around there, coming back to Burford for tea at the beautiful Bay Tree Hotel. Burford, I think, is absolutely perfect in its way, and an entirely unspoiled Cotswold town – just beautiful, with apparently not an ugly thing in it. We came back on the 4.45 coach, reaching Oxford at 6.00, for baths, and bathing my blistered heels before finishing the day with a lovely dinner at the George.

Saturday, 27 June. Shopping. In the afternoon Miss Stone from the Depôt came to tea. She looks like a Pekinese dog, exactly, and usually is very talkative and boring. She was just as chatty today, but not so boring, as she and Robert had a lot in common as to Church architecture and things historical. Vera came in for the evening, and to supper, but I suddenly had a liver attack of the 'stars and stripes' variety, which left me feeling ill and headachey.

Occasionally private and domestic life was interrupted by war news, which, as Madge said on 29 June, 'is again very bad, and everyone is very gloomy. The Germans pressing into Egypt. Something must be very, very wrong, and one almost despairs sometimes, but we *must* have faith and just do our bit as much as possible.' The following day's brief entry concluded with the words: 'More grave war-news. Oh dear, oh dear!'

Thursday, 2 July. A busy morning, getting through my work and packing, and having an early lunch, before starting our two days of sophisticated holiday

---

[2] Headington Quarry's strikingly plebeian character has been richly documented for earlier generations by Raphael Samuel in his essay, '"Quarry Roughs": life and labour in Headington Quarry, 1860–1920', found in his edited book, *Village Life and Labour* (London: Routledge & Kegan Paul, 1975), pp. 139–263. It had a population in the 1940s of some 3,800, more than ten times that of Robert's parish; many worshippers at St Michael at the North Gate came from outside the parish. Headington Quarry was a part of Oxford that was radically different from the genteel neighbourhood familiar to Madge.

as Nick's guests at Bournemouth. A beautiful summer day, and the journey there by coach (1.00p.m. to 5.30p.m.) was entrancing, through Abingdon, Newbury, Andover, Winchester, Southampton and Christchurch. We had tea at Winchester. Southampton is very badly bombed indeed. The New Forest looked most lovely in sunshine. Nick met us at Bournemouth, which appeared extremely prosperous, crowded, gay and un-bombed. The siren greeted us, too, but no-one took the slightest notice, as it evidently is a very common occurrence. Nick had a taxi out to the Branksome Tower Hotel, at Branksome, which is a beautiful part of Bournemouth, all tall pines, shrubs, trees, and well laid out roads. The hotel is enormous, and has a slightly passé air of faded splendour. We had a very nice room with a balcony. We went up to Nick's room for drinks, then sat in the pine-covered gardens, overlooking the sea, which is very much cut off by barbed wire etc. I cannot think of it as being my real beloved sea at Bournemouth, and it is even less so now. We had more drinks before dinner. Nick's only idea of a good time is drinking! It would never do for us for long, but we quite enjoy it as a change. A long chat till after midnight after the good dinner, in the large dining room with pre-war looking waiters, food and people. Poor Nick – what a life! And he pities *us* for our contented routine-like, quiet existence in an ordinary home. Ah well, one man's meat –––.

Friday, 3 July. A stormy rainy morning. I felt somewhat ill until the afternoon. Too much high living, I suppose. Breakfast in bed. Then we all went into Bournemouth, walking to West Bourne along the magnificent roads, almost overwhelmingly tree-ed and too green and rhododendron-covered for words. I felt stifled with greenery and lush foliage, and felt I couldn't breathe. Bournemouth slightly more human, though that too, whilst being most splendid and smart, is not a lovable place, like common old Brighton. It is all *too* immaculate and built too correctly and richly. We had coffee at Bobby's [department store]. Then Nick led us to the Norfolk, a very expensive and smart place, and there was more sitting about in the luxury bar for drinks – about an hour of this. Then we gave him lunch there. We went to the pictures, as it was raining, and saw Clive Brook in *Breach of Promise* – not bad. We left Nick to sleep away the drinks in there, and came out for a cup of tea and a stroll round the town to get any air there was. The evening was fine again. We decided definitely that we still don't care for Bournemouth whilst admiring its well-planned gardens and streets and its most excellent shops. We picked Nick up, and went back by bus to the hotel to change. There was dancing after dinner, and we sat and watched for hours, too tired to dance ourselves.

Saturday, 4 July. Up fairly early, and said our grateful farewells to poor pathetic Nick. A lonely man, deserted by his younger wife, and now quite well-off. It was sweet of him to have us there, and we enjoyed the rich living for just two days, but give us our quiet life, small but sufficient meals, our books and ordered existence, even my housework![3] We returned to Oxford again by coach, the same way, arriving at 3.15. We had a little shopping after tea, then supper, then the quiet read we longed for!

During the next couple of days Madge was busy cleaning the house in preparation for her mother's arrival on 7 July, which happened also to be the 83rd birthday of Danna, her mother-in-law. On the following day she and her mother went shopping together and enjoyed a coffee at the Cadena, 'even though Mrs Tyrell was at our table. I was polite to her, mostly, I fear, because of some strawberries she promised me.' On 9 July she went to the dressmaker's 'for a fitting of a cotton frock – made from a dust-sheet!'[4] On 10 July war-news was mentioned – she wished it 'would improve. Even the gallant Russians are falling back now. What an age it has been, of depressing set-backs, nearly three years. When will the tide ever begin to turn in our favour?'

---

3   Robert wrote in his diary for 4 July 1942 that, although L.N. had been generous, 'we were not happy for long in luscious hotel surroundings'. Madge later wrote of Leonard Nicholls, on 7 October 1944: 'Poor pathetic, unhappy Nick – no wonder drink is his only solace. How he manages to keep so cheerful is a wonder. I wish he could find a really nice loving 3rd wife.' (He had at the time been talking about his life in Nigeria.)

4   Still, this was an example of the advantages enjoyed by middle-class women at a time when new clothes were rationed, for Madge was at least in possession of fabric that could be turned to other and, in wartime, better use. Similarly, over three months later (18 October 1942), she, along with (probably) her mother, was able to convert 'an old table-cloth into table-napkins and tea-cloths, a virtuous Victorian occupation'. Longmate, in *How We Lived Then*, p. 250, reported that one young woman who went up to Oxford in 1943 'remembers preparing for a college dance by making a long dress out of a hospital sheet given her by her sister, a nurse. She removed the edge, cut out a halter neckline and pinned the material together at the shoulder with a gilt, arrow-shaped brooch, studded with green stones, borrowed from a fellow student. The result was impressive; a heavy white dress, gathered in at the waist and falling in folds below it like a Roman toga. At the same dance another girl sparkled in a dress made from furnishing material, and a third created a stir in a black nightdress worn beneath a pink chiffon slip.'

Saturday, 11 July. Doris on holiday for a week, so mother and I were busy all morning, housework, cooking and washing-up.[5] June came after lunch. She seems to have changed lately – and become hard, and seemingly callous, and hard to please. She used to be such a happy, easy person. She went off to Woodstock for the evening and returned triumphant after being dared to drink a combination of things which is supposed to knock out the most hardened drinker. She managed to survive, but only just, and arrived here in a giggly incoherent state. It is a great pity that she has been encouraged to drink like this, by her father [Harry] as she has such a nice, decent disposition underneath the flippancy.

Friday, 17 July. A great day – our Silver wedding day, 25 years of blessed happiness together, thank God. Married at 17, in the 3rd year of a war like this, 1917, the 7th month, the 17th day! We don't feel anything like old yet. Nor look it, I think. No-one does these days. I suppose if we had had children, we should have looked more mature! We had lovely presents, telegrams, cards, and messages – it was most lovely. We went up to town with mother on the 8.40 (Doris 'obliging' for the day). It was rather a dull rainy day, but it didn't make much difference, as we weren't out in it much. We did a little shopping, and had cups of tea at Selfridges. I bought a nice tailor-made blouse, very expensive, but it should be a good investment. We met Nita and Dick and Nance at the Regent Palace Hotel – Norman couldn't manage it – and had a merry though modest meal in the Grill Room, with a couple of modest drinks to mark the occasion, and there was lots of nice family chat. Nance had to get home then, and we others went to the Empire to see a very nice film, *Mrs Miniver*, all about an English family during the Battle of Britain and after. It was beautifully done, especially the acting of lovely Greer Garson and nice Walter Pidgeon.[6] We had cups of tea there –

---

5   'The washing up of supper, last thing at night, and the getting up in the morning,' she wrote two days later, 'are the only things we really dislike about this maid-less life.' These two exceptions were rather important, since Madge had no taste for rising early and liked to read in the evening before going to bed. 'Hard at work still,' she reported on 15 July, 'so many rooms, and all in use'. When Doris returned on 20 July, Madge's first words that day were – 'so breakfast in bed again'.
6   This iconic American film of the early 1940s was based on the 1939 novel by Jan Struther (which Madge read in 1943). It won six Academy Awards, including Best Picture, Best Director (William Wyler), and Best Actress. The film played a major role in bolstering American support for its British ally, which was suspect in some American circles for its rigid class distinctions. On 15 July Madge had seen another wartime drama, Terence Rattigan's new play *Flare Path*, 'which was all about an RAF station, the crews and their wives. It was awfully good, beautifully acted, and very moving and human, and natural.'

how different from the super-luxurious teas we used to get in that grand place. Now one had to fetch one's own, served in thick cups, and carried on an old tin tray! Funny – but somehow memorable. Mother seems to attract sirens, because, after months of silence there was an alert just as we were delving into the tube for Paddington. Actually the first I've heard in London. We came home on the 6.05 and had a final treat of dinner at the George, with a heavenly ham and salad, and strawberries and cream. Home to more telegrams and cards. A really happy day. Robert gave me a dear little Victorian silver necklace and Richmal Crompton's newest novel.[7] I gave him an 18th Century snuff box (for his saccharine tablets). Mother gave him a Queen Anne tea-spoon and cuff links, and me £1. Nita and Dick, £2 in new half-crowns! Nance and Norman, a very nice little tray. The Fryer family, some tumblers and jug. Celia [a cousin], different sorts of glasses. Danna, money (for towels). Flowers (roses) from Ruth, chocolates from Mrs Kent, a silver box from Mrs Jimenez, cards and telegrams from *lots* of people.[8]

Thursday, 23 July. Robert was rung up early to hear that his eldest brother Harry had died quite suddenly in bed, during the night. It was a great shock, as he was still young, and appeared in very good health. Robert has so much to see to now. Danna is a remarkable woman when real troubles come and was as brave as could be. She is wonderful. We couldn't go out much, as we expected so many messages. Robert went over to Aylesbury for a Rotary Club Conference. An alert at 12.30. I got up with mother.

Friday, 24 July. Robert had to catch an early train to Alton [Hampshire] to see about Harry's affairs, and I got his breakfast early and had it with him. Vera had said yesterday that her father was very ill, but we were shocked when we went round to inquire after him to hear that he had died in the early hours. Two deaths all at once, and both so unexpected. Mrs Dyer, Vera and Mabel [Vera's sister] were all marvellously brave. I can't understand how people can be so controlled and courageous. I feel as though I should never be. Mrs Dyer is even going to have her hair done this afternoon! Mother and I went to the pictures after tea, wanting to have our minds distracted from

---

7   Madge was speaking of *Mrs Frensham Describes a Circle* (1942). She thought it one of the best books she read this year.
8   Mrs Jimenez's gift was actually delivered the following day, she 'having discovered that it was our anniversary yesterday. She is so nice, and has such perfect manners.' This gift-giving seems to have been soon reciprocated, for on 9 August 'Mr and Mrs Jimenez came in after supper. One of their formal visits – very pleasant – to thank us for our silver wedding present to them.'

the sadness round us, and saw just the film to do so, *Week-end in Havana*, one of these highly improbable but entertaining Technicolor films with nice dresses and plenty for one's money. Robert got back about 10.15, tired after his busy day and much travelling.

Saturday, 25 July. Rather a nice day as to the weather, but not really as hot as it ought to be. Shopping. We sat in the garden most of the afternoon, for the first time for weeks, and chatted to Mrs Jiminez some of the time. I went round to Vera's after tea, strolling first round the [University] Parks with mother, and sitting on a seat in the sunshine. The Dyers were a little more settled down and less distressed, and carrying on the business of the pub as usual – very brave. Vera walked back with me. Kenneth Denton was there and stayed to supper, and a little piano playing and listening to gramophone records. He is a nice lad, but very 'Yorkshire'.

Monday, 27 July. Still doleful weather and doleful news, with broken nights often now, because of air-raid sirens. The enemy seems to be making a series of scattered raids during the moonlit nights.[9] I went to Mr Dyer's funeral in the afternoon when the sun came out, and in the evening went up to the Rose Hill Cemetery with Vera, to see the beautiful wreathes.[10] She is very cheery really, though of course feels her father's death very much.[11] I walked back with her, as she seems to like talking about him. This was the day that sweets were rationed, and the shops are now displaying very tempting things. Lots of people were delightedly gathered round, speculating how best they could use their coupons, as we only get 2oz a week.

Tuesday, 28 July. Robert went to Faringdon [Farringdon, Hampshire] to take Harry's funeral. I stayed, and in the afternoon read the Service to Danna at the same time that Robert would be reading it. It was rather nice to be able to do this. Mother had a field day on our grubby drawing-room suite, and made them look very much cleaner. Vera came round for an hour, and Robert returned at 8.00 and told us all about the funeral.

---

9   Many major German raids in 1942 targeted five historic towns (Bath, Exeter, Norwich, York, and Canterbury) and came to be known as the 'Baedeker raids'.
10 Robert took the funeral service in St Michael's Church. Mr Dyer's obituary spoke of his long service as a licensee in Oxford and of his work with the Oxford Licensed Victuallers' Central Protection Society (*Oxford Times*, 31 July 1942, p. 6).
11 Madge had a different view three days later: 'She seems, I think, over excited now, and on the verge of hysteria.'

Wednesday, 29 July. The weather always starts very dull, but generally gets sunny later, as if double-summer time didn't suit it. Shopping as usual. The last afternoon at the Depôt till October. There was a farewell party for nice Miss Pitts, the secretary, whom everyone loves, and who is returning to London. We shall all miss her very much. We had tea in the garden, when the weather had got really lovely. A beautiful tea of sandwiches, scones, cakes, biscuits and raspberries! Miss Pitts was given a cheque, and there was a group photograph with many 'sleeping members' in it, who always turn up for special occasions, and are never seen working! A busy evening cleaning silver etc.

'So many of these days are just alike,' Madge wrote the next day, 30 July, 'with only very small differences, so that it is very difficult to recall them once they have gone.' But there was one noteworthy event that day: 'We had a likely future curate and his wife to tea, Mr and Mrs Roberts, youngish. He was almost over-friendly and easy to entertain, she quieter and more normal. They have two young children, but I doubt if they will come as it will be difficult to find a house here.'[12] The August Bank Holiday weekend was noteworthy for 'a lovely supper [on Saturday, 1 August] of pork chops, apple sauce, and raspberries!', but otherwise unremarkable – dreary weather and 'The news is dreary too' (Monday). On Tuesday, 4 August, Robert missed the midnight train back from London and 'had to wait in the Station till 5.30a.m., poor lamb. I wondered where he was, and slept fitfully. Also there was another "alert" at 2.30.'

Further testimony to the Martins' close association with Oxford's Playhouse theatre was recorded on 5 August. 'The manageress of the Playhouse came to tea, Miss Celia Chaundy, a surprisingly young and pretty person. She appears harmless and pleasant enough, but the cast one and all appear to dislike her.' (Robert and Madge had clearly been made privy to these opinions.) The Martins, as other evidence from 1941 and 1942 shows, knew some members of this company personally and enjoyed their connections with theatrical society. 'We had Peter Copley[13] to tea, from the Playhouse,' Madge wrote on 8 September 1941. 'He is extremely pleasant, and made us feel very much at ease.' On 10 April 1942 Robert 'had to show some

---

12   See below, 27 and 29 September 1942, regarding Malcolm Pearce's departure as curate, p. 193.
13   Peter Copley (1915–2008) had a distinguished acting career that stretched from 1932 to his death in 2008, combining the London and provincial stage with films and television roles in many well-known dramas (*The Times*, 14 October 2008, p. 62). His presence in the Oxford Repertory Company followed service in the Royal Navy, from which he had been invalided out (Chapman, *Oxford Playhouse*, p. 125).

of the theatre people round the Colleges', and six days later he and Madge entertained one member of Oxford's company at home. 'We had Winifred Bury to tea, the Playhouse pianist.[14] She was the most friendly and charming of all of them so far, and they have all been nice. She took a lot of our music away to try – old musical comedy selections which she loves.' The world of the stage and its players appealed a lot to Robert and Madge.

Thursday, 6 August. Shopping, I suppose, but I can't remember really. Mother and I and Robert met [cousin] Celia [Bowen, b. 1900, daughter of Madge's mother's sister, Blanche], in at tea-time from Leeds. She is to stay three weeks. I haven't seen her for about 14 years, but she seems exactly the same to outward appearances, as ever, and looks scarcely any older in spite of her sorrows. I feel somehow rather silent and solemn in comparison – and so much more the wife and harassed housekeeper. She seems sweetly delighted with everything. She and mother get on very well, and I must try to fight down the thought that mother is fonder of her than of any of us, as I know it can't really be so – just her way of keeping us in our place, as she always did when we were children and the other children came to stay.

Friday, 7 August. Out shop-gazing and coffee-ing with mother and Celia. We all went up to our rooms to rest in the afternoon as we were tired of talking, and some, of listening. Nick came for the night, and we all went to the Playhouse to see *Rebecca* [1939, by Daphne du Maurier, based on her 1938 novel] – Vera too. It was very well done. I sat with Nick for some of the time, but he is strange at plays or films, and never takes them in. We had rather a horrid hurried dinner after, at the George, then came home for a song evening, till 2.30a.m. Nick at his most riotous, after whiskies. I played till I dropped off the seat with weariness. It is Nick's last evening of leave. He goes back to Nigeria tomorrow.

Saturday, 8 August. Miserable rainy weather – it makes shopping so dreary. Coffees at the Cafeteria. Then I went to register [for national service] – my class of 42 year olds having arrived. I expect I shall have an interview.[15] Bed

---

14 Winifred Bury (1897–1980) was a well-established musician – composer, pianist, singer, and accompanist – and had performed in concerts, radio, and early television. She was also an actress.
15 Starting earlier this year, women had been called up to register for national service according to the year in which they were born. Those born in 1921 had been called up first; now it was the turn of those born in 1899. The system is well discussed in H.M.D. Parker,

again in the afternoon, and a walk round the meadows between showers after tea. An alert sounded whilst we were out. Home to an ordinary evening. Celia joins in the reading after supper.

Monday, 10 August. Very depressing and fitful weather, more like April, with its sudden heavy showers and bursts of sunshine. I don't feel as good as I should – in my soul, as it were, and have a great difficulty in concealing my frame of mind, but I must, or I shall be sorry. Mother, Celia and I had coffee and shopped in the morning, and had the usual rather indolent afternoon. We all went to the pictures at night to see a good Mickey Rooney–Judy Garland musical film, *Babes on Broadway*.

'My diary is very dull lately,' Madge thought on 13 August. There was some truth in this self-assessment.[16] Still, there was the occasional revealing remark. On 15 August she mentioned Robert's niece, June: 'she seems even more hard-bitten than usual, after her father's death. This is her way, I think, of hiding her feelings, but I find her very restless and difficult.' The following day, a Sunday, she, Celia and Muriel walked through the University Parks and came across 'another pre-last-war scene – with a small band playing to a crowd seated in an enclosure and sunning themselves on the warm grass. … What a difference a bit of warmth makes to the poor British people – they unbend at once.' On 17 August there was a visit to Burford, 'the perfect English village'; the following day Madge had coffee in Oxford at the rather 'gloomy and quiet' Cafeteria, 'but [there] one gets served without queuing for it'; and on 19 August she saw *The Merchant of Venice* at the Playhouse. They went to this modern-dress production with sceptical minds but were 'pleasantly surprised' by what they saw – 'it was enchanting, perfectly produced and acted, with very charming settings and costumes. We really loved it.' In London on 21 August she thought 'the war has certainly changed the look of our beloved city, though her spirit remains the same'.

Manpower: A Study of War-time Policy and Administration (London: HMSO, 1957), chap. 17 and p. 491 (a volume in the *History of the Second World War, United Kingdom Civil Series*, edited by W.K. Hancock).

16 Many long-lasting private diaries fade at points, and some later regain a degree of vitality. Moreover, Madge's diary, unlike wartime diaries written for Mass Observation, had no mission to *inform* an outside reader of the diarist's experiences of life, which often gave MO diarists an incentive to carry on and try to convey useful information even when they felt sub-par. By contrast, if Madge felt dull, she made no particular effort to find things to write about.

Wednesday, 26 August. The weather still terribly hot, damp and unhealthy. Celia returned to Leeds via Derby, where she has to stay the night. Mother and I saw her off. I had dreaded her visit, for some quite unknown reason, but gradually the dear old 'Celes' came back as I knew her, and if she had been here long enough, we should have returned to the couple of giggling schoolgirls of 1911–1921! Lots of shopping and preparation for our holiday. If it is weather like this it will be *awful* in quiet little Hawkshead, but we just hope for the best. Mrs Harris and Arlette called after lunch. She is a face from the past, having been a menace years ago, now returned to a village nearby. She is worse than ever, and the child, apparently, seems forward and uncouth too. They have come from Canterbury, where Hitler's bombs failed to find them – this is unkind of me, but truly she is a *pest*. Busy packing all afternoon, and to the pictures with mother in the evening – very good English film, *The Foreman Went to France*.[17]

As in the previous year, the Martins enjoyed another late summer holiday in the Lake District, this one for two and a half weeks. Madge was thrilled with almost all her Lakeland experiences – the food, the walks, the company, the vistas, even (for the most part) the weather, which was, unsurprisingly, not always warm and sunny. She spoke of being 'in love with this part of the world' (29 August). She was very happy most days. She praised 'the beautiful fresh air' (13 September). She felt 'utterly refreshed' on the day of their departure for London and 'truly thankful for my heavenly holiday and good health' (14 September). Then there was a revealing last sentence in her diary entry for Wednesday, 16 September: 'Home on the 6.05 – straight to ecclesiastical atmosphere and maudish worries.'[18]

---

17 The script was written by J.B. Priestley, the score by William Walton. This was one of many wartime examples of close collaboration between the producers of popular culture and serious artists.
18 'Maudish' refers to Maud Pead, who, for undisclosed reasons, had become a problem for Madge, but was still being engaged and housed by the Martin household months later, despite ongoing complaints. As a cousin of Danna's, she was perhaps acknowledged to have family claims that could not be refused. On 17 February 1943, Madge wrote of 'the Maud-infested atmosphere of the home'; five weeks later (23 March) she disclosed that Maud was then sharing a room with Danna, Robert's mother – and perhaps had been for some time. More testimony as to Maud's provocative presence is found in the diary for 18 November 1944, five years after her arrival in Oxford. 'At tea-time, there was a fish-wives' row between Maud and mother, in which I had not much chance to make myself heard, but had to come

Thursday, 17 September. Back to shopping, planning, housework and domestic problems – always a horrid time till one gets used to it again. I ran into Mrs Booth on my way into town, and got a lot of my restlessness off in chatting to her and listening. Vera came to tea, which was cheering. Then we plunged straight into a whist-drive – no more thorough way of *really* getting normal again! We won 2nd prize at the drive, a military one. Oxford makes one very tired, coming back straight from the North.

Sunday, 20 September. I met Muriel on my way to Church, and had to turn back with her as she felt sick, as she often does – after wild indulgences of pork at night etc! I should feel sympathetic towards her, but there is something about her fat form and broad countenance that makes it impossible to feel anything but irritation. A luxurious reading afternoon, and Church at night with Vera. Dark now when we come out, and we have to start blacking out at 7.30! Everyone hates the thought of this winter before us, with the shortage of fuel now, to make things even worse. It is already cold, but we haven't started fires – just huddle beneath rugs. What it will be like when its gets really cold, I hate to contemplate.

Monday, 21 September. I received my papers for an interview for war-work, and went to get it over at once. They made me feel as though I were a lady of leisure, or had been, in spite of the Red Cross work, [the knitting] sub-Depôt, household shopping, housework and all, and they put me down as willing to do part-time work. I came out feeling ruffled up. One is too old at 42 to be cursorily treated after complete freedom since marriage. Still, I am willing – and am now in their hands.[19] Robert and I went to the Playhouse in the evening and saw *Ladies in Retirement* [1940, by Reginald Denham and Edward Percy] which was an excellent thriller and very well acted. We had an 'austerity' supper at the Randolph. Dear and rather 'ersatz'. I forgot

---

in, on mother's side, of course, at the end. I do believe – in fact we all do – that Maud is rapidly losing her mind, as she says such outrageous things. These rows shake me to the marrow, foolish though it may be. This was once a happy, peaceful house but since Maud came – not.' By linking here 'maudish worries' to 'ecclesiastical atmosphere', Madge again suggested her disaffection with church society.

19 The perception of Madge as 'a lady of leisure' is not surprising: in 1942, according to her own accounts, she went to the ballet 10 times and the theatre 45 times, as well as seeing 79 films.

– I had tea with Susie at the 'Racket'.[20] She was full of chat, and cheerful, as usual.

Wednesday, 23 September. I had to go to the Ministry of Labour – or the Exchange, whatever they call it, and stayed there ages filling up forms, and answering questions. It looks now as though I might actually have to work there, either from 9.00a.m. to 1.00p.m. or 1.00 to 5.00p.m. daily, including Saturdays! I can think about it, but there is apparently no alternative time for part-time work. I see that the hours are reasonable, but oh, how I shall hate my lack of freedom. No more lovely Friday walks, no more trips to town, no holidays! I quite see that it must be done, and I am quite willing, even anxious, to do my share, but one can't help feeling the lack of freedom more than some-one who has always worked. We had the new curate and his wife to tea – quite a pleasant middle-aged couple who were bombed out of their East-End home.[21] I wrote letters in the evening. It is cold now, as we daren't light fires just yet, if the fuel is to be short later on.

Thursday, 24 September. Shopping in the morning. I feel as though I cannot get really interested in anything until my future work is settled.[22] Letter writing in the afternoon, and a whist-drive at night.

Saturday, 26 September. Everyone shivering with cold. It seems very bad luck that this year, when we are asked to go without fires, if possible, till November 1st, the autumn is so much colder than usual. Perhaps it will get warm later. Shopping in the morning. Ruth to tea. She works harder than anyone I know, teaching German almost every evening, and doing the work of a huge house in the day time, yet she is an example of uncomplaining patience. She looks tired and sad sometimes. It is nice to get into bed with a hot bottle these nights.

---

20   Actually named 'The Rackett Restaurant', at 6 St Aldate's.
21   The new curate, the Rev. V.G. Kirk-Duncan, was older than Robert and from bomb-ravaged Stepney, where he had been Rector at St Philip's. According to Robert, Kirk-Duncan was 'doing post-graduate work at Magdalen College, and was to be made a Doctor of Philosophy two years later, and was to remain with us until the end of the war.' (Martin, *Church and Parish of St Michael at the Northgate*, pp. 186–7.) On 7 October 1942 Robert and Madge had tea with the Kirk-Duncans 'in their nicely furnished flat in George Street [no. 7 Three-Ways House]. They were very friendly and easy to get on with, and I think we shall probably like them very well.'
22   On 25 September she 'bought a new skirt and jumper, with the eye to a chilly unheated office during the winter'.

Sunday, 27 September. Church in the morning. Mr Pearce's last sermon here – he goes soon to more arduous work on the East Coast [Kirkley, near Lowestoft]. He is a nice conscientious young man, if sometimes precious, and will be missed. I wrote to John [in Gibraltar] in the afternoon, and went to Church again at night with Vera.

Tuesday, 29 September. Very rainy and cold. Michaelmas Day, so I went to the Services of Morning Prayer and Holy Communion at St Michael's – very sparsely attended. Shopped after, and got very wet. We had the boiler fire on for the first time today, so we had cosy meals in the kitchen after lunch to save the dining-room gas fire, in our campaign against waste in heating, which everyone is fighting this winter. Mr Pearce came to tea and had it with us in our warm but humble kitchen. He goes tomorrow. I stayed in all the evening cooking etc and Robert and I sat down there instead of in the sitting room. Queer ways!

Wednesday, 30 September. Warmer again, and sunshine – about time. Shopping. I heard from Chatham House, where I hoped to get part-time clerical war-work, that they have nothing for me at present.[23] Maybe later, so I am more unsettled than ever, and cannot make up my mind whether to wait and take no further steps till the Labour Exchange do, or plunge into the work they offer. It is a depressing state of affairs to be in. I went to Vera's to tea and, as usual, enjoyed it very much. Robert and I went to the

---

23   Chatham House, the Royal Institute for International Affairs, occupied premises in Balliol College, Oxford between September 1939 and August 1943. Oxford colleges were ideal sites for teams of researchers (and some others) needing to be relocated from bomb-threatened London. Government services were housed at several colleges: for example, most of Merton was taken over by the Ministry of Transport and half of Queen's by the Ministry of Home Security; the War Office's intelligence corps was settled at Oriel; and fish controllers were accommodated at St John's. (Brian Harrison, ed., *The History of the University of Oxford, Volume VIII, The Twentieth Century* [Oxford: Clarendon Press, 1994], p. 170.) Brasenose College was occupied by various military schools from 1940 (Brasenose College website). London University's medical students took over space at Keble College, Wadham College and St Peter's Hall (Graham, *Oxfordshire at War*, pp. 34–5). Corpus Christi College found room for some members of Chatham House and gave up some of its residential accommodation to house students from other colleges that had been taken over for non-academic purposes (Thomas Charles-Edwards and Julian Reid, *Corpus Christi College, Oxford: A History* [Oxford: Oxford University Press, 2017], p. 379). According to one estimate, about half of Oxford's colleges were 'assigned' to wartime purposes (Elton, *First Fifty Years of the Rhodes Trust*, p. 163). Teaching continued, though with an emphasis on short courses, including many for the Forces, and, relative to pre-war, the full-time undergraduates were disproportionately women (though still a minority).

Playhouse at night to see *Yes and No* [a comedy by Kenneth Horne] which we have seen before, but found amusing again. There is a good new man there, John Wentworth – or is it Richard?[24]

Saturday, 3 October. A busy morning decorating the Church with Michaelmas Daisies for the Patronal Festival tomorrow. Mrs Kirk-Duncan, the new curate's wife, helped. She is naturally a bit inclined to be too much in her element, having been a vicar's wife, and of course the 'big noise' in her sphere. Still, she might be worse. Muriel there too. The Church looks its loveliest with the varying shades of mauve and crimson of the daisies. I had tea with Muriel at the Moorish again. Then she came with me to St Barnabas Schools, where I registered for the compulsory fire-watching we have to do in future.[25] June and I cooked sausages and tomatoes for supper in the kitchen.

Tuesday, 6 October. Shopping. I feel to be in a 'Slough of Despond' [John Bunyan] just now, due to end of summer, restlessness about my future activities, cold fire-less rooms.[26] I am at last beginning to miss the business of having the huge family here to keep me too active to get dreary. I shouldn't get dreary really, as I have nothing in the world to make me so, but – there it is! The Depôt in the afternoon. Sometimes I think that this is dreary too, and that I should find myself a more active job, and leave Red Cross work to old ladies. There was a tea to welcome the new year's work [after the summer break]. I think I had a quiet sort of evening, as far as I remember.

Friday, 9 October. A nice Chiltern day for us. The usual 10.00 o'clock bus to the Lambert Arms [in Aston Rowant]. Then a leisurely ramble in our lovely heart of the Chilterns, beginning to flame with gold and brown. We picked beautiful berries and leaves for the Harvest Festival decorations, and picked

---

24   John Wentworth (1908–1989) went on to have a career in television.
25   St Barnabas schools were in Great Clarendon Street. These Fire Guard duties were the responsibility of local authorities, and women aged between 20 and 45 could be required to perform them (Terence H. O'Brien, *Civil Defence* [London: HMSO, 1955], pp. 599–600, a volume in the *History of the Second World War, United Kingdom Civil Series*, edited by W.K. Hancock).
26   'We are still holding out against having a fire in the sitting room, but it makes it very cheerless,' she had written the previous day, which was 'nasty' and damp. 'Still, we must remember how much colder it will get later on when we shall need all the fuel we can spare.' When on 10 October she did have a fire at home in the evening she was thrilled – 'such joy to have one'. Later that month she attended a meeting at the Shamrock: 'No heating yet allowed, and we were already cold and wet. This winter threatens to be a most terrible one' (26 October).

a few blackberries for a Sunday pie, had tea at Stokenchurch and returned by bus to Oxford in time to meet mother in at the Station from London, where she has been for six weeks. June here too for the night. She moves to Newbury tomorrow, on a fresh job.

Sunday, 11 October. Church with mother and Muriel in the morning. The Church resplendent again with flaming autumn colours, flowers and fruit and vegetables, and even pots of jam, cereals, one precious egg (someone's sacrifice!) and bread. Church again in the evening with mother and Vera. Crowds there, and the choir at full strength and blast, telling us in no uncertain terms that the Heavens were telling the Glory of God! Everybody loves the Harvest Festival.

Monday, 19 October. Robert, Mother and I all have colds – no wonder, with the Fuel Economy campaign,[27] and the cold weather. We shopped, and got ready for a tea-party in the afternoon. I had a bad head, but they don't hamper me as they used to do. Mrs Booth and her equally incomprehensible sister came to tea, also two American Army nurses, on leave from Ireland. They were so sweet, and looked very smart in their perky little navy uniforms. They seem so alive, and interested in everything. We enjoyed having them. An evening at home.

Tuesday, 20 October. A miserable rainy day. I feel very restless and unsettled and surrounded by cares at the moment. Doris has given notice for one thing.[28] I still don't know what war work I shall have to do. I have a horrid task of begging money from every house in St Giles for a YMCA hut, a thankless job. Fortunately I have met with only one repulse so far. The Depôt in the afternoon and at night we plunged through the torrent of rain to the theatre to see a nice little revue called *New Faces* [1940, by Eric Maschwitz]

---

27 Residents were being required by the Ministry of Fuel and Power to fill out 'household fuel assessment forms' (*Oxford Times*, 16 October 1942, p. 3). The primary objective was to restrict residential use of coal so that supplies could be used as much as possible to support the war purposes. Rationing was tightened further the following year, with strict limits on the quantity of coal a householder could purchase (*Oxford Times*, 24 September 1943, p. 3). Consumers were advised to 'Order your fuel now, but don't expect to get coal of the size or type to which you have been accustomed in the past: it may not be available either now or later.' See also Graham, *Oxfordshire at War*, pp. 151–2.
28 'Doris now wants a Sunday off every month,' she wrote on Sunday, 25 October. 'A certain amount of Dictatorship is beginning, it seems, but I feel not for long.' The war undoubtedly gave domestic servants much greater leverage in dealing with their employers.

with no stars but one of our Playhouse friends in it, Christopher Hewett.[29] We enjoyed it quite a lot.

Thursday, 22 October. I really can't be bothered to write much about these days, which are dreary to say the least, not to say definitely unpleasant, in minor domestic ways, though these are of course negligible, comparatively speaking. Still, they certainly aren't [worth] mentioning in a diary, although they occupy so much thought.[30]

Thursday, 29 October. There was a great to-do with Doris in the morning, and I had to give her notice. She has been with us for 14 years and once was a 'treasure', but has never been the same since the war, gradually growing more insolent, and working only when she felt like it. Things have been very difficult for years, and not helped any by the different personalities in the home, since war started. So, it is best that she should go, and I think that frayed nerves will settle down. I wish our other 'problem' was also solved.[31] I felt rather upset by all the shouting and recriminations, and I can't remember anything more about this day. I think I dressed a doll at night for the Red Cross Bazaar [to raise money for Prisoners of War].

Friday, 30 October. Mother and I up and doing, of course, in Doris' absence, but we quite enjoy it – up to a point! It is nice to be able to control all the food ourselves anyway. Robert spent a lot of his holiday time collecting YMCA envelopes on my behalf – a great help. Then we had a peaceful tea together at the Moorish. Only one sort of cake there now, after the new restrictions, a fruit slab. No more éclairs or ginger sponges, alas! We went to the Playhouse with Vera and saw an awfully good play, *Sheppey* [1933] by Somerset Maugham, extremely interesting and beautifully acted. Mother with Maud at the theatre. Mrs Booth had let us have two tickets for *The Merry Wives of Windsor* which she couldn't use. June came for the week-end.

---

29 Christopher Hewett (1921–2001) began his acting career at the Oxford Playhouse and made his début in the West End in 1943. He appeared in plays, musicals, films, and television in Britain and the United States, and also directed (*Independent*, 9 August 2001, p. 6).
30 Here is an explicit declaration of a form of self-censorship. Some of her concerns and worries were, for whatever reasons, rarely if ever recorded in her diary. About certain topics and people she was reluctant to be fully candid. At the beginning of her 1935 diary, just before her entry for 1 January, she wrote: 'I am trying to make resolutions for the New Year, but they are too secret to write down.' (At the end of this volume, on 31 December 1935, she confessed that 'I have entirely forgotten what the resolutions were!')
31 Madge at no point indicated what the problem was, though the most likely candidate is Maud Pead.

Saturday, 31 October. Working hard again in the morning. Mother is a marvellous worker. She does most of the cooking and the downstairs work, and I do the upstairs. We find it works out very well. Muriel appeared and did a bit of shopping for me. I met her for tea at the Moorish. A quiet evening writing to John. June in – she is a great help too, and is very sensible.

Sunday, 1 November. Everyone welcomes the beginning of November this year, as the ban on heating buildings is lifted and we feel that we can have a fire without feeling guilty. Mother and I working hard in the morning, and June lent a hand too. A restful afternoon, then Ruth came to tea. It is her birthday today. I had had a remote hope that she might be persuaded to leave her rather hard present place and come here, but she is so loyal to everyone that she is going to stick it there. Ah well, it mightn't have worked out – you never know with friends! We stayed at home at night, too tired for Church.

Thursday, 5 November. Everyone very excited and happy for once at very good news from Egypt where Rommel's forces have had a definite beating from us after 12 days' fighting. It is one of our few real victories so far, and has lightened all heads with its promise of better things to come. Fearful weather today. We expected an American soldier to tea but he failed to appear, after preparing a grand meal for him. Robert and I went in the awful rain to the military whist-drive, where we got the Booby prize!

◆

Three themes were prominent during the rest of November. First, there was much better war news, with, as Madge put it on 8 November, 'the Americans marching into North Africa, and we pursuing Rommel's army out of Egypt'. A certain optimism was in the air. 'The news is heartening these days,' she wrote on 14 November, 'and it is so nice not to dread listening to the wireless, or reading the headlines.' The next day, a Sunday, there were crowds at Church for both Remembrance and to give thanks for the victory in Egypt. 'The bells pealed this morning in celebration of it. They haven't been allowed to do so since the war started – only in case of invasion. It was lovely to hear them.'

Second, with Doris gone, Madge was much busier at home. 'I hate the actual getting up,' she admitted on 9 November, 'but quite enjoy the work when I get going.' Moreover, she thought there were advantages in not having help (10 November): 'no waste of food or gas, and much more interesting meals than before, and a great saving of money'. Still, as she added, 'I shall really have to get help before the Spring.' A search was launched, and on 17 November she thought 'we are having a "woman" twice a week, a Mrs Nutt'. Initially things did not go well. 'We expected "the woman" this morning [20 November], but as is the way with all "women", she never turned up. But as we couldn't have really found her a thing to do (all seems to keep twice as clean since Doris went), we weren't sorry really.' This insouciance was, if not feigned, certainly short-lived, for as she declared on 26 November, 'There is an enormous amount to do to keep this house as nice as it should be kept.' There was movement on the household front on 24 November. 'Mrs Nutt, our new "help", came in the morning. She seems quick and sprightly.' She was back on 27 November, 'so I was able to go out a bit with Robert'. A week later (4 December) Madge was also pleased: 'The brisk Mrs Nutt here in the morning, so I was able to get out shopping for Christmas, a little, with Robert.'

Third, lots of time was being consumed this month making dolls for December's Red Cross Bazaar. This work involved various hands. On 7 November 'Muriel looked in with a doll she had dressed for me for the Bazaar. She does things well but expects twice as much admiration as everyone else. ... I dressed small dolls at night.' Madge often reported dressing dolls – specifically on 8, 10, 11, 13, 16, 23, 25, 27, and 29 November (June helped on both these latter days). It is likely that this work occupied her on other evenings too. She was also at the Red Cross Depôt many weekday afternoons. With all this work to do, she had little time for reading. Dolls and toys loomed large in her life for several weeks. Robert ensured that a notice of the sale – 'where St Michael's is responsible for the Christmas Tree' – appeared in the *Parish Magazine* (December 1942, p. 1): 'Purchases here will not only secure Christmas presents for our children in these days when toys are so scarce, but will help our own Prisoners of War as only the Red Cross can do.' After a Mrs Wood brought her 'some dolls and toys of her own childhood for my collection' on 18 November, Madge remarked on 'how sweet' the dolls were 'of those days', and lamented 'that the Germans are not still busy making some charming toys instead of bringing misery to the world'.

Monday, 30 November. Still busy at home – and for the Sale.[32] Mother and I went to the private view of the Depôt dolls and toys in the afternoon – they have a bewildering amount. Very exhausting looking round. I haven't seen so many since the war. They should be a godsend to all who want Christmas

---

32   Madge's altered working circumstances at home and active volunteering had an impact on how she was regarded at the Labour Exchange. 'I had to go to the Labour Exchange again,' she wrote on 21 November, 'but when I told them that I had now no maid or any help in the house, she realized that until I had again I couldn't do any part-time war-work, but only go on with the Red Cross. I was relieved at this, as I don't know how I could have got through any more.'

presents for children as the shops have next to nothing in that way. An evening at home.

Tuesday, 1 December. I had a hell of a headache just when I could least cope with it. Robert and I spent most of the morning hanging about at the Cadena waiting for the Christmas tree to arrive. It came in the afternoon, and we, together with Mrs Nichol-Smith and Miss Walker, decorated it. Mother helped too, and we had tea there when my head began to go. Now all the toys have gone round, and the dolls are all dressed. I was able to have a fairly easy evening.

Wednesday, 2 December. The day of the great Red Cross Bazaar for the Prisoners of War, held at the Cadena. We scuttled through our work, and I went round with Robert at 10.00. It was supposed to start at 11.00, but an immense crowd poured in long before that, not waiting for the opening by the Duchess of Marlborough, and in no time at all the Christmas Tree and all the toys we had were sold up, and my gallant band of helpers, Miss Walker, Mrs Nichol-Smith, Mrs Eliot and Miss Masefield,[33] were besieged and nearly torn to pieces. Our things were really bargains and some were quite beautiful, so we were, I think, the first to be emptied, and took over £42, a good sum for such cheap things. The room was packed out from 10.30 to the end, and they must have made hundreds of pounds. I had lunch with Mrs Eliot at the Shamrock, as we couldn't get it at the Cadena, and tea with mother and Vera. I've never *seen* so many people at a Sale in all my life. Robert was *such* a help dressing the tree and even helping to sell in the crush. It *was* a day![34]

---

33 Judith Masefield (1904–1988), daughter of the Poet Laureate John Masefield who lived in Oxford, was an illustrator.

34 Some 900 POWs were said to be from Oxfordshire, including 200 from the City (*Oxford Mail*, 3 December 1942, p. 4). On 8 December Madge went to help 'sell some of the dolls and things left over from last week's Bazaar, at the Clarendon, but I am no seller, really, especially when the things to sell are so expensive. I have too much sympathy with the customer.' This Red Cross Prisoners of War Week included numerous special events – a concert, a dance, a flag day, a tea at the Randolph Hotel, and more – all focused on fund-raising (*Oxford Times*, 4 December 1942, p. 4).

Robert was a big supporter of Madge in her Red Cross work and often used his pulpit on Sunday to seek worshippers' help. Around a year and a half later, on Sunday, 18 June 1944, shortly after D-Day, she wrote that 'Robert made an appeal for me for the Red Cross, for pillow-cases for ambulances for the wounded from Normandy. To my astonishment, I had promises for 400, nearly.'

Saturday, 5 December. Rainy early on, but giving way to a pure turquoise sky, against which Oxford's buildings stood out, as if made of icing sugar. Lovely! Out a little with mother in the morning. I wrote some of my Christmas cards in the afternoon. We are not sending any to the Church people this year, but putting the money into war savings, so I only had about 30 instead of nearly 200 to do. I went along to what was to have been a Fire Guard training class, but as no-one else turned up, I just had a cosy chat with Mollie Counsel [of 2 Pusey Street, St Giles], the senior Fire Guard of this district. She is very charming in spite of looking most masculine – always in trousers, and even smoking a pipe. She is gentleness itself though, and everyone likes her.

Thursday, 10 December. The great whist-Drive day, and me with a headache and all! But it wasn't too bad. This is the last hot and botheration affair till Christmas, I hope. We needn't have feared that no-one would come, or that there wouldn't be enough to eat, and not enough prizes. We were besieged with people, deluged with food and drink, and over-faced with prizes, so that half the people there, including me, got one! It was really an enormous success and got over £22, I think the highest sum ever taken at a St Michael's whist-Drive. No-one seemed to mind the crush, and all appreciated the lovely pre-war food. I do wish that Hitler could have seen it. It would have convinced him, surely, that England is far from starving! The Prisoners of war, poor things, will have at least benefited to the extent of over £64 from St Michael's, with the Christmas tree takings too. I only hope they get the parcels, and not the Germans.[35]

Friday, 11 December. Still a wee bit tired, but Mrs Nutt here, so we could relax a bit. I did a bit of Christmas shopping but it is *so* difficult to find anything to buy this year, without coupons, and I come home frustrated so often. It is just my luck that even my present to Robert, which I had got rather rejoicingly, has gone awry. It was a fitted writing-case to take the place of one which was stolen some months ago, and which he used a lot.

---

35   On 23 December Madge reported that her husband was busy 'selling his old soldiers, which he had arranged most beautifully in the Morris Garage window [a high-profile location]. He is sacrificing them for the Prisoners of War Fund – and got £10 for them.' There were, apparently, many (perhaps hundreds) of gifts of items to be sold this month in aid of this fund. The items put up for sale at an auction on 10 December at the Randolph Hotel included two white jade scent bottles from the Duchess of Kent, a silver and turquoise cigarette box from the Duchess of Marlborough, a model aeroplane capable of flying made by the Oxford Police Force, and two bottles of whisky sent from the Lord Mayor of London. An American officer donated £10. The auction realized some £425. (*Oxford Times*, 11 December 1942, p. 8.)

But this very morning a detective walked in with it, recovered at Aberdeen! I am very disappointed, as I really was pleased with my choice of a gift for him, in this difficult year. Robert and I went to an amateur performance of *Love from a Stranger* [1936, based on a 1924 short story by Agatha Christie] in St Faith's Hall. One of our ex-Junior Guild girls was in it, Anne Buttrum. It was a bit tiresome, though a good play. June here for the week-end.

Thursday, 24 December. Christmas Eve! Lovely day, really the nicest in the whole year, even in war-time; and although gifts and food are very difficult this year, everyone is determined to make the best of it, and for weeks the shops have been crowded with people buying presents, cards and extra treats. The better war news, too, makes us feel that we *can* celebrate a little.

A busy morning. I decorated the font, with Muriel, and the Chancel window, and did final shopping. We have managed to get a goose! I went to see Mrs Busby in the afternoon and took her money from the Church, some bulbs from us, and two oranges – very precious now [young children always got first pick whenever oranges were available]. The usual lovely evening, decorating the house and tree with our familiar things saved year after year – the kneeling cherubs and Christ-child, and miniature fir-trees, on the mantel-shelf the 'snow-storm', crib, festoons, holly and mistletoe, and finally the gathering-up of presents, in piles, for each one. 'Stille Nacht, heilige Nacht.'

Friday, 25 December, Christmas Day. Up bright and early for the 8 o'clock Holy Communion – Vera there. I love the darkness of Christmas morning, and the brightness of the decorated Church. Home to breakfast, and then the exciting opening of our gaily-wrapped parcels. I had such beautiful things – and we had our usual display in the waiting room. I wasn't able to go to the Christmas morning service this year, as having no Doris, we had to do our usual household duties, and mother had to cook the goose, which she did beautifully – also the Christmas pudding. It was a most luxurious feast, in the stately dining room, with the lace cloth, candles, and best glass – not pigging it, as we have done, from fuel reasons, lately in the kitchen. We listened to the King's speech in the afternoon. He sounded much more confident than usual, and has a nice voice. We cut sandwiches after tea for the three guests who came in later. Muriel, Miss White, whom I have only recently got to know, and like. She is quiet but cheerful, thirty five-ish, tawny-haired, tall and slim. She is housekeeper at the Radcliffe [Infirmary]. An army sister also looked in – not the lonely soul we had expected, but rather a gay, wild and slightly tipsy young person. She stayed to the supper and a game, then, rather to our relief, left to go on duty. We played more games and sang, finishing up with the rowdy 'Excelsior'. It was quite an amusing evening, and the whole day was most happy and enjoyable. My Christmas present list over-leaf.[36]

Thursday, 31 December, New Year's Eve. Goodbye to 1942. Not such a bad year as its previous three terrible war years. It really looks as if 1943 will bring hopes for the beginning of the end, and we surely can look forward with hope, even though there may be bad patches to endure still. Anyway we don't feel so depressed as on the eve of 1942, and for me personally, I look back on it as, on the whole, a happy year, considering the war. It has brought minor changes – the children and Nancy going back to London; Robert's brother, Harry's, death; John off to Gibraltar for 18 months; Doris going, after 15 years, so that mother and I have to work extremely hard.[37] Lovely holidays, especially the Hawkshead one; an improvement in food; not so many raids, and scarcely a siren in Oxford, thank God. Sweets rationed; eggs appearing very, very seldom; towels rationed[38]; less clothes' coupons; on the whole bad weather. The Russians still doing marvellously, and Stalingrad not fallen yet; our 1st and 8th armies also doing well in Libya and Tunisia, and the Americans too. Our Air-Force now larger, at last, than that of our enemies – so that surely we should have a better year in 1943.

We were invited to a New Year's Eve party, given by Mrs Allen, at Rhodes House for American and Canadian Forces.[39] We went about 9.00 and had a really lovely time. There was dancing and community singing, led by a sprightly young American captain. They are so easy to make friends with, and no-one could feel shy with them. I danced a lot, and found myself doing the 'Conga' and other new American dances, quite adequately. I am always a bit afraid that because I don't go to many – or *any* dances – I shan't be able to do the new ones, but I managed this time. Winifred Bury and other Playhouse people were there. Rhodes House is such a beautiful place and Mrs Allen is such a charming hostess that all the parties they give

---

36 This page listed the approximately thirty presents she received and the names of their givers.
37 Describing these occurrences as 'minor' seems odd, but this is what she wrote.
38 Soap and soap flakes were also being rationed, as she noted on 9 February 1942.
39 Dorothy Allen was the wife of Carleton Allen, Warden of Rhodes House. In 1939 she presided over a household there of sixteen people. (Barbara Tearle kindly supplied this information.) The hospitality and educational activities of wartime Rhodes House, mainly for North Americans, are described by her husband in Elton, *First Fifty Years of the Rhodes Trust*, pp. 171–3.

are successes. We saw the New Year in there, the nicest and cheeriest way possible, with our friendly allies.[40] Good luck to 1943.

---

40 Robert, by contrast, did not enjoy the party: 'I was bored stiff' and 'glad to get home'.

8

Carrying On

January 1943–December 1943

Friday, 1 January, 1943. Robert has bought my diaries this year, two exercise books. I started using this sort last year, because I couldn't get a suitable diary, and have grown to like it better, as one can write exactly as much or as little as one likes. 1943 starts much more hopefully than 1942 did and we all hope that this may be the last year of war – or that the end of it may see victory in sight at least. The days are much alike – a lot of housework in the morning, as Doris is no longer here;[1] letter-writing and reading in the afternoon (the Red Cross Depôt is on holiday just now). In the evening we went to the pictures to see an amusing film, *Between Us Girls* [with Diana Barrymore and Robert Cummings], which was fun.

Saturday, 2 January. Very, very cold just now – the winter is really just starting. Out, after our usual work in the morning. I washed Danna's hair in the afternoon. It was quite black instead of snowy white, after her oil-lamp had smoked during the night, covering her and the bedroom with horrible oily smoke. Mrs Nutt and I spent a whole morning cleaning it all up. Mother and I also washed our hair. I used one of my birthday 'Drene' shampoos on mine, and at last it came soft and shiny. I haven't been able to buy a nice shampoo for years.[2]

Thursday, 7 January. Very headachey today. Where do these headaches come from? I go to bed quite free from them, and wake up with a juicy one so often. However, they often take themselves off in the evening, as this one

---

1   However, Mrs Nutt was coming two mornings a week to help with the housework, and her contributions were still being praised weeks later (5 February and 5 March 1943).
2   On 5 April 1943, when she went to the hairdresser's for a (now infrequent) permanent wave, she was there for almost five hours.

did, after going to bed with Veganins [used for headaches] and a [hot water] bottle in the afternoon. It improved so much that I was able to go to the Playhouse with Vera and mother to see *Maria Marten* again. Quite amusing, and the audience helped.³

Friday, 8 January. Extremely cold – now the really cold weather begins. Winter never really becomes very severe till about now. It is so cold that one can hardly bear to take one's clothes off properly to wash, and the only warm place is in bed with two hot bottles – and then the nights are so short. Nothing much doing today. I had another nice present from John – a pair of stockings – and how welcome.⁴ We went to a Fire Guard meeting at night, and heard again all about different and horrible types of bombs and methods of dealing with them. I feel that I should be entirely useless, especially with the new explosive sort, or the oil bomb. Heaven grant we may never have an attack here, though why we should be spared, I don't know.⁵

Monday, 18 January. The usual morning. Cup of tea at 7.40. Reluctant tearing out of bed – this is my greatest trial of no-maid conditions, as I have been

3 A 'theatrical lark', according to the *Oxford Times*, 8 January 1943, p. 7.
4 Stockings were not the only items valued by women that had become hard to get. 'I bought two pairs of corsets,' Madge wrote on 24 October 1942, 'as they are getting so short, especially the elastic ones, as we have no more rubber coming in.' After Japan's military advances in 1942, it controlled most of the world's rubber supplies, and elastic made from synthetic rubber was not satisfactory. Furthermore, as an authority on this subject has said, 'The corset industry had released a high proportion of its resources to the war effort,' especially the production of parachutes. As well, the skilled workforce was greatly reduced, imposing a further constraint on the manufacture of corsets. (E.L. Hargreaves and M.M. Gowing, *Civil Industry and Trade* [London: HMSO, 1952], p. 466, a volume in the *History of the Second World War, United Kingdom Civil Series*, edited by W.K. Hancock.) In mid-1943 Oxford's WVS put on a salvage display that focused on rubber and its use in various manufactured items. 'It created an interest, and a good deal of rubber has been brought to the depôt, especially old rubber hot water bottles.' (RVS Archive & Heritage Collection, Oxford City Narrative Report, July 1943.) See Plate 16.
5 Oxford (with one minor exception) was in fact never bombed. A map of air raids in Oxfordshire, 1940–1944, shows not a single hit on the city (Graham, *Oxfordshire at War*, p. 26). Later in the war only four V1 missiles reached the whole county, in contrast to 886 in Sussex, 412 in Essex, and 295 in Surrey (O'Brien, *Civil Defence*, pp. 431–2 and 682). Still, no one could be sure of what might happen – including Robert in his concern to protect his Church. He once appealed for three or four fire-watching volunteers, men or women who would undertake in turns to go to the Church when 'alerts' were sounded. 'Only two people are required there at a time, and if we can obtain a few more offers of help, a rota can then be arranged so that each volunteer will need to go only occasionally.' (*Parish Magazine*, August 1941, p. 3.)

used for years to breakfast in bed, because of headaches. What a good thing that I am at last growing out of them. We are always up for the 8 o'clock news, now, at present, generally encouraging. Breakfast, drawing-room fire, door brasses, hall, and rooms to Hoover and dust, bathroom etc. to do. Mother valiantly below in the kitchen and scullery, and cooking lunch. We manage to get round all right, and occasionally get a bit of shopping done. Whilst the Depôt is on holiday it is nice to be quiet in the afternoon, or I go out, as I did today, with Vera, though this was exceptional. She, mother and I went to the Playhouse at night to see *Quiet Wedding* [1938, by Esther McCracken], familiar but delightful and very well acted this time.

Tuesday, 19 January. An ordinary morning. Tuesdays and Fridays are supposed to be somewhat eased by the help of Mrs Nutt, but we still seem to do much the same, whilst she does the 'extras'. I had tea with Susie at the Shamrock, and went with her to choose a gramophone record afterwards, for her. She chose the *Coppélia* Ballet music. I washed my hair. It is long and horribly straight now.

Wednesday, 20 January. One begins to feel the usual January depression about now. The war news is still much better but there are horrible things to worry about like the Jewish massacres. If only something could be done to save some of those wretched thousands. I have just read a horrifying pamphlet on the subject, and feel very miserable but helpless about it. Robert and I went to see *Pied Piper*, the film of the splendid novel [by Nevil Shute]. It was very good indeed and we enjoyed it enormously.

Thursday, 21 January. Very busy getting rooms ready for Nita and Dick and Christopher, who hope to come for the week-end. We went to the pantomime again at night – mother, Vera, Robert and me, with the 'choir-boys' treat. The theatre manager gave us 25 lovely stalls, which was very generous. We enjoyed it again, as much, I think, as the choir-boys!

Friday, 22 January. Busy as usual – or more so in the morning. We expected Nita and Kit at 5.45, so I went to bed for a rest in the afternoon – a thing I rarely do – and they suddenly appeared before I was up, having come on an earlier train, so instead of being the 'soignée hostess' to greet them, I was taken unaware. It was lovely to see Nita and we had a nice evening chatting. Christopher is now 'dabbling in oils' and produces surrealist pictures to his own satisfaction at any rate!

Saturday, 23 January. Richard arrived to complete the family reunion, in time for lunch. Muriel and José Trafford came in for coffee in the kitchen.

José is growing into a nice, intelligent girl. A lovely afternoon. Nita, Dick, Kit and I went out to buy some cups and saucers at Bakers [at the corner of Broad Street and Cornmarket Street], for our birthday present to Nita (her birthday is on Monday). It is very hard to find cups and saucers now, so she was pleased with the pretty white ones she got. We prowled round Blackwells afterwards. I had to go to a Fire Guard stirrup-pump practice in the evening at the Welsh Commissioner's office,[6] crawling about floors, and dealing with imaginary explosive bombs. Heaven preserve me from the real thing! Nice to get home to a ham supper!

Sunday, 24 January. A morning in the home with the family – working, cooking, listening to the gramophone and lunching. The 'guests' went at 3.15 and we had to settle back to normality again. Church at night and a good sermon about the Jewish persecutions from Robert.

Wednesday, 27 January. Tired and headachey, as Robert had been called out at 2 in the morning to go to a dying woman, the first time this has happened, at this time of the day. I retired to bed in the afternoon to nurse the head, and spent an evening wrapping up Robert's birthday presents, mostly books, and getting ready for going to town tomorrow to celebrate the birthday by spending a night at the Regent Palace Hotel.

Saturday, 30 January. Oxford had an exciting week-end with two days' 'mock invasion'. Today was the 'air attack' and all shops, cinemas and theatres were closed, and civilians, except those who were taking part in the exercises, were not allowed out. It was very thrilling and rather frightening to see the enormous planes 'dive-bombing' and flying very low over the houses whilst being attacked by dummy anti-aircraft fire. A noisy but interesting day.[7]

Sunday, 31 January. The day of the 'invasion by enemy troops'. Even the churches were closed after 9.00a.m. and Robert had a strange Sunday at home. We could only hear the excitement and 'noises off', which were quite

---

6   The Commissioners of Church Temporalities in Wales was at 46 St Giles Street.
7   Robert wrote of this day in his diary: 'The Imaginary Air-raid began at 1.00. I dressed in all my ARP kit and went through the streets deserted by all but ARP people to the Church, where I climbed the Tower with an earnest young Cockney archaeologist in the Signals.' On Friday, 29 January the Oxford press published very detailed forewarnings of what was to happen during the weekend's 'Exercise Carfax' and how people should conduct themselves, which often meant staying out of the way (*Oxford Mail*, p. 3; *Oxford Times*, p. 3). Except for Civil Defence workers, the main streets were almost entirely deserted. However, it was also said that 'Everyone should be ready to assist in digging trenches, clearing road-blocks or any other duties they may be called upon to do by the military or civil authorities.'

loud. We went out after the 'all clear' sounded, into St Giles to see the tired tank corps having a hot meal, looking very dirty and oily. The day had been a very wild one, with a 70 miles an hour gale and rain. The wind was as noisy as the guns.[8]

Tuesday, 2 February. Nothing much today either [like the day before]. Danna's cousin, Mary, came over to see her for the afternoon, a sharp, practical person with a humourless 'no nonsense' air, but at least *sane*, as so many people who are in some way attached to both our families are not. I looked in at the Depôt but as the bandaging room is closed at present for want of materials from the Red Cross headquarters, I didn't stay.[9] Mrs MacGregor, the nice but sweetly distant [woman], invited me to the theatre to see Noel Coward next week.[10]

Wednesday, 3 February. Delightful weather. Really, this winter so far has been wonderful, and the news of war so much better, that it is grand to read a paper these days. Mother and I went to see Mickey Rooney in *A Yank at Eton* in the evening. It was amusing and enjoyable, but quite impossible, and must cause Etonians great mirth.

---

8 Understandably, the postmortem was extensive, given the efforts invested in the exercises (*Oxford Mail*, 1 February 1943, p. 3; *Oxford Times*, 5 February 1943, p. 5). These mock battles gave Oxford residents a modest sense of raids that they never actually had to face. Pretend-bombers 'gave the City a thrilling idea of what might be expected in a heavy enemy raid, and sharp and heavy explosions were heard in all parts of the City. Smoke bombs were also used and palls of smoke hung over the main objectives as the planes weaved and circled overhead. Wave after wave of attacking planes came over and the steady drone of their engines fill the air.' (*Oxford Times*, 5 February, p. 5.) Public statements and assessments underlined the great success of the exercises and the City's ability to defend itself (*Oxford Times*, 5 February 1943, p. 4 and 12 February 1943, p. 5).
9 The following Tuesday, 9 February, finding the bandaging room still closed, 'I went to the sewing room, where I was given the dull job of unpicking and re-stitching Red Cross labels on pull-overs. I don't think I shall go again till our own room gets going, as I miss my cronies, and there is not enough to do to justify going.' The sewing room, for her, was 'dismal', unlike the bandaging room where she had made friends and felt at ease (24 February). Occasionally her work at home involved maintaining clothes: she spent almost all the evening on 15 February 'pulling out from a white cardigan of Harry's the navy letters and insignia of the OU Lawn Tennis Club, a horrid task, but wool is precious now, and every garment may be useful'.
10 Coward's new play was *Present Laughter*, which Madge found 'amusing, smart, clever, and typical of him in his sophisticated strain' (10 February). Coward starred in two other of his plays performed this week at the New Theatre, *Blithe Spirit* and *This Happy Breed* (see 11 February).

Saturday, 6 February. June went over to Bedford for the day. It is a pity that everyone can't see what a fine girl she is. I never seem to have enough time to talk to her these busy days, and I think we should get on very well together. I always admire these people who hide their real worth under a façade of reserve. Nothing much to write about today. Meal-times are often stormy – I think it is the two opposite mothers who set an argument alight, and lead up to quarrelling pitch. I try to keep pretty mum. Anyway the house *is* alive.

Thursday, 11 February. Just a usual day – till again in the evening we went to the theatre, all of us and Vera, to see another Noel Coward play *This Happy Breed* which was as unlike yesterday's [*Present Laughter*] as possible, being homely and 'lower middle-class', a domestic saga of a Clapham Common family from 1919 to 1939. We liked it very much indeed, and think Noel Coward is remarkable – a real genius of the stage.[11]

Friday, 19 February. Robert in Brighton today, taking Mr Wills' (his god-father's) funeral. Another beautiful day [the winter was exceptionally mild]. Out with mother in the morning, looking longingly at Spring clothes and counting coupons, which don't go far. I spent most of the afternoon chatting with Mrs Jimenez, sitting in the sunshine in the garden, and being shown fascinating photographs of their home in Spain before the war. How they must miss it. Mother and I met Vera at the theatre to see [Franz Lehar's] *The Merry Widow*, a spectacular revival. We enjoyed it enormously and revelled in Edwardian romance. Cyril Ritchard was a most fascinating Prince Danilo and Madge Elliot a dignified and dazzling widow [they were in fact a married couple]. Robert returned with large book-cases for his growing library.[12]

---

11 'In this new play', according to the *Oxford Times* (12 February 1943, p. 7), 'Mr Coward has given us a sort of miniature *Cavalcade* of the 20 years between the two wars as seen by a lower middle class family. It is a vivid drawing of a piece of all too real life; there is none of the sparkling cynical wit of his earlier plays, and the younger generation who went to the theatre expecting this sort of thing mostly came away disappointed. The more experienced generation, however, found it a profoundly moving and convincing reflection of the life of the inter-war years.'

12 This shelving was necessary because of an inheritance from his late brother: on 1 February '7 large crates of Harry's books came, much to Robert's joy, although we have already more ourselves than we can find room for'. A few weeks before, on New Year's Eve 1942, Robert wrote in his diary: 'spent the whole day re-arranging my books to admit the accessions from Harry's. Histories in the morning, Heraldry in the afternoon, Divinity in the evening. I thoroughly enjoyed it.'

Saturday, 20 February. Rather a dull day after the sunny ones we've had, but still very mild. Out in the morning – and a restful afternoon. After tea, mother and I went to call on Mrs Busby and [her daughter] Ruth. We admire their uncomplaining acceptance of their lives which sound to us terribly dreary and hard working. They are wonderful.[13] Natalia and John Stucley came in for a polite call, from next door. They are home for a few days. What a very good-looking, perfect-mannered young couple they are, both so very charming, even when paying boring duty calls!

Sunday, 21 February. A funny morning. I had to go for my Fire Guard's 'wet' training in the [University] Parks, which means putting out a fire in the Fire Hut, and crawling through the smoke, with nose pressed to the floor. I rather dreaded it, as I have always had a terror of fire, but actually got quite a thrill out of it, and the speed with which my stirrup pump put out the flaming 'furniture', which was really iron foundations piled high with straw soaked in paraffin, made one feel so confident. There was only one other person, beside the nice Austrian (?) group captain[14] and we enjoyed building upon our own fires and even cleaning out the filthy hut, choking with the thick smoke, and throwing out the blackened drenched properties whilst we swept the floor. I hope I shall be as steady in the event of a real fire – but I doubt it. There was a procession in the afternoon – very long – in honour of the Russian Red Army's 25th anniversary. Strange to see Communists cheered! Mother and I watched it pass for nearly an hour – contingents of all services, and Civil Defence services etc. Quite interesting.[15] Church at night.

    Robert's bookishness was longstanding. He was once a member of Lincoln College's literary society, the Davenant Society, named in honour of William Davenant, and is pictured in a 1925 photograph of the members of the Society; and he had been general editor of the first issue of the *Lincoln Imp*, December 1920, the College's student magazine. We are indebted to Lindsay McCormack for showing us these sources in the Lincoln College Archive.

13   Mrs Busby was house-bound. On 1 October 1942, Madge, having recently returned from the Lake District and seen Mrs Busby shortly thereafter, remarked that she 'has never been out of Oxford, to visualize things like mountains and lakes'.

14   Presumably a refugee.

15   These elaborate tributes to Russia and the increasingly victorious Red Army, involving a parade of over 4,000 and nine bands, were fully covered in the press (*Oxford Mail*, 22 February 1943, p. 3; *Oxford Times*, 26 February 1943, p. 5). The saluting base was in St Giles, near Madge's home. An exhibition of photographs of Russian life was opened that week, and one shop window 'is devoted to action photographs of the Russian air force, navy and army, whilst those inside the store illustrate the training of the "Red Army", guerillas in action, how the "scorched earth" policy has been applied, the part played by women in warfare, the work of the Red Cross and so on. The exhibition gives a clear picture of the tremendous war effort of the peoples of the USSR' (*Oxford Times*, 26 February 1943).

Wednesday, 24 February. I think I met Mrs Booth for coffee at Kemp Hall after my work this morning, and went to the Depôt in the afternoon. Mrs Booth was there again.[16] We sewed coverings on buttons. We do miss our bandaging work and our old friendly room. The sewing room is a dismal one – it was the dining room, and is full of alien faces and the whirr of sewing machines.[17] Mrs Lys joined the party – an honour, was it meant to be? Mother and I went to the pictures after tea and saw *Moontide* [based on the 1940 novel by Willard Robertson] – quite an unusual film with good acting from Frenchman Jean Gabin.

Tuesday, 2 March. Mother went up to stay with Nita for a week, so I shall have a taste of what this house is like to run, on my own. Even with the help of Mrs Nutt on two mornings, it should be strenuous. Mother had done as much as possible to leave things nice for me, and made pastry to last for ages, so that I shouldn't have to bother about puddings, which is a great help. I feel rather lonely on my own, especially at washing-up times. Muriel looked in – her half-term is up today. I went to the dentist again in the afternoon for, this time, rather a painful stopping. A quiet evening.

Thursday, 4 March. Busy in the home. I wish I could look dainty and attractive whilst working, like people in magazines, but I don't seem to have the knack. I don't look my best with my hair in a scarf, and my sleeves rolled up! My favourite moment of the day is when I come downstairs, changed and washed, to a cheerful fire. Later on, I get too sleepy to enjoy it. A whist-drive at night in the Shamrock Tea Rooms. An awful squash and very cold and draughty. Almost the last for Lent, thank goodness.

Friday, 5 March. Mrs Nutt here, which saved me some of the work. She is a good, quick worker, and as sharp as a needle! I didn't go out till the evening, when we went to the theatre to see *Brighton Rock* [adaptation of Graham Greene's 1938 novel] with Vera. Another very morbid and miserable play, but well acted. Robert and I had a so-called 'dinner' at the George, but it is scarcely worth the money now.

---

16   On Monday, 1 March 'Mrs Booth and her daughter came to tea. How different they are, the mother so homely and incomprehensible, and the daughter so assured and modern. We "christened" our newly-acquired silver tea-service for them.'
17   One week before she had 'looked in at the Depôt in the afternoon. I simply can't take much interest in it now the bandaging room is closed and none of my friends are there, but I stayed chatting to Mrs McGregor.'

Sunday, 7 March. Very busy in the morning. I cooked the Sunday dinner (my first, actually, always having had maids or efficient persons to do it for me, disgraceful!) It turned out surprisingly well – to my relief.[18] May Harrison came to tea, a negative sort of person, and hard to contemplate that she is a good violinist. No temperament, except for rather a languishing voice.[19] Church at night and a peaceful read by the fire, in my lovely new long blue house-coat.

Monday, 8 March. I meant to 'take it easy' this morning but found myself scrubbing away at stairs, floors and sinks till I nearly dropped. I can see why housewives become obsessed with work. It grows on one. To rest ourselves Robert and I went to the pictures to see *The Young Mr Pitt* [starring Robert Donat, Robert Morley, and John Mills] which was rather ponderous and political but beautifully presented. I answered a letter to John in the evening. He is worrying about his future after the war and whether he shouldn't look round for a wife when he comes back. Poor lamb. He would make a sweet husband and father to someone.

Wednesday, 10 March, Ash Wednesday. I went to the Holy Communion at 11.00. I can rarely go to morning services now. It is a pity that I can never appreciate fully the Communion service, but I realise that the words are beautiful. Mother and I went to Rhodes House, where there was a recital of songs by Winifred Bury of the Playhouse. They gave us a very attractive and rather American tea first. Mrs Allen, who must be, surely, the most charming woman in Oxford, introduced a lonely young officer's wife to us, and she sat with us for the concert, which was very delightful. We like jolly Winifred Bury, and she sang very pleasingly, in her warm easy voice. It was altogether a very nice 'occasion'.

Thursday, 11 March. Work – and shopping. In the afternoon mother and I went to the Scala to see Ginger Rogers in an amusing film, *Tom, Dick and*

---

18   On Shrove Tuesday, 9 March, 'I successfully made pancakes – my first.' She was also very pleased with herself on Sunday, 11 April. 'I made – actually! – my first suet pudding, and my first batch of pastry, under mother's guidance. It made me feel like a young bride, but I've never had it to do before, and it took a war and maid-less days to make me blossom out as a "hausfrau".'
19   'May Harrison came to tea in the afternoon,' wrote Madge on 21 June 1942. 'She is pleasant but dull.' See also below, 23–24 October 1943, p. 231.

Harry, and in the evening we went to Robert's first Lenten Lantern Lecture on 'Oxford – Past and Present'. Very interesting indeed.[20]

Friday, 12 March. I went out and spent 18 coupons on a black costume. Our coupons now have to last so very long, so that one can only get about two big things a year, and I have been saving mine for this suit. It cost a lot of money, £14, but as I don't – or can't – spend much these days, it doesn't make much difference.[21] Robert and I had a walk (Hinksey to Boars Hill) – a beautiful sunny Spring day, with warm sunshine. I seem to feel rather nervy at present, and get very peevish and restless within myself – yet how lucky I am. In the evening we all went to a new J.B. Priestley play, *They Came to a City*. It was a modern allegorical play, full of ideals and longings for a better future world on earth. Priestley is an idealist and sincere, and the play was moving, and beautiful, with fine acting by John Clements and Googie Withers and all the cast.[22]

Sunday, 14 March. I went to Church in the morning for the first time for ages. Mother carried on at home. The first Sunday in Lent, and it should have been dreary, but I found it inspiring. Sometimes Church services are deadly dull and heavy, even on festive occasions, but this was full of meaning. I love the Benedicite – and the lovely anthem 'Christ in His Garden'. Robert's sermon about the Lenten array was very interesting too. No church at night,

---

20   These Thursday evening lectures on Oxford's history continued until 15 April (excepting 1 April) and were intended for the broader community. Robert, clearly, was regarded as something of an authority on the history of both the University and the City. On 29 October 1943 he and Madge 'went to an exhibition of City planning. There were fascinating photographs and pictures of Oxford, past, present and future.' Given their interests and rootedness in the centre of Oxford, it would have been surprising had they not attended such an event.
21   The cost of this coat was equivalent to roughly three weeks' wages for a semi-skilled labouring man.
22   The *Oxford Times*, 12 March 1943, p. 7, began its review with a sneer: 'There are many to whom anything from the pen of J.B. Priestley has the sanctity of Holy Writ, and they are being duly thrilled by *They Came to a City*, presented this week at the New Theatre.' However, the acting, it was allowed, 'is quite above criticism'.
  While Madge had fairly broad theatrical tastes, she did struggle to enjoy plays with dark messages. She thought Ibsen's *Ghosts* 'the most depressing play … I've ever seen, but very haunting and stirring' (1 March 1943). Ibsen's *The Wild Duck*, which she saw after the war, on 17 October 1945, 'was rather tiresome on the whole'. Her tastes in the theatre ran noticeably to sparkle and wit, with comedies and uplifting stories holding more appeal than tragedies. On 10 April 1943 she saw *Give Me Yesterday* (by Edward Percy, 1938) at the Playhouse, 'which we liked, although it was conventional. Still, mother and I love a "real romance".'

as Robert was up at the Bleibens preaching,[23] Vera came in, and we discussed – inevitably – clothes! The war news not so good again. The Germans have retaken Kharkov.

Tuesday, 23 March. More work in the morning, clearing out Danna's cupboard which is a mass of extraordinary things, mostly Maud's. Where there are two people sharing a room, who never put things away, the result is chaos.[24] I went to the Depôt in the afternoon. Nice to be in the bandaging room again, though only the irritating Miss Stone and gentle Miss Reid were there. We made field dressings. We all went to the pictures in the evening to see a strange but fine film, *Thunder Rock* [based on Robert Ardrey's 1939 play] with Michael Redgrave in the leading part. It was most absorbing.

Monday, 29 March. March is going *out* like a lion this year, with showers and high rollicking winds. There was an inspection at the Depôt in the afternoon. We had to work late, and wait for the people who, as usual, were late – Lady Louis Mount-Batten and other high-up officials of the Red Cross and Order of St John organizations. Quite a lot of old faces turned up, and there was tea afterwards. One of Mrs Lys' party teas![25] I dashed home, then out again to a concert at the Town Hall. We only went because a friend of Nita's was singing in it. It was a [free] 'popular' concert [in aid of the Merchant Navy Comforts Service], and pretty awful, so we creeped away at half-time.

Tuesday, 30 March. A *very* nice day. For once, Robert and I managed to get out for a day in the country. Mrs Nutt was here, which made it easier. We took a bus to Buckland, a nice little village, and walked across a ridge to Faringdon. We had our sandwiches in the grounds of a beautiful Elizabethan house, which was a joy to behold whilst we lunched. The wind was terrific as we battled along to Faringdon, but the country looked lovely with its haze of fresh buds. We liked Faringdon, a pretty little market-town, and spent a lot of time, and money at W.H. Smith's buying books. A nice tea there. Then

---

23   In his diary this day, Robert wrote of the Rev. Bleiben's 'nice prosperous Church'.
24   A little over a month later, on 27 April, Madge reported that 'Maud installed herself with quantities of luggage *and* the kitchen stove, as the saying is!' Later in the year (Sunday, 5 September) Maud was presented more approvingly: 'Maud seems to like having a lot to do, and is her best at these times, though she gets in dreadful muddles.'
25   Such inspections occurred from time to time. On 21 July 1942 at the Depôt 'Lady Bruce-Gardner came to see the work. She seems a homely little body, and engaged Mrs Booth and me in earnest chat about her recent illness! We had a nice honey and scones tea in the rose garden.' On Tuesday, 11 January 1944 there was a visitation headed by royalty, the Duchess of Gloucester.

back in time to wash and go to the Playhouse to see a Clemence Dane play, *Mariners* [1927] which was much better than the notices led to believe.

Monday, 12 April. It is more like May than April – and late May at that. I nearly burst with joy every Spring, and this year it has been so especially amazing that it has taken everyone by storm. We had a welcome bit of soft rain in the morning, which was badly needed. I met Susie and went shopping with her, and had tea at the Cadena, after calling on Vera beforehand and arranging about the Playhouse to-night. I had a lovely cup of tea there, too. I brought Susie back to try on dresses, and there was a young lad whom Robert had taken out to tea – a son of one of his old Bedford girl friends. Mother and I were both highly amused at him – so young, but so sophisticated! He played, atrociously, jazz music on the piano, and was pathetically naïve in spite of much large talk! Vera and I went to see *The Blue Goose* [by Peter Blackmore, 1941] at the Playhouse. We had seen it before, but had forgotten how very funny it is. We loved it. Such a warm moon-lit night.

Tuesday, 13 April. The perfect day. It is so beautiful that words are useless. Mother and I had a walk round Magdalen Island and in the Botanical Gardens in the afternoon. Addison's Walk was a picture of loveliness – a bower of fresh green, and primroses, narcissus, and daffodils starring the grass. The pink and white blossoms against the old walls and the sparkling river made us almost groan with joy! There were a lot of appreciative American soldiers there. For once an English spring comes up to all its fame of touching beauty. So often they are so disappointing. A Parochial Church Council meeting at night.

Wednesday, 14 April. Not quite such a perfect day, but still very warm. We shall take very badly to cold and rain when it comes, and rain, at least, is badly needed. An unusual afternoon for me. I went with Miss Reid, the gentle, fragile and cultured Scottish Depôt friend, to Begbroke, near Woodstock where she wanted a grave photographed. I had offered, as I am lucky enough to have a film [which was hard to get in wartime]. Begbroke is a tiny, lovely village. I photographed the tombstone which was in the cemetery of the Priory, then we looked in the tiny village church. We wanted to find a wood which someone had said was carpeted with primroses, but went to the wrong wood, which only had King-cups and which was scrubby and tiresome. Miss Reid is not strong and got tired, so we rested a bit in the field and she talked gently about Italy, where she lived for many years. This pause made us miss the bus back to Oxford, by a minute, and we had to stand waiting for another for half an hour, finally reaching her rooms for tea about 6.00. I was quite done in when I got back at 7.00, though I do like her very much, but it is a strain talking to someone who is very deaf for a long time. An alert at 1.00a.m. for half an hour.

As usual at this time of the year, the Martins were planning to enjoy a holiday in the country. This year they were returning to Somerset and had booked accommodation at Cross Lane Farm, Allerford, near Minehead. 'This part of Somerset must be about perfect,' she wrote on 28 April, the day of their arrival. She rejoiced, not only 'in the most lovely surroundings', but also – and this was clearly important – in 'being alone together at last', after being so often with other people in Oxford, some of them frequent visitors to their home,[26] 'and the prospect of walking in all this beauty'. During the following fortnight her responses to the landscape were quasi-spiritual in character. They walked almost every day. On 30 April 'I felt too happy to do anything but talk about the glories of the country-side'. They much admired the local churches. 'This is such a lovely life,' she declared on 4 May, after lots more fine walking, 'that one's mind becomes so rested and smoothed over that one almost becomes unable to think at all, and certainly to worry. It must be doing us so much good mentally and physically and I feel truly thankful for our good fortune in being able to have holidays like this.' On 13 May, 'our last day in this enchanted paradise', she thought that 'I shall take very hardly to going back to work, but the main thing is that we should be *together*.' She spent part of this day saying mental farewells. 'We paid a last visit to the church [in Selworthy], in thankfulness for the peace and happiness we have found here.'

Back in Oxford there were stresses – though on the day of their return (14 May) Maud appeared in a better light, for she 'had done a lot of work and cooking to greet us'. Madge was often on edge, and leisure time was less abundant, especially for Robert. 'I get very depressed at the amount of times I am told how tired and over-worked Robert looks,' Madge wrote on Sunday, 30 May. 'Altogether I feel very bad-tempered, inferior and low-spirited at the moment, in spite of being aware of my many blessings.' She had similar thoughts the following day: 'These days are rather a drag somehow.' But in some respects there was progress, notably becoming less nervous and more confident about cooking, for she had no choice but to learn (Sunday, 23 May). On 25 May 'I tentatively made a "batch" of pastry in the evening and it turned out extremely well, to my astonishment.' Sunday usually made for heightened challenges in the kitchen. On 30 May she was 'Busy with the Sunday

---

26   Weeks later, on 10 July, 'a very tiring day', Madge said that 'Robert and I find we are worn out by so many people especially at meal-times, and I get headachey.' At supper that day there was 'more exhausting chatter'. Her tolerance for socializing, especially hosting people who were not family, was noticeably limited.

joint and some more pastry. I am getting quite bold now, and am delighted when things turn out well.'

Tuesday, 1 June. As usual 'flaming' June came in with deluges of rain and cold wind. I went to the Depôt in the afternoon. What an effort it is to turn out for this, but I usually enjoy it when I get there, and did, especially so today. Home in a drenched state. I took a kitten in which was also wet through, and lost, and of course what to do with it now is a problem, as it will not leave us. I lit a fire in the drawing room, meaning to have a cosy evening by it, but Danna, Maud and Miss Bridgeland all came in and took possession, so I retreated to Robert's study and helped him with some typing. I liked doing it, but was very furious at being done out of the rest I much needed, and felt very tired and infuriated all evening.

The following day Madge learned of an event that distressed her – the death of the famous and (certainly for her) beloved actor, Leslie Howard (b. 1893), who was a passenger in a DC–3 that was shot down by a Luftwaffe fighter on a flight from Lisbon to Bristol on 1 June. Madge 'adored' him (2 June). 'I felt as sad as though he had been a dear personal friend, which he did seem to many who have loved him on the screen for so many years.' Her scrapbook contains five newspaper clippings (this was exceptional for her) about his death and remarkable career. Three days later – 'everything seems very depressing' – she cited the main cause of her malaise as 'the great personal sadness of Leslie Howard's death, which I somehow can't forget. He was such a perfect sort of person it seemed, and to have such a fearful though heroic death makes it all so overwhelming, somehow.' The following day she listened to the tribute to him that was broadcast by the BBC. 'It was beautiful and touching, and comforted me that he should be so appreciated and honoured in this way. Evidently many people feel the loss almost as much as though they had known him personally.' Months later, on 26 October, she, her mother and Robert saw again *The Gentle Sex*, which she thought 'A *very* nice film, with our lamented and loved Leslie Howard's voice, telling the story of the 7 ATS girls. What a great loss he is to everyone.'[27]

---

27 Leslie Howard's death features prominently in Ian Colvin, *Flight 777: The Mystery of Leslie Howard* (Barnsley: Pen & Sword, repr. 2013).

Wednesday, 16 June. Busy all morning, a bath and rest after lunch. Then we went to tea with a Mr and Mrs Hughes in Southfield Road [East Oxford]. Very friendly people. They gave us glorious flowers with exquisite bright colours which are a joy to look at now in our drawing room. Ruth came, really to see if she could come here when she leaves her present place. How I should have jumped at this once, but now with me being able to manage so much better than I ever thought, and us having to economise so drastically,[28] it is better not. However, she might possibly come and take our big guest room. She is such a truly good person, and so warm-hearted and understanding. Too good for the likes of me – that's the trouble![29]

Thursday, 17 June. The usual morning, with Muriel bursting in and flummoxing one. John [home on leave] away at Bewdley with relations. Muriel called for me to go to a whist-drive, but once more suddenly turned tail before even getting there. Is the girl right in the head? As it happened, the tables were all made up, when Robert and I got there, so, nothing loath, we came away and guiltily sneaked in to the pictures to see *Yankee Doodle Dandy* [starring James Cagney] which was very good.

Friday, 18 June. We meant to go walking today, but it just poured with rain every minute, so nothing daunted, we went up to town, leaving Mrs Smith (née Nutt) in charge.[30] We went up on the 10.20. It was so wet that we couldn't do much but have two lovely meals, forget work and Oxford, just be alone together, and see a grand Techni-color film, *The Life and Death of Colonel Blimp*, which we both loved.[31] Lunch at Selfridges, tea at the Café

---

28   While she gives no details, it may be that Robert's income as Vicar had declined, and his liability for taxes would certainly have increased. Comparing *Kelly's Directory*, 1939 and 1943, it appears that the value of the living of St Michael's declined by over 11%, or some £51, during those four years.

29   Madge had learned that winter (13 February) that Ruth Hendewerk 'is leaving her present place, so I wonder if she will come to us. She is a wonderful person and I love her, and I know she would work too hard probably [at domestic tasks], but I'm always a little afraid of mixing friendship with business.'

30   The previous Friday Madge had written that 'Mrs Nutt, my "woman", was being turned into "Mrs Smith" today, so she didn't come.' Mrs Nutt had been widowed in early 1942.

31   Others loved this film too – it was one of the most popular movies in 1943 – though not Churchill, who tried to shut it down, and others disapproving of its mildly disrespectful representation of the British Army. The film also featured an 'enemy alien', albeit an anti-Nazi, played by Anton Walbrook, who was portrayed very sympathetically. It was also exceptionally long (over two and a half hours) and inventive by the standards of most feature films of the time.

L'Europe, dinner at the Cumberland. Back on the 7.40, still in the rain, but it had been a very welcome relaxation.

Saturday, 19 June. I thought I was immune from feelings of suppressed fury and disappointment which used to make my life a misery whenever John failed to come up to my standards of him, but alas, I find that he still has this power over me, and after a brief appearance following his 5 days' absence, to say that he would see me tomorrow night just before leaving for Northern Ireland, I felt so worked up that Muriel's foolish presence drove me to lashing of tempers – though John saw none of my fury. It seems a bit thick that after a year away, he should spend so little time with me, whom he professes is his very best and only real friend. However, I do begin more and more to see that his ways and mine, his disposition and mine, and his standards and mine are as opposed as can be – yet this friendship holds firm. I gradually cooled off, went to see the Horsers, and had a busy writing evening – nothing like work!

Sunday, 20 June. Sally's 7th birthday today – bless the dear pig-tailed one! We sent her a lot of drawing things in a box, covered with scraps, and a book about the ballet, two things which especially interest her. Just now I am handicapped in my work by a painful festered left hand which keeps me awake at night, and irritates me in the mornings when I have lots of work to do. The presence of Muriel is too awful, also in the morning, especially when she becomes emotional and personal. Church in the evening with her and Vera. John, who goes to Northern Ireland tomorrow to resume his work with the Coastal Command, came in for his farewell visit. He told me that he thought that Agnes Jennings, an austere school teacher, with a lot of intelligence and no looks, had apparently acquired a 'passion' for him, and that he was beginning to be intrigued and attracted in a way, himself. The poor lamb is so shy and diffident that any woman who showed an interest in him would stand a fair chance of getting him – and this one has, I think, a certain cold charm and more to her than the usual young thing. She must be about 28 – or so.

Monday, 21 June. What with the hand and no sleep and rather a worried outlook just now, I feel a bit under the weather. I rang up to say good-bye and good-luck to John, who has a long journey before him, and a dangerous job at the end of it. I wish he had never left Gibraltar – at least he was safe there. I was suddenly given nine coupons by Robert, so with great joy, went to order a grey-ish suit, which I always wanted even when I went and bought a black one. It is funny now, the way one is only allowed *so* many pleats and pockets because of the shortage of cloth. I am lucky, being small, and can have the maximum, and *four* pockets if I wish! Robert and I went to the pictures after tea to see *The Moon and Sixpence* [adapted from Somerset Maugham's 1919 novel] a most interesting film about Gaugin the painter. The hand so painful, however, that it dominated the picture.

Wednesday, 23 June. I am not enjoying this little batch of time at all, and do not sleep well. Neither have I any interest in my work, though my hand is improving now. Thank goodness, when one is grown-up one realises that all moods pass. It is not like being a child – though sometimes one feels as unreasonable as one.

Thursday, 24 June. Beautiful weather today, and I was able to bask in the sunshine instead of going to rest upstairs, which was nice, though not so good for one's back-ache. Mrs Jimenez and I went together to the Food Office to get the new ration books, and stood 2½ hours in a queue, in what must surely be the most depressing district in Oxford [St Ebbe's]. Home, late and tired, to a scratch supper.

Friday, 25 June. The day wasn't so sunny as yesterday, but we decided to get into the country for a bit, so we took the 11.30 train to Kingham, and walked over fields and faintly pleasant country to Bourton-on-the-Water. We had sandwiches in a warm corner of a field, against a hay stack, and felt very glad that we had come, as we always do. I felt more and more at peace than I have for some days. The country soothes me as nothing else can. We reached Bourton, which for some reason, didn't look its charming self today, and found we had *just* missed the Oxford train. As there was no other till 7.50 and we had tickets for the Playhouse, we hired a taxi to Kingham, some 8 miles away. It was such a leisurely one, that again we missed the Oxford train, and had to wait for the 4.50. We got tea, after waiting a long time, at the hotel there. I think this degraded waiting for meals is one of the most trying things of the war. We just had time to get clean before going to see *Of Mice and Men* at the Playhouse. It was very well acted, but not really my 'mould'.[32]

Saturday, 26 June. Beautiful weather just now. I had a nice letter from John – full of self reproach and regrets. He will just have to think out his own

---

32   This gritty play, adapted from John Steinbeck's novel, was said by the *Oxford Times*, 25 June 1943, p. 7 to be 'moving' and 'acted with sincerity and fine sympathy … The play has moments of deep pathos.'

future – I cannot help him in 'matters of the heart'. He will learn. We went up to tea at Miss Slade's. Her garden is exquisite and a joy to behold. I stayed on after Robert had left and listened to Miss Slade, who is a strange mixture of matter-of-fact-ness and beauty-lover. She has lovely things in her house, and has 'green fingers'. I came home at 7.00, in the warm evening.

Tuesday, 29 June. Glorious day again. I was able to get out for a little, in the morning, as Mrs Nutt [surname crossed out] Smith was here, and take my coupons to the tailor with Vera, as I wanted her approval of the material. The Depôt in the afternoon – quite nice. A Mr and Mrs Allen came to call after tea. She was a Depôt member at one time – rather a shrew, but friendly. He is simple and nice. Vera and I went to the Fire Guard lecture in Regent College at 8.00. It dealt mainly with the system of co-operation between Fire Guards and the NFS (Regular National Fire Service) in the event of a raid. Quite interesting. I wonder if we shall ever have to do these hazardous deeds? Other people have had to, but it seems incredible that we ever should. Let us trust that Oxford will be spared.

Thursday, 1 July. Lots of pastry making – cherry pie, red-currant tarts and meat patties – and a morning visit from Winifred Bleiben, which lightened things up a lot.[33] A rest, a bath, and a bask in the garden after lunch. I went in solemn solitariness to see Fred Astaire in *You Were Never Lovelier*. I think he is a supreme dancer, and has the pathetic but cheeky charm of a mongrel puppy. Ruth came in later. She wants to come and live in our big spare room!

Sunday, 4 July. A very busy morning. Sometimes I seem to do far too much, others, just slack around. I polished the floors of four rooms, did a lot of washing, cleaned out a cupboard, and cooked roast pork, onions, peas, potatoes and red currant tart, finally washing up and cleaning out the oven. I sank thankfully into a garden chair for the afternoon after that, with the Sunday papers, letter writing, and one ear on Bach from the wireless. Church at night. Robert had had a very hard day too, with lots of services, and a call to a dying woman after Evensong.

Monday, 5 July. A letter from John. He seems in the very depths of despair, remorse and bewilderment over this Agnes Jennings affair. I wonder how it will all turn out. I think I know just what is troubling him, and I am very frightened that he will do something hasty, just because she is paying him

---

33 Her entry for the previous day had concluded with the words: 'I wish I didn't always feel so strung up lately.' By contrast, 2 July was 'a very happy day' of mostly country walking.

attention. Neither Susie or I like the idea of him belonging to this particular family, but we must trust that things will turn out for his ultimate happiness.[34] I wrote what I hope was a soothing letter to him in the afternoon. Robert and I went to see a good film, *Shadow of Doubt* [1935 mystery] after tea. Later on Pansy [Robert's sister 'Panny'] came to stay for a fortnight.

Tuesday, 6 July. Work, with Mrs Smith and Pansy to help, so that we managed to get out for coffee in the morning even. The Depôt in the afternoon. Mrs Booth *and* Miss Walker both turned up for the first time this term, so it was fun. I had tea with an agitated Susie (because of John's affair). We got soothed with *strawberries* – a great treat – and one another's views on the subject. Susie is much against the whole thing, and wants me to use all my influence against it, but I shall not do this, as I don't know the girl much, and don't want to interfere, though I cannot think it is a right thing for my nice John. There is something horrid about it – perhaps the shady family? We all went to the Playhouse to see *The Little Foxes* [by Lillian Hellman, 1939] an unpleasant but well acted play.

Wednesday, 7 July. Danna's 84th birthday. She had quantities of flowers, cards, letters and telegrams. Panny helped me in the house, but though she does do all she can, I find I get most confused, and would *far* rather be on my own, however hard it is.[35] Maud came for a festive lunch, and Danna opened all her cards and presents after it. I had tea with Miss Whyte in her Beaumont Street flat – I like her very much I think. She has done up her rooms very charmingly. We are both cat-worshippers. I went on to the pictures all by myself to see *Star Spangled Rhythm* [a patriotic musical] – not so good – and *The Silent Village*, which was.[36] I went to see Vera after, and found her depressed and upset at having to go into the Acland Home [in

---

34 Mr and Mrs Jennings had been appointed resident caretakers of St Michael's Church Hall in 1935. By 1940, Mrs Jennings was the Church Hall steward and Mr Jennings worked elsewhere. Mr Jennings was also a musician, as was Agnes, and played for Church social events. (We are indebted to Barbara Tearle for this information.)
35 'I find I *cannot* get along when anyone is working around me in the kitchen,' she wrote the following day, 'and I long to get back to my own rather fussy ways.' On Tuesday, 13 July she was left alone: 'Lovely even to work, with the kitchen all to myself.' She was sometimes tiring of having so much company (10 July): 'Robert and I find we are worn out by so many people, especially at meal-times, and I get headachey.' The following day she wrote of 'supper for 7 and more exhausting chatter'. With Panny's departure early on 22 July, 'we had the first breakfast alone together, for a long time. It was very restful – and quick.'
36 This was a short 1943 documentary, directed by Humphrey Jennings, honouring Czech villagers murdered by the Nazis.

Banbury Road] next week for two nights for an internal adjustment. Poor Vera always dreaded that she should have to do anything like this. Back to supper and a sing-song in Danna's birthday honour.

———◆———

Subjects that in earlier years were mentioned infrequently gained prominence in 1943. Food was one. Gifts of fresh eggs were much appreciated (15 March and 24 April), at a time when powdered egg was already a standard substitute for the real thing. On 8 July Winifred brought 'red currants and kippers for me – very kind' and Madge and Robert were able to enjoy 'the lovely kippers' together at supper. The following day Diana and June arrived, the former 'sweetly bringing a basket full of good things to eat – a chicken, eggs, bacon, tea, lard, margarine and chops! Most generous and thoughtful. June, too, contributed to the larder.' (Diana also 'brought generous rations' on Friday, 22 October when she came to stay for the weekend.) July 10 brought a thrilling surprise: 'I was sent six *BANANAS* from Ireland, a nearly forgotten taste, last experienced in Autumn, 1939. I just love them, and had two, with *cream*, there and then!'[37] Scarce foods were now being given as gifts on special and festive occasions, as Madge's lists of the presents she received attest (for example, butter, sugar, plums, an apple). On 14 July, after a Red Cross meeting, she had tea at the Depôt – 'it was rather pleasant, as a lot of the people I like were there, and we had tea with raspberries, in the lovely rose garden'. Sunday dinner may have continued relatively unchanged (though perhaps with smaller portions), for on the morning of 25 July she was preparing 'the joint and vegetables etc.'

———◆———

Monday, 26 July. The weather really *is* flaming July at last, and I love it. Just an ordinary morning, I think, and a laze in the garden in the afternoon. We went out to 'supper' with Mr and Mrs Corry. He is a surgeon, and Robert christened their little girl not long ago. We found that 'supper' was a superb meal of soup, salmon and salad, and ices, with wines, and coffee after. They have a beautifully furnished house in the Woodstock Road [no. 113], and a lovely garden. They are very friendly, but we feel as though we don't really

---

37 The scarcity of bananas in wartime was often remarked on and later remembered. The subject is imaginatively discussed in C.M. Peniston-Bird, '"Yes, we had no bananas": sharing memories of the Second World War', in Mary Addyman, Laura Wood, and Christopher Yinnitsaros, eds, *Food, Drink, and the Written Word in Britain, 1820–1945* (London: Routledge, 2017).

belong to this world of dinner-parties and rich-nesses, and we are much more comfortable in our meek setting, by our own fireside.

Monday, 2 August. Bank-holiday Monday. Would that we were at Scarborough as we invariably were at this time before the war. Shall we ever be there again? Certainly, things seem much more hopeful now than ever before in the war news. I didn't go out all day. Just an ordinary working morning, a rest in the afternoon, and an evening painting dolls' masks for the Red Cross before supper.[38] I am in rather a deflated state of mind and body at present.

Thursday, 5 August. Very, very busy dashing about getting the house right, and doing last minute cooking etc. Muriel in, so I put her to ironing, which was a help. We had rain for the first time for ages. The farmers wanted it, I believe. Mother and [cousin] Celia arrived after tea. Mother looks like the one who has been working hard for three months, and I like the one who has had the holiday. It appears that Auntie Beatrice has grown a very tiresome and unpleasantly snobbish person to live with. I think *I* should soon feel quite worn out by the unceasing chatter which must go on where she [mother] has been staying. Celia looks no older and may still be the excitable and garrulous girl of 1915. Teaching evidently either ages one quickly or turns one into the perpetual school-girl.

Saturday, 7 August. Quite coldish. Last week was unbearably hot. I seem to be a bit at sea as to housework now and almost regret having to turn over the kitchen work to mother, who also prefers it to the other sort. I went out again with Celia. I fear I must seem quiet and dull to her, who is so loquacious. She seems to be so very wrapped up in her school and 'little ones' that I don't think she takes in much of our doings, though she is so warm-hearted and generous. She helped me paint some of the interminable dolls' faces in the evening.

Tuesday, 10 August. Shopping and cooking in the morning. I went to the station in the afternoon to meet Nance, Roger and Sally. Mother followed in a belated taxi. It seemed like old times to have so many of my family round the table again, merrily chattering away.[39] We all walked in the [University]

---

38   She had one hundred dolls' masks to paint before September for that year's Christmas Bazaar (27 July 1943). This would prove during the following weeks to be a time-consuming job.
39   She mentioned another pleasure the following day: 'Lots of us to share the housework.'

Parks after tea – also like old times. Likewise the family supper-table, and the cups of tea after.

Thursday, 12 August. The weather quite sunny and warm so after lunch Celia, Nance and I took the children for a steamer trip to Abingdon. We had to queue up for a long time at Folly Bridge, and then only got 'standing room' on the 2nd steamer. However we managed to perch comfortably on the tarpaulin of the 'saloon' below and quite enjoyed the very leisurely trip. We had to queue again at Abingdon for the bus back to Oxford, and after missing one and waiting an hour altogether, we just got back with five minutes to spare before the Playhouse. Robert and mother brought welcome cups of tea in thermos flasks which we surreptitiously had in the interval. The play was *Poison Pen* [by Richard Llewellyn, 1938] and very good too in a way. We quite liked our funny day in spite of queues and crowds.[40]

Friday, 13 August. Mother and Celia went to stay with Nita in the afternoon. Celia, Nance and I had coffee at the Cadena in the morning. Celia's week has seemed very fleeting and I just haven't had time to be with her privately, so there was no chance of renewing our childhood's friendship. Robert, Nance and I went to see a most brilliantly funny film, *I Married a Witch* [a romantic comedy starring Veronica Lake and her magnificent hair] which we all liked a lot. Maud kept an eye on the children. I replied to a letter from John. I cannot believe that he is really going to spend a week with Agnes Jennings as part of his leave, which ironically starts in the middle of our own [forthcoming] holiday. My mind is very full of him and this affair. It is incredible that he should be so intrigued with such a plain, supercilious school-teacher as she is. Not his type at all – and she is so very clever and dominating. Oh dear, my poor old John.

Monday, 16 August. Heavenly weather. We skipped through our work and shopping, had an early lunch, and all, except Robert, went on the river for a long afternoon and evening. We took tea, and went up past the Cherwell Hotel [in North Oxford], right up, until it got strangely dismal, excavated, and seething with grinning Italian prisoners-of-war, who flashed white teeth at us, and cried 'Belissimma' [i.e., extremely beautiful] or some

---

40 Over-crowded buses were not uncommon. 'One woman returning to the Oxfordshire village of Enstone from a shopping trip in Oxford remembers how the "bus became so full that people had to sit on the stairs". When Woodstock Hill proved too much for it, several passengers got off and walked to the top, like passengers on an eighteenth-century mail-coach.' (Longmate, *How We Lived Then*, pp. 318–19.)

Italian-sounding word.[41] We retreated hastily, and found a pleasant place for tea and a bask in the sun. A leisurely paddle back, and home at 8.00. Kenneth Denton was there, and had supper with us.

Wednesday, 18 August. A busy morning, transforming, rather sadly, our big pleasant 'attic' room, which always seems to belong to the children and is haunted by happy family parties, into a bed-sitting-room for Ruth Hendewerk, who comes in on September 1st. I am very fond of Ruth, but I sometimes wonder why on earth I ever consented to let her have the room, and so cheaply too, although I'd rather have her than someone who would pay much more, if it has to be. I somehow couldn't get out of the situation – and it may work out all right. Nance and I went shopping and had coffee at the Shamrock. Miss Hardman is the soul of kindness. The family left in the afternoon. I have so loved having them. I wish my sisters lived nearer. I should not have time for the sort of mad depression that is upon me now, regarding the person who has had the power to make me so ever since the friendship began [with John Hall].

I meant again to do some preparations for our holiday, but again it was too hot for anything but sitting in the garden. In spite of being so busy, Robert and I went to the Playhouse to see *Goodness, How Sad* [by Robert Morley, 1937] which we had seen before, but enjoyed even more, this time. Alas, double-summer-time has ceased since Sunday and at 10.00 o'clock we came out into our first black-out since early Spring. Everyone hates it so, though when one gets used to it, there is a great beauty in the dark buildings against the starry sky. One notices the stars so much more, now there are no rival electric lights to dim them.

Thursday, 19 August. A busy day – it always is, just before going away on holiday. Hectic, but exciting. Miss Whyte and Marcia Parsons (née Cripps) both called in the midst of my morning's work, the former to bring back books, and gaze adoringly on Monty and Joey, the latest kittens, beautiful at three weeks and named after General Montgomery and Stalin, who had both achieved victories the week they were born. I like Miss Whyte very much. She is quietly friendly and rather nice to look at, with her thick mane of tawny hair and smiling eyes. I spent all the afternoon packing, and called on poor old Mrs Busby in the evening. I'm afraid she will not live very long,

---

41 There was a camp for Italian POWs at Harcourt Hill, North Hinksey (Graham, *Oxfordshire at War*, p. 67).

though sometimes these bed-ridden people linger for years.[42] I never can believe that in another evening we shall be far away from home. I'm glad we know and love the place we are going to. I always long for holidays to come, but at the last minute am often full of regret at leaving our comfortable home with all its familiarities. However I soon get to love everywhere I am with Robert, and feel just as reluctant to come back. I shall especially be loath to return this time because of all this strange business of John and his affaire!'[43]

This holiday was again in Somerset, in the Minehead area: the first week at a cottage in Bossington; the second week with Nita, Dick and their son Christopher in three bedrooms at Brendon. Nearby Lynmouth, she said, 'was lovely as ever, but almost entirely occupied by American troops and their untidy possessions' (29 August). On her second day back in Oxford, 4 September, she had occasion to reflect on the course of the war. 'I'm glad that it isn't four years ago, when all was still unknown, and war had been declared, as it were, yesterday. We have been through some fearfully anxious times, but it does look now as though things were moving towards certain victory, however long it may take. Yesterday we invaded the "toe" of Italy.'

Madge's return to Oxford was brief, for on 8 September she and Robert were off on another week's holiday, this time to Painswick in Gloucestershire. From there they could enjoy the Cotswold countryside and visit a few towns, including Gloucester and Stroud. One event in Gloucestershire was a reminder of the scarcities that were increasingly looming over everyday lives – and how various commodities were acquiring more and more value. On 10 September she spent 'the

---

42 Mrs Busby was the one ill person whom Madge, officially titled St Michael's 'Church Visitor', visited regularly – around once every couple of months. 'Poor soul,' she wrote after seeing her on 31 July 1943, 'it is awful for her, bed-ridden in a small stuffy bedroom. She is beginning to lose her remarkable spirits, and it will be a good thing when she is taken, as I think there is no hope for her recovery now. Ruth, the daughter, is wonderful.' Mrs Busby in fact bounced back (18 September, 24 December 1943) and was still alive at the end of the war.
43 On 3 September, the day she arrived back home after this holiday, she wrote: 'Why is Oxford so depressing a place to *return* to? I love it at all times except on these occasions.' John showed up that evening 'and we had hours to discuss nothing but his "affairs of the heart". He seems serious about Agnes, but by no means happy. In fact he looks quite worn out and miserable. I feel contented, anyway, about one thing – that he still comes to me with all his problems and confidences. He goes away with her for a week, tomorrow, to stay in her cottage at Rochester. This is done so often by most young men these days, but it seems highly unconventional of the strictly brought-up, fastidious John, and he is half defiant, half afraid. We understand one another completely, which is a comfort.'

usual evening' at the house in Painswick where they were staying, 'except that the dog, Topsy, ate half my chocolate ration for the month, when I wasn't looking. Quite a dismal thing to happen to one!'

Sunday, 26 September. Still exceptionally cold for the time of year. An ordinary Sunday morning. I'm afraid I rather like these non-Churchy Sunday mornings, though I enjoy the evening services. Two visits to Church was always too much for my rebellious heart, in one day.[44] There was a procession in remembrance of the 'Battle of Britain' three years ago this month, and Vera and [her sister] Mabel, mother and I stood in St Giles to watch it.[45] Afterwards they came back to tea. Church at night, special prayers for 'Battle of Britain Sunday'. Robert had been busy taking a service in the Town Hall, lunching with the Mayor and other people connected with it, then appearing on the 'Saluting platform' watching the march past.

Tuesday, 28 September. Out shopping with mother, and a coffee, as it was a 'Mrs Smith' morning. The first Depôt Day in the afternoon. We are only meeting once a week apparently – lack of Red Cross material, they say, but it looks much more like lack of helpers. It was very chilly there, and none of my special cronies were there, except the angelic Miss Reid, so the time rather dragged, and it was nice to be back to a warm home, and cosy evening by the fire.

Saturday, 2 October. I was busy decorating the altar and sanctuary window with Michaelmas daisies, ready for the Dedication Festival tomorrow.[46] Mother and I met Nita and Richard in the afternoon. They are to stay a week. Nita looked *very* nice in a sumptuous camel-hair coat and saucy red

---

44 Religious fervour was not Madge's forte. On Michaelmas Day, 29 September, she went to Church in the morning. 'I wish I could feel more deeply about the Communion Service. I can't expect to get much serenity from it till I do.' By contrast, she enjoyed decorating the Church for festive services, attending them, and the rituals and music associated with ceremonial occasions.

45 These ceremonies and religious services to commemorate the Battle of Britain, and the many people and organizations involved in them, were described in detail in the *Oxford Times*, 1 October 1943, p. 5. The Bishop of Dorchester 'said that they were gathered together with millions of their fellow citizens in town and country, to give thanks to God with grateful hearts for a mighty deliverance'.

46 The following Saturday she decorated the Church for the Harvest Festival (10 October): 'The Church looked beautiful with candles, silver, festive hangings, and the vivid flowers and fruit.'

hat, and a new 'perm'.[47] We had a cosy evening chatting and supping and reading, as we used to do when they came to see Kit when we had him during the Blitz.

Sunday, 3 October. A domestic morning. In the afternoon a visit from May Harrison – pleasant, gracious, and queenly. She and Beatrice are giving a concert in three weeks [see 24 October], at which I have to sell programmes. Nita and I went to Church at night and shouted festival hymns.

Monday, 4 October. Just perfunctory work in the morning, then out for holiday coffee and the delicious Cadena buns. It is fun doing anything, however small, with the family [Nita and Richard were visiting]. Out again in the afternoon, and at night. Robert's first Ruridecanal Conference meeting, as Rural Dean. He, as chairman, brightened it up a bit, but apart from him, it was as deadly as ever.

Tuesday, 5 October. I haven't heard from John for a long time. It is depressing being all at sea with him, and slightly unfriendly, like this. I wonder when it will all come right again. Out again to coffee. In the afternoon Nita came with me to the Depôt and saw some of the dolls and toys we are making for the Red Cross Bazaar. We all went, after tea, to see that superbly acted film *Un Carnet de Bal* [1937]. We had seen it twice before and still think it is brilliant.

Wednesday, 6 October. Work, shopping, and coffee-ing in the morning and shopping with Dick and Nita in the afternoon. Poor Ruth had a telegram from Berlin, months old, to say that her sister, who is a teacher there, has had everything she possessed destroyed by 'enemy action' – that by *our* bombers. What a tragic war this is! We had a singing evening – all our old favourites.

---

47 Madge was undoubtedly fashion-conscious, which included an attentiveness to how hair was presented – her diary includes a number of drawings of hair-dos. On the lower half of the page after her diary entry for 24 October 1938, she had drawn an elegant-looking head with an upswept hairstyle, accompanied by the words: 'I dressed Nancy's hair up in the fashionable new "Edwardian" style. Mine is too short.' On 19 May 1939, when she was in Bedford for a Martin family gathering, she had waxed enthusiastic about Robert's nine-year-old niece, Priscilla Telford (daughter of Panny): 'she has the most beautiful hair I am ever likely to see in my life – really like spun-gold, and falling in soft waves and curls on her small neck, each wave shimmering as if it was lighted from within. Marvellous.' Madge was visually sensitive, interested in style and colour, and had something of an artist's eye, especially regarding women's dressing.

Friday, 8 October. Nita and Dick went soon after breakfast. It was so nice to have them. More and more I realise that my real and only happiness lies in my husband, my own family and my home, and all the small joys to be got out of simple things which are bound up in all these. Friends are essential – but families are the best. The weather perfect again – out shopping with mother in the morning. She, Robert and I to the pictures at night to see two enjoyable films, *Hello, Frisco, Hello* [a musical] and *Apache Trail* [a Western].

Tuesday, 12 October. After waiting a long long time to hear from John, I now got one of his new type of pompous, priggish, defiant and rude ones. He proposes to silence these mythical 'slanderous tongues' by getting engaged to Agnes in the summer. No-one can believe that he really can be in love with such a very unattractive and supercilious female. It is all very strange. I helped to sell shoes at a Rummage Sale, in St Paul's school-room, in the morning. Mrs Dudden was with me, which made it quite amusing. It was in aid of the Greek Relief Fund.[48] I had lunch with nice Mrs Nicol-Smith, at the Moorish, then went on to the Depôt for an afternoon's bandaging. A cosy evening, painting dolls' faces etc.

Friday, 15 October. The headache still there [from the day before] till the evening. Out in the morning. I visited Mrs Horser in the afternoon. Much as I like people, I do not like the 'Vicar's wife' visits.[49] Mother and I to the Playhouse at night to see an amusing play, *After October* [by Rodney Ackland, 1936].

Monday, 18 October. Out in the morning, when we had finished work. Mr and Mrs Hughes to tea. They are great stand-by's of All Saints. He is meek

---

48 There was a collection for Greece at Sunday evening's Church service on 17 October.
49 Two days before, in the afternoon, she and Robert 'visited the "sick and needy" and took them things from the Harvest Festival'. Madge compared herself, unfavourably, with her friend, Winifred Bleiben several months later, on 12 March 1944. 'Winifred is a most active and efficient parson's wife, deservedly popular, and she makes me feel worldly, frivolous, lazy, and thoroughly inadequate – not a nice feeling at all.'

While we have no knowledge as to how others viewed Madge as a parson's wife, it is possible to portray the work that a third party might have observed her to do both before and during the war, and the contrast between the two. Consider, as evidence, the first eight and a half months of 1938, well before she was drawn into war-related work with the Red Cross. According to her diary, in the evenings she went to some eight or nine Guild-sponsored whist-drives and a few Church meetings; and her daytime Church-related tasks during these roughly 250 days, including home visits, represented perhaps the equivalent of two full days' work. So leisure at that time (and she was away from Oxford for about ten weeks) was for her overwhelmingly more prominent than work.

and silent, and she garrulous and homely – never stops talking. We had to push them off – very nearly – as we had seats for the theatre to see *The Man Who Came to Dinner*, a very sophisticated American play [by Moss Hart and George Kaufman, 1939], cruelly amusing, but that's all.

Saturday, 23 October. Torrents of rain most of the day. Busy in the morning. Muriel came for half-term, and later June for the weekend. We had a vast tea-party – ten of us. The Harrison cousins, May, Beatrice and Margaret, arrived for a concert they are giving tomorrow for [the exiled] King Haakon's Norway Relief Fund. They are all good-looking, though Beatrice and Margaret are wild and 'arty' in voice and appearance. May is more normal altogether. We quite enjoyed them, though.[50] We all went to the Playhouse to see James Bridie's *The Black Eye* [1935] which was charming in a naïve, refreshing style.

Sunday, 24 October. Lots of us for breakfast and lunch – the girls helping very kindly. In the afternoon, the whole household – Ruth, too, and even Danna and Maud, and Muriel – went to the concert in the Sheldonian, which was packed. A beautiful concert. May Harrison (violin), Beatrice (cello), Margaret (piano), Sofi Schönning (soprano) and Eric Britten (piano). King Haakon was there himself, and Diana [June's sister, visiting for the weekend] had the honour of giving him his programme. The music was mostly [Edvard] Grieg with some [Frederick] Delius [a close friend of and collaborator with the Harrisons]. The soprano was utterly beautiful and we liked May very much too; she looks *exactly* like our Queen, and plays beautifully. The King made a very charming speech and everyone was thrilled to see him there.[51] Too tired for church. Diana played gramophone records for us. She is a very simple, nice girl. No wonder everyone likes her.

---

50   The three Harrison sisters were well-established and prominent performing musicians. May was the eldest (b. 1890), Margaret the youngest (b. 1899), and Beatrice (b. 1892) the most famous (see *Oxford Dictionary of National Biography*). They were also cousins of Robert, through the Martins, and both families had childhood connections with the Indian subcontinent.

51   Madge pasted a copy of the programme and a newspaper account into her diary. Public events to aid Continental allies and underline the solidarity of the Allied cause were commonplace in wartime Britain. King Haakon reminded his audience that, after the German invasion of his country, Norway's large merchant marine 'was ordered to report to British ports and he was proud that not one man disobeyed the command'. The concert realized almost £160. (*Oxford Mail*, 25 October 1943, p. 3.)

Wednesday, 27 October. We went to lunch, mother, Robert and I, at the American Red Cross Club, which was the old Clarendon Hotel.[52] We were some of a party, and there were two young and friendly American women organizers, and the pleasant man who runs it. They showed us all over the beautifully appointed rooms, dormitories and kitchens etc, then we had lunch in the big spacious canteen, which is also the ball-room. Everything is spot-less, even luxurious, and runs like clock work. Most enjoyable. I rather want to help there after the Red Cross Sale is over – in the canteen [this did not happen]. To the Scala with Muriel in the evening – one good but gloomy film which we'd seen before, *The Stars Look Down* [starring Michael Redgrave], the other light and nonsensical, but fun [*Over She Goes*], with Stanley Lupino, who was a really good comedian. A lovely star-lit night.

Friday, 5 November. A holiday for Robert, so he went to look at some churches at Banbury. We just shopped and coffee-d. I wrote letters in the afternoon. We all went to the theatre at night to see a new Terence Rattigan play, *While the Sun Shines*. It was in his best manner – gay, wise and brilliant dialogue. Michael Wilding, Jane Baxter, and other very good actors.[53] Our own Oxford repatriated Prisoners of War were there, with the Mayor. What

---

52 As Malcolm Graham has pointed out, Americans were by now often seen in Oxford (Graham, *Oxfordshire at War*, pp. 70–4); their prominence is central to the article 'Our American Guests' in the *Oxford Times*, 17 July 1942, p. 4. Madge later wrote (4 December 1943) that the big Saturday crowds included 'American forces and our own soldiers and airmen, on weekend leave.' At the opening performance on 8 November 1943 of *There Shall Be No Night* at the New Theatre, for members of the Forces only, 'every seat was occupied by officers and other ranks of all the Services, including a very high proportion from the American Army' (*Oxford Times*, 12 November 1943, p. 5). While Americans were crucial to winning the war, their actual presence in Britain was frequently unwelcome – as many diaries written for Mass Observation richly attest. One expression of concern came from Oxfordshire's Women's Voluntary Services 'The USA army is expected in several places in Oxfordshire very shortly. Areas are being reserved for battle practices. Some places to which they have already come are getting very anxious about the way they treat the girls to drink and we are doing what we can to encourage cafes being started, instead of their being forced into public houses, but the scarcity of accommodation makes this very difficult' (RVS Archive & Heritage Collection, County Narrative Report for October/November 1943).
53 The *Oxford Times*, 5 November 1943, p. 7, was similarly enthusiastic, saying that 'the brilliant sunshine of first-rate comedy permeates the production from start to finish. The audience responds immediately to its sparkle and spontaneity, and anyone who sees it is assured of an evening entertainment of the highest order.' The comedy was set in the war, and featured both British and American characters. Praise had also been bestowed the previous year on Rattigan's *Flare Path* – 'the finest new play the British stage has seen for years' – with its realistic portrayal of the 'ever-present underlying tension of life on a bomber station of the RAF in war-time' (*Oxford Times*, 17 July 1942, p. 7).

a thrill for them to see such a show, and a jolly crowded theatre, after their long time of misery. We enjoyed ourselves hugely.

Tuesday, 9 November. Robert and I went to the Town Hall to see the election of the new Mayor in the morning. It was an interesting ceremony, until the speeches started – and almost everyone on the Council seemed to want to get up and hold forth. We had sherry after, in the Mayor's Parlour, and met him and his wife, both nice homely people,[54] also Quintin Hogg [b. 1907], our Conservative member [since a 1938 by-election], who is also extremely nice. We seem to be oozing in, on the fringes of Oxford Society, willy-nilly. The Depôt in the afternoon, and the Playhouse at night, but *Heartbreak House*, Shaw's odd play, bored and exasperated us, so we walked out before the third act.

Wednesday, 10 November. I try not to think about John, who hasn't written for weeks now, and appears to have deserted me forever. He has been in Iceland, I believe, and Susie and his 'girl friend' have both heard, but not I. When I *do* think about it, I feel bitter and hurt, but I am much too busy really to worry about him.[55] I went to the Depôt again in the afternoon, painting my *endless* faces, and at night went into Mrs Harcourt's to talk about this Merchant Seamen flag day. Mrs Ridler came too. Mrs Harcourt is so much nicer than she appears and strangely easy to talk to.[56]

Thursday, 11 November, Armistice Day. A very hectic important day for us. Robert was inducted, at [the City Church of] St Martin and All Saints [in High Street], in the afternoon, and made City Rector. Everyone from home went, and it was a really beautiful ceremony. The Bishop of Dorchester inducted him. The Mayor and Corporation attended, in their robes, and a lot

---

54 Harry Charles Ingle (1870–1949), a retired bank manager, represented Summertown on the Oxford City Council.
55 Her emotions had also been apparent in previous entries. 'I feel I have lost *my* John forever,' she wrote on 19 September, 'and cannot begin afresh on a new footing. I want to retain his friendship, but I fear it will be most difficult if he marries Agnes. After more than 20 years, it is hard to give this up.' She revisited this anxiety on 25 October: 'What *is* happening to John? He really seems to have cast me off completely, in this new passion for Agnes. I really feel as though he has passed entirely out of my life as a personal friend.' On 15 November she finally received a letter from him (it had taken three weeks to arrive from Iceland): 'It was quite a nice letter for these days, and I answered it in a friendly way. He is disturbed in mind.'
56 This flag day was to be held on Saturday, 20 November and Madge was worried about being responsible for supervising twenty-eight flag-sellers: 'I was never born to organize!' (30 October). In her seventies Madge recalled as a child 'being of a timid nature' – and 'to this day, [I] have never been "capable" – always unsure of myself' ('A Yorkshire Childhood', p. 10).

of robed clergy. The Bishop spoke very nicely indeed, and everything went off splendidly. Lots of people in the congregation. I felt quite nervous and overwhelmed by so much honour and dignity. We went to an At Home at the Rector [of Lincoln College] and Mrs Munro's, in the Rector's Lodgings. All very nice and select! – with the Bishop, the Mayor, and all the 'narks' [i.e., annoying persons] of both churches.[57] The Munros are nice but rather terrifying, I always think. At night I had my annual Red Cross Whist Drive, this time for the Prisoners of War. It was a huge success, and crowded out, and we made more than last year – over £29.

Friday, 12 November. Shopping with mother. We met Mrs Harber and had coffee with her at the new 'Ross' Café [7a High Street] – nice but dilatory. I had to go to a meeting given by the Mayor in the 'Mayor's Parlour' for the Merchant Navy flag seller organizers. Quite pleasant. It is strange to find myself amongst this sort of 'society'. The Mayor seems most pleasant and unassuming. We went to the theatre at night to see a very fine play, *There Shall Be No Night* [by Robert E. Sherwood, 1940]. Alfred Lunt and Lynne Fontanne, the American 'stars', and very good they are. It was a tragic tale of modern Greece.

Saturday, 20 November. The coldest, foggiest day yet – and this was my Merchant Navy Flag Day. Mrs Harcourt and I had to be at the local Depôt (Wyatt's in St Giles) off and on until 5.00.[58] I went at 12.00 and sat in solitary gloom all through their lunch hour. A strange experience, all alone in an echoing iron-mongers'. Mrs Harcourt kept me company from 2.30, and we chatted pleasantly. She gets nicer for knowing, as most people do. The flag-sellers returned, chilled and blue with heavy tins and empty trays. Home at last. Kenneth Denton here to tea, and the evening, and Muriel came to dress a doll.

Monday, 22 November. Out shopping and coffee-ing with mother. We had Mr and Mrs Jones to tea in the afternoon. He is the manager of the Westminster Bank, a typical business-like but affable man. She is youngish

---

57 A copy of the 'Form of Service' – sixteen pages of high-quality paper – is included in Robert's diary. Six ancient Oxford parishes would now be under the charge of one clergyman. Robert, according to the Bishop, 'was one who knows his City and is known, respected and loved by all within it.' (*Oxford Mail*, 12 November 1943, p. 3.) With his various offices and with St Michael's continuing to draw worshippers from a distance, Robert was a key figure in the Church's work in the centre of Oxford.
58 The goal during the week was to raise at least £5,000 for the Merchant Navy Comforts Service (*Oxford Times*, 19 November 1943, p. 5).

and smart. A quiet evening sewing away at dolls. I finished a red-haired one, dressed in late Eighteenth Century costume à la Lady Hamilton, and also a be-spangled fairy-queen for the top of the Christmas tree.

Tuesday, 23 November. Now we have no 'woman',[59] we have to work very hard in the mornings. I loathe trying to get the bath spotless more than anything. The Depôt in the afternoon. I am beginning to know the names of the people in the sewing room where we all congregate now to stuff, assemble, be-wig and dress the hundreds of dolls for the Bazaar. I had tea with Miss Masefield. She is as elusive and shy as a wild pony, but I like her. We went to the theatre at night to see Turgenev's *A Month in the Country*, which was enchanting. Michael Redgrave was most heart-stirring in his early Victorian suits, and Valerie Taylor looked lovely as Natalia. The settings were beautiful, too, and we agreed that it was a very sympathetic, clever and charming comedy.

Wednesday, 24 November. Hard work in the morning. Depôt in the afternoon, and an evening at home dressing, I hope, the last doll.

Thursday, 25 November. A letter from John. He evidently really intends to marry Agnes. I tremble for his future happiness, though one never knows. Busy at the Depôt in the afternoon arranging the very expensive dolls, ready for tomorrow's Private View. I met mother at the Ritz for tea, and then Robert joined us to see *King's Row*, a good but somewhat long and morbid film.

Friday, 26 November. I was at the Depôt from 10.30 to 5.00 selling dolls at the Private View. Tiring but interesting. They gave us a sandwich lunch, and tea there. Lord Nuffield came, and the Duchess of Marlborough. He is self-effacing and one cannot believe he is the richest man in England. Very tired at the end, but recovered after a rest.

Saturday, 27 November. A strange day. Very miserable weather and dark. John suddenly rang up after lunch. I had not expected him just yet, so was a bit flustered. He came round to see me in the afternoon, bringing lots and lots of bars of heavenly chocolate – corn in Egypt – and some silk stockings, also beyond rubies. He was strangely nice and not at all queer, as his letters

---

59 Mrs Smith had just had a baby. On Sunday, 5 December Madge mentioned for the first time 'doing my own washing'. The following year, on 22 February, she 'had a new char-woman for the first time, a Mrs Payne, a real old scrubbing country woman'. But Mrs Payne's employment, for whatever reason, was notably irregular (26 June 1944).

have been. I can't make out if he really wants to marry Agnes for his own sake – or not. If so, he is being very materialistic about the whole matter. Anyway, we had an awfully nice chat. I had to hurry away to go to tea with the Bishop of Dorchester and Mrs Allen, who were entertaining the head of the Church Army, and Mr and Mrs Lunt from St Aldates, young Mr Martin and Captain Sharpe, also of the Church Army.[60] They were all very kindly, and young Mrs Lunt is sweet. Robert joined us, very late, when he returned from Banbury, very tired and mentally exhausted. I feel these days too tense – not sleeping well.

Monday, 29 November. Sometimes the size of this house gets me down, with its passages and stairs, occupied rooms, tramping feet, telephone bells, and visitors. It is really too much of a good thing, even with both mother and me working hard at it. I had a tea party to price the Christmas tree things, Mrs Booth, Miss Walker and Mrs Eliot. It was quite fun, as they are all familiar and friendly souls. John came in later in the evening – pleasant but a bit stolid.

Tuesday, 30 November. A busy day, mostly preparing for the Bazaar tomorrow. We were round at the Town Hall all the afternoon and early evening, up to the knees in dolls and toys. An enormous Christmas Tree we had to deck, being dirty and exhausting work, but we had willing helpers. John looked in very briefly after lunch – only five minutes. It should be a marvellous show tomorrow.

Wednesday, 1 December. The day of the great Red Cross Bazaar in aid of the Prisoners of War.[61] I went round [to the Town Hall] before 10.00 and was there till 6.30. The crowds were beyond belief, and we were besieged,

---

60   In the *Parish Magazine* for August 1941, p. 3, Robert had written about one aspect of the Church Army's welfare work and how parishioners could help. 'In the ground of the GWR Station, there is a Church Army canteen which is fulfilling a very present need in providing food and beds for members of HM Forces. This is served almost entirely by voluntary workers, and St Michael's has undertaken to be responsible for the night shift on alternate Sundays. For more than six months several young friends of St Michael's have gone regularly, once a fortnight, and worked all through the night from 10p.m. until 7 o'clock in the morning. Their faithfulness to this duty has been remarkable. But several of them have now been obliged to resign it.' Thus the need for another two or three volunteers. 'This work is strenuous while it lasts and it means foregoing a night's sleep, but it does constitute a real service to the men who are winning the war for us.'
61   There had been a long build-up to this big event: Madge first wrote of painting dolls' masks in late July, and wrote on and off about this work for months thereafter. A lot of labour was involved, on her part and the part of many other women. At least one civic reception for

overwhelmed, hemmed in and nearly knocked out by the hordes of women anxious to find cheap toys for Christmas. The Christmas Tree itself was emptied quite early, and we were sold out long before closing time at 7.00. We snatched a very welcome lunch at the Master of Pembroke's Lodgings, and tea, with mother and Robert, at the Rackett. Welcome oasis in the midst of turmoil. John looked in twice and helped by taking money to the bank. I had a nice lot of helpers – Miss Walker, Mrs Eliot, Mrs Booth, Miss Masefield, and two from the Church, Mrs Shead and Mrs Wood. The tree made over £108, nearly three times as much as last year. I should think the whole total must run into the thousands. It was exhausting, but fun too. I could scarcely totter home, but felt refreshed after a wash. John came in at 9.00 for a final talk of his affairs, till after 11.00. He is a dear thing, in spite of everything, and has a special warm corner in my affections. He goes to Rochester to stay with Agnes tomorrow.[62]

Making dolls was not quite over: Madge spent the afternoon of 8 December sewing one, and another the next evening. This continuing work was 'for a supplementary sale on Saturday [11 December], when they hope to bring the Stalls' total from over £800 to £1000' (7 December). There were other happenings too – or non-happenings. On Sunday, 5 December there was to have been carols at New College, but 'all the boys have Influenza, so it had to be cancelled. There is a very bad epidemic of that now. Almost everyone else seems to have it, or has had it.' The streets of Oxford were full of life, especially at the end of the week: 'shopping in Oxford on a pre-Christmas Saturday afternoon is a stampede', she wrote on 11 December. That evening she and Robert had dinner with the Provost of Worcester College and Mrs Lys, who headed the Depôt there, at his lodgings. 'They were very kind, and gave us a lovely dinner, and entertained us charmingly. The house looks lovely at night. The Provost is a very nice old man.'[63] Work at the Depôt was not quite finished: on

---

ex-prisoners of war had already been held (*Oxford Mail*, 2 November 1943, p. 2). It was said that £3,742 15s 6d was raised at this day's sale (*Oxford Times*, 3 December 1943, p. 8).
62 The engagement of John Hall and Agnes Jennings was announced in February 1944, they were married in August, and their son was born in October 1945. John pretty much disappears from Madge's diary from mid-1944. When he does resurface, on 14 July 1945, he is said by her to be 'staid', 'solid' and 'dull'. He visited Madge on 12 September 1945: 'I had my first talk, tête à tête, for about two years.' John was then going to a new job in Pontypool, Wales and apparently was resolved to live his life without much to do with Madge.
63 Madge remarked on 19 October 1943 that Mrs Lys, the University organizer for the Red Cross, 'is at her best at formal and social occasions'. On 18 June 1942 around thirty members of St Michael's Guild visited Worcester College and were shown around by the

14 December Madge was there 'sewing labels on knitted garments. Not many there, but those few were charming, as most of the Depôt members seem to be.'

Thursday, 16 December. Very bleak, cold and dreary, inside *and* out.[64] The 'Christmas spirit' sometimes gets lost, with so many people of such varying characters in the house, all with strong wills. How much everyone is in need of a complete and lovely holiday – all the world over. Truly this war has been as much of a Battle of nerves as anything else. I had a bad headache, and went to bed with it, but it didn't help much. But I can't complain as, unpleasant and exhausting as they are, they are nothing compared with those of earlier times. Mother and I went with Vera to see *Jane Eyre* at the Playhouse. Old-fashioned, but strangely moving and satisfying after so many modern off-hand plays.

Friday, 17 December. Foggy and murky. Shopping, *alone*, in the morning. Out with Robert in the afternoon, and to tea at Fullers before seeing a film, *The Flemish Farm*, which was a fairly good English war one [with a musical score by Ralph Vaughan Williams]. Our Prime Minister has pneumonia.

Saturday, 18 December. The dreariest, darkest, wettest day this year, I should think. The spirits of the house have recovered, at last, after a dreary couple of days. Out busy shopping in the morning, and up to the Bleibens to tea in the afternoon. Peter drove me up. Winifred and I had the afternoon all to ourselves, which was lovely. She saw me to the bus. June was here for the night. I think she has only recently recovered from the shock of her father's death, and is now her sunny interesting self again. She is a very nice girl, I think, and Diana, too, so ready to help always. She is improving vastly in looks too, and looks most attractive in her Land Girl's uniform.[65]

Provost, 'and Mrs Lys allowed them to look over the Depôt, and gave them a very good tea, which impressed them all a lot'. Otherwise, Madge did not particularly like her: at the Depôt on 19 November 1943 she found 'Mrs Lys at her most foolish and aggravating. She has such a silly giggle.' On the other hand, months earlier, on 22 January 1942, Madge was working in the bandaging room and wrote that 'Mrs Lys had a kind chat with me about wool and household difficulties, being unexpectedly nice, just as I had made up my mind that I didn't really like her.'

64   This was a time when the supplies of coal for consumers were being deliberately cut, in order to satisfy the increasing war-related demand for fuel, some of it because of the growing numbers of American Forces in the country.

65   On 25 October, at the end of Robert's two nieces' visit to 1 Wellington Place, Madge wrote: 'I think highly of them both. June has the more character, but Diana is the sweeter.

Sunday, 19 December. Work as usual in the morning – mother cooking. June doing the brass work as I never have time to do, myself. She went in the afternoon. To Church with mother and Vera at night.

Monday, 20 December. My 44th birthday, and I still feel at times a foolish 18! A crystal clear frosty day. We all got up early as we were off to town on the 10.20. Ruth very kindly helped to look after Danna so that mother could come up with us. I had an exciting early morning breakfast, looking at my beautiful presents. I do seem to have wonderfully kind friends and relations. We caught the 10.20 and had a very comfortable journey. Mother went straight to Nancy's, and we went to Oddenino's [on Regent Street] to park our bags before having lunch (rather utility) at the Regent Palace Hotel. We did some shop-gazing at book shops and dress-shops and hunting for Robert's special chocolate all the afternoon [he was diabetic], and had tea at a funny café, the 'Bull-dog', in Bond Street – so sadly bombed, in parts – then went back to change and have cock-tails before going to the Lyric to see Jack Buchanan in *It's Time to Dance* – rather a poor musical comedy, and not half good enough for our dear Jack, who still looks attractive and dances as well as ever, and whose personality is so engaging. We went across to the Trocadero for supper. The worst of these early war-time shows is the awkwardness of the meal-times. One gets far too hungry after them, and not hungry enough before. We had a floor-table, and were able to watch the dancing. So many sweet young things of both sexes, in uniform, the men of all the allies, Belgium, French, Poles, Czechs, Canadians, Americans, Norwegians, Danes, mixing with the fewer English. Fascinating to watch. Back to the comfortable but over-heated hotel. Much too air-less to sleep, and the siren went off, apparently on the hotel roof, at 2.00a.m. until 2.30. A very happy birthday indeed.

The rest of 1943 highlighted the usual seasonal activities. Food appears to have been ample, and there was 'even sherry to drink' on Christmas Day, along with a goose and a chicken.[66] However, no Boxing Day pantomime was offered in Oxford this year 'because of theatre staff shortage'. Unusually, the Martins gave a private

Nice girls both.'
66 'Even Maud called an Armistice,' said Madge on 25 December, 'and gave very nice presents, though refused to have lunch with us. She came to tea, however.' The difficult Maud had been briefly noticed several weeks earlier, on 17 November, when 'Robert and Maud had "words". It was coming to her.'

party on 30 December – apparently the first they had given since the start of the war – with a total of fourteen in attendance, including their own household. 'We had all sorts and types of games, simple and semi-intellectual, and a treasure hunt, and everyone seemed to enjoy themselves, and everyone approved of everyone else.' On New Year's Eve, a mostly quiet day spent recovering from the previous evening's efforts, her final words were: 'Goodbye to 1943. Not too bad a year as far as the war-news went, and very hopeful for 1944. I do so *wonder* if peace will come next year. Everyone is talking of it, but then they always do. Well, here's hoping!' She revisited this tentative optimism the following day, in her first entry of the New Year. 'Everyone seems eager and anticipatory of good things to come after more than four years' war. How many times I seem to have started my diary, hoping that the end of the year will bring peace.' Robert's concluding words that evening were: '1943 has been a blessed year for the war effort, and brings us real hope of peace in '44. It has made me Rural Dean and City Rector, swelling my pride, and kept us happy together.'

Epilogue[1]

Peace, of course, did not come until 1945, and Madge wrote with enthusiasm when it did. 'The Day we have waited for [8 May], for nearly six years, and at last, here it is, miraculous, exciting, wonderful! Lovely weather, streets be-flagged, happy crowds, dancing in the streets, singing everywhere, infectious happiness.' The press in Oxford – as almost everywhere else in the country – reported in detail on these public festivities. There were great crowds of people, 'happy, good-humoured, noisy and properly determined to make the most of the occasion'. In the pubs and hotels 'there were many toasts between sailors, soldiers and airmen of the United Nations'. The complete ending of wartime blacking-out was suitably celebrated. 'Floodlighting of some of Oxford's famous buildings fitly signalised the end of the war black-out. The crowds greatly appreciated the striking beauty of Magdalen tower and the front quadrangle, Merton and New College towers, St John's and Lincoln quad. The New Theatre was also lit up.' Bonfires were lit in almost all parts of the city, some large, others in side streets where they were 'generously fed by the residents with old chairs, bedsteads, mattresses, packing cases and any other materials which came to hand'. Little in the way of drunkenness was observed.[2]

These were memorable days, and they are prominent in Madge's diary – as they were in many other diaries composed in May 1945. On VE Day 'There were short services in the morning and evening (the real Thanksgiving Service will be on Sunday).[3] We went to both – packed churches, thankful people. Mr Churchill spoke

---

1   Madge's diary for most of 1944 and early 1945 generally lacks substance and vigour, and many entries are short. A sense of dénouement predominates; evidence of novelty and unexpected events diminishes. Of course, the war news was mostly good; some previous anxieties about wartime living, notably the prospect of invasion, were no longer so acute; and Madge never again mentioned one troubling personal threat – the possibility that she might have to do paid work outside the home.
2   *Oxford Times*, 11 May 1945, p. 8.
3   'The great day of National Thanksgiving,' she wrote on Sunday, 13 May. 'Busy in the morning. I listened to the service from St Paul's, which the Royal Family and Winston

in the afternoon, quietly, and no boasting. The Jimenez came in to listen. The King spoke at 9.00 – and they came again, also the Bleibens, and Ruth and a friend. We listened to his modest speech, and drank sherry happily and rather dazedly. Then sang rollicking songs before going out to see the sights.' There were 'Enormous crowds shouting, cheering, singing, dancing. Huge bonfires fed by ARP properties, magnesium bombs, great logs of wood, chairs, tables, ladders etc. with dancing rings of young people circling them, beautiful flood-lit buildings, lighted windows, torch-light processions, and a good-humoured gaiety with no rowdy-ism. We all got parted in the singing throng at Carfax [Oxford's central junction] but Robert and I went about together, happier than for years, remembering it all, for ever, light after darkness! Our own house was beautifully be-decked with flags and every window a blaze of light – after 5 years and more. We all met at last for cups of tea before going to bed at 1.00a.m. Thank God for this day of days.'[4]

The following day, 9 May, was a second official holiday. 'One of the nicest things is to hear the weather forecast on the wireless again – such a peace-time feature. Even to hear of "stationary depressions" is exciting. All the morning was spent at the United Missions Bazaar at the Town Hall, where St Michael's had a cake-stall. In spite of difficulties – no buses today etc. – we sold out in an hour and made over £15. … Lunch at the Shamrock, and a much-needed rest in the afternoon. The Bleibens asked me to go to Woodstock with them for dinner as Robert was dining in College. I was delighted. I met them on the 7.00p.m. bus, and we had a nice dinner at the Marlborough Arms, with cider cup, and a lovely cheerful atmosphere all round. Woodstock looked sweet, with miniature flags to match its tiny buildings. Back on the 9.20, and Robert and I went out again into the gay town to see more crowds, even huger bonfires, and the glory of Merton College chapel, flood-lit against the deep blue sky. How thankful we must be, for ever, that our lovely Oxford Buildings have been spared bombing raids.'

While war in Europe was over, Japan was still fighting. When it did accept defeat and the news reached 1 Wellington Place, a little after midnight on 15 August, there was rejoicing and celebrating with glasses of sherry. VJ Day, she wrote, 'was comparatively quiet. Not so much riotous excitement, less festive decorations, smaller crowds than on VE Day. We all went to the short Thanksgiving service at 11.00, at

---

Churchill and a great crowd of important people, as well as the general public, attended. Very beautiful. There was our own Thanksgiving Service at St Michael's in the evening [she attached the printed programme]. I still can't believe it is true!'

4   At the top of this entry for 8 May 1945 she pasted a Union Jack and at the end a distinctively marked penny stamp, accompanied by her comment, 'Even the post-office celebrates! Victory V and 2 bells' (the images on the postmark). In his diary, Robert wrote that this was 'One of the Great Days of our Life. … I got the flags from the tunnel where they have reposed since the Coronation 8 years ago, and set them out.' He had bought sherry especially 'for this great day'. 'Thank God. Thank God,' were the concluding words to his entry. It was, he said, 'a memorable week' (11 May).

St Michael's.' They had 'lovely decorations at home, and fairy-lights in the apple-tree'. The evening in town was 'Not anything like so exciting as the 1st Victory day.' Still, as she said two days later, 'The war is *really* over. Impossible to comprehend. Everyone still in festive mood.' This sense of exhilaration came back to her on several of the following days. On 23 August, returning home from the Playhouse 'in the *dazzlingly* lighted St Giles was wonderful. The war memorial was flood-lit. Oh think back on 1939 – and be glad.' She was thrilled to be able to return with Robert two days later to Scarborough, a place where she was almost always happy. 'We cannot believe that we are here again,' she remarked on 26 August. 'It all seems too good to be true.' For her, in a way, after the interruption of war, real life was being restored. 'Six years ago today', she wrote on 3 September, 'we were feeling in the depths of misery at the outbreak of war. How differently we feel now, thank God, and how long ago it seems.' Pre-war holiday destinations could now be revisited. Being back in 'Our dear Scarborough' marked a happy taste of freedom after 'all the weary war years' (4 and 7 September 1945).[5]

* * *

'Oh, why do I keep a diary?' This was a question Madge asked herself on 10 June 1944. Her answer was: 'I think I only do it because it gives a sort of permanence to our doings.' 'Permanence' may have meant different things to her. It probably meant, in part, an aid to her memory, and to keeping matters of significance fresher in her mind and adequately recorded. The desire to keep such a record is supported by the fact that each volume of her diary includes a list of films and plays seen that year, usually with the exact date attached. 'Permanence' may also have suggested a desire to compose a record that could be passed on to posterity, especially when she had no children. Indeed, it may well be that, since the absence of children meant that she had time on her hands, diary-keeping was one agreeable way of filling this time, and that as the years passed it became an aspect of ordinary routine (especially when she did not demand a lot of her writing). Whatever her motives in the 1930s and early 1940s, her diary became a well-rooted habit – a habit that in fact continued until 1989, when she turned 90.[6]

---

5   Their days in Scarborough were full of some of the usual genteel seaside pleasures that had been absent in wartime, though one, on 4 September, was perhaps not entirely genteel. 'We went to "The Bouquets" [a Northern troupe of entertainers] in the evening for a change. They still have Murray Ashford and Edgar Sawyer, who are so funny together. We laughed till we cried at the crude humour.' The Bouquets played at the Spa Theatre and were promoted as 'A bunch of refined personalities tied up with a ribbon of originality' (*Scarborough Mercury*, 7 September 1945, p. 12). We are grateful to Angela Kale at the Scarborough Library for this information.
6   Madge died on 18 September 1990. She had been a widow for twenty-four and a half years.

Most importantly, for posterity Madge Martin's diary offers an intimate portrayal of a life lived just before and during a world war – a life of a different sort from most of the lives that have so far been revealed in published wartime diaries and letters. Madge's world in, say, 1937 to 1938 was comfortable and in many ways untroubled – 'placid' was a word that both she and Robert used favourably – though her many and severe headaches must have weighed heavily on her happiness. In the early 1940s she was still able to enjoy many of, for her, the standard pleasures of life, especially through reading and the creative arts, being out-of-doors, and taking holidays, albeit not on the Continent or even at a major English seaside resort. However, she shared with almost everyone else normal war-worries – about her sisters and their families in blitzed London, for example. She often presided over a much larger number of residents in her household, and thus had many fewer opportunities to be solitary and serene; and she both had to and was inclined to work significantly harder at home – the departure of servants was important – as well as volunteering as a war-worker, mainly with the Red Cross. These were major changes. She was, though, able to avoid compulsory paid work, which probably would have meant a part-time office or clerical job in Oxford, and certainly would have interfered with her leisure preferences. Her home and her holidays and her Oxford social life and festive occasions continued to be central to her existence. She had to make *some* sacrifices – but not a lot (and she did acknowledge her good fortune).

This is a diary that opens a window on to some of the features of life for wartime England's lower gentility and professional classes. It shows how some of these women and men, in one notably privileged, prosperous, and fortunate city – and one married woman in particular – thought about their lives, responded and adapted to wartime pressures, and kept themselves going during these years when their country's very survival was, for the first time in generations, acutely under threat.

Appendix A

Madge Martin and John Hall

'It is an awful thought that I am now much happier writing to him [John] and getting letters from him, rather than the exciting but troubling presence of him here' in Oxford: these were Madge's words on 24 August 1941. Later that year, on 4 November, when she heard that John was on his way home on a fourteen days' leave, her initial reaction was to feel confused and flustered. But then he 'came in and had supper with us, and afterwards a talk in the waiting room, absolutely as of yore, just as though he had never been away all these months. ... I never fail to marvel at this strange but firm friendship. We are as different from one another as is possible for any two people to be, yet, I believe, we shall be the best of friends all our lives.' The role of John Hall in Madge Martin's life was so central and her feelings about him so intense that some attempt to understand their relationship seems warranted. And on this matter readers of her diary are likely to have come already to their own conclusions, with perhaps a variety of plausible perspectives to offer. Here are ours.[1]

First, Madge's feelings towards John appear to have involved a prominent maternal element that was otherwise unfulfilled, given her lack of children. More than once she wrote of him as 'a lamb' or her 'ewe lamb'. The part of Oxford where he lived 'has vivid memories of a small ginger head', she once remarked of a time twenty years earlier (30 December 1942). On 19 May 1936 'I felt as proud as a mother-hen and fussy over his well-being' after he had given blood at the Radcliffe Infirmary. 'Fancy, my little "Johnnie" 31,' she wrote on his birthday, 22 April, in 1942. 'It doesn't seem possible somehow.' On occasion she expressed mixed feelings about him growing up (though was mostly glad that he did grow up, if not always in ways she approved of). They were becoming 'polite strangers to one another', was her view on 1 March 1931, 'which is only to be expected, as it was a little boy in whom I was first interested, not a lanky youth of 19'.

---

1   There is much more about John in Madge's diary entries that have not been selected for reproduction, almost all of which is in the same spirit as what is printed.

Sometimes Madge tried to pull back. John, she wrote on 12 October 1930, 'still has the power to make me feel angry but otherwise I am delightfully free from his sway now'. (As time would show, she was not.) On the last day of this year, looking back reflectively, she thought that 'John has almost ceased to worry me, and I can laugh at things that would have caused me much grief at one time'. On 30 August 1931 she wrote about liking him 'much better now, though I have lost my love for him'. A decade later (6 June 1941) she recalled her 'early turbulent feelings when John was a boy'.

These turbulent feelings were not confined to times well past. They persisted through the 1930s and early 1940s, and are often detailed in her diary. John lived for a fortnight with Robert and Madge just after his mother died, and she acknowledged that 'my mind is mostly confused by having John here – a mixed blessing indeed, as he always has this bemusing effect on me' (4 March 1936). She was distressed at the thought of 'not having him under my roof now' (2 March 1936). Some days later (24 March 1936) she strove for a degree of objective understanding. 'What an enormous part John has played, in the last 13 years of my life – for better, or worse. I suppose for the better, as he has kept me, at least, from becoming stodgy and has been a kind and loving friend, the last years anyway.' Friendship was, for her, the key value – and she never wrote of any other friend with such intensity. John was special. 'I'm the only one he can talk to properly' (26 May 1936). 'He is a truly satisfying friend to have and would never let you down' (31 May 1936). But it was a volatile relationship that was marked – as she said the last day of that year – by 'all sorts of ups and downs which rend me asunder'.

Madge often thought of their friendship – she considered herself John's 'greatest friend' (15 February 1940) – in a rather custodial fashion, as if an important part of her purpose in life was to pay close attention to his welfare and assess carefully his character, maturity, and state of mind. On 28 September 1941 she wrote him a letter, 'trying to be kind, tactful, but firm, in reply to some of his rather worrying questions'. He 'is slightly less tongue-tied than he used to be, in general company', she declared on 21 March 1942, 'but not much'. At the same time she was highly sensitive to how he treated her, whether badly (in her eyes) or agreeably. On 8 January 1941 he 'said a lot of very nice things about our long friendship, and the effect it had on him'. Such appreciative words from him always made her happy.

He sometimes hurt her. She was sensitive to perceived slights – when his visit to her was (she thought) too short, when he chose to spend time with others in preference to her (30 March 1930), or was otherwise insufficiently attentive. She could also be jealous. On 21 February 1940 she discovered that John had given an RAF badge not only to her, but also to two other women, another (probably middle-aged) married woman and his sister. She had thought his gift to her was 'my exclusive property', and was sadly disappointed that it was not – 'just a wholesale giving away to all his women-folk, that's all! This fact is depressing me.'

Madge, by her own testimony, was not a resolute or forceful person, and her friendship with John may have allowed her to play a stronger part socially than she usually played. Since they met when he was only 12 and she 24, it was natural for her, from the start, to be dominant, more open with her opinions, more self-confident, and generally directive. With most people in her life from 1929, she seems to have been reactive, often hesitant, even timorous, and certainly in no way pushy. With him, by contrast, she could feel more in command – a feeling that he probably balked at, and sometimes argued against, after he became a man. He comes across in her diary as almost the only person in Oxford to whom she sometimes acted assertively.[2]

There was also a degree of equality in their relationship that may have been even more important. On 8 January 1942, as one of his leaves from the RAF was ending, John visited Madge for a chat and they exchanged 'pleasant and cheerful confidences'. With the possible exception of Vera, he was probably the only person outside the family with whom she enjoyed such a familiar, often 'easy' relationship. Madge was a shy woman. In some ways Oxford society did not suit her. (Perhaps this is why she so often felt depressed after returning home from a holiday.) University people readily caused her to feel socially awkward and inferior. She was quick to acknowledge her own lowliness.

Then there was Oxford's sometimes oppressive conventionality. Stefan Collini has remarked on 'the ritualised bonhomie of many senior common rooms' – Robert, moreover, was also a Mason – and 'the experiences of the wives exposed to the unforgiving social protocols of inter-war north Oxford'.[3] Madge was ill-at-ease with these protocols. Her academic background was thin – formal education had ended for her at the age of sixteen – and early marriage had deterred her from learning to do a lot on her own. Nor had she been able to exercise the responsibility of motherhood. While her husband was a member of the senior common room of one college and chaplain of another and at least on the margins of the University's culture of learning,[4] she certainly was not – beyond supporting its rugger teams. Her friendship with John was important (we speculate) not only because it was longstanding, it was also felt by her to be a relationship that did not regularly require her to put on an act dictated by rigid social conventions.

2   While Madge was often irritated with Muriel Smith, whom she found childish, it is unclear to what extent if at all she took her on in argument. If she did, such incidents were rarely reported. The negative feelings about other people who appear in Madge's diary were probably infrequently spoken aloud, except to John, and almost certainly to Robert.
3   Stefan Collini, 'Rabbits Addressed by a Stoat', *London Review of Books*, 13 July 2017, p. 27.
4   As well as writing on the history of his Church, Robert had also done research for a biography of the churchman, non-juror, and antiquarian George Hickes (1642–1715), and left seven of these notebooks to Lincoln College, which are currently held in its archive. His close connection with this college for all of his adult life is highlighted in his obituary in the *Lincoln College Record, 1965–66*, p. 25. (Lindsay McCormack kindly advised us on these sources.)

The deep impact John often had on her is further confirmed by a remarkable passage in her diary for 19 January 1937. 'If things go on as dismally as they are doing at present,' she wrote, 'I shall have no heart to keep a diary any more. The year has been hellish so far, and I see no reason why it should ever change, as far as John is concerned ... I must now start to regard [him] as no more important than any of my other friends – he has hurt me so much in such a self-righteous way, I can do nothing else.' The following day she added the words: 'The comforting thought is, that the more John upsets me, the more, then, [I] turn to Robert for happiness.' Given the premise that having only one emotional pillar (a good husband) is to court vulnerability, perhaps John often served for Madge as a second pillar, albeit a much less reliable one.

Appendix B

Madge Martin's Reading

—◆—

' … books are my great happiness and relaxation' (14 January 1943)

Each year Madge compiled a list of the books she had read, usually singling out her favourites, which are noted at the end of this Appendix. She read 51 books in 1940, 56 in 1943, and either 62 or 63 books in each of the other four years. The great majority were novels. When a title was non-fiction, she often identified it as such. We have checked each title and its author's name in the British Library catalogue and corrected her errors, which were numerous. A few authorial names were pseudonyms. We have added in square brackets the year of publication, which Madge's lists did not supply. Strikingly, she read very few books published before 1930.

Books read by Madge Martin in 1939

Jane Allen, *I Lost My Girlish Laughter* [1938]
Anne Parrish, *Mr Despondency's Daughter* [1938]
Margaret MacKay, *Like Water Flowing* [1938]
Caroline Seaford, *Dear Emily* [1938]
Barbara Willard, *Set Piece* [1938]
Kathleen Wallace, *Ancestral Tablet* [1938]
Howard Spring, *O Absalom!* [1938]
Cecil Roberts, *They Wanted to Live* [1939]
Mary Mitchell, *Who Pays?* [1939]
Martin Armstrong, *Victorian Peep-show* [1938] (autobiography)
John Brophy, *The Ridiculous Hat* [1939]
Jean Ross, *Flowers without Sun* [1938]
Louis Bromfield, *The Rains Came* [c. 1937]
John Brophy, *Man, Woman and Child* [1938]
Margaret Halsey, *With Malice Toward Some* [1938] (non-fiction)
Irene Rathbone, *When Days Were Years* [1939]

Irene Rathbone, *We That Were Young* [1932]
Anne Meredith, *The Stranger* [1939]
Beverley Nichols, *Revue* [1939]
Richmal Crompton, *Merlin Bay* [1939]
Joanna Cannan, *They Rang Up the Police* [1939]
W. Somerset Maugham, *Christmas Holiday* [1939]
Constance Inskip, *Pink Faces* [1939]
Morchard Bishop, *Two for Joy* [1938]
Storm Jameson, *Here Comes a Candle* [1938]
Eleanor Dark, *Waterway* [1938]
Barbara Worsley-Gough, *Learn to be a Lady* [1938]
Josephine Kamm, *Nettles to my Head* [1939]
Francis Brett Young, *My Brother Jonathan* [1928]
Margaret Iles, *The Burden of Tyre* [1939]
Rose Wilder Lane, *Let the Hurricane Roar* [1933]
Margery Sharp, *Harlequin House* [1939]
Martin Armstrong, *The Snake in the Grass* [1938]
Marguerite Steen, *The Marriage Will Not Take Place* [1938]
Mazo de le Roche, *Growth of a Man* [1938]
G.B. Stern, *The Woman in the Hall* [1939]
Dorothy Whipple, *The Priory* [1939]
Rachel Field, *All This, and Heaven Too* [1939]
Doreen Wallace, *Old Father Antic* [1937]
Pamela Hansford Johnson, *World's End* [1937]
Caroline Seaford, *The Velvet Deer* [1937]
Mary Borden, *Passport for a Girl* [1939]
E.M. Delafield, *Three Marriages* [1939]
Rachel Ferguson, *Alas, Poor Lady* [1937]
Doreen Wallace, *A Handful of Silver* [1939]
Agnes Sligh Turnbull, *The Rolling Years* [1936]
Ladies Must Live: An Autobiography [1939]
Francis Iles, *As for the Woman* [1939]
Elizabeth Goudge, *Towers in the Mist* [1938]
Noel Streatfeild, *Luke* [1939]
Leo Walmsley, *Love in the Sun* [1939]
Leonora Starr, *Hear the Bugle* [1937]
Howard Spring, *Heaven Lies About Us* [1939] (autobiography)
Noël Coward, *To Step Aside* [1939] (short stories)
Annemaria Selinko, *Everything Will Be Better Tomorrow* [1939]
Pamela Wynne, *Choose from the Stars* [1938]
Margery Lawrence, *The Bridge of Wonder* [1939]
D.E. Stevenson, *Miss Bun, the Baker's Daughter* [1938]
Pamela Wynne, *Love's Lotus Flower* [1939]

J.B. Priestley, *Let the People Sing* [1939]
Jean Ross, *We are Shadows* [1939]
Elizabeth Goudge, *Sister of the Angels* [1939]

Books read by Madge Martin in 1942

Stella Gibbons, *The Rich House* [1941]
Hugh Walpole, *The Blind Man's House* [1941]
Josephine Bell, *Martin Croft* [1941]
Philip Gibbs, *The Long Alert* [1941]
Angela Thirkell, *August Folly* [1936]
C.B. Cochran, *Cock-a-doodle-do* [1941] (non-fiction)
James Laver, *Nymph Errant* [1932]
Rachel Field, *Time out of Mind* [1935]
Kay Ambrose and Arnold L. Haskell, *Balletomane's Sketch-Book* [1942] (non-fiction)
Cecil Beaton, *Cecil Beaton's Scrapbook* [1937] (non-fiction)
Noel Streatfeild, *I Ordered a Table for Six* [1942]
Eunice Buckley, *Family from Vienna* [1941]
Don Portbury, *Brief Hour* [1939]
Edith Pargeter, *Ordinary People* [1941]
Arnold Haskell, *Dancing Round the World* [1937] (non-fiction)
Charles Norris, *Seed* [1930]
Marjorie Mack, *The Red Centaur* [1939]
Stella Morton, *The Convoys Pass* [1941]
Doris Leslie, *The House in the Dust* [1942]
Angela Thirkell, *Cheerfulness Breaks In* [1940]
Dorothy Whipple, *After Tea* [1941] (short stories)
Stuart Engstrand, *Norwegian Spring 1940* [1941]
Cecil Beaton, *New York* [1938] (non-fiction)
Edna Ferber, *Saratoga Trunk* [1942]
Joyce Cary, *A House of Children* [1941]
Betty Miller, *Farewell Leicester Square* [1941]
Mary Ellen Chase, *Windswept* [1941]
Rhys Davies, *Tomorrow to Fresh Woods* [1941]
Kathleen Norris, *The Venables* [1941]
John Marquand, *H.M. Pulham, Esquire* [1942]
Kathleen Wallace, *The Singing Tree* [1941]
Batsford non-fiction, *The Streets of Paris* [not found]
Margaret Lane, *Faith, Hope, No Charity* [1935] (second time)
Richmal Crompton, *Mrs Frensham Describes a Circle* [1942]
Monica Dickens, *One Pair of Feet* [1942] (non-fiction)
Nevil Shute, *Pied Piper* [1942]
Doreen Wallace, *The Spring Returns* [1940]

Joanna Cannan, *Snow in Harvest* [1932]
Rosamond Lehmann, *The Weather in the Streets* [1936]
Nevil Shute, *Landfall* [1940]
Rumer Godden, *Breakfast with the Nikolides* [1942]
Phyllis Bottome, *London Pride* [1941]
Francis Brett Young, *A Man about the House* [1942]
Lin Yutang, *A Leaf in the Storm* [1942]
Ellen Glasgow, *In This Our Life* [1941]
J.B. Priestley, *Blackout in Gretley* [1942]
Angela Thirkell, *Marling Hall* [1942]
Vincent Sheean, *Bird of the Wilderness* [1942]
Jean Ross, *Women in Exile* [1942]
Vicki Baum, *Grand Opera* [1942]
Lin Yutang, *The Importance of Living* [1938] (non-fiction)
Margery Nugent, *Fenella* [1942]
Louis Bromfield, *Wild is the River* [1941]
Phyllis Waite, *My Heart in Him* [1942]
Hugh Walpole, *Rogue Herries* [1930] (second time)
Frank Tilsley, *What's in it for Walter?* [1942]
Ruth Manning-Sanders, *Elephant* [1940]
Dorothy Cowlin, *Winter Solstice* [1942]
Dorothy Cowlin, *Penny to Spend* [1941]
Edith Pargeter, *She Goes to War* [1942]
Elizabeth von Arnim, *The Jasmine Farm* [1934]
Frank Reynolds, *Off to the Pictures* [1937] (non-fiction)
Phyllis W. Manchester, *Vic-Wells: A Ballet Progress* [1942]

Books judged by Madge Martin as 'The Best' or 'Enjoyed Most' during each of the six years 1938–1943

1938

Margaret Mitchell, *Gone with the Wind* [1936] (outstanding)
Noël Coward, *Present Indicative* [1937]
Sarah Campion, *Unhandsome Corpse* [1938]
Catherine Meadows, *Friday Market* [1938]
Nina Warner Hooke, *Own Wilderness* [1938]
Geoffrey Uther Ellis, *There Goes the Queen* [1935]
J.B. Priestley, *Wonder Hero* [1933]

1939

Irene Rathbone, *We That Were Young* [1932]
Irene Rathbone, *When Days Were Years* [1939]

Howard Spring, *O Absalom!* [1938]
Martin Armstrong, *Victorian Peep-show* [1938]
Louis Bromfield, *The Rains Came* [c. 1937]
Dorothy Whipple, *The Priory* [1939]
G.B. Stern, *The Woman in the Hall* [1939]
J.B. Priestley, *Let the People Sing* [1939]
Caroline Seaford, *The Velvet Deer* [1937]
Noël Coward, *To Step Aside* [1939]
Elizabeth Goudge, *The Sister of the Angels* [1939]
Rachel Ferguson, *Alas, Poor Lady* [1937]

1940

Stella Gibbons, *My American* [1939] (outstanding)
Ernest Raymond, *A Song of the Tide* [1940] (outstanding)
Richard Llewellyn, *How Green was My Valley* [1939]
Sinclair Lewis, *Bethel Merriday* [1940]
Michael Sadleir, *Fanny by Gaslight* [1940]

1941[1]

Ernest Raymond, *A Family That Was* [1929]
Ernest Raymond, *Child of Norman's End* [1934]
Compton Mackenzie, *Carnival* [1912]
Emery Bonett, *Never Go Dark* [1940]
Angela Thirkell, *High Rising* [1933]
Christopher Morley, *Kitty Foyle* [1940]
Richmal Crompton, *Narcissa* [1941]
Margaret Irwin, *Still She Wished for Company* [1924]
Alison Uttley, *The Farm on the Hill* [1941]
Doris Leslie, *Royal William* [1940]
Lilian Prior, *These Times of Travail* [1941]
Eleanor Farjeon, *A Nursery in the Nineties* [1935] (non-fiction)

1942

Stella Gibbons, *The Rich House* [1941]
Nevil Shute, *Pied Piper* [1942]
Margery Nugent, *Fenella* [1942]
Dorothy Cowlin, *Winter Solstice* [1942]
Richmal Crompton, *Mrs Frensham Describes a Circle* [1942]

---

1   She wrote at the top of this list of books: 'No outstanding ones. The very best were the old ones, read again.'

Noel Streatfeild, *I Ordered a Table for Six* [1942]
Rachel Field, *Time out of Mind* [1935]
Phyllis Bottome, *London Pride* [1941]
All the books on Ballet, and the twice-read novels.

1943

Jerrard Tickell, *Soldier from the Wars Returning* [1942] (outstanding)
Eleanor Farjeon, *Golden Coney* [1943] (outstanding)
William White, *Journey for Margaret* [1942]
Rachel Field, *And Now Tomorrow* [1942]
Jan Struther, *Mrs Miniver* [1939]
Eiluned Lewis, *The Captain's Wife* [1943]
Kathleen Wallace, *Without Signposts* [1941]
Vicki Baum, *Marion Alive* [1943]
Irina Skariatina, *In Your Glad Heart Tamara* [1943]
Margaret Mann Phillips, *Within the City Wall* [1943] (non-fiction)
Kay Ambrose, *The Ballet-Lovers' Pocket-Book* [1943] (non-fiction)
Kitty Barne, *While the Music Lasted* [1943]
Honor Croome, *O Western Wind* [1943]

Bibliography

Primary sources

Oxfordshire History Centre (OHC)

Acc. 5374   St Michael at the North Gate, *Parish Magazine*
PAR211/1/R3/7   St Michael at the North Gate, Parish Registers
PAR211/1/R5/1   St Michael at the North Gate, Parish Registers
PAR211/2/A1/5   St Michael at the North Gate, Vestry Minutes 1871–1955
PAR211/4/F1/8   St Michael at the North Gate, Parish Accounts
PAR211/3/A1/3   St Michael at the North Gate, Parochial Church Council Minutes 1942–1944
P5   Diaries and correspondence of Robert and Madge Martin 1911–1988
P5/C2   Madge Martin's correspondence 1915
P5/C3   Robert Martin's correspondence 1915–1966
P5/1J   Robert Martin's diaries 1911–1965
P5/2J   Madge Martin's diaries 1916–1988
P5/P3   Photograph albums 1921–1965

Royal Voluntary Service Archive & Heritage Collection, Devizes, Wiltshire (RVS Archive & Heritage Collection)

WRVS/HQ/NR/R6/1940-CB/OXF WVS Narrative Report for Oxford City, September and October 1940
WRVS/HQ/NR/R6/1941-CB/OXF Oxford City Narrative Report, March and September 1941
WRVS/HQ/NR/R6/1943-CB/OXF Oxford [City] Narrative Report, February, May and July 1943
WRVS/HQ/NR/R6/1943-OXF/OXF CO County Narrative Report for October/November and December 1943

In private hands
Madge Martin, 'A Yorkshire Childhood 1899–1913'

Newspapers

Cheshire Chronicle
Hendon and Finchley Times
Irish Times
Lincoln College Record
Lincoln Imp
Oxford Mail
Oxford Times
Scarborough Mercury
The Times
Worcester College Record 1939–1944

Reference works

Crockford's Clerical Directory (several years)
Kelly's Directory of Oxford, Abingdon, Woodstock, and neighbourhood, with street plan, 45th ed. (Kelly's Directories Ltd, 1939)
Kelly's Directory of Oxford, Abingdon, Woodstock, and neighbourhood, 48th ed. (Kelly's Directories Ltd, 1943)
Oxford Dictionary of National Biography

Secondary sources

Allen, Sir Carleton, 'The Rhodes Scholars and Oxford 1931–52', in G. Elton, *The First Fifty Years of the Rhodes Trust and the Rhodes Scholarships 1903–1953* (Oxford: Basil Blackwell, 1955), pp. 129–82

Brooks, Robin J., *Oxfordshire Airfields in the Second World War* (Newbury: Countryside Books, 2001)

Chapman, Don, *Oxford Playhouse: High and Low Drama in a University City* (Hatfield: University of Hertfordshire Press, 2008)

Charles-Edwards, Thomas and Julian Reid, *Corpus Christi College, Oxford: A History* (Oxford: Oxford University Press, 2017)

Collini, Stefan, 'Rabbits Addressed by a Stoat', *London Review of Books*, 13 July 2017, p. 27

Colvin, Ian, *Flight 777: The Mystery of Leslie Howard* (Barnsley: Pen & Sword, repr. 2013). First published 1957

Complete speeches, see James, Robert Rhodes, ed., *Winston S. Churchill: His Complete Speeches, 1897–1963*

Elton, Godfrey, Baron Elton, ed., *The First Fifty Years of the Rhodes Trust and the Rhodes Scholarships 1903–1953* (Oxford: Basil Blackwell, 1955)

Gardiner, Juliet, *Joining the Dots: A Woman in her Time* (London: William Collins, 2017)

Garnett, Maxwell, *A Lasting Peace … With some chapters on the basis of German co-operation* by H.F. Koeppler (London: Allen & Unwin, 1940)

Graham, Malcolm, *Oxfordshire at War* (Stroud: Alan Sutton, 1994)

Hargreaves, E.L. and M.M. Gowing, *Civil Industry and Trade* (London: HMSO, 1952). A volume in the *History of the Second World War, United Kingdom Civil Series*, edited by W.K. Hancock

Harrison, Brian, ed., *The History of the University of Oxford, Volume VIII, The Twentieth Century* (Oxford: Clarendon Press, 1994)

James, Robert Rhodes, ed., *Winston S. Churchill: His Complete Speeches, 1897–1963* (London: Chelsea House, 1974, 8 vols). Cited as *Complete Speeches*

Korda, Michael, *With Wings Like Eagles: A History of the Battle of Britain* (New York: HarperCollins, 2009)

Longmate, Norman, *How We Lived Then: A History of Everyday Life during the Second World War* (London: Pimlico, 2002). First published 1971

Malcolmson, Patricia and Robert, eds, *The View from the Corner Shop: The Diary of a Yorkshire Shop Assistant in Wartime, Kathleen Hey* (London: Simon & Schuster, 2016)

—— *Wartime Cumbria, 1939–1945: Aspects of Life and Work* (Cumberland and Westmorland Antiquarian and Archaeological Society, 2017)

Malcolmson, Robert, ed., *Love and War in London: A Woman's Diary 1939–1942, Olivia Cockett* (Waterloo, Ontario: Wilfred Laurier University Press, 2005)

Martin, R.R., *Beating the Bounds of the Parish of St Michael at the North Gate, Oxford* (1961), pamphlet

——*The Church and Parish of St Michael at the Northgate, Oxford* (Oxford, 1967)

Mazower, Mark, *What You Did Not Tell: A Russian Past and the Journey Home* (New York: Other Press, 2017)

Meyrick, Ian, *Oxfordshire Cinemas* (Stroud: Tempus, 2007)

O'Brien, Terence H., *Civil Defence* (London: HMSO, 1955). A volume in the *History of the Second World War, United Kingdom Civil Series*, edited by W.K. Hancock

Parker, H.M.D., *Manpower: A Study of War-time Policy and Administration* (London: HMSO, 1957). A volume in the *History of the Second World War, United Kingdom Civil Series*, edited by W.K. Hancock

Peniston-Bird, C.M. '"Yes, we had no bananas": sharing memories of the Second World War', in Mary Addyman, Laura Wood, and Christopher Yinnitsaros, eds, *Food, Drink, and the Written Word in Britain, 1820–1945* (London: Routledge, 2017)

Samuel, Raphael, '"Quarry Roughs": life and labour in Headington Quarry, 1860–1920', in Raphael Samuel, ed., *Village Life and Labour* (London: Routledge & Kegan Paul, 1975), pp. 139–263

Thorsheim, Peter, *Waste into Weapons: Recycling in Britain during the Second World War* (New York: Cambridge University Press, 2015)

What Is the Oxford Group? by 'The Layman with a Notebook' (London: Oxford University Press, 1933)

Whipple, Dorothy, 'One Dark Night', reprinted in her *Every Good Deed and Other Stories* (London: Persephone Books, 2016), pp. 223–33

Index

Many matters involving Madge Martin and her husband are indexed as subjects rather than under her or his name. Place-names, family members, and personal friends (e.g., the Cadena, named cinemas, train stations, Vera Dyer, John Hall, Madge's mother) are usually not indexed when they are mentioned only in passing, absent any noteworthy detail or comment (this absence is a regular feature of Madge's private diary: she was not writing to inform outsiders). The same applies to most named visitors, people visited, and fellow Red Cross volunteers. Public figures and events are almost always indexed. Since Madge says something about the weather almost every day, weather events are rarely indexed, and only when they were in some sense extreme. 'Passim' is used mainly when a proper name or subject appears on average at least once every two pages, usually in passing, over at least half a dozen pages.

For places in Oxfordshire and neighbouring counties see the entries for country walks and Maps 3 and 4.

actors
    Ahearne, Brian, 104
    Ameche, Don, 91
    Arden, Eve, 41n
    Arthur, Jean, 83
    Ashford, Murray, 243n
    Astaire, Fred, 32, 70, 103, 221
    Barnes, Barry, 96, 130
    Barrymore, Diana, 204
    Barrymore, John, 123
    Barrymore, Lionel, 18
    Bartholomew, Freddie, 33
    Baxter, Jane, 232
    Bell, Marie, 27
    Bergman, Ingrid, 177
    Best, Edna, 1
    Boyer, Charles, 140n
    Brook, Clive, 182
    Brown, Pamela, 165
    Buchanan, Jack, 132
    Buttrum, Anne (née Elsie Harris), 116–17, 119, 140, 201
    Buttrum, Dudley, 116–17, 119
    Byron, John, 126
    Cagney, James, 218
    Chaplin, Charlie, 26
    Churchill, Diana, 130
    Clements, John, 213
    Colbert, Claudette, 87, 134
    Colman, Ronald, 178
    Cooper, Gary, 63, 129
    Copley, Peter, 187
    Culver, Roland, 130
    Cummings, Robert, 204
    D'Albie, Julian, 157
    Dare, Zena, 40
    Darnell, Linda, 177
    Davis, Bette, 27, 78
    de Havilland, Olivia, 89
    Deval, Jacques, 166
    Donat, Robert, 86, 212
    Drew, Ellen, 66
    Durbin, Deanna, 98, 102
    Elliott, Madge, 209
    Evans, Clifford, 149n
    Evans, Winifred, 165
    Fairbanks, Douglas Jr, 41n
    Farrell, M.J., 158
    Faye, Alice, 114
    Fonda, Henry, 87
    Fontanne, Lynne, 234
    Ford, John (film director), 111

INDEX

Gabin, Jean, 211
Gable, Clark, 17
Garland, Judy, 80, 126, 129, 189
Garson, Greer, 184
Gielgud, John, 140n
Grant, Cary, 27, 142, 145n
Hale, Binnie, 96
Harker, Gordon, 132n
Harris, Elsie, *see* Buttrum, Anne
Harrison, Rex, 94, 95
Hay, Will, 171
Henjie, Sonja, 101
Henson, Leslie, 96
Hepburn, Katherine, 27, 145n
Hewett, Christopher, 196
Hillier, Wendy, 26
Hobson, Valerie, 57
Holloway, Stanley, 96
Hopkins, Miriam, 78
Howard, Leslie, 26, 145
  death of, 217
Jolson, Al, 91
Jones, Griffith, 88
Karloff, Boris, 99
Keaton, Buster, 177
Lake, Veronica, 225
Leeds, Andrea, 91
Lockwood, Margaret, 73n
Lombard, Carol, 65, 104
Loy, Myrna, 18, 61
Lunt, Alfred, 234
Lupino, Stanley, 232
MacDonald, Jeanette, 58
MacMurray, Fred, 102
Matthews, Jessie, 95
Milland, Ray, 66, 117, 134
Mills, John, 212
Montgomery, Robert, 92
Morgan, Frank, 119n
Morley, Robert, 36, 128, 212
Nesbitt, Cathleen, 130
Nicholson, Norah, 165
Niven, David, 40, 89, 172
Oberon, Merle, 180
Olivier, Lawrence, 57
Owen, Granville, 167
Perry, John, 158

Pickford, Mary, 26
Pidgeon, Walter, 184
Power, Tyrone, 177
Price, Dennis, 72
Price, Vincent, 99
Rathbone, Basil, 99
Rawlings, Margaret, 40
Redgrave, Michael, 73n, 137, 214, 232, 235
Reed, Carol (film director), 73n
Richardson, Ralph, 57
Richter, Frederick, 165
Ritchard, Cyril, 96, 209
Rogers, Ginger, 32, 35, 70, 157, 167, 172, 177, 212
Rooney, Andy, 19
Rooney, Mickey, 33, 72, 80, 117, 126, 129, 189, 208
Sawyer, Edgar, 243n
Shearer, Norma, 36
Sherwood, Robert, 166
Sim, Alistair, 132n
Skelton, Red, 41n
Stack, Robert, 119n
Stanwyck, Barbara, 102
Stewart, James, 83, 96, 145, 119n, 132n, 167
Sullavan, Margaret, 36, 96, 119n, 132n, 140n
Taylor, Robert, 61
Taylor, Valerie, 235
Temple, Shirley, 70, 91, 112
Thorndyke, Sybil, 31
Todd, Ann, 18
Tracy, Spencer, 18, 177
Turner, Lana, 177
Vanbrugh, Irene, 30
Veidt, Conrad, 49
Walbrook, Anton, 100, 218n
Wallace, Nellie, 98
Wentworth, John, 194
Wilding, Michael, 232
Williams, Emlyn, 31, 128
Withers, Googie, 213
Wyngard, Diana, 100
Young, Loretta, 40, 117
Young, Robert, 119n

INDEX

Addison's Walk, 215
Air Raid Precautions (ARP), 22, 96, 100, 102, 103, 207n
air-raids/alerts, 52, 53, 90, 94, 104, 105, 107, 112–21 passim, 124, 130–1, 186, 189, see also London, air-raids
airfields, 100n, 127
Allen, Mrs Dorothy, see Rhodes House, Allen, Mrs
Americans in Oxford, 232
Anderson, George (visiting American clergyman), 37, 38, 41, 42
authors/playwrights
    Ackland, Rodney, 230
    Ardrey, Robert, 214
    Balderston, John, 120
    Ballan, George, 139n
    Barrie, J.M., 140
    Blackmore, Peter, 215
    Bottome, Phyllis, 119n
    Bridie, James, 231
    Christie, Agatha, 201
    Crompton, Richmal, 185
    Coward, Noël, 208, 209
    Dane, Clemence, 215
    Dawson, A.E.W., 113
    Denham, Reginald, 191
    du Maurier, Daphne, 188
    Dumas, Alexandre, 65
    Edmonds, William D., 87
    Egan, Michael, 125
    Ellis, Geoffrey Uther, 34
    Fagan, James Bernard, 30
    Farjeon, Eleanor and Herbert, 80
    Ford, Robert, 55
    Garnett, Maxwell, 73n
    Greene, Graham, 211
    Greenwood, Walter, 149n
    Hackett, Walter, 114
    Hamilton, Patrick, 100
    Hart, Moss, 231
    Hay, Ian, 25, 118
    Hellman, Lillian, 222
    Herbert, A.P., 30
    Herman, Henry, 41
    Hilton, James, 97
    Hodge, Merton, 144
    Horne, Kenneth, 194
    Houseman, Laurence, 35
    Ibsen, Hendrik, 130n, 213n
    Johnson, Philip, 92
    Jones, Henry Arthur, 41
    Kaufman, George, 231
    Koeppler, H.F., 73n
    Lehar, Franz, 209
    Llewellyn, Richard, 225
    Lonsdale, Frederick, 130
    Maschurtz, Eric, 195
    Maugham, Somerset, 127, 196, 220
    McCracken, Esther, 114, 206
    Milne, A.A., 136
    Mitchell, Margaret, 25n
    Morley, Robert, 226
    Niemöller, Martin, 88n
    Novello, Ivor, 109, 141
    Page, Elizabeth, 142
    Percy, Edward, 191, 213
    Philpotts, Eden and Adelaide, 90, 135
    Pitt, George, 174
    Priestley, J.B., 139n, 190n
    Rattigan, Terence, 66, 184n
    Robertson, Willard, 211
    Shaw, George Bernard, 86, 123, 147, 233
    Sherwood, Robert E., 234
    Shute, Nevil, 206
    Smith, Dodie, 111
    Steinbeck, John, 96, 111, 220n
    Stratton-Parker, Gene, 127
    Struther, Jan, 184n
    Sturges, Preston, 125
    Turgenev, Ivan, 235
    Turner, John Hastings, 141
    Van Druten, John, 148
    Vaughan, Hilda, 30
    Vosper, Frank, 143
    Wells, H.G., 137
    Wharton, Edith, 78
    Whipple, Dorothy, 56n
    Williams, Emlyn, 94
    Winter, Keith, 147
    Wodehouse, P.G., 55n, 118

ballet, 138, 158, 166, 171
    Margot Fonteyn, 166

INDEX

Robert Helpmann, 166
bandages, *see* Red Cross War Depôt
Barnett House Institution for Social and Economic Studies, 80
'Battle of Britain' remembrance, 228
bazaars, *see* Red Cross, Bazaar
'beating of the bounds', 134, 171–2
Bedford, 2
Begbroke, grave photographed, 215
Bekonscot, *see* model villages
Belgium, capitulation, 83
Birmingham, 107
Bishop of Dorchester (Gerald Allen), 19, 28, 82, 233–4, 236
Bishop of Jamaica (Edmund Sara), 28
black-out, 47, 50, 55, 56, 99, 103, 113, 114, 119, 191, 226, 241
Blewbury, Berkshire, 89
books, 209–10, 214
    Alice in Wonderland, 120
    Gone with the Wind, 24–5, Plate 11
    The King's Service, 25
    A Lasting Peace, 73n
    Mrs Frensham Describes a Circle, 185n
    There Goes the Queen, 34
    on Edmund Dulac's pictures, 93
    see also Appendix B, 249–54
Bourdillon, Miss A.F.C., 33, 80
British Expeditionary Force, 83–4
British/Municipal Restaurants, 160
Bruce-Gardiner, Lady Gertrude, 74, 156n, 214n
Buckingham Palace, 108, 109
Burford, 'just beautiful', 181, 189
buses/coaches, 50, 128–9, 152, 225n
    to Bournemouth, 182–3
    to London, 123

Cadena Café, 17, Plate 15; and passing references throughout the volume
    'marvellously cheerful', 53
    'the liveliest place in Oxford at present', 54
    'the only cheerful place in Oxford at the moment', 78
Canadians, 90, 163
canteens, 109–10, 236n

card games, 33, 114, 120; *see also* whist
cattle market, 85
Central Hospital Supply Service, 55n; see also Red Cross War Depôt
Chamberlain, Neville, 21–3
Chatham House (RIIA), 193
Cherwell, River, 114, 143n
Christ Church Meadows, 59, 103, 125
Church Army, 143, 236
Churchill, Winston, 68, 80, 95, 108, 165, 167, 218n, 238, 241–2
circus, 136
class-consciousness, 38, 55n, 67, 74, 105, 129–30, 130n, 150, 169, 223–4, 233, 234
clothes
    and coupons, 137, 142, 155, 209, 213, 219–20, 221
    evening, 30
    fabric selection, 60
    fittings, 26–7, 29, 31, 62, 76, 90, 110, 129, 155, 183
    maintaining, 208n
    purchasing, 26, 48, 59, 76, 111, 113, 184, 192n, 213
    visits to dressmaker, 28, 40, 109, 127
    visits to tailor, 24, 25n, 123, 155
    see also stockings, trousers
corsets, 205n
country walks, 17, 77
    in 1938: 20, 27, 29, 38
    in 1939: 43, 48, 49, 50, 61, 63
    in 1940: 71, 75–6, 79, 83–4, 85, 87, 89, 90, 92, 98, 100, 102, 103, 104, 110–11, 115, 119
    in 1941: 124, 125–6, 127, 128–9, 132, 134–5, 136, 137, 138, 140, 147
    in 1942: 181, 189, 194–5
    in 1943: 213, 214, 220, 221n
cowardice, *see* Martin, Madge, cowardice
crowded streets, 35, 106, 110, 112, 117, 155, 159, 171, 237
Czechoslovakia, 21, 47, 58, 222n
curates, 90
    Jenkins, Kenneth, 19, 22, 30, 31, 34, 35, 39, 41, 85, 144
    Kirk-Duncan, V.G., 192, 194

Pearce, Malcolm, 94, 97, 99, 115, 164, 166, 167, 170, 193

Dance, Eric, and the Oxford Playhouse, 30n
dancing, 23, 45n–46n, 202, 239
Dandridge, Doris, *see* servants, Dandridge, Doris
diaries, xin, 9
disagreeable places, 29n (Cowley), 89 (Didcot)
dolls, 198–9, 224, 230, 235–7
double summer time, 132, 169, 226
Dragon School, 37, 158
Dunkirk, 84, 122
Dyer, Vera and family, *see* Martin, Madge, feelings/facts about friends

editorial practice, xi–xii, 154
Egypt, 197
Elton, Godfrey, 1st Baron Elton, 99, 126
'enemy alien', 53, 93; *see also* refugee (German), Ruth Hendewerk
evacuees, 50, 52n, 108–9, 110, 113n, 117–18, 119n, 152n
　accommodating them, 108–9
　Madge Martin's sisters' families self-evacuate, 50–72 passim (1939), 111–48 passim (1940–1), 167–8
excursions
　Abingdon, 225
　Thame, 128–9
　see also country walks
Exercise Carfax, *see* 'mock invasion'

'facial', 27, 101–2
Falmouth, Viscountess, 74
films (usually seen at a cinema in Oxford), 44
　49th Parallel, 159
　Andy Hardy film, 164
　Andy Hardy Gets Spring Fever, 71–2
　Apache Trail, 230
　Arise, My Love, 134
　Babes in Arms, 80
　Bachelor Mother, 172
　Back Street, 140n
　Beau Geste, 63
　Between Us Girls, 204

Black Sheep of Whitehall, 171
Boy from Barnardo's, 33
Boy Trouble, 49
Blockade, 29
Blood and Sand, 177
Breach of Promise, 182
Bringing up Baby, 27
Broadway Serenade, 58
Cardinal Richelieu, 88
Carefree, 32
Un Carnet de Bal, 27, 180, 229
Christmas in July, 125
Climbing High, 95
Curly Top, 70
Divorce of Lady X, 26
The Doctor Takes a Wife, 117
Dr Cyclops, 110
The Drum, 113
Drums Along the Mohawk, 87
The Earl of Chicago, 92
Escape, 132
Everybody's Baby, 59
Everything Happens at Night, 101
First Love, 98
Flashbacks, 26
The Flemish Farm, 238
The Foreman Went to France, 190
French Without Tears, 66
Gas-light, 100
The Gentle Sex, 217
Gone with the Wind, 24
The Grapes of Wrath, 111
The Great Profile, 123
Gulliver's Travels, 76
Having a Wonderful Time, 41
Heart of the North, 94
Hello, Frisco, Hello, 230
Hold My Hand, 114
How Green Was My Valley, 176
I Married a Witch, 225
Inspector Hornleigh on Holiday, 132n
It's a Date, 102
Jezebel, 27
Judge Hardy and Son, 93
Judge Hardy's Children, 19
King's Row, 235
Kipps, 137, 138

Kitty Foyle, 157
Laddie, 127
Laugh It Off, 111
The Life and Death of Colonel Blimp, 218
Lillian Russell, 114
Love on the Dole, 149
Lucky Night, 61
Lucky Partners, 178
Lydia, 180
Made for Each Other, 65
Man in the Iron Mask, 65
Marie Antoinette, 36
The Midas Touch, 96
The Moon and Sixpence, 220
Moon Over Miami, 168
Moontide, 211
The Mortal Storm, 119
Mr Jekyll and Mr Hyde, 177
Mr Smith Goes to Washington, 83
Mrs Miniver, 184
Newsboys' Home, 94
North-West Mounted Police, 129
Of Mice and Men, 96
The Old Maid, 78
Out West with the Hardys, 126
Over She Goes, 232
Pastor Hall, 88
The Philadelphia Story, 145
Pied Piper, 206
Pimpernel Smith, 145
Le Puritain, 29
Pygmalion, 26
Q Planes, 57
Raffles, 89
Rebecca, 188
Remember the Night, 102
Romance á la carte, 29
Secret Journey, 111
Shadow of Doubt, 222
The Ship Around the Corner, 132n
Shopworn Angel, 36
The Silent Village, 222
Sixty Glorious Years, 31
South Riding, 18
The Spy in Black, 49
Stagecoach, 55

Star of the Circus, 35
Star Spangled Rhythm, 222
The Stars Look Down, 73n, 232
Stolen Heaven, 33
The Story of Vernon and Irene Castle, 71
Strange Boarders, 33
Strike Up the Band, 129
Swanee River, 91
Ten Days in Paris, 94
Test Pilot, 17
That Uncertain Feeling, 149
The Thief of Bagdad, 147
Three Comrades, 40, 127
Thunder Rock, 214
Tom, Dick and Harry, 212–13
The Tower of London, 99
The Tree of Liberty, 142
A Trip to Paris, 40
Trouble Chaser, 167
Two's Company, 29
Victoria the Great, 31
Viennese Nights, 59
Vigil in the Night, 104
Vivacious Lady, 35, 167
We Are Not Alone, 97
Wee Willie Winkie, 91
Week-end, 186
Wings of the Morning, 87–8
A Yank at Eton, 208
Yankee Doodle Dandy, 218
You Can't Take It With You, 36
You Were Never Lovelier, 221
You Will Remember, 128
Young Man's Fancy, 88
The Young Mr Pitt, 212
Young Tom Edison, 117

Finland, 73, 84
fire, 20–1, 27, 96, 210
fire-watching, 121, 194, 200, 205, 207, 210, 221
flag-selling, 233–4
France/Paris, 55, 62, 85–93 passim
friends and acquaintances
    Acton family (parishioners), 27, 66
    Allen, Mr and Mrs (Red Cross Depôt worker), 79, 82, 93, 221

INDEX

Barrett, Miss (dressmaker), 40, 62, 109, 127, 129
Blencowe family (parishioners), 25, 39, 178
Booth, Mrs (parishioner, Red Cross Depôt worker, bazaar helper), 87, 92, 109, 112, 191, 195, 196, 211, 214n, 222, 236, 237
Boyce, Miss (dressmaker), 28, 29, 31
Butler, Mrs and Miss (parishioners, Red Cross Depôt worker), 74, 100
Buttrum, Anne and Dudley *see* actors
Cline, Miss, 126
Counsel, Mollie (fire guard), 200
Earey, Mr and Mrs, 31
Egerton, Miss (violin teacher), 90–1
Eliot, Mrs (Red Cross Depôt worker), 115, 143, 199, 236, 237
Fryer family, 95, 155, 158, 185
Gray family (parishioners), 28, 33, 139
Hall, Susie (parishioner), 6, 18, 26, 75, 82, 140, 165, 172, 192, 206, 215, 222, 233
Harber family (parishioners), 122, 139, 234
Hardman, Miss (parishioner), 65, 164, 226
Hughes, Mr and Mrs, 218, 230–1
Maclagan family, 110, 130n
Masefield, Judith (Red Cross bazaar helper), 199, 235, 237
McGregor/Macgregor, Mrs (Red Cross Depôt worker), 114, 208, 211n
Nichol-Smith/Nicol-Smith, Mrs (Red Cross bazaar helper), 199, 230
Potter, Mr and Mrs, 23, 28
Reid, Miss (Red Cross Depôt worker), 214, 215–16, 228
Russell family (parishioners), 138–9
Spurling, Miss (Red Cross Depôt worker), 99
Stone, Miss (Red Cross Depôt worker), 181, 214
Storr, Mrs (parishioner), 59
Thomas, Louise (choreographer) 36, 37
Walker, Miss (Red Cross Depôt worker, bazaar helper), 118, 127, 129, 144, 178, 199, 222, 236, 237
Warland family, 53, 132
White/Whyte, Miss, 201, 222, 226
Wood, Mrs (Red Cross bazaar helper), 198, 237
see also curates; hardships of others; Martin, Madge, facts/feelings; neighbours; Jennings, Agnes; Nicholls, Joy; Nicholls, Leonard; Oxford Playhouse; parishioners; Pead, Maud; refugee (German); servants

Gardiner, Juliet, 1
gas cooker/electric kettle, 110
gas-masks, 22, 53, 54, 55, 83–4, 127
German lessons, 27, 34, 36, 66
Germany, *see* Hitler; Nazis
Gotch, Bernard (artist), 88–9, 141
Greece, 120, 230
guiding (by Robert Martin), in Oxford, 104, Plate 7
Guy Fawkes Day, 35n, 68

hair/hairdressing, 32, 38, 86, 91, 98, 121, 147, 204, 206, 229n, Plate 12
Hall, John, *see* Martin, Madge, facts/feelings about friends, Hall, John
Harcourt family, *see* neighbours, Harcourts
hardships of others, 122
  Busby, Mrs, 45, 98, 117, 201, 210, 226–7
  Horser, Mrs, 61, 84, 91, 99, 111, 219, 230
  Odlum, Jack, 45
Harvest Festival, 26–7, 62, 114, 194–5, 228n, 230n
Headington Missionary Festival, 180–1
Headington Quarry, 181
Hendewerk, Ruth, *see* refugees (German), Hendewerk
Hitler, Adolf, 47, 61, 66, 81, 92, 100
  negotiations with, 21–5
Hogg, Quintin, MP, 233
holidays, 17, 43; *see also* country walks; London

Austria, 17
Bournemouth, 181–3
Brighton, 17
Cornwall, 77, 130–1
Derbyshire, 105–6
Gloucestershire, 227–8
Lake District, 151–2, 190
Paris, 17, 62
Portmeirion, North Wales, 17
Scarborough, 17, 47, 48, 100, 101, 224, 243
Somerset, 43, 216, 227
Wales, 171
household, of Madge Martin, 4, 6–7, 17, 19n
'enormous', 114, 117, 119, 120
family tensions, 117, 121, 159, 163–4, 190n–191n, 209, 217
housework/cleaning, cooking, 52, 57, 105, 119, 121, 137–9, 141, 148, 162, 168, 184, 197–8, 201, 204, 206, 211–24 passim, 235, 236; *see also* servants

identification cards, 98
illness, 30, 72, 219–20, 237
brother-in-law (Richard), 97, 101–2
chickenpox, 122
Robert Martin, 49, 151
see also Madge Martin, headaches
India, 27
Intercession services, 49, 81, 93, 94, 98, 99, 101, 109, 111, 115
invasion, fear of, 109, 110, 114; *see also* 'mock invasion'
Ireland, 147
iron railings, 91
Italy/Italians, 85n, 86, 120, 227
POWs, 225–6

Jamaica Church Aid Association, 28, 50
Jennings, Agnes (and John Hall), 219–37 passim
Jews, murder of, 206
Jimenez family *see* neighbours, Jimenez family

knitting, 29, 36, 56, 73, 110, 160–1, 171, 176, 180, 191

Lincoln College, 3–4, 28, 50, 64n, 93n, 171, 172n, 234
Littlemore Mental Hospital, 155
London, 29, 63
air raids, 69, 107–15 passim, 129, 130, 133
bomb damage, 110, 142, 145
Madge Martin's love for, 43
visits to, in:
1938: 31–2, 36, 37–8, 40
1939: 43
1940: 96
1941: 142, 145
1942: 175–6, 184–5, 189
1943: 207, 218–19, 239
Luther, Martin, 169

Magdalen Island/Park, 22, 115, 120, 215
Marlborough, Duchess of, and the Red Cross Bazaar, 199, 200n, 235
marriage certificates/registers, 99, 112
Marston estate, 54
Martin, Madge, 244, Plates 1 and 6
character and values, 4, 44–7, 71, 233n
childlessness, 5, 184, 245
church attendance, 60, 64, 68, 89, 92, 95, 125, 130, 133, 135, 144, 165–8 passim, 212, 213
courtship, 2–3
cowardice, 79, 80–1, 92, 95, 97, 99
depressed mood, 36, 46, 72, 87, 98, 117, 157, 164, 189, 220, 221n, 216
diary-writing, xi–xii, 1–2, 9, 78n, 163, 196, 204, 241n, 243
discomfort with Oxford, 4–5
fear of others, 93
feelings/facts about family, 7, 149
Celia (cousin), 190, 224–5
Danna (mother-in-law), 1, 2n, 91, 93, 142, 185, Plate 2
mother, 7, 125, 188, Plate 9
sisters (Nita and Nancy) and families, 1, Plate 4
visits to Oxford, 18–24, 101–4,

146–8, 155, 159, 206–7, 224–6, 228–30
  see also evacuees, Madge Martin's sisters' families; Pead, Maud
 feelings/facts about friends
  Bleiben, Winifred and/or Peter, 7, 33, 34, 62, 79, 81, 100, 131–2, 174, 230n
  Dyer, Vera, 1, 7, 24, 31, 34, 35, 36, 57, 60, 83–103 passim, 185–6; and passing references throughout the volume
  Hall, John, 5–6, 31, 35, 40, 42, 51, 53, 54, 64, 66, 70, 75, 97, 142–6 passim, 157–8, 212, 219, 226, 229, 233, 245–8,
  Plate 6; *see also* Jennings, Agnes
  Smith, Muriel, 7, 21, 33, 37, 53, 71, 80, 84, 86, 103, 191, 218, 219, 247n
  see also Nicholls, Leonard; refugee (German), Ruth Hendewerk
 feelings/facts about fellow volunteers at the Red Cross Work Depôt, 65, 67, 99, 79, 82, 107
  Mrs Holmes-Dudden, 105, 230
  Mrs Lys, 55, 58, 74, 237n–238n
  see also Red Cross War Depôt, social relations
 headaches (of Madge Martin), 21, 31, 33, 40, 41, 42–3, 68, 92n; and passing references throughout the volume
 marriage, 2–4
  happy, 5, 44, 70, 184
  pleasure/contentment, 44, 46, 64, 69, 70, 87, 149, 150, 153, 230
 religious views, 45–6, 228
 self-criticism/inferiority, 4, 46, 74, 97, 120, 150, 180, 188, 230n, 247
 upbringing and education, 1–4
 volunteer work, 195, 196, 199n; *see also* Red Cross War Depôt
 see also household, family tensions
Martin, Robert, Plates 2 and 7
 income, 6n–7n, 218n
 made City Rector, 233–4
 military service and studies, 2–4
 relatives, 7, 125
  Harry (brother), 93, 124, 143, 144, 185–6, Plate 2
  June (niece), 7, 85–102 passim, 184, 189, 209, 238
  Pansy (Telford), aka Panny (sister), 8, 172–7, 222
  see also Pead, Maud
 sermons/talks/writings, xii, 68, 73, 115, 164n, 207, 210n, 213, 247n
 upbringing, 2n
Mass Observation, 6, 189n, 232n
Merchant Seamen, 214, 233–4
Mesopotamia (Oxford), 114
Milham Ford School, 135
model villages
 Bekonscot, 38, 75
 Bourton-on-the-Water, 49
'mock invasion', 207–8
Mountbatten, Lady, 214
munitions work for women, 178–9
music, 6, 84, 103, 115, 126, 147, 149, 163, 170n, 173, 178, 188, 202, 206, 212, 215, 221, 231
 D'Oyly Carte Opera Company, 175
 Gilbert and Sullivan, 62, 78
  The Gondoliers, 135, 175
  H.M.S. Pinafore, 125
  The Mikado, 82, 136
  Patience, 81, 158
  The Pirates of Penzance, 37, 78
  Ruddigore, 79
  Trial by Jury, 78
 London Philharmonic Orchestra, 118, 128
 London Symphony Orchestra, 157
 The Merry Widow, 209
 see also Sheldonian Theatre
musicians
 Britten, Eric (pianist), 231
 Bury, Winifred (singer), 188, 202, 212
 Desmond, Astra (singer), 84
 Fields, Gracie (singer), 148
 Harrison, Beatrice (cellist), 229, 231
 Harrison, Margaret (pianist), 231
 Harrison, May (violinist), 84, 212, 229, 231
 Marova, Maria (soprano), 39
 Naylor, Bernard (organist), 39

Rushworth, Adrian (church organist), 18, 19n, 85, 118n
Sargent, Malcolm (conductor), 118, 157
Schönning, Sofi, 231
Smith, Cyril (pianist), 157
Wood, Henry (conductor), 157

national service for women, 188, 191, 192, 193, 198n
Nazis, 68n, 73, 80, 81, 222n, Plate 10
neighbours
    Harcourts, 93, 150, 171, 233, 234
    Jimenez family, 98, 141, 177, 185, 209, 210, 220, 242
New College, 87, 89, 115, 119, 140, 164
New Zealand troops, 104
newspapers, late arrival of, 108
Nicholls, Joy, 64n, 135, Plate 5
Nicholls, Leonard ('Nick'), 2, 8, 64, 174–5, 182–3, 188, Plate 5
North Country miner, 106
Norway, relief for, 231
    King Haakon, 231
Nuffield, Lord, 55n, 235

Oxford
    depressing, 227n
    election of Mayor, 233
    heritage, 88n–89n, 213n
    never bombed, 205, 242
    population, 117n
Oxford colleges
    evacuees, 108n–109n
    in wartime, 193n
Oxford Playhouse
    manager, Celia Chaundy, 187
    opening, 30
Oxford University Drama Society, 140

pantomime, 69, 162, 206, 239
Paris, *see* France
parishioners, 8, *see also* friends and acquaintances
Parson's Pleasure, 143
peace, 24, 25
    celebrations, 241–3

Pead, Maud, 149–50, 171, 172, 180, 190n–191n, 216, 239n
Penn, Buckinghamshire, 38, 75
'phoney war', 72
picnic, 85–6
plays (most seen at the Playhouse in Oxford), 213n
    After October, 230
    Ambrose Apple John's Adventure, 114
    And So to Bed, 30
    Autumn Crocus, 111
    Baa-Baa Black Sheep, 118
    Berkeley Square, 120
    A Black Eye, 231
    The Blue Bird, 112
    The Blue Goose, 215
    The Body Was Well Nourished, 132
    Brighton Rock, 211
    Castle of Perseverance, 37
    Cavalcade, 209n
    The Corn is Green, 31
    A Cup of Coffee, 125
    The Dancing Years, 141
    Dear Brutus, 140n
    The Devil's Disciple, 86
    The Doctor's Dilemma, 156
    The Dominant Sex, 125
    Elizabeth of Austria, 37
    Fanny's First Play, 38
    Flare Path, 184n
    The Fourth Wall, 136
    Fresh Fields, 109
    Ghosts, 213n
    Give Me Yesterday, 213n
    Goodness, How Sad, 226
    Hedda Gabler, 130n
    Heartbreak House, 233
    Jack and the Beanstalk, 69
    Jane Eyre, 238
    It's Time to Dance, 239
    Ladies in Retirement, 191
    The Letter, 127
    The Lilies of the Field, 141
    The Little Foxes, 222
    Love from a Stranger, 201
    Lover's Leap, 92
    Major Barbara, 147

The Man Who Came to Dinner, 231
Maria Marten, 205
Mariners, 215
The Merchant of Venice, 189
The Merry Wives of Windsor, 196
A Midsummer Night's Dream, 176
A Month in the Country, 235
Mrs Warren's Profession, 123
Much Ado About Nothing, 140
A Murder Has Been Arranged, 94
Murder on the Second Floor, 143
New Faces, 195
Nine o'clock Sharp, 102
Of Mice and Men, 220
On Approval, 130
Playhouse Revue, 95, 98, 99, 101, 103
Poison Pen, 225
Present Laughter, 209
Quiet Wedding, 114, 207
The Runaways, 135
The Scarlet Pimpernel, 72
She Too was Young, 30
Sheppey, 196
The Shining Hour, 147
The Silver King, 41
Somebody Knows, 148
Spring Meeting, 158
Spring Tide, 139
Sweeney Todd, 174
There Shall Be No Night, 234
They Came to a City, 213
They Knew What They Wanted, 165
This Happy Breed, 209n
Tovarich, 166
The Two Bouquets, 80
Up and Doing, 96
While the Sun Shines, 232
The Wind and the Rain, 144
The Wild Duck, 213
Yellow Sands, 90
Yes and No, 194
see also music, Gilbert and Sullivan
playwrights, *see* authors
Poland/Warsaw, 50, 55, 59, 73
prisoners of war, 198, 199, 200, 232–3, 236–7
public houses in Oxford

Lamb and Flag, 120
Roebuck, 171–2
The Turf, 18n, 149, 186

Radcliffe Infirmary, 33–4, 36, 39, 41, 201
RAF
 fighters, 103, 104, 110
 Warrington camp, 70
 see also airfields
rationing, 73, 95, 116, 143, 148, 152, 168, 170, 175, 183, 186, 202, 220, 228, *see also* clothes, and coupons; scarcities
Red Cross, 108n, 199, 232
 Bazaar, 196, 198–9, 224, 229, 235, 236–7
 collections for, 82
Red Cross War Depôt (at Worcester College), 55–74 passim, 79–99 passim, 107–23 passim, 127–32 passim, 140, 178, 194, 211, 214, 217, 228, 237–8, Plate 14
 inspection of, 74, 156, 214
 social relations at, 67–8, 74, 77n, 79, 105, 107, 112, 116, 120n, 125, 150, 159, 169, 172, 180, 187, 208, 222, 223
 see also knitting
refugee (German), Ruth Hendewerk, 8, 19, 27, 33, 41, 47, 48, 50, 53, 66, 78, 93, 100–1, 104, 120, 150, 192, 197, 229, Plate 8
 move to 1 Wellington Place, 218, 221, 226
 (Spanish) *see* neighbours, Jimenez family
Regent's Park College, 96
religion, 99n
 Oxford Group, 173–4
 see also Madge Martin, religious views
Rhodes House, 99, 108
 Allen, Mrs (wife of the Warden), 202–3, 212
Ripon Hall, 104
royalty, 47, 81n–82n
 Duchess of Kent, 156, 200n
 Edward VIII (later Duke of Windsor), 82n
 George V, 81n–82n
 George VI, 47, 134–5, 201, 242

Princess Elizabeth, 115–16
Queen Elizabeth, 21, 47, 68
rugby, 41
Russia, 48, 60, 148, 159, 210

St Edward's School, 138
St John's College, 6, 91n
St Luke's Church, 124
St Michael at the North Gate, 4, 8, 66, 91n, 170, 181n, 236n
    glebe land, 115
    organ, 18–19, 25
    see also 'beating of the bounds'; curates; knitting; whist
St Philip and St James School, 54
St Swithin's Day, 95, 144
scarcities, 139, 148, 191, 202, 207, 219–20
    food, 68, 122, 123, 126, 131, 147, 223, 227–8
    fuel, 191–7 passim
    rubber, 205n, Plate 16
schooling (for nephews), 54, 114–19 passim
Scouts and Guides, 102, 132–3, 158
servants, 18–19, 32–3, 34, 38, 39, 41, 74, 83, 105, 107–8, 116, 197–8, 206
    loss of, 57, 74, 205–6, 235
    Doris Dandridge (maid), 20, 38, 39, 44n, 63, 74, 88, 100–1, 116, 119, 195, 196, 120, 121, Plate 3
Sheldonian Theatre, 38, 118, 181, 231
ships, 21, 52, 57, 64, 135, 136, 166, 167, 225
shopping, 41, 56–65 passim; see also rationing
stirrup pump, 93, 207, 210
stockings, 26, 88, 117, 170, 205, 235
strawberries, 183, 222
Switzerland, 48, 54

theatrical society, 23n–24n, 165, 187–8, 202
trains, 151, 175–6
tree-felling, 102

trousers, 95, 99, 129, 169, 200
Turkey, 65

University Parks, 35, 48, 53–4, 60, 79, 83, 100, 103, 114, 123, 137, 138, 186, 189, 210, 224–5

walking, see country walks; holidays; University Parks
Walton Street, 29
war
    anxiety, 21–2, 48, 51, 73, Chap. 3 passim, 113, 121–2, 162, 181
    optimism, 24–5, 81, 197, 201, 202, 240
war depôt, see Red Cross War Depôt
war savings, 105, 131, 166, 200
war work see munitions work for women; national service for women
wartime meals, pre-war standard, 138, 140, 223; see also rationing; scarcities, food
weather
    and air-raids, 110, 120
    cold, 70, 72, 205
    gale, 40–41
weddings, 85, 119, 124, 138–9, 141
whist, 20, 28, 32, 34, 37, 65, 81, 113, 115, 118, 121, 125, 138, 155, 165, 191, 197, 200, 211, 218, 230n, 234
West Wycombe, 63, 126
windows, preventing splinters, 111
'Woman's Fair' at Olympia, 40
Women's Voluntary Services (WVS), 108n, 109n–110n, 172n, 232n
Worcester College, 55, 57, 61, 67, 123, 129, 156, 237
    dinner with Provost, 237
    see also Red Cross War Depôt

Yorkshire, 2n, 95, 142n, 148, 149, 186